ARBIT␣␣␣
IN
CHINA

REGULATION OF
ARBITRATION AGREEMENTS
AND PRACTICAL ISSUES

ARBITRATION IN CHINA

REGULATION OF ARBITRATION AGREEMENTS AND PRACTICAL ISSUES

Gu Weixia

Assistant Professor, Faculty of Law
University of Hong Kong

若汝春文敏陸春斧正。

引建筐 上
2012.03.20

SWEET & MAXWELL   THOMSON REUTERS

Published in 2012 by

Thomson Reuters Hong Kong Limited
trading as Sweet & Maxwell
10/F, Cityplaza 3,
Taikoo Shing, Hong Kong
www.sweetandmaxwell.com.hk

Affiliated Companies

AUSTRALIA
Thomson Legal and Regulatory Limited
100 Harris Street
Pyrmont NSW 2009
www.lawbookco.com.au

CANADA
Carswell
One Corporate Plaza
2075 Kennedy Road
Toronto, Ontario M1T 3V4
www.carswell.com

MALAYSIA
Sweet & Maxwell Asia®
No 17 Jalan PJS 7/19
Bandar Sunway
46150 Petaling Jaya
Selangor Darul Ehsan, Malaysia
www.sweetandmaxwellasia.com

NEW ZEALAND
Thomson Reuters
Level 1, Guardian Trust House
15 Willeston Street
Wellington 6011
www.thomsonreuters.co.nz

SINGAPORE
Sweet & Maxwell Asia®
18 Science Park Drive
Singapore 118229
www.sweetandmaxwellasia.com.sg

UNITED KINGDOM / EUROPE
Sweet & Maxwell
100 Avenue Road, London NW3 3PF
www.sweetandmaxwell.co.uk

UNITED STATES OF AMERICA
West Group
610 Opperman Drive
Eagan, Minnesota 55123
www.westgroup.com

Typeset by Innodata Isogen, Inc.

Printed in China

ISBN 978 962 661 476 1

© 2012 Thomson Reuters Hong Kong Limited

FOREWORD

Every foreign company that makes a contract with a Chinese counterpart should absorb the wisdom of this book, either directly or through its lawyers. Serious disputes often occur in business transactions, especially when the parties are from different commercial and legal cultures and systems. Given China's rapidly expanding economic prominence and ever closer cooperation with the world's enterprises, both at home and abroad, the number of international contract disagreements involving Chinese entities can be expected to continue to increase. Many cannot be resolved through "friendly consultation" or informal mediation. The assistance of some type of formal institution is often necessary to decide matters or at least stimulate the parties toward the negotiated or mediated settlement that had previously eluded them. In view of the abiding distrust of China's courts by both foreigners and Chinese and the reluctance of Chinese firms to put their fate in the hands of foreign courts, which foreigners also frequently criticize, the parties frequently prefer arbitration.

Yet under what auspices should arbitration take place? How should the process be administered? Who should serve as arbitrators, and how should they be appointed? What procedures should the arbitration tribunal follow? What law should it apply? To what extent and how should there be review of the arbitration award? What if a party fails to honor the award? These and many other questions have to be considered when contracts are negotiated, long before any dispute over their interpretation might arise. Yet, different legal systems and arbitration organizations do not provide uniform answers to these questions, despite a steady trend toward the standardization of arrangements.

Among the major trading nations, the arbitration arrangements established by the People's Republic of China stand out as the most distinctive — in theory, law, institutions and, above all, practice. Although Chinese and foreign law professors, lawyers and other experts specializing in international arbitration have published a large number of valuable analyses of the PRC's relevant multilateral and bilateral international agreements and its domestic legislation, regulations, judicial documents, and arbitration awards, what has been lacking is an overall study that frankly links this increasingly impressive body of legal material to real life circumstances. This is the outstanding feature of this fine book. It not only deals with the questions posed above but also contextualizes them, evaluating the operation of relevant institutions, norms and procedures in the light of political and social reality. For one reason or another, too many other commentators on China's arbitration have felt compelled either to skirt unpleasant topics or content themselves with oblique references.

Professor Gu helps us understand how China's pre-Communist authoritarian political-legal traditions, its Communist government's organization and ideology, its unusually prominent and protean network of social relations compendiously described as "guanxi" and its grave problems of corruption lead to a dispute resolution environment that, despite some superficial similarities with conventional international arbitration alternatives, often fails to inspire confidence. The more one learns about the actual operation of this system, the greater one's caution in dealing with it. That is why non-transparency about internal operational details is so important to those who are responsible for administering most of China's arbitration organizations. In 2006, the world's arbitration experts were stunned when China's police detained the country's best-known arbitration specialist, who was then leading its flagship institution, the China International Economic and Trade Arbitration Commission (CIETAC). Yet the case was cloaked in silence greater than that which accompanies the arrest of a Politburo member or a Supreme People's Court Vice President. Nor did the subsequent prosecution, conviction, imprisonment and eventual release of Wang Shengchang lift the veil significantly. The credibility of one of China's most visible economic and legal institutions could have been destroyed if we had been allowed to peer behind the curtain in this and other reported cases of alleged corruption.

Fortunately, the situation is far from hopeless. As Professor Gu makes clear, the Beijing Arbitration Commission has become the national pacesetter in implementing necessary reforms, and CIETAC itself has been taking steps to bolster trust in its integrity. Without greater compliance with international standards and greater transparency about the handling of concrete cases, however, skepticism will continue to be the watchword.

This book does not pretend to be the last word on its important subject, but it takes us further than we were. It will surely stimulate not only lively and more informed discussion but also the additional empirical research that is necessary to foster more accurate comprehension of China's international commercial arbitration in practice. I hope we can count on Professor Gu to pursue this critical work. She is a young and able scholar who has just made a remarkable contribution.

Jerome A. Cohen
Professor and Co-director, US-Asia Law Institute,
New York University Law School
Adjunct Senior Fellow for Asia, Council on Foreign Relations
November 2011

PREFACE

This book is an attempt to consider some of the thorniest challenges facing the arbitration regime in China during the country's transition to a market economy and its ongoing progress to establish a rule of law. Historically, Chinese arbitration was scarred by the heavy-hand of governments as part of the administrative governance network. As China has clearly indicated its intention to move towards deepening marketization and globalization, provisions have to be made to ensure that the Chinese arbitration system is consistent with international standards. A corresponding wave of reform was launched in 1994, when the first Arbitration Law was implemented, initiating the trend of voluntary arbitration in China to facilitate economic development and attract foreign investment. Nevertheless, a system of arbitration rooted in a developing country which is undergoing social, political and economic transformations remains plagued by many pervasive shortcomings. One of the most contentious issues in the rising use of arbitration in China today is that party and tribunal autonomy is not satisfactorily protected. In this regard, the Arbitration Law and its ancillary rules have been criticized as defective on the regulation of arbitration agreements.

By exploring the dynamics of the evolving regulations that pertain to or affect arbitration agreements in China since the promulgation of the Arbitration Law, this book delves into the integrity and quality of Chinese arbitration role players (arbitral commissions, tribunals, and people's courts). Moreover, this book considers both theoretical and practical aspects of the Chinese arbitration system and seeks to analyze the penetration of judicial and institutional initiatives — arbitration reforms led by the Supreme People's Court and China International Economic and Trade Arbitration Commission (CIETAC) over the past decade — in order to test the extent to which these arbitration reforms have really improved the situation. As revealed in the book, the fundamental problem of the Chinese arbitration system is that state control over arbitration is still pervasive. Formally, the Arbitration Law is overly rigid. Empirically, this book points out that the functioning and development of arbitration has proceeded under various constraints imposed by the country's transitional economy, limited political liberalization, and an under-developed judiciary.

Drawing on the comparison between China and global trends, this book argues that prospective legislative reform should take advantage of the world's best experience of international arbitration norms. The argument that there are practical constraints impacting on Chinese arbitration refers to the distorted state control over arbitration outcomes, by way of political and administrative influences with respect to the formation of the arbitral tribunal and the infrastructures of both arbitration commissions and people's courts. Hence, this book suggests some specific reforms to decouple state control from the arbitration system, which are necessary and feasible for tackling the practical constraints. This book emphasizes that Chinese arbitration commissions should be restructured and decoupled from local governments in order to achieve independence and self-sufficiency. In addition, the China Arbitration Association should be empowered to qualify and train arbitrators. Finally, this book advocates that Chinese government influence on arbitration should be exercised by way of a legal system, with modern arbitration legislation as ante-control, and, if parties fail to abide by the law in conducting arbitral proceedings, effective judicial review should step in as post-control.

Features of the book

In general, the publication of this book should enrich the literature on Chinese arbitration in the English-speaking world. It is one of the first books in the English language on contemporary Chinese arbitration written from comparative and empirical perspectives. At a more specific and technical level, this book has a few features in its coverage and analysis.

First, this book articulates a dynamic theory of arbitration agreements in the international commercial arbitration context and applies it to all major stages of the arbitral procedure in China — validity requirements at the drafting stage, relationship with the tribunal's jurisdiction and power, and finally, judicial review by the people's courts. The interpretation and implementation of these agreements at different stages and various levels have resulted in a unique system of arbitration, often referred to as *arbitration with Chinese characteristics*.

Secondly, the book presents abundant empirical evidence from a vast volume of existing studies in both the Chinese and English literature with respect to the Chinese arbitration system and its reforms — especially, evidence from some of the most influential Chinese arbitration commissions such as CIETAC and Beijing Arbitration Commission — and makes necessary comparisons. The empirical and comparative perspectives of this book make it a useful source for those interested in not only the progress made in Chinese arbitration institutions, but also the broader political and economic dimensions of Chinese arbitral developments.

Thirdly, this book relates academic inquiries to practice and policy concerns. Various problems with arbitration in China, which both academics and practitioners are concerned about, are discussed and their possible solutions are provided in the book. These problems and solutions can prompt further academic inquiry, and are also of practical use to readers. Finally, the topics discussed include a wide range of issues that have received serious attention from the Chinese government, especially that of its arbitration reformers, who have pushed for legislative reforms which hopefully will take place in the not too distant future.

Gu Weixia
Hong Kong
December 2011

ACKNOWLEDGEMENTS

My initial interest in arbitration arose while I was a law student at the East China University of Political Science and Law in Shanghai, where I had the good fortune of taking an undergraduate course on international commercial arbitration skillfully taught by Professor Liu Xiaohong. I am grateful to Professor Liu for helping develop my lifelong interest in arbitral studies. Afterwards, I was lucky to have Professor Zhang Xianchu as my postgraduate research supervisor, who supervised me throughout my Master's and Doctor's degree studies at the University of Hong Kong and to whom I owe tremendous gratitude. Professor Zhang inspired me on the academic career and provided me with vigorous training on comparative legal research, particularly with respect to China's commercial law reforms during the market transition, where the studies in this book have developed from. My thanks must also go to my co-supervisor, Professor Katherine Lynch, who devoted much of her precious time to nurturing me in the broader horizons of international arbitration norms.

I owe a special debt to Professor Jerome A. Cohen, my former teacher at the Law School of New York University. Professor Cohen is, of course, a world-renowned scholar of the Chinese legal system, who has trained generations of Chinese law specialists in the West. He has abundant experience in Chinese arbitration and has witnessed the progress of Chinese arbitration gradually interacting with the world. He was among the first batch of foreign arbitrators appointed by China's flagship arbitral institution, the China International Economic and Trade Arbitration Commission (CIETAC). In this regard, his kind sharing with me of the expertise of handling CIETAC arbitration cases from foreigners' perspectives is deeply appreciated. It has indeed been the greatest honor and privilege for me to have been associated with Professor Cohen, first as his student under the Fulbright scholarship program, and now as the beneficiary of his writing the Foreword to this book.

Sincere thanks are due to my colleagues at the Faculty of Law, University of Hong Kong, in particular, Dean Johannes Chan, Professor Albert Chen, Professor Zhang Xianchu and Professor Fu Hualing, for their encouragement and support to me in completing the research and writing of this book. They have been extremely generous in mentoring me as a young colleague over the years, and have given me many valuable opinions on managing various fronts of my job as a young academic.

I also wish to acknowledge that some of the research work leading to the publication of this book has been supported by the National Social Science Research Fund (Project code 11BFX143) and the Seed Funding for Basic Research at the University of Hong Kong (Project code 201001159002). The editors at Sweet & Maxwell, particularly Neerav Srivastava and Abdul Azeem Ali, have been very kind and patient with me in the preparation of the manuscript, particularly as the birth of my son delayed the submission by a number of months.

Earlier drafts of three chapters have been published elsewhere. Chapter 4 appears in "The Changing Landscape of Arbitration Agreements in China: Has the SPC-led Pro-arbitration Move Gone Far Enough", 22 (2) *New York International Law Review*

(2009) 1–56. Chapter 6 appears in "The China-styled Closed Panel System in Arbitral Tribunal Formation — Analysis of Chinese Adaptation to Globalization", 25 (1) *Journal of International Arbitration* (2008) 121–150. Chapter 7 appears in "Judicial Review over Arbitration in China: Assessing the Extent of the Latest Pro-Arbitration Move by the Supreme People's Court in the People's Republic of China", 27 (2) *Wisconsin International Law Journal* (2009) 221–269. The kind permission for the inclusion in this book of updated and revised versions of these chapters is acknowledged.

Finally, I must record my deepest gratitude to my family — my parents, my husband, and my little boy, Victor — whose lasting love and unswerving support during the many hours consumed by this project, have, in fact, made the writing of this book possible. This book is dedicated to them.

Gu Weixia
Hong Kong
December 2011

TABLE OF CONTENTS

CHAPTER 4   VALIDITY OF ARBITRATION AGREEMENTS

CHAPTER 5   ARBITRAL JURISDICTION

CHAPTER 6   PANEL ARBITRATOR SYSTEM AND TRIBUNAL FORMATION

CHAPTER 7   JUDICIAL INTERVENTION AND ENFORCEMENT

CHAPTER 8   CONCLUSION AND DIRECTION FOR FUTURE REFORM

APPENDICES

TABLE OF CASES

TABLE OF LEGISLATION

ABBREVIATIONS

AAA	American Arbitration Association
BAC	Beijing Arbitration Commission
BHC	Beijing Higher People's Court
B/L	Bill of Lading
BPG	Beijing People's Government
CAA	China Arbitration Association
CCOIC	China Chamber of International Commerce
CCP	Chinese Communist Party
CCPIT	China Council for Promotion of International Trade
CIArb	Chartered Institute of Arbitrators
CIETAC	China International Economic and Trade Arbitration Commission
CISG	Convention on International Sales of Goods
CJV	Contract Joint Venture
CLOUT	Case Law on UNCITRAL Text
CMAC	China Maritime Arbitration Commission
ECAC	Economic Contract Arbitration Commission
EJV	Equity Joint Venture
HKIAC	Hong Kong International Arbitration Centre
ICC	International Chamber of Commerce
LCIA	London Court of International Arbitration
LHPC	Local Higher People's Court
NPC	National People's Congress
NPCSC	National People's Congress Standing Committee
NYC	Convention on the Recognition and Enforcement of Foreign Arbitral Award (New York Convention)
SAC	Shanghai Arbitration Commission
SAIC	State Administration of Industry and Commerce
SCC	Stockholm Chamber of Commerce
SIAC	Singapore International Arbitration Centre

SHC	Shanghai Higher People's Court
SOE	State Owned Enterprises
SPC	Supreme People's Court
SZAC	Shenzhen Arbitration Commission
TCAC	Technology Arbitration Commission
UN	United Nations
UNCITRAL	United Nations Commission on International Trade Law
WTO	World Trade Organization

CHAPTER 1

REGULATORY FRAMEWORK OF ARBITRATION IN CHINA

Chapter 1 presents an introduction to the domestic and international background **1.001** of China's arbitration system. The first part discusses the relevance of arbitration to China as an economy in transition from central planning to the market in an age of rapid integration of the world economy. Following this discussion will be a review of the regulatory framework of arbitration in China. In this regard, different types of arbitration regulations will be featured such as statutes, administrative notices, judicial interpretations, rules of arbitration commissions, and international and regional agreements. The third part depicts China's ongoing motivation in establishing the China Arbitration Association and implication of its establishment for the country's arbitration reform. Finally, it clarifies the relationship between arbitration and the courts in China.

1. ARBITRATION AND LEGISLATIVE DEVELOPMENT SINCE 1978

Disputes are an inevitable concomitant of international trade and cross-border **1.002** investment. As the world has become more complex, countries are judged by the mechanisms that they put in place to resolve such disputes. Litigating cross-border business disputes in national courts poses various problems and uncertainties given the potential involvement of several different legal systems.[1] Arbitration is today regarded as an indispensible tool designed to afford parties engaged in international trade and investment the requisite degree of certainty and confidence they rightly demand for dispute resolution in international transactions.[2] Development of international arbitration norms is largely fuelled by the expectation of the global business community, and has been under heavy influence of the modernisation and harmonisation waves shaped by the New York Convention of 1958 (NYC),[3] UNCITRAL Model Law on International Commercial Arbitration of 1985,[4] and International Chamber of Commerce Rules of Arbitration of 1998 (ICC Rules).[5]

Since 1978, with China entering into the era of "reform and opening up", the drive **1.003** towards economic modernisation via the policy of attracting foreign investment has been pressing. Over the past three decades, in tandem with increased trade and

---

[1] Thieffry and Thieffry, "Negotiating Settlement of Dispute Provisions in International Business Contracts", (1990) 45 *Journal of Business Law*, 577.

[2] For detailed discussion, see Fabien Gelinas, "Arbitration and the Challenge of Globalization", (2000) 17 *Journal of International Arbitration*, 117.

[3] The official title of the NYC is the Convention on the Recognition and Enforcement of Foreign Arbitral Awards. The NYC has paid tremendous contribution to international arbitration by providing a unified platform across the globe as regards the enforcement of arbitral awards. For a historical account of the development of the NYC, see Albert Jan van den Berg, *The New York Convention of 1958* (Deventer: Kluwer Law, 1981). See, as well, discussions *below* under the heading "International agreements".

[4] The Model Law is drafted by the United Nations Commission on International Trade Law (UNCITRAL), for the purpose of harmonising arbitration laws of different countries in the course of economic globalisation. For a general account of the Model Law and its relationship with the NYC, see Holtzman and Neuhaus, *A Guide to the UNCITRAL Model Law on International Commercial Arbitration: Legislative History and Commentary* (The Hague: Kluwer Law & Taxation, 1989).

[5] The International Chamber of Commerce (ICC), being the earliest established arbitration institution in the world, is the forerunner of international arbitration rules. See, generally, Lawrence Craig, William Park and Jan Paulsson, *International Chamber of Commerce Arbitration* (3rd ed.) (New York: Oceana Publications, 2000).

investment opportunities, China has witnessed a corresponding rise in the number of commercial disputes, in particular Sino-foreign business disputes. Foreign investors who require reasonable assurance that their commercial interests will be adequately protected vis-à-vis their Chinese partners, call for an efficient, effective, and fair mechanism of dispute resolution to be established. Although China has promulgated an impressive body of laws and regulations concerning foreign trade and investment, their enforcement has been less than satisfactory. It has been argued that a judicial system rooted in an administrative governance society which is undergoing economic and political transformation such as China remains plagued by many pervasive shortcomings.[6] There are further wider concerns against Chinese courts such as the slow pace in processing cases, lack of professional judges, varying quality of law enforcement across the nation, influence of local politics and social pressures over judicial decisions, despite the continuing efforts that China has made in improving the quality of its judiciary.[7] These difficulties are compounded also due to the fact that the judiciary can not be reformed in a manner and at a pace sufficient to satisfy the requirements of foreign investors. Traditionally, Chinese enterprises have preferred the settlement of disputes via the Chinese judicial process. However, there is also a general understanding among foreign investors that domestic judicial process is underdeveloped. Arbitration is then considered as an alternative to solve the problem at negotiations.[8] Chinese entities have since then relied heavily on the arbitral process for providing foreign co-operative partners with the confidence and reassurance required to encourage trade and investment.

1.004   In general, although Chinese entities prefer the settlement of disputes through domestic arbitration, foreign parties may not. This is not only owing to the relatively higher costs attached to overseas arbitration, but also the language barrier to Chinese entities contained therein.[9] The growing tendency amongst foreign investors to seek international arbitration before a neutral arbitral body (such as ICC Court of Arbitration) has not alleviated the concerns of a Chinese business community that remains sceptical of receiving a fair hearing overseas. The government in Beijing then sought instead to tackle the problem through the development of a competent system of arbitration, by providing reputable arbitration laws and improving the prestige and competence of domestic arbitration commissions.[10] A corresponding wave of reform was launched in 1994, when the Arbitration Law was enacted beginning the trend of independent and voluntary arbitration in China as a means of facilitating economic development and attracting foreign investment. Provisions have been made to ensure that the Chinese arbitration system is consistent with international arbitration standards. Of equal importance are the ongoing expansion of arbitration commissions in China and their inclusion of larger numbers of foreign legal and technological

---

[6]   Donald Clarke, "Empirical Research into the Chinese Judicial System," in Erik Jensen and Thomas Heller (eds), *Beyond Common Knowledge: Empirical Approaches to the Rule of Law* (Stanford: Stanford University Press, 2003), 164–192.

[7]   Benjamin Liebman, "China's Courts: Restricted Reform", (2007) 191 *The China Quarterly*, 620–643.

[8]   Gu Weixia and Robert Morgan, "Improving Commercial Dispute Resolution in China", [2005] 1 *Asian Dispute Review*, 6–9.

[9]   Jingzhou Tao, *Arbitration Law and Practice in China* (The Hague: Kluwer Law, 2003), 10.

[10]   *Ibid.*

experts on the commission panel, a move designed not merely to help enhance their international character but also to wipe out the partisan concerns of foreign investors. These developments demonstrate the important role that arbitration plays in the development of the Chinese economy and its integration with the global economy. In consequence, instead of seeking recourse through people's courts, arbitration has become the preferred method of resolving commercial disputes between Chinese and foreign parties.

2. SOURCE OF REGULATIONS ON ARBITRATION

Pursuant to the Legislation Law promulgated in March 2000, legislation in China can be classified into six categories, under which the hierarchical order is as follows:
1.005

(1)   Constitution;

(2)   National laws passed by National People's Congress (NPC) and its Standing Committee (NPCSC);

(3)   Administrative regulations passed by the State Council;

(4)   Administrative rules passed by various ministries and commissions directly under the State Council;

(5)   Local regulations passed by provincial-level local people's congresses (LPC) and their standing committees (LPCSC);

(6)   Local rules passed by local governments.[11]

Passed by the NPC, the Arbitration Law is a national-level statute directly below the Constitution, with administrative notices on arbitration promulgated by the State Council following immediately in the legislative hierarchy. In addition, although the judiciary is not delegated with any legislative power under the Legislation Law, the Supreme People's Court (SPC) does exercise *de facto* rule-making power in China under the Organic Law of People's Courts by way of interpreting and clarifying national laws in judicial practice and these interpretations act as legal authorities in the court room.[12] With respect to the rules of arbitration commissions, they do not carry the force of law under the Chinese legislative jurisprudence. However, arbitration is supposed to be carried out in accordance with a set of agreed rules, and due to the institutional arbitration system in China, it must be a set of rules of a chosen arbitration commission.[13] Hence, arbitration commission rules are broadly regarded
1.006

---

[11]   Li Yahong, "The Law-making Law: A Solution to the Problems in the Chinese Legislative System?", (2000) 30 *Hong Kong Law Journal*, 120–140.

[12]   Article 33 of the Organic Law of People's Courts, adopted by NPC in 1979 and amended in 1983 and 2006; see also the Resolution on Strengthening the Works for Interpretation of Law, issued by NPCSC in 1983. However, the scope of SPC's interpretative power is not clearly defined between *interpreting law* and *making law* although there may be literal distinction that legislation is the act of making a law, while interpretation is the art of process of ascertaining the meaning of existing laws.

[13]   Articles 16 and 18 of the Arbitration Law. See more discussions in Chapters 2 and 4.

as part of the legal framework of arbitration in China and the rules largely govern arbitral proceedings. Lastly, international conventions and agreements signed by China also form part of the regulatory framework on arbitration, by virtue of art.142 of the General Principles of Civil Law.[14]

(a) Arbitration Law 1994

1.007   Being a civil law jurisdiction, statute provides the primary source of law in China for the arbitration regime. As the first ever arbitration statute in China, the Arbitration Law was adopted by the NPCSC on 31 August 1994 and came into force on 1 September 1995.[15] The promulgation was praised as a "milestone in Chinese arbitration history", "a major milestone in the development of China's legal system",[16] and was acclaimed widely both at home and abroad.[17] This 80-article law is generally applicable to all arbitration conducted within China over a wide range of economic disputes on the basis of voluntary agreement to arbitrate. It is divided into eight chapters, dealing with the contents of arbitration agreements,[18] establishment of arbitral tribunals and procedural rules,[19] as well as means to vacate and enforce arbitral awards.[20] There are two main reasons for the promulgation of the Arbitration Law. The first is that the rapidly changing economic and legal environment demands reform of the Chinese arbitration system. The second reason is that commercial arbitration is increasingly used in China, but the outdated domestic arbitration regime has hindered its development.[21] To meet these needs, the law explicitly sets out the following four principles:[22]

> (1)   Principle of party autonomy (*xieyi yuanze*): arbitration must be based on an agreement in writing and it is unlawful for any arbitration body to seize a case in the absence of arbitration agreement;[23]

---

[14]   Article 142 of the General Principles of Civil Law (passed by NPC in 1986) provides that where a case involves foreign parties, the Chinese courts are directed to apply the terms of international treaties and conventions to which China is a signatory even when such provisions conflict with other relevant provisions of domestic law.

[15]   Arbitration Law of the People's Republic of China (*Zhonghua Renmin Gongheguo Zhongcai Fa*), reported and translated in *China Law and Practice*, 7 November 1994, 23–27.

[16]   Michael J. Moser, "China's New Arbitration Law", (1995) 1 *World Arbitration & Mediation Report*, 9.

[17]   See, for example, Michael J. Moser, "China's New Arbitration Law", (1995) 1 *World Arbitration & Mediation Report*, 9; Chen Dejun, "The New Milestone in the Arbitration History of Our Country (Woguo Zhongcaishi shang de Lichengbei)", (1994) 4 *Journal of Arbitration and Law (Falu yu Zhongcai)* 2-18; Chen Min, "The Arbitration Act of the People's Republic of China—A Great Leap Forward" in *China International Commercial Yearbook (1994–1995)*, 77–101; Guiguo Wang, "The Unification of the Dispute Resolution System in China", (1996) 13(2) *Journal of International Arbitration*, 5–44; Ge Lui and Alexandra Lourie, "International Commercial Arbitration in China: History, New Developments, and Current Practice," (1995) 28 *Journal of Marshall Law Review,* 539.

[18]   See Arbitration Law, Chapter 3: Arbitration Agreement, describing the validity of an agreement and jurisdictional issues.

[19]   See Arbitration Law, Chapter 4: Arbitration Proceedings, setting out the general procedure from initiation of proceedings until conclusion of proceedings.

[20]   See Arbitration Law, Chapter 5: Application for Setting Aside Arbitration Award, providing the grounds for the setting aside of awards and remedy measure; and Chapter 6: Enforcement, providing the grounds for the refusal of enforcement of awards and remedy measures.

[21]   Katherine Lynch, "The New Arbitration Law", (1996) 16 *Hong Kong Law Journal*, 104.

[22]   The basic principles are provided under Chapter 1 of the Arbitration Law entitled "General Provisions".

[23]   Article 4 of the Arbitration Law states that the parties' submission to arbitration shall be "on the basis of both parties' free will and an arbitration agreement reached between them".

(2)   Principle of either arbitration or litigation (*huocai huosong*): where the parties have reached a valid arbitration agreement, the agreement shall be honoured and the court shall not accept the case;[24]

(3)   Principle of independence (*duli zhongcai*): arbitration shall be conducted independently according to the law and shall not be subject to administrative or judicial interference;[25]

(4)   Principle of finality (*yicai zhongju*): arbitral award shall be final, regardless of whether they are international or domestic.[26]

Generally, the gap with international standards has been narrowed, and the Chinese arbitration statute in respect of main principles converges with modern arbitration norms that have been accepted all over the world. Although the Model Law has never been officially adopted in China, it was said to have served as a guiding reference during the drafting of the Arbitration Law.[27] Dr Wang Shengchang, ex-Secretary-General of China's leading arbitration institution, the China International Economic and Trade Arbitration Commission (CIETAC), persuasively argues that, "The basic framework and underlying principles embraced in the Arbitration Law 1994 are more or less the same with the UNCITRAL Model Law".[28] The streamlined legislation and process, which is substantially shorter than those for ordinary civil procedures in the Chinese courts, have been nudging disputants not already disposed to arbitrate into the arbitral fora.[29]   **1.008**

(b) State Council notices

The State Council (SC), being the highest executive branch of the government, can enact "administrative regulations" under the Chinese legislative jurisprudence. As to arbitration, the SC promulgated several notices for the purpose of implementing the Arbitration Law, particularly for guiding the work of local arbitration commissions which take shape only after the Arbitration Law took effect in 1995.   **1.009**

In 1995, the SC issued a notice concerning the re-organisation of local arbitration commissions (the 1995 Notice).[30] It mandates that the re-organisation work must   **1.010**

---

[24]   Article 5 of the Arbitration Law provides that the people's court shall not accept the case if there is an agreement to arbitrate between the parties, unless the agreement is null and void.

[25]   According to Article 8 of the Arbitration Law, the arbitration shall be carried out independently and shall be free of interference from administrative organs, social organizations or individuals.

[26]   Article 9 of the Arbitration Law gives the arbitration a "single and final" arbitral award system. Hence, the court and the other arbitration commission shall not accept a case that have been heard and rendered the arbitral award by an arbitration commission.

[27]   Wang Shengchang, "The Globalization of Economy and China's International Arbitration", paper delivered at the Seminar on Globalization and Arbitration jointly sponsored by the International Chamber of Commerce (ICC) and the ICC China, Beijing 15 October 2002.

[28]   *Ibid.*

[29]   James V. Feinerman (Georgetown University Law Centre), "The History and Development of China's Dispute Resolution System", in Chris Hunter *et al*, *Dispute Resolution in the PRC: A Practical Guide to Litigation and Arbitration in China* (Hong Kong: Asia Law & Practice Ltd Press, 1995), 11. For discussions about a comparison between civil litigation and arbitration in commercial dispute resolution mechanism in China, see Gu Weixia and Robert Morgan, "Improving Commercial Dispute Resolution in China", [2005] *Asian Dispute Review*, 6–9.

[30]   Notice Concerning the Improvement of the Work on the Re-Organization of Arbitration Commissions, issued by the General Office of the State Council in April 1995.

be "led and assisted" by many governmental departments,[31] which purports to help structure the newly-established local arbitration commissions, as short of being addressed under the Arbitration Law. The SC guidelines have, however, been challenged as defeating the Arbitration Law objective on the non-governmental status of the arbitration commissions due to unavoidable government influence in the commission infrastructure.[32] A year later, the SC issued another clarification with regard to the arbitral jurisdiction of local arbitration commissions (the 1996 Notice).[33] Prior to the time the Arbitration Law was promulgated, hundreds of economic contract arbitration commissions established within government agencies at various levels handled domestic arbitration cases. Foreign-related arbitration was then monopolised by CIETAC for general commercial disputes and the China Maritime Arbitration Commission (CMAC) for maritime-related disputes.[34] The 1996 Notice, however, entitles local arbitration commissions to arbitrate foreign-related disputes and by doing so, seeks to dilute the impression of "dual-track" division under the Arbitration Law on the basis of jurisdiction. In the meantime, foreign investment enterprises (including Chinese-foreign equity joint ventures, Chinese-foreign co-operative joint ventures and wholly foreign-owned enterprises) who previously found themselves within the domestic arbitration regime, can now submit their investment disputes to CIETAC under the new development.[35] Some local arbitration commissions have since then grown rapidly and accepted significant numbers of international cases,[36] although generally foreign parties are reluctant to select local arbitral bodies because of their inexperience with respect to handling of foreign-related arbitrations.[37] International arbitrations are still largely conducted before CIETAC and CMAC, which continues to pose practical challenges towards the SC-led blurring jurisdiction motive.

(c) Judicial interpretations

1.011   With respect to judicial interpretations, the SPC has been playing an important role in the regulatory landscape of Chinese arbitration, because of its double roles as both a *de facto* rule-making power-holder and the highest judiciary in China. The SPC has from time to time formed the view that part of the Arbitration Law is too general and vague. Hence, it has issued many judicial interpretations for filling the practical gap.[38]

1.012   Most of these judicial interpretations take the form of "replies" or "notices", where the SPC gives directives to lower courts for their handling of specific arbitration cases.[39]

---

[31]   *Ibid.*

[32]   Yang Lin, "On the Legal Status of Arbitration Institution—Revisiting the Arbitration Law of Our Country (Lun Zhongcai Jigou de Falu Diwei—Jianji Woguo Zhongcaifa de Xiugai)", (2005) 6 *Arbitration and Law (Zhongcai yu Falu)*, 52–53.

[33]   Notice Concerning Several Issues to be Clarified for the Purpose of Implementing the PRC Arbitration Law, issued by the General Office of the State Council in June 1996.

[34]   See more discussions at Chapter 2, "Dual-track Arbitration".

[35]   CIETAC has expanded the jurisdiction to cover domestic disputes under its 2000 version rules amendment, in response to the State Council Notice.

[36]   For example, the Beijing Arbitration Commission. See more discussions in Chapters 5 and 6.

[37]   John Mo, *Arbitration Law in China* (Hong Kong: Sweet & Maxwell, 2001), 35; Daniel R. Fung and Wang Shengchang (eds), *Arbitration in China: A Practical Guide* (Hong Kong: Sweet & Maxwell, 2004), para 2-26.

[38]   Explanations on the "Several Regulations on How People's Court Should Handle Foreign-related Arbitration (Draft Provisions for Opinion Solicitation)", issued by the SPC on 31 December 2003.

[39]   Mo, *Arbitration in China* (2001), 37.

An example of these "replies" is the SPC Reply to the Hubei Provincial High Court in 1999 concerning the effect of an arbitration clause undergoing contract assignment (the Hubei Reply).[40] As regards "notices", the SPC, through issuing a series of notices in 1995 and 1998, established the "pre-reporting system" (*youxian baogao zhidu*) among people's courts on the enforcement of foreign-related arbitration.[41] These notices are important because they provide that only the SPC has the final say in deciding whether to enforce foreign-related arbitration agreements and awards in China. In consequence, it is now mandatory to report to and obtain the approval of the upper-level courts, and ultimately the SPC, for any decision that would revoke, or deny enforcement of a foreign-related arbitral agreement or award. By interpreting so, the highest-level judiciary aims at offsetting the local influences on arbitration enforcement.[42] In the meantime, albeit they are not authorised with official judicial interpretative power, local higher people's courts in some developed regions have issued more liberal judicial opinions for promoting arbitration in the region.[43] Among them, the Beijing Higher People's Court published its judicial opinion on arbitration in 1999, followed by the Shanghai and Sichuan Higher People's Courts in 2001 and 2003 respectively.[44]

Most recently, in September 2006, to consolidate its sporadic judicial replies and notices on specific arbitration cases, the SPC published the very impressive interpretative document entitled the SPC Interpretation on Several Issues Relating to the Application of the Arbitration Law (the 2006 Interpretation).[45] The newly issued judicial interpretation represents the latest, most comprehensive and systematic attempt by the SPC in codifying its past judicial opinions on arbitration and provides explicit clarification to certain issues that left a vacuum by the Arbitration Law, for example, the effect of the arbitration agreement in split clauses (where both arbitration and litigation are chosen).[46] The 2006 Interpretation is highly regarded as the prelude for the future reform of the Arbitration Law.[47] The content indicates that the judiciary, in a rather purposeful and liberal manner, attempts to further encourage the development of arbitration in China to align with international norms and standards.

1.013

---

[40] See case report by Wang Shengchang, "Arbitration Agreement and Ascertaining of Its Validity", in CIETAC (ed), *Symposium Essays on Economic and Trade Arbitration Across the Taiwan Straits* (Beijing: China Law Press, 2001), 18–20. See also discussions in Chapter 4.

[41] SPC Notice on Some Issues Concerning Foreign Arbitration and Arbitration in Foreign Countries, Fa Fa (1995) No. 18, SPC Notice on the Fee and Time Limit of Recognition and Enforcement of Foreign Arbitration Awards, Fa Shi (1998) No. 28; and SPC Notice on Some Issues Concerning Setting Aside Arbitration Awards Related to Foreign Elements by the People's Court, Fa Fa (1998) No. 40.

[42] *Ibid.* See more discussions in Chapter 7.

[43] According to Chinese jurisprudence, only the SPC enjoys the *de facto* rule-making power by its publication of judicial interpretations. The SPC judicial interpretations are binding on all lower courts in China. See Huang Jin and Du Huanfang, "Chinese Judicial Practice in Private International Law", (2008) 7 *Chinese Journal of International Law*, 227 (exemplifying the trend of lower Chinese courts interpreting arbitration law).

[44] See discussions in Chapter 4.

[45] SPC Interpretation on Several Issues Relating to the Application of Arbitration Law, promulgated by the SPC on 23 August 2006, and with effect on 8 August 2006.

[46] See discussions in Chapter 4.

[47] *Ibid.* See more discussions in Chapters 4 and 7.

(d) Arbitration commission rules

1.014   As aforementioned, given China's institutional arbitration system, the rules of arbitration commissions play a critical role in the promotion of arbitration practice, particularly in respect of arbitration proceedings. The importance of arbitration rules in China is further reflected in the fact that under the Arbitration Law and Civil Procedure Law, a court can set aside or refuse to enforce an arbitral award if the formation of the tribunal and conducting of the procedure violate the rules governing the arbitration concerned.[48]

1.015   As the earliest established arbitration institution in China, CIETAC has been playing an irreplaceable role in the Chinese arbitration practice. Since its inception in 1956, CIETAC has amended its arbitration rules on six occasions[49] to reflect the international trend of enhancing arbitral procedure flexibility. The most recent amendments were introduced in May 2005.[50] The CIETAC rules are mainly procedural rules concerning the formation of the arbitral tribunal, conduct of hearings and production of evidence. These rules are important as they bind parties, counsels and arbitrators. Parties who choose CIETAC are governed by less stringent evidentiary burdens after comparison with those applicable to the courts.[51] In more recent years, with a continuing effort to attract a larger caseload and improve competitiveness, CIETAC has expanded its jurisdiction to cover more disputes and engaged in the international trend of drafting specialised rules for catering to specialised disputes. For example, in addition to arbitration rules for general commercial disputes, CIETAC has also published the Arbitration Rules for Financial Disputes (the Financial Arbitration Rules), with its most recent amendment taking place in 2005.[52] CMAC, which handles most of the maritime disputes in China, has its own rules specifically designed for shipping cases. The CMAC rules have been revised on several occasions, the latest revision having taken place in 2004.[53] It is possible that in the future there are more specialised arbitration commissions covering specialised areas of law, for example securities and intellectual properties, to deal with increasingly complex and sophisticated commercial disputes.[54] If this happens, each of these specialised arbitral bodies created may also draft their own arbitration rules.

---

[48]   Article 58(3) of the Arbitration Law see also art.217(3) of the Civil Procedure Law.

[49]   The six occasions took place in 1988, 1994, 1995, 1998, 2000, and 2005 respectively.

[50]   The CIETAC rules were most recently revised and adopted on 11 January 2005, effective as from 1 May 2005.

[51]   For example, an arbitral tribunal is obliged to collect evidence on behalf of parties when it believes this to be necessary (art.37.1 of 2005 CIETAC Rules). However, under cl.3 of the Evidence Rules issued by the SPC (effective on 1 April 2002), a claimant is required to prove its own claim and cannot rely on the court (as used to be the case) to collect and investigate the evidence on its behalf.

[52]   The CIETAC Financial Arbitration Rules was first adopted in 2003, and then amended in 17 March 2005 with effect from 1 May 2005.

[53]   The CMAC rules were most recently revised on 5 July 2004, effective as from 1 October 2004.

[54]   There were discussions on the establishment of a securities arbitration commission in China following the issuance of the *Securities and Futures Disputes Arbitration Circular* by the Legal Affairs office of the State Council and China Securities Regulatory Commission in 2004. See Sanzhu Zhu, *Securities Dispute Resolution in China* (England: Ashgate, 2007), 214–219.

At the same time, there have been around 200 local arbitration commissions established   **1.016**
as a result of the promulgation of the Arbitration Law.[55] Most of them are situated in
major cities. Each local arbitration commission then published its own set of arbitration
rules. Therefore, arbitration rules of the Beijing Arbitration Commission (BAC) are
different from those of the Shanghai Arbitration Commission, and they may still be
different from those of the CIETAC.[56] Among the local arbitration commissions,
BAC has been recognised as a rising star of arbitration rule-making in China drawing
experience of both CIETAC and international arbitral bodies. The current BAC rules,
which feature more autonomous and streamlined arbitral procedure, were amended in
September 2007 and put into effect in April 2008.[57]

(e) International agreements

To facilitate its integration into the global economy, China has entered into a number   **1.017**
of international conventions. Pursuant to the Chinese jurisprudence, in cases where
provisions of the international conventions are applicable, they will take precedence
over counterpart provisions contained in domestic legislations save for the reservations
that China has made during accession.[58] In the realm of arbitration, the NYC 1958
remains the most important framework as regards China's involvement in the
international arbitration.

China acceded to the NYC in December 1986.[59] The accession largely encouraged   **1.018**
the use of arbitration in China because arbitral awards rendered in China can be
reciprocally recognised and enforced in other member states. As of October 2010,
there are over 144 signatories to the NYC,[60] making arbitration truly international.
It is noteworthy that China made two reservations in respect of the application of the
NYC. First, the application must be based on "reciprocity", i.e. where a country is
not a member state to the NYC, for recognition and enforcement of arbitral awards in
China, parties will have to rely on relevant judicial assistance agreements which China
has entered into with the certain country or region.[61] In this respect, for example,
an agreement has been signed on mutual enforcement of arbitral awards between

---

[55]   Gao Fei, Interview with Lu Yunhua, Chief of the Department of Coordination on Government Legal Affairs
       Office of the Legislative Affairs of the State Council (Fang Guowuyuan Fazhiban Zhengfufawuxietiaosi Sizhang
       Luyunhua)" (hereinafter referred to as "Interview with Luyunhua"), (2008) 2 *Arbitration and Judicature in
       China (Zhongguo Zhongcai yu Sifa)*, 3.
[56]   See more discussions in Chapter 6.
[57]   A brief of the 2008 BAC Arbitration Rules can be viewed at http://www.bjac.org.cn/rule/index.html.
[58]   Article 142 of the Civil Procedure Law. SPC reaffirmed this approach through its *Conference Summary of a
       National Work Conference on Economic Adjudication*, issued on 16 May 1993.
[59]   Decision on China Joining the Convention on the Recognition and Enforcement of Foreign Arbitral Awards,
       adopted by the NPCSC on 2 December 1986 and effective from 22 April 1987. Subsequently, a notice was issued
       by the SPC on 10 April 1987 to direct its lower courts to comply with the contents of the NYC when dealing with
       recognition and enforcement of arbitral awards.
[60]   A brief of the member states of the NYC can be viewed at the New York Convention library, http://www.
       newyorkconvention.org/new-york-convention-countries/contracting-states.
[61]   Denis Brock and Kathryn Sanger, "Legal Framework of Arbitration", in Fung and Wang (eds), *Arbitration in
       China: A Practical Guide* (2004), para 2-30.

China and Hong Kong.[62] The agreement is significant because, after the reversion of Hong Kong to Chinese sovereignty on 1 July 1997, the NYC could not apply between China and Hong Kong as they are no longer two separate states albeit Hong Kong is authorised with a high degree of judicial autonomy under the "One country, Two Systems".[63] Hence, the agreement has effectively paved the way for Hong Kong awards to be enforced in China, and vice versa. The second reservation that China has made relates to the restriction to a "commercial" dispute, i.e. the NYC is only applicable to arbitral awards arising from disputes of a commercial nature, with the exception of investment disputes between foreign investors and the host nation which receives the investment.[64] Such disputes should then be under the auspices of the 1963 Convention on the Settlement of Investment Disputes between States and Nationals of Other States (Washington Convention) to which China became a party in February 1990.[65]

3. China Arbitration Association

1.019   Article 15 of the Arbitration Law provides for the establishment of a China Arbitration Association (CAA), which should be a non-governmental and self-disciplinary body designed as a social organisation with corporate status for the purpose of supervising all arbitration commissions and arbitrators in China.[66] Each arbitration commission, including CIETAC and CMAC, are thus required to become members of the CAA. Whilst the Arbitration Law has provided for the founding and legal status of the CAA, the incorporation has not, as yet, been materialised, with the result that Chinese arbitration commissions operate without a dedicated supervisory and co-ordinating body. It has been further provided under the Arbitration Law that pending the establishment of the CAA, arbitration commissions can formulate their own interim rules.[67] For long, CIETAC and CMAC had been under the organisation of China Chamber of International Commerce with respect to the enactment of arbitration rules given their historic classification as foreign-related arbitration commissions.[68] But the title of foreign-related arbitration commissions has become merely a metaphorical

---

[62]   Memorandum of Understanding Concerning the Mutual Enforcement of Arbitral Awards between the Mainland and Hong Kong (Hong Kong-Mainland Mutual Enforcement Agreement), signed by both sides on 21 June 1999. Subsequently, in 2000, the Hong Kong Legislative Council amended the Arbitration Ordinance (Cap.341) to reflect the changes. The SPC in China then issued a judicial interpretation to render it part of the domestic law.

[63]   Before the sovereign reversion in 1997, arbitral awards in Hong Kong and China can be mutually enforced between each other given Hong Kong's colonial status under the United Kingdom, the latter being a member state of the NYC. The judicial assistance agreement signed between Hong Kong and China also shares experience to the situation in Macao since its handover from Portugal to China in 1999.

[64]   See fn 58 above.

[65]   The Washington Convention forms the basis for the International Center for the Settlement of Investment Disputes (ICSID) that was founded by the World Bank in 1966 in response to the demand for competent and efficient conciliation and arbitration services for the resolution of disputes between investing governments and foreign investors. Article 25(1) of the Washington Convention provides that the jurisdiction of the ICSID shall extend to any legal dispute arising directly out of an investment between a contracting state (or any constituent subdivision or agency of a contracting state designated to the ICSID by that sate) and a national of another contracting state.

[66]   Article 15, Arbitration Law.

[67]   Article 75, Arbitration Law.

[68]   Article 66, Arbitration Law.

term since the blurring of jurisdiction between CIETAC, CMAC, and local arbitration commissions in 1996. More problems rest with local arbitration commissions. Arbitration rules of more than 200 local commissions differ from each other and this has led to inconsistent arbitral practice in China. One of the objectives of the CAA would then be to consult the membership over the formulation of uniform arbitration procedural rules.

Many argue that the CAA should have been established following the effect of the   **1.020**
Arbitration Law in 1995 and further delay is inexcusable.[69] The reasons for the pending establishment are manifold. There are debates among the Chinese arbitration circle regarding the legal status of the CAA and specifically, whether it can really achieve non-governmental status and self-discipline under the administrative governance system in China.[70] Further arguments relate to the technical functions and structure of the CAA. For example, whether it would be necessary to include the training and qualifying of arbitrators within the ambit of the CAA; in addition, whether branches shall be set up within the CAA. Scholars seem to favour a simple structure without branches for avoiding unnecessary bureaucracy and expenditures within the organisation.[71] Arbitration administrators and practitioners are, however, more inclined towards branches being set up in major Chinese cities for easier promotion and training in the locality.[72] These issues are important and will be further examined in the concluding chapter as regards the way forward for the CAA and its associated arbitration reform in China.

4. RELATIONSHIP BETWEEN ARBITRATION AND THE COURTS

The involvement of the courts with respect to arbitration is necessary and unavoidable   **1.021**
in China due to following reasons. To begin with, courts, particularly the SPC, issues judicial interpretations which constitute an important source of regulations on arbitration. The particular role of the SPC in the promotion and enhancement of arbitration has been highlighted in previous discussions. In addition, in China, courts have the sole power to grant and enforce interim measures of protection to assist arbitration proceedings. These interim measures include property and evidence preservation orders upon party and arbitral tribunal's request.[73] Courts also exercise the final check over arbitral jurisdiction, i.e. to rule on whether the arbitration agreement or clause is existent or valid. Pursuant to the Arbitration Law[74] and subsequent SPC judicial interpretations,[75] where parties dispute the validity of their arbitration

---

[69] See Wen Ge, "On the Lingering Establishment of the China Arbitration Association: Worries by Arbitration Academics and Practitioners", available at http://www.china-arbitration.com.

[70] *Ibid.*

[71] See Lin Yifei, "The China Arbitration Association and the Reform of the Arbitration Institutions", (2005) 62 *Arbitration in Beijing*, 28.

[72] See Liu Jimin, Secretary-General of the Shenyang Arbitration Commission, "Some Considerations on the Character of China Arbitration Association", accessible at http://China-arbitration.com.

[73] Article 68, Arbitration Law.

[74] Article 20, Arbitration Law.

[75] SPC Reply on Several Issues of Ascertaining the Validity of the Arbitration Agreement, Fa Shi [1998] No. 27, issued by SPC on 26 October 1998.

agreement and one party requests the arbitral tribunal for a determination whilst the other party approaches a people's court for a similar determination, once the decision has been rendered by the tribunal, the court will seize its jurisdiction.[76] Some authors conclude the above judicial involvement as courts' *supportive* role towards arbitration (the first limb of courts' relationship with arbitration beginning with the letter "s").[77]

1.022   More powerfully, courts scrutinise arbitral awards, which they are asked to enforce or set aside. This is often summarised by arbitration commentators as courts' *supervisory* role over arbitration (the second limb of "s").[78] One of the outstanding features of the judicial scrutiny over arbitration in China is that different standards are applied to domestic and foreign-related awards under the dual-track system whereas domestic awards are more severely scrutinised.[79] On the one hand, in line with art.V(2) of the NYC and international practice, courts in China can only examine procedural aspects of a foreign or foreign-related award,[80] save for the public policy or social public interest ground where China does not have a fixed definition.[81] Immediately after the promulgation of the Arbitration Law, the SPC established the complicated "pre-reporting" system upon lower-level courts where enforcement of foreign and foreign-related arbitral awards would be extra-protected.[82] The "pre-reporting" system has aggregated the favoured judicial treatment towards the foreign-related regime in China. On the other hand, however, courts are empowered to review a domestic award both on its merits and on its procedures. The Arbitration Law states explicitly that, in addition to the legal grounds in respect of procedural issues, when a domestic award is presented to the court for enforcement, it can be set aside on the following two grounds: (1) the evidence on which the arbitral award has been given is false; and (2) the counter-party has concealed evidence which is material to affect the fairness of the award.[83] Accordingly, a party to a domestic award can refer to a mistake in the fact-finding process to achieve its purpose of having the award set aside, in addition to procedural irregularities. The reason courts in China have been granted the power to review the merits of domestic awards is untold in the legislative annotation on the Arbitration Law, although many believe that it is mainly due to the concerns that local arbitration commissions are less experienced and sophisticated than CIETAC and CMAC and the quality of arbitral awards so rendered require substantive supervision.[84] But CIETAC and CMAC, post the 1996 Notice on blurring jurisdiction, can hear domestic disputes as well. The design of the Arbitration Law, when putting

---

[76]   See more discussions in Chapter 7.

[77]   For example, Jingzhou Tao, *Arbitration Law and Practice in China* (2nd ed.) (The Hague: Kluwer Law International, 2008), paras 98–99.

[78]   *Ibid.*

[79]   See more discussions in Chapter 2.

[80]   Chapter 6 and art.71, Arbitration Law; see also art.258, Civil Procedure Law.

[81]   There are reports that people's courts in some parts of China had denied enforcement of foreign arbitral awards quoting the "public policy" ground simply because the enforcement could endanger the economic interests of state owned enterprise. To that extent, it is challenged whether "public policy" is a shield where the Chinese government could exercise favouritism or local protectionism. See Gu Weixia, "Public Policy under New York Convention: Application in Greater China", (2010) 1 *Journal of Comparative Law*, 90–99.

[82]   See discussions above.

[83]   Article 58, Arbitration Law.

[84]   Brock and Sanger, "Legal Framework of Arbitration", in Fung and Wang (eds), *Arbitration in China: A Practical Guide* (2004), para 2-84.

together the subsequent guidelines from the SC, creates practical confusion. There are further confusions when an award is to be enforced in Hong Kong under the mutual enforcement arrangement, because courts in Hong Kong will not review the merits of awards rendered in China, whether domestic or foreign-related.[85] Hence, if the party against whom an application for enforcement of a Mainland domestic award is sought has property situated in both Hong Kong and China, the meticulous successful party may shop the jurisdiction and choose Hong Kong for enforcement so as to avoid the unbalanced judicial review across the border.[86] It is hoped that this practical loophole can be rectified in the future.

---

[85] Article 7, Hong Kong-Mainland Mutual Enforcement Agreement.
[86] Articles 2(3) and 7, Hong Kong-Mainland Mutual Enforcement Agreement.

SALIENT FEATURES OF ARBITRATION IN CHINA

Chapter 2 summarises the three salient features of the Chinese arbitration system **2.001** for the purpose of studying their impact upon the practice of arbitration and in addition, latent impact upon the future of Chinese arbitration development. It first reviews the institutional adherence in the Chinese arbitration regime, particularly its denial of *ad hoc* and foreign arbitrations that has been challenged in the international arbitration community. The second part addresses the dual-track distinction and highlights its impact on the organisation and operation of China's arbitration commissions, most importantly the China International Economic and Trade Arbitration Commission (CIETAC), which is closely associated with China's ongoing arbitration internationalisation. The last part discusses the harmonious feature of the Chinese arbitration, in particular its emphasis on conciliation in the arbitral proceedings, as has been given much attention under the rising awareness of due process in arbitration.

1. System of Institutional Arbitration

(a) Institutional adherence in Chinese arbitration

Modern commercial arbitration can be divided into two types: institutional and *ad hoc* **2.002** arbitration. An institutional arbitration is one that is administered by an arbitration institution, which provides a set of ready-made arbitration rules to be applied by both tribunals and parties.[1] On the contrary, an *ad hoc* arbitration refers to any type of arbitration not administered by an institution.[2] Generally, each type of arbitration has its strengths and weaknesses. By choosing institutional arbitration, parties can rely on the resources and expertise of the institution for carrying out the arbitral proceeding. On the other hand, because *ad hoc* arbitration is that of a "tailor-made" type, the distinctive advantage is that it satisfies the specific needs of the parties in accordance with the particular facts of the case.[3] The compatibility between institutional and *ad hoc* arbitration reflects the relevant degree of state control on party autonomy in a given jurisdiction.[4] Worldwide, almost all countries recognise *ad hoc* arbitration. However, *ad hoc* arbitration has never existed as a dispute resolution method admitted by the Chinese legislation, nor has it been protected in Chinese arbitral practice.

Prior to when the Arbitration Law came into effect, foreign-related arbitration **2.003** was handled by foreign-related arbitration institutions, i.e. CIETAC and the China Maritime Arbitration Commission (CMAC).[5] Arbitration cases involving domestic

---

[1] There are many arbitration institutions around the world, to name a few, the International Court of Arbitration of the International Chamber of Commerce (ICC Court), London Court of International Arbitration (LCIA), American Arbitration Association (AAA), and Hong Kong International Arbitration Centre (HKIAC).

[2] The parties may design a set of *ad hoc* procedures in an arbitration agreement, or refer to a set of ready-made *ad hoc* arbitration rules, such as the UNCITRAL Arbitration Rules.

[3] For detailed discussions, see Alan Redfern and Martin Hunter, *Law and Practice of International Commercial Arbitration* (4th ed.) (London: Sweet & Maxwell, 2004), para 1-104.

[4] *Ibid.*

[5] Decision of the Government Administrative Council of the Central People's Government Concerning the Establishment of a Foreign Trade Arbitration Commission within the China Council for the Promotion of International Trade, adopted on 6 May, 1954 at the 215th Session of the Government Administration Council.

economic contracts were then handled by the Economic Contract Arbitration Commissions (ECACs) and Technology Contract Arbitration Commissions (TCACs).[6] Hence, only specific institutions could conduct arbitration cases in the pre-Arbitration Law stage in China. The institutional emphasis may be further reflected from the then provisions of relevant laws prescribing arbitration, where only institutional arbitration was mentioned. Article 14 of the Law on the Sino-Foreign Equity Joint Venture (1979)[7] stated:

> "Disputes arising between the parties to a joint venture which the Board of Directors fails to settle through consultation may be settled through conciliation or arbitration by *an arbitration institution* of China or through *an arbitration institution* agreed upon by the parties".

2.004 By analogy, in the Law on Sino-Foreign Co-operative Joint Venture (1988), disputes were required to be conducted under a *Chinese arbitration institution* or *other arbitration institutions*.[8] Other legislations had shared a similar approach towards the point where only institutional arbitration was prescribed.[9] These provisions offered a historic footnote to the continuing institutional adherence in the subsequent drafting of the Arbitration Law.

2.005 The Arbitration Law promulgated in 1994 confirms the institutional arbitration system. Article 16 requires that an arbitration agreement must contain a designated arbitration commission; otherwise the agreement will be invalid.[10] As Kang Ming, Vice Secretary-General of CIETAC, points out, the institutional adherence in arbitration roots in the traditional Chinese respect to the power of office:

(1)   The political culture in China emphasises the role of institutions rather than individuals which inhibited legislators from allowing *ad hoc* arbitration;

(2)   Most enterprises were state-owned, preferring to follow the government office line which advocated institutional arbitration.[11]

---

[6]   Article 2 of the Provisional Regulations Concerning the Administration of Organization for Technology Contract Arbitration Institutions.

[7]   Sino-Foreign Equity Joint Venture Law, adopted by the 2nd Session of the Fifth National People's Congress on 1 July 1979.

[8]   Article 26 of the Law on Sino-Foreign Co-operative Joint Venture, adopted by the 1st Session of the Seventh National People's Congress on 13 April 1988.

[9]   Besides the foregoing, there are other similar examples, such as art.27 of the Regulations of the PRC on the Exploitation of Offshore Petroleum Resources in Co-operation with Foreign Enterprise (1982), art.26 of the Regulations of the PRC on Exploitation of Onshore Petroleum Resources in Co-operation with Foreign Enterprise (1982), art.37 of the Foreign Economic Contract Law (1985, annulled in 1999), and Chapter 28 of the Civil Procedure Law (1991).

[10]   Article 16 of the Arbitration Law states that an arbitration agreement shall contain (1) an expression of intention to apply for arbitration; (2) matters for arbitration; and (3) a designated arbitration commission.

[11]   Kang Ming, "*Ad Hoc* Arbitration in China", [2003] *International Arbitration Law Review,* 200.

Thus, for the purpose of regulating arbitration institutions, Chapter II of the Arbitration Law makes special provisions for the establishment,[12] organisation,[13] and legal status[14] of an arbitration commission. Accordingly, ECACs and TCACs, which used to be attached to different governmental departments for resolving domestic economic disputes, terminated their operations on the date of entry into force of the Arbitration Law, and new arbitration commissions were reorganised by locality in accordance with the Arbitration Law. CIETAC and CMAC retained their official status as foreign-related arbitration commissions being separately regulated under Chapter VII of the Arbitration Law.[15] These different types of arbitral bodies administer the arbitral proceedings by formulating their own rules under the exclusive supervision of each commission's secretariat.

2.006

(b) Denial of *ad hoc* and foreign arbitration

Two major problems have been associated with the unitary institution system of Chinese arbitration: denial of *ad hoc* arbitration and in addition, denial of arbitration administered by foreign arbitral bodies.

2.007

The Arbitration Law endorses institutional arbitration and does not expressly forbid the practice of *ad hoc* arbitration. Notwithstanding the foregoing, Dr John Mo argues on two grounds that the practice of *ad hoc* arbitration is not protected in China.[16] First, an arbitration agreement submitting a dispute to *ad hoc* arbitration is not valid as the designation of an "arbitration commission" is one of the required components of a valid arbitration agreement under the Arbitration Law. Second, an award made through *ad hoc* arbitration is not enforceable because it will be set aside or refused following an invalid arbitration agreement under arts.58, 63, 70 and 71 of the Arbitration Law.[17] Indeed, in the recent case of *People's Insurance Co of China, Guangzhou v Guanghope Power* in 2003, the Supreme People's Court (SPC) struck down an arbitration clause providing for *ad hoc* arbitration in China.[18]

2.008

The absence of *ad hoc* arbitration gives rise to both theoretical and practical problems. Article I s.2 of the New York Convention (NYC) provides that arbitral awards shall include not only institutional awards but also *ad hoc* awards. As a member state to the Convention, Chinese courts are obliged to recognise and enforce all arbitral awards rendered in other contracting states including those obtained through *ad hoc* arbitration. By contrast, *ad hoc* awards rendered in China cannot be recognised and enforced either in China or in another member state. Chinese courts have to declare the nullity and invalidity of an *ad hoc* arbitration agreement if the applicable law is

2.009

---

[12] Articles 10 and 11 of the Arbitration Law.
[13] Article 12 of the Arbitration Law.
[14] Article 14 of the Arbitration Law.
[15] Article 66 of the Arbitration Law.
[16] John Mo, *Arbitration Law in China* (Hong Kong: Sweet & Maxwell Asia, 2001), 56.
[17] These Articles concern the grounds for setting aside and refusing enforcement of arbitral awards, among which the foremost reason is the invalidity of an arbitration agreement, including *ad hoc* arbitration agreements.
[18] *People's Insurance Company of China, Guangzhou v Guanghope Power* [Min Si Zhong Zi] No. 29 of 2003, SPC of China.

the Chinese law, i.e. the Arbitration Law; and courts of the other contracting states to the Convention may refuse to enforce an *ad hoc* arbitral award following an invalid arbitration agreement that is made in China in accordance with art.V s.1(a) of the NYC.[19] For example, in Hong Kong, *ad hoc* arbitration is very popular and *ad hoc* arbitral awards rendered in Hong Kong can be recognised and enforced in China, but not the other way round.[20] The current system gives rise to conflicting practices in people's courts in China as regards the enforcement of both arbitration agreements and arbitral awards.

2.010   With respect to arbitrations conducted by foreign arbitration institutions, the Arbitration Law neither explicitly permits nor prohibits the practice from taking place in China.[21] The issue has been numerously addressed, with particular focus as to whether an arbitration following the ICC Rules can be lawfully conducted within China and produce an enforceable award.[22] In this regard, Chapter II of the Arbitration Law which deals specifically with arbitration commissions in China, sets out the requirements for the establishment of such commissions and makes it quite clear that they are to be organised by the local people's governments, registered with the local departments of justice, conform to a number of constitutional requirements and be subject to supervision by the China Arbitration Association.[23] Chapter VII of the Arbitration Law further provides for the establishment of foreign-related arbitration commissions (CIETAC and CMAC) by the China Chamber of International Commerce. The organisation of foreign-related commissions must also conform to the requirements set out in Chapter II referred to above.[24] Accordingly, as a foreign arbitral body, it is difficult to see how the ICC can be squeezed comfortably, if at all, within these provisions.[25] The current system seems to close the door to not only *ad hoc* arbitration practice, but also institutional practice conducted by foreign arbitral bodies. Hence, arbitration in China is monopolised by Chinese

---

[19]   Article V s.1(a) of the NYC states that, "Recognition and enforcement of the award may be refused … only if the parties to the agreement were, under the law applicable to them, under some incapacity, or *the said agreement is not valid under the law to which the parties have subjected it* or, failing any indication thereon, *under the law of the country where the award was made*". For example, two parties, one from England and the other from Hong Kong, reached an arbitration agreement, stating that "arbitration in Beijing governed by the China Arbitration Law". Whether the arbitration can be conducted is in doubt because under the applicable law and the law of the place of arbitration—Beijing, the arbitration agreement is null and void since there is no designated arbitration commission. Supposing it is conducted and an *ad hoc* arbitral award is made, the court for which the winning party seeks enforcement of the arbitral award may refuse to enforce the award according to the law of the place of the arbitration.

[20]   Prior to 1 July 1997, the NYC applied as between China and Hong Kong. After Hong Kong's handover to China, China and the Hong Kong Special Administrative Region reached an agreement on the recognition and enforcement of arbitral awards. This agreement became effective on 1 February 2000.

[21]   "Conducting arbitration" in this context means to choose China as the site of arbitration, regardless of whether the hearings take place in China.

[22]   See discussions on the topic "ICC Arbitration in China", in the *Roundtable on Arbitration and Conciliation Concerning China*, ICCA Congress Series No. 12, 12–14 May 2004, Beijing; compiled in Albert Jan van den Berg (ed), *New Horizons in International Commercial Arbitration and Beyond: ICCA Congress Series No. 12* (The Hague: Kluwer Law International, 2005).

[23]   Article 15 of the Arbitration Law.

[24]   Article 65 of the Arbitration Law.

[25]   See speech by Robert Briner, "Arbitration in China Seen from the Viewpoint of the International Court of Arbitration of the International Chamber of Commerce", see fn 22 above.

arbitration commissions.[26] Such institutional monopoly, however, entails inherent risks. Chinese arbitration commissions, lacking competitive pressures from *ad hoc* arbitration and foreign institutional arbitration, will feel themselves complacent with the bureaucratic practice and finally lose the competitive edge when the Chinese arbitration market gradually liberalises under the country's WTO commitment of legal service opening.

(c) Impact upon arbitral practice

The unitary institutional system impacts significantly on arbitral practice in China. To begin with, the validity requirements of the arbitration agreement are constrained. Pursuant to art.16 of the Arbitration Law, an arbitration agreement containing no or unclear arbitration institution will be deemed as null and invalid. In this context, except those very experienced parties with excellent draftsmanship, most arbitration agreements which fail to include the proper identity of an arbitration institution will be declared void. In addition, because the Chinese law does not provide for the legal status of either *ad hoc* arbitration or arbitration conducted by foreign arbitral bodies seated in China, arbitrating disputes solely by Chinese arbitration commissions limits the freedom of parties to determine the way they want to resolve disputes and thus does not comply with the principle of party autonomy. Under Chinese arbitral regulations, since the 1996 State Council Notice (and subsequently CIETAC rules revision in 1998), parties may choose either to submit their disputes to a local commission or non-local arbitration commission, i.e. CIETAC or CMAC. In practice, however, parties usually submit their disputes to the arbitration commission where they are located. Apart from geographic convenience, more often than not, the influence from the local government on the drafting of standardised arbitration agreements contributes to the localisation of arbitral choices, which severely restricts the parties' autonomy and interests.[27]

2.011

Moreover, the jurisdictional autonomy of the arbitral tribunal is undermined. Due to an over-emphasis on institutions, the jurisdiction of the arbitral tribunal is considered in the first place that of the arbitration commission, where the commission rather than the tribunal enjoys *competence-competence* in ruling on the effect of arbitration agreement.[28] The institutional influence has resulted in the improper enlargement of the powers by the commission which threatens the autonomy and power of the party-appointed arbitral tribunal. Another problem rests with the appointment of arbitrators and correspondingly, constitution of the arbitral tribunal. Under the Arbitration Law, CIETAC, CMAC and local arbitration commissions are required to set up panel lists of arbitrators for their institutional establishment. The selection of arbitrators from the

2.012

---

[26]   Song Lianbin, "From Ideology to Rules: Several Issues Worthy of Attention in Revising the Arbitration Law (Linian Zouxiang Guize: Zhongcaifa Xiuding ying Zhuyi de Jige Wenti)", (2005) 52 *Arbitration in Beijing (Beijing Zhongcai)*, 6–7.

[27]   Some local governments frequently use so-called "red-headed documents" to request local enterprises and companies to modify their standard contracts that contain an arbitration clause solely designating the local arbitration commissions.

[28]   See discussions in Chapter 5 of this book.

respective list of the administering arbitration commission is mandatory[29] until the practice is very recently challenged by CIETAC.[30] In most cases, those whose names are not included in the arbitrator panels are excluded from the parties' scope of choices even if they are highly qualified. Many have argued for the abolishment of the panel system as against the principle of party autonomy.[31]

2.013   Lastly, under the unitary institutional system, Chinese arbitration commissions play a more active role in the supervision of arbitration. Hence, procedural autonomy of the parties is largely restricted to institutional arrangement of the rules of the relevant arbitration commission that administers the case. The scope of institutional review can be very wide, including the effect of arbitration agreements, arbitral jurisdiction, qualifications of arbitrators, arbitral procedure, and finally, the quality of arbitral awards.

2. System of Dual-track Arbitration

(a) Definition of "domestic" and "foreign-related" arbitration

2.014   The second feature of the Chinese arbitration system is its dual-track division (*shuangguizhi*) between the domestic and foreign-related regimes.[32] Arbitration in China has been clearly developed from these two tracks, with different arbitral procedures for each, and different standards of judicial review applying to each. The "dual-track" division used to refer to different types of disputes and their resulting jurisdictional bifurcations among CIETAC, CMAC and local arbitration commissions.[33] Such criteria of division have been changed after the Arbitration Law came into effect and the jurisdictional bifurcation has been merged since the 1996 State Council Notice on blurring of the jurisdiction between domestic and foreign-related cases.[34]

2.015   One interesting phenomenon in the Chinese civil and commercial legislative literature is that the term "international" is seldom used. Instead, "foreign-related" (or "foreign element") is frequently employed. The preference for using the term "foreign-related" is a special characteristic of Chinese legislation since its reform and opening up policy in late 1970s and for serving the interests of foreign investors.[35] In lieu of the term

---

[29]   China is perhaps one of the only two jurisdictions in the world that require arbitrators to be appointed from panels maintained by the arbitration commissions. The other being, Venezuela; see Famon J. Alvins and Victorino J. Tejera-Prerez, *The International Comparative Legal Guide to: International Arbitration* (Boston, NY: Global Legal Group, 2004), Chapter 41.

[30]   See discussions in Chapter 6 of this book.

[31]   *Ibid.*

[32]   The division has been called by Chinese arbitration academics as the "dual-track" system. See Wang Shengchang, *Resolving Disputes in the PRC: A Practical Guide to Arbitration and Conciliation in China* (Hong Kong: FT Law & Tax Asia, 1997), 19–25.

[33]   Jingzhou Tao, *Arbitration Law and Practice in China* (The Hague: Kluwer Law International, 2004) para 1-32.

[34]   See also discussions in Chapter 1.

[35]   Xiabin Xu and George D. Wilson, "One Country, Two—International Commercial Arbitration—Systems", (2000) 17 *Journal of International Arbitration*, 48.

"foreign-related", basic laws in China fail to give an explicit answer.[36] Yet, some inference can be sought from art.178 of the Several Opinions on the Implementation of the General Principles of Civil Law,[37] which provides that a foreign element will exist where:

(1) One party or both parties to the contract are foreign entities, foreign legal persons or stateless persons;

(2) The subject matter of the contract is located in a foreign country; or

(3) The act which gives rise to, modifies or extinguishes the rights and obligations under the contract, occurs in a foreign country.[38]

Besides the three criteria above, pursuant to the Reply to Several Issues Concerning the Implementation of the Foreign Economic Contract Law,[39] cases involving persons, companies or organisations of Hong Kong, Macao and Taiwan are referred to as foreign-related. This situation remains unchanged with regard to Hong Kong and Macao in the post-handover period. Thus, an arbitration would be deemed as "foreign-related" where it relates to disputes arising out of a contract with a foreign element. **2.016**

Compared to art.1 of the UNCITRAL Model Law, a significant difference may be noted in respect of the criterion of the "foreign" element. Under art.1(3)(c) of the Model Law, the parties may "create" an international element by expressly agreeing that the subject matter of the arbitration agreement relates to more than one country.[40] One should recognise that this is a subjective rather than objective test, which offers parties greater autonomy to tailor their arbitration to international regimes. However, the criteria envisaged by Chinese guidance are limited to objective situations. **2.017**

(b) Bifurcations between the two tracks

Prior to the time the Arbitration Law was promulgated, ECACs subordinated to governmental agencies at various levels handled domestic arbitration cases, on the basis of mandatory jurisdiction. Foreign-related arbitration, however, was monopolised by CIETAC as regards general commercial disputes and CMAC as regards maritime disputes, governed by the CIETAC and CMAC arbitration rules respectively. Domestic arbitrations in the pre-Arbitration Law stage can be characterised as administrative in nature, lacking party autonomy, independence, and the binding effect of arbitral **2.018**

---

[36] The statutory expression of "foreign-related" may be found in the Civil Procedure Law, Foreign Economic Contract Law, General Principles of Civil Law and Arbitration Law. Unfortunately, none of these basic laws has given an explicit definition of "foreign-related" in their stipulations.

[37] The Opinion was issued by the SPC on 26 January 1988.

[38] Following the "Civil Code Judicial Interpretations", similar opinions were issued by the SPC relating to the China Civil Procedure Law (1991). See art.304 of the Opinions Relating to Several Issues Arising form the Implementation of the Civil Procedure Law (the Civil Procedure Law Interpretations), issued by the SPC in 1992.

[39] The instructions were laid down under para I (2) of the Reply, which was issued by the SPC on 19 October 1987.

[40] See art.1(3)(c) of the Model Law.

awards.[41] Although there was a genuine acknowledgment of the need for a viable institution of dispute resolution alternative to court litigation,[42] the then Chinese government chose to employ domestic arbitration in an instrumentalist manner rather than embracing it as an institution. The subordination of ECACs to administrative powers made their level of institutionalisation and systemisation much laggard behind the then foreign-related arbitration regime, i.e. CIETAC and CMAC. The main features of domestic arbitration in the pre-Arbitration Law era are concluded as follows:

(1)   Domestic arbitration is purely conducted on territorial jurisdiction. Parties have no right to choose arbitration institutions nor could they select arbitrators.

(2)   Domestic arbitral tribunals are established within the local government. All arbitrators are government officials and appointed by the chairman of the relevant ECAC.

(3)   The domestic arbitral process is conducted in an administrative-review manner and arbitral awards are not final but subject to appeal to a higher-level administrative authority.[43]

2.019   These deviations from the accepted norms of arbitration clearly harmed the reputation of Chinese domestic arbitration regime and could not meet the needs of the country's marketisation.

2.020   On the other hand, even without a legal infrastructure, the Chinese government did not hesitate to set up the institutionalisation of the foreign-related arbitration commissions. The Foreign Trade Arbitration Commission (FTAC) and the Maritime Arbitration Commission (MAC) were established as early as 1956 and 1958 to handle China's foreign-related disputes, which were renamed CIETAC and CMAC in 1988.[44] Before the Arbitration Law came into effect, major distinctions of the foreign-related arbitration are summarised below.

(1)   CIETAC and CMAC conduct foreign-related arbitral cases pursuant to the principle of consensual jurisdiction.

(2)   In CIETAC and CMAC's arbitral proceedings, parties have the right to choose arbitrators from the commission roster.[45]

---

[41]   Jiang Xianming and Li Ganggui, Study of Chinese Arbitration Law (*Zhongguo Zhongcai Faxue*) (Nanjing: Southeast University Press, 1996), 28.

[42]   Legislative Affairs Commission of the Standing Committee of the National People's Congress of the PRC (ed), *Arbitration Laws of China* (Hong Kong: Sweet & Maxwell Asia, 1997), 18.

[43]   Will W. Shen and Iris H Y Chiu, "Arbitration in China: History and Structure", in Fung and Wang (ed), *Arbitration in China: A Practical Guide* (2004), para 1-35. See also, Gou Chengwei and Zhang Peitian, *Practical Handbook of Arbitration (Zhongcai Shiyong Quanshu)* (Beijing: China University of Politics & Law Press, 1993), 7–10.

[44]   "The International Commercial Arbitration Institutions of China" in Legislative Affairs Commission of the NPCSC of the PRC (ed), *Arbitration Laws of China* (1997), 119–121.

[45]   Foreign-related arbitration commissions in China, even before the Arbitration Law came into effect, maintained its own roasters of arbitrators in accordance with its arbitration rules. Both CIETAC and CMAC have their roasters of arbitrators which include arbitrators of both Chinese and foreigners.

(3)   Arbitral awards rendered by CIETAC and CMAC are final and binding on the parties which stand in sharp contrast to the appealable awards under the domestic regime.[46]

Evidently, at the pre-Arbitration Law stage, the real arbitration system in China was only the foreign-related arbitration system, which had been under the exclusive jurisdiction of CIETAC and CMAC. They were described as fully autonomous arbitration bodies acting independently of both the China Council for Promotion of International Trade (CCPIT)[47] and the Chinese government. Ever since then, CIETAC and CMAC have gradually earned the reputation as important fora for resolving international disputes in China. On the contrary, the then domestic arbitration was in fact a system of administrative adjudicature. Development of the domestic regime did not pick up until the Arbitration Law was promulgated in 1994, which marked a vital step in Chinese arbitration history.   **2.021**

The Arbitration Law covers both domestic and foreign-related arbitrations, with a set of well-recognised principles that are fundamental to bridge the gap between the Chinese arbitration system and international norms and makes it clear that these general principles will equally apply to both regimes.[48] The scope of arbitration has also been expanded to cover all matters relating to contractual or property rights, with the exception of labour and agriculture disputes, which are outside commercial arbitrability.[49] Despite the unified attempt, the Arbitration Law continues with the "dual-track" policy by differentiating foreign-related arbitration and treating them separately from domestic arbitration. For the purpose of the division, Chapter VII (arts.65–73) of the Arbitration Law particularly regulates the foreign-related regime and prescribes a series of privileges exclusively reserved to foreign-related arbitration, which are lined up below.[50]   **2.022**

(1)   Only the China Chamber of International Commerce (CCOIC) has the privilege to establish foreign-related arbitration commissions (art.66). Domestic arbitration commissions are established on the basis of locality, subordinated to local justice administrations and hence, called local arbitration commissions (arts.10–15).

---

46   For detailed comparisons and contrasts, see Mo, *Arbitration Law in China* (2001), 58–64. See also Li Hu, "Feature International – An Introduction to Commercial Arbitration in China", (2003) 58 *Dispute Resolution Journal,* 78.

47   The two institutions operated under the auspices of the CCPIT, which acted as the then China's international chamber for commerce. The CCPIT was founded in 1952. Its mandate was to promote and co-ordinate China's economic and trade relations with foreign countries. At the time when it was established, CCPIT was an adjunct to the then Ministry of Foreign Trade, and its status now is that of a non-governmental economic and trade organisation.

48   These principles are: (a) respect for party autonomy; (b) independence from the administration; (c) final adjudication; and (d) awards based on established principles of law and evidence which are legally recognised and enforceable. See Chapter I (arts.1–9), "General Provisions" of the Arbitration Law.

49   See arts.2 and 3 of the Arbitration Law. Labour arbitration and arbitration of contractual disputes arising from farming of collectively-owned land, are reserved for special administrative arbitration commissions or special government authorities outside the system of commercial arbitration. See arts.77 of the Arbitration Law.

50   See Chapter VII (arts.65–73), "Special Provisions Concerning the Foreign-related Arbitration" of the Arbitration Law.

(2)   Foreign-related arbitration commissions may decide upon their own organisation structure. For example, the maximum number of members for a local arbitration commission is 16 (art.12), but there is no exact limit for that of a foreign-related arbitration commission (art.66).

(3)   Different rules govern the application for interim measures of protection in domestic (art.46) and foreign-related (art.68) arbitrations, where rules of the latter are more flexible and user-friendly.[51]

(4)   As to level of court in exercising judicial support and supervision, for foreign-related regime, the jurisdiction to review the validity of an arbitration agreement (art.20), order interim measures (art.28), set aside (arts.58–61) or enforce an award (arts.62–64) is rested with the people's court at the intermediate level (arts.68, 70 and 71, making reference to arts.258, 259 of the Civil Procedure Law). In the case of domestic arbitration, the competent court is at the lowest basic level, except for setting aside of a domestic award which shall be applied to an intermediate people's court.

(5)   Lastly, on the grounds to exercise judicial supervision, for setting aside or refusing enforcement of domestic arbitral awards, the review involves even substantive matters such as the effect of the evidence on which the award is based (art.58). However, in the case of a foreign-related award, the grounds for setting aside and denial of enforcement (arts.70 and 71, making reference to art.260(1) of the Civil Procedure Law) are limited within the scope of procedural aspects.[52]

2.023   Besides provisional differences within the Arbitration Law, there are also bifurcations with respect to judicial approaches by people's courts which further strengthen the dual-track disparities in the post-Arbitration Law period. In this regard, as aforementioned in Chapter 1, the SPC established a "pre-reporting" system in relation to the recognition and enforcement of foreign-related arbitration.[53] The system requires that only after the SPC has confirmed the findings may the intermediate people's court rule to refuse recognition or enforcement of foreign-related arbitral agreements and awards.[54] Hence, higher-level people's courts would not interfere with positive enforcement rulings made by the lower levels, but a negative ruling must be subject to "pyramidal scrutiny" by the provincial-level higher people's court and eventually by the SPC. The "pre-reporting" system further extended to the time limits relating to recognition and enforcement. It is stipulated that the court receiving the application for enforcement must report within *two* months after the negative ruling is rendered and must accomplish mandatory enforcement within *six* months since

---

[51]   See also Tao, *Arbitration Law and Practice in China* (2004), 98.

[52]   For example, art.58 stipulates that the intermediate people's court shall set aside the award on the request of one of the parties if "(4) the evidence on which the award is based was forged; (5) the other party has withheld the evidence which is sufficient to affect the impartiality of the arbitration …" Besides, an award shall be set aside if the court determines that it violates the public interest.

[53]   Notice on the Relevant Issues Concerning the Handling of Foreign-related Arbitration and Foreign Arbitration, issued by the SPC on 28 August 1995.

[54]   See paragraph 2 of the Notice; see also discussions on this topic in Chapter 7.

parties' application.[55] By strictly following the SPC stipulations, a refusal or delay in handling enforcement matters of foreign-related arbitration would be deemed as exceptional rather than usual. Arguably, the "pre-reporting" system aggravates the unbalanced treatment in the judicial supervision over the two tracks.

On the other hand, the jurisdictional divisions between the two tracks have now been blurred. As previously mentioned, the State Council, through its 1996 Notice, prescribes that a local arbitration commission is entitled to receive and arbitrate foreign-related disputes.[56] It is noteworthy that the 1996 Notice changes significantly the original dual-track system predicated on the difference of jurisdiction, where local arbitration commissions were not allowed to receive cases with foreign-related elements; nor could foreign-related commissions accept domestic cases. There have been different opinions with respect to the jurisdiction blurring. Amongst them, while some criticised for its practical confusion and lack of legislative competence,[57] more believed that the 1996 Notice helped to deprive the monopolised jurisdiction of CIETAC and CMAC over foreign-related disputes.[58] But other concerns remain. Although there are now more than 200 local arbitration commissions competing with CIETAC and CMAC for the foreign-related arbitration market, it would be difficult for these local arbitration commissions to match CIETAC and CMAC regarding expertise and experience in dealing with finance, trade, transport and maritime disputes involving foreign parties. CIETAC and CMAC have not only a wealth of experience in handling these sophisticated commercial matters but the panel of arbitrators consisting both of Chinese and foreign experts in these areas. Whilst CIETAC has led the way in increasing the number of foreign experts listed on its panel (from none in 1988 to three in 1989 to 146 today, nearly a third of total),[59] local commissions have lagged behind. Few of them have appointed foreign nationals to their panels.

2.024

As the largest, oldest, and most experienced arbitration institution in China, CIETAC has been a critical actor in witnessing and framing the Chinese arbitration system. The initial purpose of the CIETAC establishment is for settling business disputes arising from contracts and transactions between Chinese and foreign companies. For many decades, CIETAC has been representing the level of internationalisation of the Chinese arbitration and moreover, been leading the evolution of arbitration practice in China. Many have argued for the irreplaceable role of CIETAC: (a) CIETAC has received the

2.025

---

55 Stipulations on the Issues Relating to Fees-Charging and Time Limits for Handling Cases in Respect of Recognition and Enforcement of Foreign-related Arbitral Awards and Foreign Arbitral Awards, issued by the SPC on 21 October 1998.

56 Notice of the General Office of the State Council Concerning Several Issues to be Clarified for the Purpose of Implementing the PRC Arbitration Law, Guo Ban Fa [1996] No. 22, issued on 8 June 1996 by the General Office of the State Council.

57 For example, art.260 of the Civil Procedure Law clearly adopts the wording "the award rendered by a foreign-related arbitration commission". Since "1996 Notice" has abolished the previously-named "foreign-related" arbitration commission of CIETAC and CMAC, if a party applies to a court for refusing to enforce a foreign-related arbitral award rendered by a domestic arbitration commission, or better to be called as local arbitration commission, which legal source shall take precedence and which Article should the court apply, Arbitration Law or the Civil Procedure Law or both? Regarding the criticism on the "Notice 1996", see Song Lianbin, *Studies on Jurisdictional Problems in International Commercial Arbitration (Guoji Shangshi Zhongcai Guanxiaquan Yanjiu)* (Beijing: China Law Press, 2000), 143.

58 *Ibid.*

59 Available at the CEITAC website, http://cn.cietac.org/Query/zhongcaiyuanNewen1.asp.

largest caseload of international arbitration in the world; (b) the rules and practices of CIETAC have significantly influenced not only the drafting of the Arbitration Law,[60] but also the rules and practices of the local arbitration commissions.[61] Prior to the implementation of the Arbitration Law, CIETAC had almost monopolised foreign-related arbitration in China. Nowadays CIETAC has widened its jurisdiction to cover both domestic and foreign-related disputes.[62] This change makes CIETAC in line with the worldwide trend in unifying international and domestic arbitration regimes.

(c) Impact upon arbitral practice

2.026   Although there is no longer a jurisdictional division between CIETAC, CMAC, and local arbitration commissions, the dual-track system has been deep rooted in the Chinese legal and arbitration system and has impacted significantly the arbitral practice.

2.027   To begin with, parties to foreign-related arbitration agreements enjoy a wider range of choices as regards arbitration institutions. Pursuant to art.128 of the Contract Law, parties to a contract with foreign element(s) may choose to submit their disputes to arbitration either within or outside China.[63] Foreign-related parties may thus have their disputes arbitrated by either Chinese arbitration commissions or other arbitration institutions abroad. It is perceived that the implied meaning of art.128 is to limit the capacity of parties to domestic arbitration agreements to arbitrate outside China. Since foreign arbitration outside China involves both institutional and *ad hoc* arbitrations, parties to foreign-related disputes thus have more choices of types of arbitration.[64] By contrast, parties to domestic disputes can only choose to arbitrate under the auspices of institutional arbitration administered by Chinese arbitration commissions because no legal protection has thus far been given to *ad hoc* or foreign arbitration conducted in China.

2.028   The dual-track system has further led to unbalanced choices of arbitrators. Most arbitration commissions in China provide two panels of arbitrators, with one for foreign-related disputes and the other for domestic disputes. The foreign-related panel has consisted of both Chinese and foreign nationals. Foreign arbitrators, including those from Hong Kong, Macao and Taiwan are however excluded from the domestic panel. As such, parties to domestic disputes are confined to the domestic arbitration commissions and in addition, with only Chinese arbitrators available for their choices.[65]

---

[60]   From 1991 to 1994, the experts of CIETAC had been working hard for the drafting of the Arbitration Law and had put forward many important proposals for the legislation of arbitration. After the Arbitration Law was promulgated in 1995, the experts began to participate in the drafting of the plan for reorganisation of domestic arbitration commissions and model arbitration rules, carter of association and the ethical rules of the arbitrators.

[61]   See Wang Wenying, "Distinctive Features of Arbitration in China: A Historic Perspective", (2006) 23 *Journal of International Arbitration*, 49–53.

[62]   The expansion of CIETAC jurisdiction to cover domestic disputes reflected by its 2000 Arbitration Rules was treated as its immediate responsive act to the State Council "1996 Notice".

[63]   See, para 2 of art.128 of the Contract Law.

[64]   But foreign-related parties are still limited to refer to *ad hoc* arbitration in their agreement if they adopt the Arbitration Law as the governing law of the arbitration agreement.

[65]   See "Stipulations for the Appointment of Arbitrators", http://www.cietac.org/.

The qualifications of arbitrators are also different. For domestic arbitrators, conditions are strictly stipulated in both the Arbitration Law and institutional rules. Appointment of foreign arbitrators is more flexible and their inclusions in the panel depend largely on the discretion of the relevant arbitration commission. For example, the conditions of being listed as an arbitrator on the CIETAC foreign-related panel can be relaxed appropriately.[66]

There are bifurcations in arbitral hearings as well. The updated CIETAC Rules in 2005 mandate an arbitral tribunal for domestic cases to have a record of hearing in writing which *shall* be signed by the members of the tribunal, the person who takes the notes, the parties and other participants to the arbitration.[67] On the other hand, rules for foreign-related arbitration are more flexible and discretionary. Tribunals of foreign-related cases *may* make a record in writing and *may* ask the parties to sign the document *when it considers necessary*.[68]

2.029

Lastly, the degree of judicial support and supervision over the two tracks is drastically different. The unequal judicial treatment is evidenced by the level of people's courts involved that provide judicial assistance with respect to interim measures of protection. For foreign-related disputes, property or evidence preservative measures should be applied to the people's court at the intermediate level; while the application for domestic disputes is just filed through the basic-level.[69] It is generally perceived that intermediate courts have more expertise and experience in dealing with complicated issues than basic courts.[70] Therefore, foreign-related arbitration are treated by courts in a more prudent and friendly manner. In respect of the supervisory scheme, as previously discussed, the SPC decrees a pyramidal "pre-reporting" system to ensure that the effect of foreign-related arbitral agreements and awards will not be denied without justifiable grounds. There is as such less interference in the judicial review of, and more esteem to the party autonomy in foreign-related arbitration.

2.030

The distinctions between the two tracks have been criticised as artificially and inappropriately regulated, resulting in legal contradictions. Since there are no longer foreign-related arbitration commissions in China after the 1996 blurring jurisdiction, an urgent task is to omit the expression "foreign-related arbitration commission" from the Arbitration Law. The task has become even more urgent when CIETAC extended its jurisdiction to receive domestic cases in 2000. The amendment to the Arbitration Law is necessary to ensure consistency between different Chinese regulations on arbitration.[71] There are even aggressive proposals as to the abolishment of the dual-track

2.031

---

[66] Article 2(2)(5) of the Stipulations for the Appointment of Arbitrators, jointly promulgated by CIETAC and CMAC on 1 September 1995, revised in 2000 and 2005 respectively.

[67] Article 64 of the 2005 CIETAC Arbitration Rules.

[68] Article 35 of the 2005 CIETAC Arbitration Rules.

[69] Article 17 of the 2005 CIETAC Arbitration Rules.

[70] In China's judiciary system, from intermediate courts above, a special tribunal called "Civil Division No. 4" is set which deals specifically with foreign-related commercial cases including enforcement of foreign-related arbitration agreements and awards. For more discussion, see Gu Weixia and Robert Morgan, "Improving Commercial Dispute Resolution in China", [2005] *Asian Dispute Review*, 7–9.

[71] John Mo, "Dilemma of 'Foreign Related Arbitration in PRC", [1999] *Arbitration and Dispute Resolution Law Journal*, 257–264.

system so as to avoid the impression of unequal treatment.[72] In this respect, the author concurs with Professor Schmitthoff that one of the notable characteristics of modern arbitration regulation is its distinction between international and domestic regimes. It is impossible for a country to exercise the same degree of control; generally, support is given to the international arbitration in the form of special regulations and laws for promoting international trade.[73]

2.032   With respect to China, the dual-track legislative technique has been emphasised for the particular sake of attracting more foreign investment, which traces back to the fledging marketisation level of China as a developing nation. It is submitted that the Arbitration Law employs the common method of legislation worldwide in dividing the two tracks, but the contents of the regulations on both tracks must be relatively comparable so that preferential bias to the foreign-related regime will not be a level playing field. Moreover, regulations on both tracks need to be improved and be in line with international standards. It might be plausible to adopt the Model Law for the foreign-related regime, which precedes the domestic regime historically in China. The foreign-related regime could be attempted as a pilot project of China's arbitration reform so that the domestic regime can gradually benefit from its experience in order to later integrate with international practices. However, because of their late start in institution-making and ongoing association with local administrative powers, local arbitration commissions lack integrity and quality as compared with CIETAC and CMAC. The improvement of arbitration rules by these local commissions also leaves much room to be pursued.

3. SYSTEM OF HARMONIOUS ARBITRATION

(a) Heritage from Chinese legal culture

2.033   The third trait of the Chinese arbitration system associates with its arbitration procedure being carried out in a harmonious manner, which has been phrased as "harmonious arbitration" in the scholarly context.[74] Such "harmony" is realised through the exercise of conciliation in the arbitration proceeding to seek an amicable settlement for restoring relations. The combination of arbitration with conciliation is not only the outstanding feature of CIETAC, but also prevailing practice in all Chinese arbitration commissions. For long, conciliation has been enjoying a prominent status in the dispute resolution system in China, which originated in the indigenous Confucian culture and Chinese legal traditions. Professor Holtzman sharply pointed out that legal culture and tradition play a critical role in the selection of an appropriate dispute resolution mechanism:

---

[72]   Song Lianbin, Zhao Jian, Li Hong, "Approaches to the Revision of the 1994 Arbitration Act of the People's Republic of China", (2003) 20 *Journal of International Arbitration,* 184.

[73]   Chia-Jui Cheng (ed), *Clive M. Schmitthoff's Selected Essays on International Trade Law* (The Hague: Kluwer Law International, 1988), 628.

[74]   Wang Shengchang, "The Relation between Arbitration and Conciliation", (2004) 49 *China law,* 88.

"Modern dispute resolution, although couched in the language of sociology—and indeed often in a jargon of their own—reflect techniques used for centuries in settling disputes in its own cultures and legal system."[75]

To appreciate the Chinese approach to dispute resolution, one must contemplate its cultural roots. In particular, the Confucian ideas of "harmony is valuable" (*heweigui*), "moderation in all things" *(zhongyong)* and the rule of propriety (*li*)[76] have formed the philosophical basis of the means of dispute resolution alternative to the lawsuit.[77] Accordingly, the Chinese ethical principles exist to secure a sense of communal harmony, which are then translated into cultural dictates as to how parties should relate to each other. Disputes are seen as a deviation from peace and harmony and hence, they are more often internalised through negotiation as a non-binding, voluntary dispute settlement process which enhances the possibility that parties will settle their disputes by way of mutually acceptable agreement, rather than by a binding third-party order. There is cultural disposition for *li*, emphasising the "right ordering" in the dispute resolution so that relationship may be preserved and accommodated. In this respect, Lauchli asserts that:

2.034

"Conciliation or mediation, with its advantage of restoring relations, is a natural extension of the Confucian ethics, and therefore has the longest standing position in Chinese tradition, and is pervasive in China."[78]

Thus, the Arbitration Law provides that if parties suggest conciliation, the tribunal is obliged to conduct it.[79] The legislation fits exactly into the Chinese morality culture. According to the legislative annotations, the main purpose for providing conciliation is to "help the parties maintain and promote their co-operations after the dispute is settled".[80]

2.035

There is also a strong impact received from Chinese legal traditions, which provide the fertile soil for the fostering of harmonious arbitration atmosphere between the parties. In Chinese legal history, the perception of lawsuit has been linked with punishment against "wrongs". As a result, adjudication institutions are largely for the purpose of determining guilt and wrongfulness, and enforcement is largely criminal or administrative in nature. In the ancient Chinese legal system, the threshold for criminal offences was extremely low. Heavy criminal penalties were imposed not only in criminal cases but also in certain cases that should be civil in nature. The fact

2.036

---

[75] Holtzmann, Workshop on *The Peaceful Settlement of International Disputes: Future Prospects*, at Hague Academy of International Law, September 1990, quoted in Redfern and Hunter, *Law and Practice of International Commercial Arbitration* (2004), 40.

[76] Confucius identified five cardinal relationships that needed to be honored to achieve a stable social order: father and son, ruler and subject, husband and wife, elder and younger, friend and friend. *Li*, or propriety, arose from the observance of these relationships. See Xin Ren, *Tradition of the Law and Law of the Tradition: Law, State, and Social Control in China* (Connecticut, London: Greenwood Press, 1997), 19–36.

[77] Urs Martin Lauchli, "Cross-Cultural Negotiations, With A Special Focus on ADR with the Chinese", (2000) 26 *John Marshall Law Review*, 1045.

[78] *Ibid.*, 1065–1066.

[79] Article 51 of the Arbitration Law.

[80] Legislative Affairs Commission of the NPCSC of the PRC (ed), *Arbitration Laws of China* (1997), 78.

that criminal penalties were applied to civil disputes frightened people away from the door of the court and geared an expectation of harmonious dispute resolution method among the general Chinese public.[81] As conciliation afforded people a method to settle their disputes that was socially acceptable in the light of the Confucian ethic and group moralities, it gained great popularity in Chinese legal history. In conclusion, the important harmonious feature of conciliation has been reputed as an integral part of the dispute resolution system rather than an alternative to court litigation in Chinese legal history.[82] These influences form a sound legal and historic base for the harmonious exercise of arbitration today.

2.037   Before the illustration as regards to how conciliation has been engaged in arbitral proceedings in China, one terminology issue must be clarified. In the context of international dispute resolution, both mediation and conciliation are important methods, although there has been slight difference between the two. Mediation entails a third neutral party for helping the disputants achieve the amicable settlement while conciliation is friendly negotiations directly between the two disputing parties.[83] Under provisions of the Model Law, only mediation is mentioned. However, in the context of Chinese arbitration, both terms have been used interchangeably to describe the same scope, whether a third-party is involved in assisting parties' amicable settlement.[84] The following discussion adopts the term "conciliation".

(b) Emphasis on conciliation in arbitration proceedings

2.038   The emphasis on conciliation in arbitral proceedings has been a long-standing practice in China. Prior to the Arbitration Law coming into effect, there had been regulations stipulating that arbitration institutions should conduct conciliation first.[85] Conciliation was also employed widely to deal with disputes arising from Sino-foreign business contracts.[86]

2.039   The Arbitration Law confirms such emphasis and specific provisions are provided in guiding the conciliation practice in arbitration:

> "The arbitral tribunal *may* carry out conciliation prior to rendering an arbitral award, but if both parties voluntarily seek conciliation, the tribunal *shall* conciliate the case. The tribunal *shall* make a written conciliation statement and then make an arbitral

---

[81]   On these issues of Chinese legal traditions, see generally, Ding Linghua, *History of Chinese Legal System (Zhongguo Falv Zhidu Shi)* (Beijing: China Law Press, 1999).

[82]   Stanley B. Lubman, *Bird in a Cage: Legal Reform in China after Mao* (California: Stanford University Press 1999), 23.

[83]   James T. Peter, "Med-Arb in International Arbitration", (1997) 8 *American Review of International Arbitration*, 83.

[84]   Wang, "The Relation between Arbitration and Conciliation", 88; see also Jun Ge, "Mediation, Arbitration and Litigation: Dispute Resolving in the People's Republic of China", (1996) 15 *UCLA Pacific Basin Law Journal*, 123–124.

[85]   For example, art.25 of the Rules of Economic Contract Arbitration, issued by the National Administration for Industry and Commerce on 22 August 1983 and repealed on 1 September 1995.

[86]   Cheng Dejun, Michael J Moser and Wang Shengchang, *International Arbitration in the People's Republic of China: Commentary, Cases and Materials (2nd ed.)* (Hong Kong: Butterworths Asia 2000), 95.

award in accordance with the settlement agreement should a settlement agreement be reached."[87]

Pursuant to it, parties may reach an amicable settlement through conciliation after they submit to arbitration; and if they so request, the tribunal is obliged to conciliate the case. Arbitrators may act as conciliators.[88] The outcome of a conciliation so conducted by arbitrators enjoys the legal effect as an arbitral award enforceable under the NYC across the globe.[89] This brings to the concept of combining conciliation with arbitration in China, simply the "Con-Arb", which means that in the process of arbitration, arbitrators will conduct conciliation in accordance with the parties' wishes.[90] Practical experience shows that there are many advantages when the Con-Arb approach is adopted. First, separate proceedings can be avoided and benefits of both conciliation and arbitration are made available to the parties at the same time. Second, the likelihood of achieving a successful dispute resolution outcome through conciliation is higher due to the harmonious atmosphere created. Lastly and most importantly, the settlement with conciliation incorporated can keep and promote the friendly cooperative relationship between the disputing parties.[91]

2.040

In respect of CIETAC's arbitration practice, over fifty percent of the parties agreed to have Con-Arb for their expectation of maintaining harmonious business relationship after the arbitration. Statistics show that in the period from 1983 to 1988, about 50 per cent of CIETAC cases were settled through conciliation by arbitrators; the figure maintained from 1989 to 2000.[92] These days, CIETAC still enjoys a steadily successful rate in the range of 20–30 per cent.[93] In late 1980s, CIETAC Rules had provided the Con-Arb approach by arbitrators, "If an amicable settlement was reached by the parties through conciliation, the tribunal should render an award in accordance with the contents of the amicable settlement".[94] Since then, CIETAC has amended its rules several times for improving the system.[95] In the latest updated rules in 2005, CIETAC has established a very comprehensive system under its art.40 with respect to the combined approach.

2.041

First, conciliation must be based on the absolute free will of parties so as not to infringe upon parties' lawful rights and interests in the subsequent arbitration.[96] The arbitral tribunal may provide conciliation service to both parties in an appropriate way.[97] In addition, none of the parties shall be prejudiced by the information revealed in the

2.042

---

[87]   Articles 49, 51, 52 of the Arbitration Law.
[88]   Wang, "The Relation between Arbitration and Conciliation", 88.
[89]   Paragraph 2 of art.51 of the Arbitration Law.
[90]   Wang, *Resolving Disputes in China* (1997), 51.
[91]   "An Interview to Tang Houzhi" in Wang Shengchang (ed), *The Theory and Practice of Combining Arbitration with Mediation (Zhongcai yu Tiaojie Xiangjiehe de Lilun yu Shiwu)* (Beijing: China Law Press, 2001), 292–305.
[92]   CIETAC website, http://cn.cietac.org/Mediation/index.asp?hangye=1.
[93]   *Ibid.*
[94]   Mediation or conciliation was formally stipulated in the 1989 CIETAC Arbitration Rules, which was the first provision concerning Med-Arb in Chinese arbitration practice.
[95]   The 1989 Rules was the 2nd version of CIETAC Rules. The CIETAC has had its rules updated in 1994 (3rd version), 1995 (4th version), 1998 (5th version), 2000 (6th version). The current rules are the 7th version, which has been effective since 1 May 2005.
[96]   Article 40(2) of the 2005 CIETAC Arbitration Rules.
[97]   Article 40(3), *ibid.*, "The tribunal may conciliate the case in the manner it considers appropriate".

subsequent arbitration proceedings if conciliation fails.[98] Parties have two options following the conciliation procedure:

(1)   If conciliation fails or if the tribunal believes that further efforts to conciliate will be futile, parties may request a termination of conciliation and proceed with the arbitration;[99]

(2)   If conciliation is successful and a settlement agreement has been reached during the arbitral process, parties may request the tribunal to make an arbitral award in accordance with the agreement thereof.[100]

2.043   Such "consented award" is then capable of being recognised and enforced under the NYC and national arbitration laws, which is boasted as the most attractive selling point of the combined practice. In the words of Cheng, Moser and Wang, this brings about a magical transformation from a non-binding private dispute resolution agreement to a binding and enforceable quasi-judicial award.[101]

2.044   The 2005 CIETAC Rules allow parties great freedom in the design of their dispute resolution process by incorporating various Con-Arb methods both prior to and in the course of arbitral proceedings, and taking place both inside and outside the tribunal. Previous CIETAC rules only protected conciliation within the arbitration proceedings, without taking into account parties' private conciliation efforts prior to the commencement of arbitration proceedings and outside the tribunal room.[102] To encourage parties to conciliate as well as to make the result of their conciliation agreement legally enforceable by subsequent simplified arbitration proceedings, an important provision has been added:

"If the parties reach a settlement agreement by themselves through conciliation without involvement of the arbitration commission, either party may, based on an arbitration agreement concluded between them that provides for arbitration by CIETAC and the settlement agreement, request CIETAC to constitute an arbitral tribunal to render an arbitral award in accordance with the terms of the settlement agreement."[103]

2.045   These new techniques provide a set of flexible and effective means for private conciliation efforts to be recognised.

(c) Impact upon arbitral practice

2.046   As illustrated above, conciliation has been emphasised in both Chinese arbitration legislation and institutional practice due to its tribute of amicable settlement.

---

[98]   Article 40(8), *ibid.*, "where conciliation fails, any opinion, view or statement … by either party or by the tribunal in the process of conciliation shall not be invoked as grounds for any claim, defense or counterclaim in the subsequent arbitral proceedings, judicial proceedings or any other proceedings".

[99]   Article 40(4) and (7), *ibid.*

[100]   Article 40(5) and (6), *ibid.*; see also art.49 of the Arbitration Law.

[101]   Chen, Moser and Wang, *International Arbitration in the People's Republic of China* (2000), 58.

[102]   See, for example, arts.41–43 of the 2000 CIETAC Arbitration Rules.

[103]   Article 40(1) of the 2005 CIETAC Arbitration Rules.

However, there are concerns with respect to the confusing role between an arbitrator and a conciliator. Cheng, Moser and Wang have underlied the significance of a "Con-Arbitrator", who they remarked as "the natural outcome of conciliation-oriented arbitration":

> "Arbitrators may act as middleman and 'peace-talker' at different times in the same proceedings. Arbitrators who have acted as conciliators are not prohibited from resuming their appointed roles as arbitrators later if the conciliation fails."[104]

Despite the Con-Arbitrator's flexibility and cost-saving benefits, the Chinese harmonious approach stands in sharp contrast with the due process requirement in dispute resolution where conciliation and arbitration are taken as two entirely separate procedures and the mixing of which is perceived to be harmful for the neutrality and sanctity of arbitration.[105] Such concern is most relevant if conciliation fails. Because parties involved in conciliation are encouraged to be as frank as possible to present both their strengths and weaknesses in facts, an arbitrator who has attempted conciliation may be influenced by allegations rather than evidence, and may consider matters not known to the other party. There are further concerns that these allegations may be subsequently used in arbitration which could endanger the arbitral award to be compromised.[106] For example, based on art.40(3) of the 2005 CIETAC Rules, "the arbitral tribunal may conciliate the case in the manner it considers appropriate". This leaves the Con-Arbitrator with great room for discretion as to how the Con-Arb process should be conducted. There is a high likelihood that *ex parte* private caucuses between the Con-Arbitrator and one of the parties could happen. Con-Arbitrators who are anxious to "push" for a settlement may elicit information from the parties and this would violate party's procedural justice. According to Moser, a Con-Arbitrator's power under art.40(3) raises issues of coercion and violation of due process if the tribunal considers it "appropriate" to pressure parties towards settlement.[107]

2.047

Moreover, the Chinese traditional respect for harmony has called the resilience of personal relations and networks (*guanxi*) within the operation of the arbitral tribunal.[108] As previously discussed, China adopts a closed panel system in the formation of tribunals where parties are obliged to choose arbitrators within the panel list of the arbitration commission which administers the case. Hence, personal relations within the tribunal could be delicate particularly when most of the panel arbitrators are drawn from internal staffs of the administering arbitration commission or government officials who share acquaintance with each other in the same local community.[109] The

2.048

---

[104] Chen, Moser and Wang, *International Arbitration in the People's Republic of China* (2000), 12.

[105] In China, arbitration and conciliation are combined in an on-going process. See negative comments by Lauchli, "Cross-Cultural Negotiations, With a Special Focus on ADR with the Chinese", 1069.

[106] Wang, "The Relation between Arbitration and Conciliation", 88.

[107] Michael J. Moser, "Commentary on Arbitration and Conciliation Concerning China" in van den Berg (ed), *ICCA Congress Series No. 12* (2005), 94.

[108] See Arias, Jose and Tomas Gomez, "Relationship Marketing Approach to Guanxi", (1998) 32 *European Journal of Marketing*, 145–156; see also Hui Chin and George Graen, "Guanxi and Professional Leadership in Contemporary Sino-American Joint Ventures in Mainland China", (1997) 8 *Leadership Quarterly*, 451–465.

[109] See more discussions in Section 2 of Chapter 6.

staff and official arbitrators afraid of breaking the personal ties tend to accommodate among the tribunal for reaching the "amicable" majority opinion. The cultural root of "amicability" is indeed strong in China's mode of dispute resolution process. Confucianism and collectivism remain powerful restraints on the penetration of Western due process principles.[110] The supremacy of personal ties over institutional obligations is obvious in China, which affects the selection and application of international legal norms. Hence, the "amicability", for the sake of keeping personal relations, may challenge due process and formal legal institutionalism when China further embraces the interaction with modern legal norms.[111] Western scholars advocate that "free-will" and "due process rights" of parties are paramount and must be protected utmost in modern commercial arbitration. But the traditional Chinese legal culture and its transitional marketisation level implies an inherent problem in China's legal modernisation process under the wave of globalisation including arbitration. According to Professor McConnaughay:

> "The traditional Chinese perspective embodies a traditional Chinese supposition that the written contract is tentative rather than final, a source of guidance rather than determinative and subordinate to other values such as preserving the relationship and avoiding disputes. All of these may control far more than the written contract itself how a commercial relationship adjusts to future contingencies."[112]

2.049 Party autonomy could therefore be undermined when relationship or collective considerations take precedence over contractual obligations. Arguably, the problem of party autonomy and due process may find an answer with Chinese characteristic that makes the CIETAC Con-Arb approach still suitable for China. In a recent occasion, CIETAC leaders persuasively argued that such "amicable settlement", though with impartiality and independence concerns, is to ensure on the one hand the deference to the Con-Arbitrator who enables greater flexibility and efficiency as to how harmony can be restored whilst on the other hand to respect parties' willingness and pleasure of enjoying peace and harmony.[113]

4. CONCLUSION

2.050 Chapter 2 has analysed three salient features of the Chinese arbitration system, i.e. institutional, dual-track and harmonious arbitration. Delving into these features, this chapter is an attempt to explore their underlying social and cultural backgrounds

---

[110] Pitman B. Potter, *The Chinese Legal System: Globalization and Local Legal Culture—Series of Routledge Studies On China in Transition* (London & New York: Routledge, 2001), 5.

[111] Pitman B. Potter, "Legal Reform in China: Institutions, Culture, and Selective Adaptation", (2004) 29 *Law & Social Inquiry*, 474.

[112] Philip J. McConnaughay, "Rethinking the Role of Law and Contracts in East-West Commercial Relationships", (2001) 41 *Vanderbilt Journal of International Law*, 427. An excellent discussion was provided on the differing perceptions and understandings of contract, party autonomy, marketisation and their interrelationship between the East and the West.

[113] Wang, "CIETAC's Perspective on Arbitration and Conciliation Concerning China", in van den Berg (ed), *ICCA Congress Series No. 12* (2005), 41.

and in addition, how these features may exert influence upon China's current arbitral practice and prospective arbitration development.

With respect to the system of institutional arbitration, historic experience shows that arbitration in China has been unitarily conducted by Chinese arbitration commissions. Thus far, *ad hoc* arbitration is not yet recognised in China, which largely restricts parties' autonomy and interests in arbitration. The denial has brought about paradoxes and confusions in both arbitration theory and practice. Institutional services provided by foreign arbitral bodies are also barred under the Chinese institutional arbitration monopoly. China's accession to the WTO and its commitment to comply with the open market rules may impose a challenge on such an institutional monopoly, as it may amount to discrimination against parties' increasing transactional autonomy as well as a sense of discrimination against foreign arbitration service providers. These issues continue to pose challenges alongside China's ongoing integration with the world market and international arbitration norms.

2.051

On the dual-track arbitration system, China is in a sense much more sophisticated than that of many other countries. It must be admitted that the country is still in the process of maturing its rather new arbitration system, which began to take shape only after the Arbitration Law took effect in 1995. At present, China has a theoretically unified regime of arbitration where both the domestic and foreign-related arbitrations have been subject together to the guidance of the Arbitration Law. In fact, however, it is a bifurcated system. The foreign-related arbitration regime is relatively separate from and enjoys more favourable treatment than their domestic counterpart at different stages of the arbitral proceeding. This has been legally supported under the Arbitration Law and practically endorsed by the SPC judicial interpretations. With respect to the practice of foreign-related arbitration, CIETAC has long maintained a higher level of professionalism and thus has been more trusted by foreign investors as compared with local arbitration commissions. The dual-track system predicts the unbalanced development of the two tracks in future.

2.052

Finally, when considering the Chinese distinction of maintaining harmony in arbitration, cultural expectations over the law must not be overlooked. The Confucius amicable dispositions play a critical role in comprehending the CIETAC Con-Arb practice and its perceived flexibility as well as critiques. The *guanxi* culture, on the top of that, exerts delicate psychological impact upon the Chinese arbitrators within the tribunal in reaching their amicable decisions. Hence, cultural factors will still play an invisible yet critical role along China's arbitration modernisation process.

2.053

To sum up, the historic, social, and cultural context of understanding arbitration remains important in China as the textual reading of the Arbitration Law may not fully embrace the inside spirit of the infrastructure of the country's arbitration regime. Economic globalisation has called upon China to embrace internationally recognised arbitral norms and principles, such as party autonomy, equal treatment, due process and formal institutionalism. To foster a credible arbitration system, China has attempted to overhaul its out-dated perceptions and practices. But

2.054

there are constraints imposed by the transitional economy as well as its associated immature rule-of-law system. In the meantime, there remain impacts from the traditional harmonious and collective culture penetrating into arbitration ideologies and practices. As such, the modernisation of China's arbitration needs time to fit into a formerly administrative-dominant legal framework and relationship-centered society on the one hand and a booming yet fledging market economy on the other hand.

REGULATION OF ARBITRATION AGREEMENTS AND PRACTICAL ISSUES

Chapter 3 locates the regulation of arbitration agreements in the wider context of the Chinese arbitration system and its development. It begins with a review of the relevance and importance of the regulation of arbitration agreements in order to reflect the delicate relationship among key role players in the Chinese arbitration system. The discussion then moves on to review the literature on the regulation of arbitration agreements in China since the promulgation of the Arbitration Law. It is notable that the regulation in the regime is largely deficient, leading to party and tribunal autonomy constrained. The last part draws a broader picture of the landscape of the regulation of arbitration agreements by introducing relevant practical issues pertaining to or affecting arbitration agreements in China. These issues exemplify the most distinctive Chinese characteristics of arbitration law and practice, while reflecting on a more limited extent of international standards with respect to party and tribunal autonomy. They also provide the scope for discussion in subsequent chapters of this book.

1. Importance of the Regulation of Arbitration Agreements in China

(a) Party and tribunal autonomy

As mentioned in Chapter 1, among the various ways of settling business disputes in China, arbitration has become a preferred means for resolving trade and investment disputes between Chinese and foreign parties. Although promulgated as a "milestone" in China's arbitration history,[1] over more than a decade of practice, the Arbitration Law has been criticised as being much tainted by local standards and thus insufficient in reflecting the international trend supporting arbitration.[2] One of the most contentious issues in the rising use of arbitration in China is that party and tribunal autonomy is not satisfactorily protected.[3] Some provisions of the Arbitration Law are too rigid and greatly restrict the autonomy of the parties, which further restrict the autonomy of the tribunal.[4] This adversely affects the flexibility of arbitration procedures, causing delay and inefficiency in arbitration. Further, the lack of detailed rules on the exercise of arbitral power by arbitrators has made the provisions soft legal constraints.[5] As a result, parties find their arbitration agreements arbitrarily interpreted by Chinese judges for minor drafting defects; in addition, arbitral tribunals chosen do not perform independently and impartially as they have been expected of what arbitration should be

---

[1] See discussions in Chapter 1.

[2] See, for example, Bei Hu, "Key Arbitration Center Loses Western Appeal", *South China Morning Post*, 13 May 2002, 4; Jane Moir, "Foreign Business are Being Urged by Their Lawyers Not to Go to China's Official Arbitration Commission", *South China Morning Post*, 3 October 2001, 4; Wang Shengchang, "The Arbitration Law after China's Accession to the WTO", (2002) 37 *China Law*, 76; Charles Kenworthey Harner, "Arbitration Fails to Reduce Foreign Investors' Risk in China", (1998) 8 *Pacific Rim Law and Policy Journal*, 393.

[3] Song Lianbin, "From Ideology to Rules: Several Issues Worthy of Attention for the Revision of PRC Arbitration Law (Linian Zouxiang Guize: Zhongcaifa Gaige ying Zhuyi de Jige Wenti)", (2005) 52 *Arbitration in Beijing Quarterly (Beijing Zhongcai)*, 3–4.

[4] *Ibid.*, 176.

[5] *Ibid.*, 178.

under the rather new Arbitration Law.[6] According to some leading Chinese arbitration scholars, "The key problem with the Arbitration Law is that not enough attention was paid to the contractual characteristic of arbitration. Party autonomy as the cornerstone of arbitration is there in form but not in spirit".[7] Indeed, this is an area where the regulation of arbitration agreements needs attention for the new-round arbitration reform in China.

3.003   Arbitration agreements are traditionally considered as the threshold of arbitral processes where the parties show their willingness to arbitrate and the tribunal derives its jurisdiction.[8] Recently, these agreements are more aptly identified as the core of an arbitration system because their regulation reflects the extent of party autonomy and tribunal autonomy. The regulation determines the freedom and scope that parties have in the drafting of arbitration agreements and thus affects the design of their dispute resolution process in the given jurisdiction. The international trend has been to comfort parties with more freedom and wider scope in the drafting so as to encourage the use of arbitration to resolve business disputes.[9] Parties are free to stipulate in their arbitration agreements almost any matters such as disputes to be arbitrated, numbers of arbitrators and ways of appointing them to the tribunal, and most importantly, specifications on the arbitral procedure, subject to the mandatory requirements of the national arbitration legislation.[10]

3.004   The definition of arbitration agreements in China is not much of an issue in the Arbitration Law. However, the scope of arbitral matters that may be included in arbitration agreements in China is much more restricted. For example, the procedural details are controlled under arbitration commission rules which parties are not allowed to modify;[11] further, parties are not allowed to choose *ad hoc* arbitration.[12] Other matters following the arbitration agreements which have been taken for granted elsewhere however become sensitive issues in China such as the tribunal's *competence-competence* to determine its own jurisdiction.[13]

(b) Delicate relationship among key arbitration players

3.005   The regulation of arbitration agreements in China is very distinctive. One aspect of this distinctiveness is that parties are required to stipulate a definite Chinese

---

[6]   United States-China Commission Meeting on 14 June 2001: Hearing Statement before the First Public Hearing of the US-China Commission by Professor Jerome A. Cohen of the New York University Law School where he remarked, "The longer my experience as either an advocate or an arbitrator in disputes presented to CIETAC, the graver my doubt have become about its independence and impartiality".

[7]   Song Lianbin, Zhao Jian and Li Hong, "Approaches to the Revision of the 1994 Arbitration Act of the People's Republic of China", (2003) 20 *Journal of International Arbitration,* 174.

[8]   Julian D.M. Lew (ed), *Contemporary Problems in International Arbitration* (London: Sweet & Maxwell, 1978), 36; J.C. Schultz and A.J. van den Berg, *The Art of Arbitration* (Deventer: Kluwer Law and Taxation Publishers, 1982), 7–9.

[9]   Redfern and Hunter, *Law and Practice of International Commercial Arbitration* (2004), 7.

[10]   Other matters may include choice of applicable law, exclusion of judicial review and appeal. *Ibid.*

[11]   See more discussions in Chapter 6.

[12]   See more discussions in Chapter 4.

[13]   See more discussions in Chapter 5.

arbitration commission. The choice of the commission is a special legal requirement for the substance of validity under art.16 of the Arbitration Law.[14] In this sense, defective arbitration agreements, i.e. agreements without specifying a clear identity of the arbitration commission, are treated as void.[15] The very reason for imposing this rule is the sole institutional feature of the Chinese arbitration system. Hence, the threshold of arbitrating in China has become extremely high. The arbitration commission chosen will then determine the tribunal formation and procedural details.[16] It thus raises the issue of quality and integrity of these Chinese arbitration commissions.

The other distinctive feature concerns the process of ruling on the validity of arbitration agreements and hence defining the scope of arbitral jurisdiction. Under art.20 of the Arbitration Law, it is the arbitration commission or people's court, instead of the arbitral tribunal, that makes the ruling.[17] Additionally, in the case where competing jurisdiction arises between a court and an arbitration commission, it is the people's court that prevails over the arbitration commission on jurisdiction determination.[18] On the one hand, the Chinese special way of dividing arbitral power between the arbitration commission and arbitral tribunal is spotted. In this regard, tribunals seem less powerful than commissions and the particular role of arbitration commissions within Chinese arbitration system has been brought to attention.[19] On the other hand, the prevalent judicial power over arbitration is reflected.[20] It therefore raises the issue of imbalanced power division among the key role players in the Chinese arbitration system. **3.006**

As such, the study on the regulation of arbitration agreements reflects the delicate relationship among these key role players in the Chinese arbitration system—the arbitration commission, arbitral tribunal and people's court; the quality and integrity of the respective role player; and how party autonomy and tribunal autonomy are to be affected by this triangular relationship. These issues amplify the major pitfalls of the entire Chinese arbitration system. The tackling of them is both the trigger and focal point of the prospective reforms for the entire arbitration system in China. **3.007**

Despite the high importance of these issues, the current regulatory framework is not satisfactory that has been much criticised for constraining parties' arbitral autonomy and interest. In this regard, it has been argued that the Arbitration Law promulgated in 1994 is deficient and that many other rules ancillary to it have been inconsistent and even contradictory.[21] **3.008**

---

[14] Article 16 of the Arbitration Law.
[15] Article 18 of the Arbitration Law.
[16] See more discussions in Chapter 4 on the "validity requirements".
[17] Paragraph 1 of art.20 of the Arbitration Law.
[18] Paragraph 2 of art.20 of the Arbitration Law.
[19] See more discussions in Chapter 5 on the "arbitral jurisdiction".
[20] See more discussions in Chapter 6 on the "judicial enforcement of arbitration agreements".
[21] See, for example, John Mo, "Dilemma of Chinese Arbitration System" (1999), 98; Song, Zhao and Li, "Approaches to the Revision of the 1994 Arbitration Act of the PRC" (2003), 174; Jerome A. Cohen, "Time to Fix China's Arbitration", (2005) 2 *Far Eastern Economic Review*, 168.

2. CONSTRAINED PARTY AND TRIBUNAL AUTONOMY IN CHINESE ARBITRAL PRACTICE

(a) Inherent deficiency of the Arbitration Law

3.009   The argument that the Arbitration Law is deficient towards the regulation of arbitration agreements is mainly reflected in two aspects. First, some of the provisions are too rigid and greatly restrict the autonomy of the parties, which further restrict the autonomy of the tribunal.[22] Second, many important provisions as to the parties' procedural freedom in arbitration are lacking from the text of the Arbitration Law, leaving a major loophole in the arbitral practice.[23]

3.010   It has been argued that the legal requirements concerning the validity of arbitration agreements in China are overly strict because under international practice, an agreement is valid as long as the parties' intention to arbitrate is manifested.[24] However, as already mentioned in previous chapters, the Arbitration Law denies the effect of agreements with an innominate or unclear identity of the arbitration commission such that *ad hoc* arbitration is not recognised in China.[25] As a matter of fact, parties arbitrating in China are barred from enjoying the flexibility of those self-tailored arbitration procedures. Similarly, it has been argued that the Arbitration Law forbids the arbitral tribunal to determine the validity of arbitration agreements and therefore its own jurisdiction, which significantly departs from the international practice of *competence-competence*.[26]

3.011   The fact that arbitral jurisdiction determination and merit adjudication have been apportioned to two different bodies indeed prolongs the procedure and causes a waste of human resources.[27] It has been further criticised that the Arbitration Law discriminates against the autonomy and interest of the parties to domestic disputes by adopting a "dual-track difference" within the Arbitration Law.[28] Based on that,

---

[22]   Ge Liu and Alexandar Lourie, "International Commercial Arbitration in China: History, New Developments and Current Practice", (1995) 28 *John Marshall Law Review*; John Mo, "Dilemma of Chinese Arbitration System", (1999) 6 *Arbitration and Dispute Resolution Journal;* Song, Zhao and Li, "Approaches to the Revision of the 1994 Arbitration Act of the PRC" (2003) 20 *Journal of International Arbitration*, 174.

[23]   Jiang Xianming and Li Ganggui, *Study of Chinese Arbitration Law (Zhongguo Zhongcai Faxue)* (Nanjing: Southeast University Press, 1997), 2; Xie Shisong, *Commercial Arbitration Law (Shangshi Zhongcai Faxue)* (Beijing: Higher Education Press, 2003), 4; Kang Ming, *A Study on Commercial Arbitration Service (Shangshi Zhongcai Fuwu Yanjiu)* (Beijing: China Law Press, 2005), 3–4.

[24]   Song, Zhao and Li, "Approaches to the Revision of the 1994 Arbitration Act of the PRC" (2003), 175.

[25]   See more discussions in Chapter 2 on the "*ad hoc* arbitration".

[26]   Song Lianbin, Studies on Jurisdictional Problems in International Commercial Arbitration (Guoji Shangshi Zhongcai Guanxiaquan Yanjiu) (Beijing: China Law Press, 2000), 89; Feng Kefei, "The Theory of Competence-Competence and Its Practical Application in Our Country (Guanxiaquan/Guanxiaquan Lilun jiqi zai Woguo de Shijian)", (2002) 71 *Arbitration and Law Journal (Zhongcai yu Falu)*, 58.

[27]   Kang, *A Study on Commercial Arbitration Service* (2005), 27.

[28]   See Chapter VII of the Arbitration Law (arts.66–73), entitled "Special Provisions for Arbitration Involving Foreign Elements". See also, Mo, "Dilemma of 'Foreign-Related' Arbitration in PRC", (1999) 2 *Arbitration and Dispute Resolution Law Journal*, 18; Wang Shangchang, "The Arbitration Law after China's Accession to the WTO", (2002) 37 *China Law*, 68.

parties whose disputes carry no foreign elements[29] were not allowed to choose the China International Economic and Trade Arbitration Commission (CIETAC) and the China Maritime Arbitration Commission (CMAC) in their arbitration agreements due to their status as "foreign-related arbitration commissions" under the Arbitration Law[30] until the jurisdiction is later blurred.[31] Indeed, the different concept with respect to "foreign-related dispute" under the jurisprudence of Civil Procedural Law[32] and "foreign-related arbitration commission" under the Arbitration Law have caused practical confusion in the handling of arbitral jurisdiction. The fact that Sino-Foreign joint ventures and foreign-invested enterprises (FIEs) are defined as Chinese domestic companies where only local arbitration commissions are available only aggravates the problem until the practice is later picked up by CIETAC Rules since 1998.[33]

Another principal weakness of the Arbitration Law that has been under considerable criticism is its absence of regulation on the parties' procedural autonomy. It has been argued that the Arbitration Law fails to prescribe the extent to which parties can modify or deviate from the rules of the arbitration commissions in their arbitration agreements for designing the dispute resolution process, i.e. whether the legislative silence means rejection or affirmation.[34] It has as well been much challenged that the Arbitration Law makes no provision for either the summary procedure or power of the parties to deal flexibly with specific issues arising from the arbitral proceeding by means of agreement.[35] It has been further argued that the Arbitration Law neglects the necessary power of the party and tribunal for a flexible-oriented arbitration which has thus subjected their procedural interest to the hands of the "powerful" arbitration commissions.[36] In this regard, despite the critical role of these arbitration commissions

3.012

---

[29] Under the judicial interpretations of General Principles of Civil Law (Civil Law Judicial Interpretation), a dispute can be considered as "foreign-related" if it satisfies any of the following three conditions: (1) either of the party is a non-Chinese citizen; (2) the subject-matter of the dispute is not in China; (3) the establishment and change of the legal relationship takes place outside China. This interpretation applies to the circumstances of Hong Kong-, Macau- and Taiwan-related disputes.

[30] Articles 66–70 of the Arbitration Law.

[31] CIETAC and CMAC were established as to cater for resolving foreign-related business and trade disputes under the Arbitration Law. The jurisdiction is blurred by both the State Council Notice in 1996 and subsequent CIETAC and CMAC Rules revision in 1998. See below for more discussions.

[32] See art.304 of Civil Procedure Law Judicial Interpretation (1991). Similar provisions can be found in art.178 of the General Principles of Civil Law Judicial Interpretations (1988). The author argues that the concept of "foreign-related arbitration commission" should be discarded from the revised Arbitration Law, see discussions under the heading "Conclusion: State Control vs. Party Autonomy "in Chapter 6.

[33] Corresponding to the State Council Notice on blurring the jurisdictions between the two types of arbitration commissions in 1996, CIETAC updated its rules and expanded its jurisdiction to domestic disputes accordingly in 1998. See more discussions by Xiabin Xu and George D. Wilson, "One Country, Two – International Commercial Arbitration – Systems", (2000) 17 *Journal of International Arbitration*, 48.

[34] Lynch, "The New Arbitration Law" (1996), 2; Wang, "The Arbitration Law after China's Accession to the WTO" (2002), 32; Cohen, "Time to Fix China's Arbitration" (2005), 25.

[35] Zhao Jian, "Reviews and Prospects: Chinese International Commercial Arbitration at the Turn of the Century (Huigu yu Zhanwang: Shiji Zhijiao de Zhongguo Guoji Shangshi Zhongcai)", (2001) 51 *Arbitration and Law (Zhongcai yu Falu),* 72; Song, Zhao and Li, "Approaches to the Revision of the 1994 Arbitration Act of the PRC" (2003), 174; Kang, *A Study on Commercial Arbitration Service* (2005), 27; Kong Yuan, "Revision of China's 1994 Arbitration Act—Some Suggestions from a Judicialization Perspective", (2005) 4 *Journal of International Arbitration*, 22.

[36] Chris Hunter (ed), *Dispute Resolution in the PRC: A Practical Guide to Litigation and Arbitration in China* (Hong Kong: Asia Law & Practice Press, 1995), 103; Song, Zhao and Li, "Approaches to the Revision of the 1994 Arbitration Act of the PRC" (2003), 174.

in formulating procedural rules in China, the Arbitration Law lacks implementation schemes to ensure the quality and integrity of these commissions. It has been critically pointed out by several authors that the Arbitration Law cherishes good wishes of leading qualified arbitration commissions in China, but fails to lay down detailed rules in realising them.[37]

(b) Inconsistent ancillary rules

3.013   Due to the inherent deficiencies of the Arbitration Law in regulating these issues, some other documents (such as judicial interpretations, administrative documents and institutional rules on arbitration) have come to address the problems. For more than a decade, unfortunately, they appear sporadic and inconsistent rules from different sources and are criticised for having even worsened the practice.

3.014   First, as discussed in previous chapters, given the institutional feature of the arbitration system in China, the rules of arbitration commissions have become a significant source on arbitral procedure in addition to the Arbitration Law. As the most experienced arbitration institution in China,[38] CIETAC has substantially developed its rules over the years for attracting more disputes.[39] Meanwhile, there have been approximately 200 local arbitration commissions established in major Chinese cities following the promulgation of the Arbitration Law.[40] Each local commission has thus published its own set of arbitration rules based on the Arbitration Law and its local conditions. Therefore, rules of the Beijing Arbitration Commission (BAC) differ from those of the Shanghai (SAC) and Shenzhen (SZAC) Arbitration Commissions; and they may still be different to those of CIETAC.[41] The lack of uniform standards in formulating rules on the arbitral procedure in China opens the door for institutional discretion by the arbitration commissions. Furthermore, the fact that revisions to these rules are often confidential under the commission secretariat only adds to the inconsistency and uncertainty.[42]

3.015   A second aspect of the ancillary rules that has been subject to considerable concern is the frequent and parallel issuing of judicial interpretations on arbitration by both the central and local judiciaries. As previously illustrated, the Supreme People's Court (SPC)

---

[37]   Song, "From Ideology to Rules: Several Issues Worthy of Attention for the Revision of PRC Arbitration Law" (2005), 6; Kong, "Revision of China's 1994 Arbitration Act" (2005), 22; Gu Weixia and Robert Morgan, "Improving Commercial Dispute Resolution in China", (2005) 1 *Asian Dispute Review*, 6.

[38]   CIETAC was established as early as 1956. For a brief history of CIETAC, see Wang Wenying, "Distinctive Features of Arbitration in China: A Historic Perspective", (2006) 23 *Journal of International Arbitration*, 49.

[39]   See discussions in Chapter 1.

[40]   Gao Fei, Interview with Lu Yunhua, Chief of the Department of Coordination on Government Legal Affairs Office of the Legislative Affairs of the State Council (Fang Guowuyuan Fazhiban Zhengfufawuxietiaosi Sizhang Luyunhua)" (hereinafter referred to as "Interview with Luyunhua"), (2008) 2 *Arbitration and Judicature in China (Zhongguo Zhongcai yu Sifa)*, 3.

[41]   See BAC Rules, available at http://www.bjac.org.cn/program/rule.htm; SAC Rules, available at http://www.accsh.org/accsh/node5/index.html; SZAC Rules, available at http://www.szac.org/guide.asp; and CIETAC Rules, http://www.cietac.org.cn/help/index.asp?hangye=10.

[42]   Pitman B. Potter, *The Chinese Legal System: Globalization and Local Legal Culture— Series of Routledge Studies on China in Transition* (London & New York: Routledge, 2001), 38; Wang Wenying, "Comparative Research on Arbitration Rules and Revisions of the CIETAC Rules (Zhongcai Guize Bijiao Yanjiu ji Maozhong Guize de Xiugai)", (2005) 94 *Arbitration and Law (Zhongcai yu Falv)*, 68.

enjoys *de facto* rule-making power whereby its judicial interpretations are treated as "quasi-laws" for filling the practical gaps of the legislation.[43] With respect to the regulation of arbitration agreements, dozens of judicial interpretations have been issued by the SPC.[44] The fact that there are many judicial clarifications does not in itself cause the practical difficulties. The problem however lies in SPC's sporadic ways of clarifying the arbitral issues and moreover, its uncertain interaction with the judicial opinions from the Local Higher People's Courts (LHPCs).[45] Since most of the SPC interpretations have been issued as replies to specific questions raised by the lower level people's courts until they were consolidated very recently in late 2006,[46] they have come as scattered and sporadic pieces of documents from time to time and thus hard to follow in arbitral practice.[47] Nevertheless, LHPCs in some economically better developed areas have at the same time issued more liberal judicial opinions for promoting arbitration in the locality although they lack judicial interpretative powers officially.[48] Moreover, it is much criticised that the allocation of power of the judiciary versus arbitration in China is very imbalanced because the people's court can empower itself to seize the arbitral jurisdiction when it wishes by way of publishing judicial interpretations.[49]

Lastly, the administrative documents laid down by the State Council have been claimed **3.016** as deteriorating rather than remedying the Arbitration Law deficiencies. Among those many documents, as aforementioned, in 1995, the State Council issued a clarification, the 1995 Notice, concerning the re-organisation of arbitration commissions post the Arbitration Law promulgation. The 1995 Notice has been challenged as defeating the Arbitration Law objective on the non-governmental status of the arbitration commissions due to unavoidable government influence in the commission infrastructure.[50] A year later, the State Council issued another clarification, the 1996 Notice, to allow local arbitration commissions to receive foreign-related arbitral disputes. The 1996 Notice seeks to abolish the monopoly of foreign-related arbitrations by foreign-related arbitration commissions (CIETAC and CMAC) and as such to remedy the Arbitration Law deficiency on the "dual-track" discriminations. However, again, the blurring jurisdiction has been criticised for failing to take into account the lack of experience of most local arbitration commissions in handling foreign-related disputes.[51] In this

[43] Resolution on Strengthening the Works for Interpretations of Laws by the Standing Committee of National People's Congress in 1981, under which the SPC was given the power to interpret national laws in relation to issues arising from the application of law to concrete issues. See also art.33 of the Organic Law of the People's Court (2006).

[44] See discussions in Chapters 4 and 7.

[45] John Mo, *Arbitration Law in China* (Hong Kong: Sweet & Maxwell Asia, 2001), 87; Jingzhou Tao, *Arbitration Law and Practice in China* (The Hague: Kluwer Law International, 2004), 32; Fung and Wang (ed), *Arbitration in China: A Practical Guide* (2004), para 2-47. See discussions in Chapter 1, under the heading "Judicial Interpretations"; see also discussions in Chapter 4, under the heading "Judicial Opinions by the LHPCs".

[46] Judicial Interpretation on the Application of the Arbitration Law, issued by the SPC in August 2006 and took into effect in October 2006.

[47] See discussions in Chapters 2 and 5.

[48] For example, the Beijing Higher People's Court issued its judicial opinions on arbitration in 1999, followed by the Shanghai Higher People's Court in 2001 and Sichuan Higher People's Court in 2003.

[49] Wang Shengchang, *Resolving Disputes through Arbitration in Mainland China* (Beijing: China Law Press, 2003), 79; Fung and Wang (ed), *Arbitration in China: A Practical Guide* (2004), para 2-65.

[50] See discussions in Chapter 1.

[51] See discussions in Chapter 1.

sense, the administrative decisions have been argued for giving rise to more practical confusion.[52]

(c) Pervasive state control over arbitration

3.017   The author agrees with the critique that limited protection to party and tribunal autonomy is owed to the deficiencies of the Arbitration Law and its inconsistent ancillary rules. Compared with modern international arbitration norms, the Chinese regulation has serious shortcomings. Although arbitration in China, like its other branches of the legal system, displays Chinese characteristics,[53] those characteristics should not deviate substantially from international standards. Therefore, discussions in the following chapters of this book will go further in examining the relative shortage of the regulation of arbitration agreements in China after comparing it with the modern international arbitration norms such as the UNCITRAL Model Law, the ICC Rules and English Arbitration Act 1996.

3.018   The author however does not agree with the critique that restricted party and tribunal autonomy are solely attributable to the regulatory defects and hence reform should only focus on remedying provisional failures. In criticising the restrictions, one has to be aware that most of the existing literature, if not all, relies mainly on the examination of the written laws and rules. As such, textual deficiencies are blamed as natural causes of the constraints on party autonomy and party interest. The critique, however, fails to take into account the empirical aspect that is more subtle in the Chinese legal system. Studies have shown that a significant gap exists between the written law and law in practice in China, particularly during its market transitions.[54] The conflicts and pressures resulting from the entire economic, political and administrative transitions tend to make the written regulations (laws, rules, etc), no matter in what form and from what source, vulnerable under political ideology and administrative supremacy.[55]

3.019   This stand seems to lead to the conclusion that the critique regarding the constrained party and tribunal autonomy in China on the sole basis of its regulatory deficiency is incomplete. Further, the existing literature fails to provide a satisfactory answer as to the continuing insufficiency in the protection of party autonomy and interest in arbitration in China despite the active regulatory reforms undertaken by the SPC and CIETAC over the past decade.[56] In this regard, the author raises the question whether there are any constraints, beyond the already identified regulatory deficiencies, which pose more serious practical challenges to party and tribunal autonomy. In addition,

---

[52]   Mo, *Arbitration Law in China* (2001), 35; Fung and Wang (ed), *Arbitration in China: A Practical Guide* (2004), para 2-26.

[53]   This is justified because a legal system cannot exist without being influenced by the local culture. See Randall Peerenboom, "Globalization, Path Dependency and the Limits of Law: Administrative Law Reforms and Rules of Law in the People's Republic of China", (2001) 19 *Berkeley Journal of International Law*, 58.

[54]   Wang Guiguo and Wei Zhenyin (ed), *Legal Developments in China: Market Economy and Law* (Hong Kong: Sweet & Maxwell Asia, 1996), 7; Randall Peerenboom, *China's Long March towards Rule of Law* (Cambridge University Press, 2002), 197.

[55]   Peerenboom, *China's Long March towards Rule of Law* (2002), 196.

[56]   By improving the rules of arbitration commissions and issuing more systematic judicial interpretations on the arbitration agreements and associated matters. See discussions in substantive chapters.

the author raises the further question whether these supposed practical constraints intervene into the Chinese arbitration system as a whole and its development generally so that reforms should target broader aspects. The hypothesis is that state control still constitutes the fundamental problem of the Chinese arbitration system. Formally, the Arbitration Law is overly rigid. Empirically, the author attempts to prove the extent to which political and administrative influences as practical constraints have encroached upon the Chinese arbitration system.

For example, in China's move from a planned to a market economy, the State still 3.020 wishes to exercise considerable control over market activities including dispute resolution for maintaining socioeconomic stability. Such "control" has then been translated to the institutions such as arbitration commissions, for controlling the outcome of arbitration. This suggests administrative taints of the Chinese arbitration commissions on the one hand and a monopoly of institutional arbitration by Chinese arbitration commissions on the other hand. As such, a rigid requirement is imposed to include a definite Chinese arbitration commission into the arbitration agreement. *Ad hoc* arbitration, due to the unpredictability of its final result, might be considered a realm outside state control and hence a deviation from the socioeconomic stability. Other questions may include, whether, over more than a decade, Chinese arbitration commissions and arbitral tribunals have achieved the object of being non-governmental and professional so that arbitration business can be really independent and market-oriented. These questions tend to lead to a number of other practical issues which pertain to or arise out of the regulation of arbitration agreements that are worthy of careful examination.

3. PRACTICAL ISSUES PERTAINING TO OR AFFECTING ARBITRATION AGREEMENTS IN CHINA

For the purpose of the discussion in following chapters, as a working definition, 3.021 "regulation of arbitration agreements" refers to the "regulation and practice of arbitration agreements in China". Specifically, it refers to the evolving regulations that pertain to or arise out of arbitration agreements in China, and more importantly, the actual implementation of these regulations since the promulgation of the Arbitration Law. The study envisages the following aspects of practical *issues* in China's arbitration regime, as will be dealt with in detail from Chapters 4 to 7 of this book: validity scope of arbitration agreements (Chapter 4); tribunal's competence in determining the effect of arbitration agreements and hence, arbitral jurisdiction (Chapter 5); formation of the arbitral tribunal (Chapter 6); role of the people's court in supervision of arbitration agreements and accordingly, arbitral enforcement (Chapter 7).

The *issues* listed above are not exhaustive of all the aspects arising from the 3.022 regulation and practice of arbitration agreements in China. However, they represent some of the thorniest problems of the Arbitration Law and the entire Chinese arbitration system. This study is limited to the current and most important issues facing arbitration in China today; to some extent these issues also exemplify the distinctive Chinese characteristics of arbitration law and practice, whilst reflecting to a more limited extent of international standards with respect to party autonomy and tribunal autonomy.

(a) Arbitral jurisdiction and tribunal formation

3.023　The direct effect of an arbitration agreement is to oblige parties to honour the commitment to refer their disputes to arbitration and hence, to provide the important basis for the jurisdiction of the arbitral tribunal.[57] Not only does a valid arbitration agreement confer arbitral jurisdiction, but also the tribunal itself has the competence to rule on the existence and validity of arbitration agreements. The principle of *competence-competence* is among the most crucial rules of international arbitration.[58] In addition to jurisdictional establishment, the arbitration agreement serves the basis of powers of the arbitral tribunal as well as specifics of the arbitral proceeding. Arbitration is more flexible than litigation as the parties can design into the agreement their procedural specifics. The tribunal is then able to tailor the procedure on basis of the agreement of the parties. Modern international arbitration norms unanimously recognise that the will of the parties should govern the submission to arbitration and the arbitration procedure *in toto*.[59]

3.024　Chapter 4 reviews the validity of arbitration agreements in China. The review is to recount the rigid regulations on the validity under the Arbitration Law and to assess the recent regulatory endeavors brought by the judiciary on liberalising the party's drafting autonomy. In particular, this chapter addresses the institutional monopoly in the Chinese arbitration system and examines its continued reluctance to recognise *ad hoc* and ICC arbitration agreements in China.

3.025　Chapter 5 concerns the tribunal's competence to determine the arbitral jurisdiction. It looks into the distorting administrative interventions with respect to the institutional infrastructure of Chinese arbitration commissions and in association, questions the pressures on the exercise of arbitral autonomy. In this regard, efforts by some leading Chinese arbitration commissions such as CIETAC and BAC on restoring the tribunal's *competence-competence* are featured in this chapter, albeit they are much struggling under the political and administrative shadows.

3.026　Chapter 6 shifts the focus to parties' procedural autonomy with a special focus on their autonomy and interest in forming tribunals. The analysis purports to identify the gap between Chinese and international arbitration practices and probes into the difficulty of why parties cannot appoint arbitrators according to their own wishes in China. It further conducts a critical examination of the integrity and quality of the arbitral tribunals and unveils the threat it exerts on party autonomy and interest.

---

[57]　Emmanuel Gaillard and John Savage *et al*, *Fouchard Gaillard Goldman On International Commercial Arbitration* (The Hague: Kluwer Law International, 1999), 198–218.

[58]　*Ibid.*, 395.

[59]　*Ibid.*

(b) Judicial intervention and enforcement

The indirect effect of an arbitration agreement is to exclude the dispute from the jurisdiction of the national court.[60] Pursuant to the indirect effect, if one party commences proceedings in a national court, that party is considered in breach of that arbitration agreement. In the circumstance, the court has a statutory duty to decline to exercise its jurisdiction and to stay the judicial proceedings in favour of arbitration even if the validity of the arbitration agreement is in suspension.[61] The Model Law and the New York Convention (NYC) both emphasise the essential of giving effect to the arbitration agreement wherever possible.[62] With respect to national legislations, the English Arbitration Act mandates courts with the general duty to enforce arbitration agreements and to stay judicial proceedings pending arbitration.[63] These duties are seen as the important aspects of judicial support that national courts provide with the arbitration, although the court reserves the power of supervision. Nowadays, national courts in modern jurisdictions are more and more found to read into the poor drafting and endeavour to give effect to arbitration agreements as far as possible, so that party autonomy can be "expanded" to the widest reach. In this regard, it is important to what extent the court performing the review would respect the tribunal's understanding and ruling of the effect of arbitration agreement; or whether they will make an arbitrary determination of their own. The fact that whether national courts are more willing to affirm the legal effect of the arbitration agreement has become one of the most crucial parameters in assessing the arbitration-friendliness of a jurisdiction.[64]

3.027

Chapter 7 thus deals with the topic of judicial intervention and enforcement. It involves an in-depth empirical analysis of the enforcement reports of defective arbitration agreements in China, and delves into the status quo of the current judicial review system with respect to the protection of party autonomy and interest in arbitration. Additionally, recent court reforms initiated by the SPC will be discussed so as to evaluate their relative effect on the improvement of arbitration enforcement in China.

3.028

---

[60] The indirect effect of arbitration agreements in excluding courts' jurisdictions is sometimes quoted as "negative effect" by the Continental legal authors. See, for example, Gaillard and Savage (ed), *Fouchard Gaillard Goldman On International Commercial Arbitration* (1999), 402.

[61] Klaus Peter Berger, "Understanding International Commercial Arbitration", in Center for Transnational Law (ed), *Understanding Transnational Commercial Arbitration* (Munster, Germany: Quadis Publishing, 2000), 11–13.

[62] Article II(3) of the NYC provides: "The court of a contracting state, when seized of an action in a matter in respect of which the parties have made an agreement within the meaning of this article, shall at the request of one of the parties, refer the parties to arbitration, unless it finds that the said agreement is null and void, inoperative or incapable of being performed". See also, similar provisions in art.8(1) of the Model Law.

[63] Section 9(1) of the English Arbitration Act; see also art.1458 of the French Code of Civil Procedure.

[64] Xie Shisong, *Commercial Arbitration Law (Shangshi Zhongcai Faxue)* (Beijing: Higher Education Press, 2003), 152.

VALIDITY OF ARBITRATION AGREEMENTS

As outlined in previous chapters, one distinctive feature of the regulation of arbitration agreements in China is that parties are required to include a definite arbitration commission in their agreements.[1] The choice of the commission is a rigid substantial requirement for validity under the Arbitration Law. Moreover, there is a serious shortage of regulation with respect to the "written" form such as under what circumstances the parties' consent to arbitrate can be recognised.

4.001

Chapter 4 first reviews the rigid regulation of validity under the Arbitration Law by outlining its gap with international arbitration norms such as jurisprudences of the UNCITRAL Model Law and English Arbitration Act 1996. It is important to note that from an international perspective, the requirements for validity in both form and substance have been very liberally construed in order to respect the parties' drafting autonomy and the effect is given wherever possible. The second part of the chapter focuses on the judicial efforts by both the central and local judiciary on relaxing the legislative rigidity. The commitment made by the Supreme People's Court (SPC) through its most recent judicial interpretation on arbitration in late 2006 is specifically examined. The third part provides a critical analysis of the continued institutional monopoly of Chinese arbitration before this chapter ends with some legislative proposal for gradually liberalising *ad hoc* arbitration in China.

4.002

1. CRITIQUE ON THE VALIDITY REGIME UNDER THE ARBITRATION LAW

(a) Overly rigid conditions

The crucial statutory provision that governs the validity of arbitration agreements in China is art.16 of the Arbitration Law, which stipulates:

4.003

> "An arbitration agreement *shall* include arbitration clauses stipulated in the contract and agreement of submission to arbitration that are in *writing* before or after disputes arise."[2]

Further,

> "An arbitration agreement *shall* contain the following particulars: (1) an expression of intention to arbitrate; (2) matters for arbitration; and (3) a designated arbitration commission."[3]

It is clear from the first paragraph of art.16 that parties' agreement to arbitrate must be made in writing. The writing requirement tends to clarify the issue of whether parties

4.004

---

[1] Parties whose arbitration agreements involve foreign elements are entitled to choose foreign arbitration institutions. See also discussions below under the heading "Ad Hoc and ICC Arbitration Agreements in China".

[2] First paragraph, art.16 of the Arbitration Law.

[3] Second paragraph, art.16 of the Arbitration Law.

have actually consented to arbitration.[4] That said, however, the Arbitration Law fails to define what constitutes a written form or to what extent the written form is sufficient.[5] With respect to this issue, an indirect answer may be found by referring to art.11 of the Contract Law[6] which stipulates that "written contracts" refer to "contracts *signed* in written instruments such as letters and electrically or electronically transmitted documents".[7] This jurisprudence, however, has been restricted to "*signature-based consent*" without taking up the scenario in which the consent to arbitrate could be manifested by other means. It is true that consent will be easily established if the arbitration agreement is signed by both parties. However, this may not always be the case in modern arbitration practice. According to a premier international arbitrator, Jingzhou Tao, the "written" requirement shall be stipulated dynamically in light of the rapid development of modern means of communications and for the convenience of transactions.[8] Problematic situations often arise as to whether a non-signatory third party can be bound by the arbitration agreement, a situation that seen frequently with the rising use of arbitration in China;[9] in particular, to what extent the "written form" can be upheld in cases of contract assignment, agency relationship, etc.[10] The Arbitration Law is silent on all these issues and the vague regulation under art.16(1) could be interpreted to deny the validity of arbitration agreements when the consent is given in a different capacity, until the practice is later resolved by the SPC through a series of judicial replies and opinions.[11]

4.005   In addition to the "written" requirement for consent, substantive requirements must be met for an arbitration agreement to be considered valid. As required by the second paragraph of art.16, the effectiveness of an arbitration agreement is dependant on the existence of three conditions: (1) an expression of intention to arbitrate; (2) matters for arbitration; and (3) a designated arbitration commission.[12] While there is not much dispute regarding the first two conditions, the third one, a "designated arbitration

---

[4]   The Legislative Affairs Commission of the NPCSC of PRC (ed.), *Arbitration Laws of China* (Hong Kong: Sweet & Maxwell Asia, 1997), 55.

[5]   See Wang Shengchang, *Resolving Disputes in the PRC: A Practical Guide to Arbitration and Conciliation in China* (Beijing: China Law Press, 1997), 78; see also Li Hu, "Setting Aside an Arbitral Award in the People's Republic of China" (2001) 12 *American Review of International Arbitration*, 10.

[6]   The Contract Law came into effect in 1999, which supersedes and unifies the now abolished Economic Contract Law, Foreign Economic Contract Law and Technology Contract Law.

[7]   Article 11 of the Contract Law.

[8]   See Jingzhou Tao, *Arbitration Law and Practice in China* (The Hague: Kluwer Law International, 2004), 96.

[9]   See Kun Liang, "The Comparative Analysis of the Existing Chinese and English Arbitration Systems from Arbitration Agreement Perspectives", (1999) 13 *Columbia Journal of Asian Law*, 35 (noting that there are still unanswered questions concerning the amount of force to be given to an arbitration agreement's effect on a non-signatory); see also Nanping Liu, "A Vulnerable Justice: Finality of Civil Judgments in China", (1999) 13 *Columbia Journal of Asian Law*, 94 (stating that for a non-signatory, it is important to assess the nature of a Chinese judgment in terms of recognition and enforcement).

[10]   See Wang Liming, "An Inquiry into Several Difficult Problems in Enhancing China's Uniform Contract Law" (Keith Hand translates), (1999) 8 *Pacific Rim Law & Policy Journal*, 381.

[11]   See Kun Liang, see fn 9 above, 35 (observing that while strict written requirement exists in the statute, there is no need for the agreement to be signed by the parties).

[12]   According to Qiao Xin, to establish the effectiveness, the three particulars must be ascertained together, if not clearly spelt out together in the arbitration agreement. See Qiao Xin, *Comparative Commercial Arbitration (Bijiao Shangshi Zhongcai)* (Beijing: China Law Press, 2004), 173.

commission", has raised considerable concern and criticism for being overly rigid.[13] Pursuant to art.18 of the Arbitration Law:

> "If an arbitration agreement has failed to set forth the arbitration commission to hear the matter or has failed to define it clearly, the parties may remedy the defect by a supplementary agreement. In the absence of a valid supplementary agreement, the arbitration agreement is invalid."[14]

By virtue of this provision, the choice of the arbitration commission must be specified (which excludes the possibility of *ad hoc* arbitration).[15] Moreover, it must be clearly specified or at least made clear in a supplementary submission; otherwise the arbitration agreement will be void. As such, the most typical defects in concluding the arbitration agreement in China would be incorrect or inconclusive references to the choice of arbitral commission, which has been referred to as "defective or pathological arbitration clauses" in Tao's commentary on the Chinese arbitration practice.[16] The following case may provide an illustration on how the stringent requirement of "specificity of an arbitration commission" has worked in real life:

4.006

> "The claimant and respondent signed a cooperation contract in 1996. Article 39 of the contract read that 'any dispute under the contract should be arbitrated under the Shanghai International Trade Promotion Commission Foreign-related Arbitration Commission'. After the dispute arose, the parties resorted to the CIETAC Shanghai sub-commission, but the commission ruled that 'since the arbitration commission agreed does not exist, and no subsequent supplementary submissions are available, the arbitration clause has to be voided under arts.16 and 18 of the Arbitration Law, and thus the jurisdiction cannot be entertained'."[17]

Indeed, there have been many reports that not only the China International Economic and Trade Arbitration Commission (CIETAC) but also local arbitration comissions suffered greatly from the "killing provisions" (arts.16 and 18)[18] and that the parties' arbitral desires can be defeated if the arbitration agreements failed to clearly provide the institutional identity.[19] These defects and pathologies may involve the situations such as selecting two arbitration commissions together, providing merely the place of arbitration or institutional rules without nominating the arbitration commission,

4.007

---

[13] See discussions below.

[14] Article 18 of the Arbitration Law.

[15] See discussions below.

[16] See Jingzhou Tao, *Arbitration Law and Practice in China* (2004), 34, 51.

[17] *Re Contract for the Sale of Cold-Rolled Steel Plate* (Case No. 2), compiled in CIETAC (ed.), *Selected Jurisdictional Decisions of the CIETAC (Zhongguo Guoji Jingji Maoyi Zhongcaiweiyuanhui Guanxiaquan Jueding Xuanbian)* (Beijing: China Commercial Publishing, 2004), 318–319.

[18] See Song Lianbin, "From Ideology to Legislation: Several Issues to Pay Attention to for Reforming the Arbitration Law (Linian Zouxiang Guize: Zhongcaifa Xiuding Yinggai Zhuyi de Jige Wenti)", (2005) 52 *Arbitration in Beijing (Beijing Zhongcai)*, 2.

[19] See Zhao Jian, "Looking Back and Looking Ahead: China's International Commercial Arbitration Crossing Centuries (Huigu yu Zhanwang: Shijinzhijiao de Zhongguo Guoji Shangshi Zhongcai)", (2001) 51 *Arbitration and Law (Zhongcai yu Falu)*, 105; see also Jun Ge, "Mediation, Arbitration and Litigation: dispute Resolution in the People's Republic of China", (1996) 15 *UCLA Pacific Basin Law Journal*, 130.

quoting incorrectly the name of the arbitration commission, etc.[20] As a result of the over-rigid substantive mandates, parties are not only excluded the opportunity of using *ad hoc* arbitration in China,[21] but their intention to arbitrate could be easily denied under the Chinese distinctive "defective-led-void" mechanism in regulating arbitration agreements.[22] The Arbitration Law fails to resolve the problems, bringing about much difficulty in arbitral practice and leaving wide room for judicial interpretations.

(b) Significant gap with international arbitration norms

(i) *Form of consent*

4.008   In examining international arbitration norms, the prevalent approach is, rather than stick to a strict signature-based form of consent, to find that the "written" requirement be satisfied as long as the communication provides sufficient proof of the written agreement.[23] Further, courts generally uphold the effect of the arbitration agreement as to its non-signatory parties.[24]

4.009   The Model Law provides the form requirement of arbitration agreements to ensure that parties have agreed to go to arbitration, but at the same time caution is given so that the parties will not be dissuaded from arbitration simply due to stringency of the form.[25] Article 7(2) has thus been designed to encompass the circumstances broadly.[26] Under this provision, much jurisprudence has been developed by jurisdictions that have adopted the Model Law, and the general theme of this jurisprudence is that the "written" requirement can be flexibly established either as a mere formality condition or as a rule of evidence.[27] This can be proved either by an arbitration agreement through conduct or by an exchange of correspondence, incorporation by reference or through statements of claim and defence.[28] In this scenario, a Canadian court[29] has

---

[20]   See discussions below under the heading "Judicial Effort on Relaxing the Legislative Rigidity".

[21]   See discussions below under the heading "Ad Hoc and ICC Arbitration Agreements in China".

[22]   Song Lianbin, Zhao Jian and Li Hong, "Approaches to the Revision of the 1994 Arbitration Act of the PRC", (2003) 20 *Journal of International Arbitration*, 174.

[23]   See Peter Kucherepa, "Reviewing Trends and Proposals to Recognize Oral Agreements to Arbitrate in International Arbitration Laws", (2005) 16 *American Review of International Arbitration*, 414; see also Olagoke O. Olatawura, "The 'Privity to Arbitration' Doctrine: The Withering of the Common – Law Privity of Contract Doctrine in Arbitration Law", (2005) 16 *American Review of International Arbitration*, 465.

[24]   See James M. Hosking, "The Third Party Non-Signatory's Ability to Compel International Commercial Arbitration: Doing Justice without Destroying Consent", (2004) 4 *Pepperdine Dispute Resolution Law Journal*, 472; see also Michael P. Daly, "Come One, Come All: The New and Developing World of Non-signatory Arbitration and Class Arbitration", (2007) 62 *University of Miami Law Review*, 103.

[25]   See Peter Binder, *International Commercial Arbitration in UNCITRAL Model Law Jurisdictions* (London: Sweet & Maxwell, 2000), para 2-014.

[26]   Article 7(2) of the Model Law: "The arbitration agreement shall be in writing. An agreement is in writing if it is contained in a document signed by the parties or in an exchange of letters, telex, telegrams or other means of telecommunication which provide a record of the agreement, or in an exchange of statements of claim and defence in which the existence of an agreement is alleged by one party and not denied by another".

[27]   See Pieter Sanders, *The Work of UNCITRAL on Arbitration and Conciliation* (The Hague: Kluwer Law International, 2004), 67; see also Chistoph Liebscher, "Interpretation of the Written Form Requirement Art. 7(2) UNCITRAL Model Law", (2005) 8 *International Arbitration Law Review*, 164; see also Alvarez, Kaplan and Rivkin, *Model Law Decisions: Cases Applying the UNCITRAL Model Law on International Commercial Arbitration (1985–2001)* (The Hague: Kluwer Law International, 2003), 37–54.

[28]   *Ibid.*

[29]   Canada adopted the Model Law in 1988, which was among those first Model Law jurisdictions in the world.

held that art.7(2) of the Model Law does not require correspondence regarding the arbitration agreement to be signed by the parties.[30] In a similar vein, the Supreme Court of Bermuda[31] held that an arbitration agreement is valid if "the applicant's written contract constituted an offer which was accepted by the respondent's conduct … 'the acceptance need not be in writing but may be inferred by conduct' … ".[32] Influenced by the English Arbitration Act in its domestic regime and the Model Law in its international regime,[33] Hong Kong has construed art.7(2) even more liberally by its legislation. Section 2AC of the Arbitration Ordinance[34] makes it clear that "arbitration agreement in writing" includes any means by which information can be recorded[35] with a wide array of illustrative examples.[36] In particular, s.2AC clarifies the portion of art.7(2) of the Model Law that deals with "incorporation of arbitration agreements by reference". Modelled after s.5(6) of the English Arbitration Act, the section provides that "[t]he reference in an agreement to a written form of arbitration clause or to a document containing an arbitration clause constitutes an arbitration agreement if the reference is such as to make that clause part of the agreement".[37] Indeed, courts in Hong Kong have interpreted this provision very liberally by stating that "what the tribunal or court must determine, as a matter of construction, is whether parties intended to incorporate an arbitration agreement and there is no need for words specifically incorporating it".[38] Likewise, the writing requirement has been construed liberally under case laws in the United Kingdom. In a pair of recent cases, the English Court of Appeal concluded that an arbitration clause contained in standard conditions of contract was properly incorporated by reference through an "incorporation clause" into the final contract and binding, although no specific reference was made to the arbitration clause in the incorporating provision.[39]

Moreover, the practice of extending the arbitration agreement to non-signatory third parties has been generally accepted. Although the Model Law does not deal with this issue directly, national courts in its receiving jurisdictions have successfully developed the jurisprudence in favour of this extension.[40] In terms of contract

4.010

---

[30] *Case Law on UNCITRAL Texts* (hereafter referred to as "CLOUT"), case 365: *Schiff Food Products Inc v Naber Seed & Grain Co* [1996] 149 Sask. R. 54, Saskatchewan Court of Queen's Bench, Canada (1 October 1996).

[31] Bermuda adopted the Model Law in 1992.

[32] *Skandia International Insurance Co and Mercantile & General Reinsurance Co*, CLOUT case 127, Supreme Court of Bermuda (21 January 1994).

[33] Hong Kong adopted the Model Law in 1996 to govern its international arbitration regime by its revision to the Arbitration Ordinance, listed as Part II. Domestic arbitrations taking place in Hong Kong still follow pretty much the English Arbitration Act 1996, listed as Arbitration Ordinance Part I.

[34] Arbitration Ordinance (Cap.341).

[35] Section 2AC(4) of the Arbitration Ordinance.

[36] Section 2AC(2)(a)–(f) of the Arbitration Ordinance: "The agreement is in writing if it is made by an exchange of written communication; or although not itself in writing, it is evidenced in writing; or although made otherwise than in writing, it is recorded in writing; or there is an exchange of written submission in arbitral or legal proceedings in which the existence of an agreement otherwise in writing is alleged by one party and not denied by the other party (waiver of objection)".

[37] Section 2AC(3) of the Arbitration Ordinance. See also s.5(6) of the English Arbitration Act.

[38] *Astel-Peiniger Joint Venutre v Argos Engineering & Heavy Industries Co Ltd* [1995] 1 HKLR 300.

[39] *The Epsilon Rosa (No 2)* [2003] 2 Lloyd's Rep 509; and *Sea Trade Maritime Corp v Hellenic Mutual War Risks Association (Bermuda) Ltd* [2007] 1 All ER (Comm) 183.

[40] See Michael P. Daly, "Come One, Come All: The New and Developing World of Neon-signatory Arbitration and Class Arbitration", (2007) 62 *University of Miami Law Review*, 102.

assignment, the prevailing notion is that if a party has agreed to an arbitration agreement, its assignee is bound by it.[41] This view of arbitration clauses and contract assignees has been endorsed by a series of cases in Germany.[42] In one such case, the Federal Court held that the buyer of real estate is bound by the arbitration clause in a tenancy agreement concerning the same property entered into by its old owner (the seller).[43] Likewise, Singapore[44] has supported the effect of the arbitration agreement on legal successors where the High Court decided that the receiver in an insolvency proceeding was bound by an arbitration agreement concluded by the insolvent debtor.[45] Similarly, the court in Canada confirms that an agent of a party giving consent to arbitration can bind its principal if the main contract where the arbitration clause appears binds the principal as well.[46] The validity of arbitration agreement in the circumstances of agency relationship is as well recognised in Hong Kong[47] and Austria.[48] Additionally, the "long-arm" effect of arbitration agreements on the non-signatory third party is confirmed under the case laws of the English Arbitration Act. A couple of very recent cases in the English Court of Appeal held that the validity of arbitration agreement will be presumed in contract assignment and in subrogation unless there is a clear restriction in the arbitration agreement stating that the arbitration clause cannot be transferred.[49]

(ii) *Specificity as to arbitral institution*

4.011   With respect to the substantive contents for an arbitration agreement to be valid, under the prevailing practice of the international arbitration community, an agreement is valid as long as the parties provide the scope of arbitrable disputes (arbitrability) and show their intention to arbitrate.[50] Beyond these core ingredients, there are some other considerations that may be included, such as the institution chosen, place of arbitration,

---

[41]   See generally, Alan Redfern and Martin Hunter, *Law and Practice of International Commercial Arbitration* (4th ed.) (London: Sweet & Maxwell, 2004), 151.

[42]   Germany adopted the Model Law in 1999.

[43]   See Norbert Horton, "The Arbitration Agreement in Light of Case Law of the UNCITRAL Model law", [2005] *International Arbitration Law Review*, 148 (discussing two cases handed down by the German Federal Court which held that legal successors to a contract are bound by arbitration agreements contained therein); see also Stefan Kroll, "German Court Enforces Domestic Award Against a Third-Party Non-signatory to the Arbitration Agreement" (case comment), [2007] *International Arbitration Law Review*, N18-9.

[44]   Singapore adopted the Model Law in 1998.

[45]   *Concordia Agritrade Pte Ltd v Cornelder Hoogewerff Pte Ltd*, High Court of Singapore (13 October 1999), reprinted in [2001] *International Arbitration Law Review*, N42-3.

[46]   *Automatic Systems Inc v E.S. Fox Ltd and Chrysleer Canada Ltd*, CLOUT case 74, Ontario Court of Appeal, Canada (25 April 1994).

[47]   *Chung Siu Hung v Primequine Corp*, CLOUT case 44, High Court of Hong Kong (28 September 1999).

[48]   Austria adopted the Model Law in 2001. See *Carter v Alsthom*, Court of Appeal in Vienna, reprinted in [2001] *International Arbitration Law Review*, 123.

[49]   *Wealands v CLC Contractors Ltd* [2000] 1 All ER (Comm) 30; *X Ltd v Y Ltd* [2005] BLR 341; both cases have been reprinted in Philip Yang Liang-Yee, *Arbitration Law: From 1996 UK Arbitration Act to International Commercial Arbitration (Zhongcaifa: cong 1996 yingguo Zhongcaifa dao guoji shangwu zhongcai)* (Beijing: China Law Press, 2006).

[50]   The prevailing notion is that there are two essentials which should be contained in every effective arbitration agreement: (1) the agreement to arbitrate (intent to arbitrate), (2) scope of the agreement (arbitrability). See Redfern and Hunter, *Practice of International Commercial Arbitration*, 3–4; see also Liu Xiaohong, *Jurisprudence and Empirical Research of International Commercial Arbitration (Guoji Shangshi Zhongcai Xieyi de Fali yu Shizheng Yanjiu)* (Beijing: Commercial Publishing House, 2005), 51–2, 57–9.

method of appointment and qualification of the arbitrators and the applicable law, among others.[51]

These principles guiding an arbitration agreement's substantive validity are clearly shown in arts.7(1) and 8(1) of the Model Law. Article 7(1) stipulates that parties should put into their arbitration agreement all or certain disputes they want to subject to arbitration.[52] In addition, pursuant to art.8(1), the court shall refer the parties to arbitration unless it finds the agreement is null and void, inoperative or incapable of being performed.[53] Thus, under the Model Law framework, an "arbitration institution" has been suggested for inclusion as one of the relevant considerations rather than an indispensable element for valid construction.[54] The Working Group of the Model Law thought they should not set out separate grounds for the validity of the arbitral agreement apart from the "intention to arbitrate" and "scope of arbitration", mainly because the formulation of an exhaustive list would cause many defective arbitration agreements and lead to lengthy litigation challenging jurisdiction both at the outset and during award enforcement.[55] The Model Law prefers the "intent over defect" rule of interpretation, which does not follow the strict textual interpretation and upholds the parties' drafting autonomy as much as possible.[56]

4.012

Under the Model Law jurisprudence, the adopting jurisdictions have generally made considerable efforts to give effect to the parties' agreement to arbitrate and intentions rather than stick to the seemingly uncertain language on arbitration institution. National courts have always attempted to uphold an arbitration clause, unless the uncertainty is such that it is difficult to make any sense of it under art.8(1).[57] The Court of Appeal in Hamburg gave effect to an arbitration clause that simply used the language, "Arbitration-Hamburg Institution".[58] The German Federal Court subsequently pointed out that an arbitration agreement can validly refer to two different courts of arbitration and the claimant will be given the choice between

4.013

---

[51] *Ibid.*

[52] Article 7(1) of the Model Law: "Arbitration agreement is an agreement by the parties to submit to arbitration all or certain disputes which have arisen or may arise between theme in respect of a legal relationship, whether contractual or not".

[53] Article 8(1) of the Model Law: "A court before which an action is brought in a matter which is the subject of an arbitration agreement shall, if a party so requests not later than when submitting his first statement on the substance of the dispute, refer the parties to arbitration unless it finds the agreement is null and void, inoperative or incapable of being performed".

[54] See Paul A. Gelinas, "Arbitration Clauses: Achieving Effectiveness", in Albert van den Berg (ed), *Improving the Efficiency of Arbitration Agreement and Awards: 40 Years of Application of the New York Convention: ICCA Congress Series No. 9* (The Hague: Kluwer Law International, 1998), 47.

[55] See UN Commission on International Trade Law (UNCITRAL), *Report of the Working Group on International Contract Practices on the Work of Its Third Sessions*, U.N. Doc. A/CN.9/216 (16–26 February 1982), para 25; see also Binder, *International Commercial Arbitration in UNCITRAL Model Law Jurisdictions* (2000), para 2-010; see also Stephen R. Bond, "How to Draft an Arbitration Clause" (1989) 2 *Journal of International Arbitration*, 65.

[56] See Julian D. M. Lew, *Comparative International Commercial Arbitration* (The Hague: Kluwer Law International, 2003), para 7-25.

[57] See Redfern and Hunter, *Practice of International Commercial Arbitration* (2004), para 3-69; see also Elizabeth Shackelford, Note, "Party Autonomy and Regional Harmonization of Rules in International Commercial Arbitration", (2006) 67 *University of Pittsburg Law Review*, 900.

[58] Hanseatisches Oberlandesgericht Hamburg [OLGZ] (Trial Court for Select Civil Matters) (24 January 2003), Germany.

the two options.[59] An extreme case showing the tendency of courts to interpret an agreement in favour of finding a technically defective arbitration agreement valid in the Model Law jurisdictions is in *Lucky-Goldstar International (HK) Ltd v Ng Moo Kee Engineering Ltd* where the High Court of Hong Kong held the arbitration clause was valid even though it said "arbitration in a third country and in accordance with the rules of International Arbitration Association".[60] The High Court found that the arbitration clause sufficiently indicated the parties' intention to arbitrate. In the words of Justice Kaplan, "The arbitration agreement was not inoperative or incapable of being performed since arbitration could be held in any country other than the countries where the parties had their places of business".[61]

4.014   The United Kingdom has taken a similar approach, and English courts tend to give the widest interpretation of defective arbitration agreements and to grant the tribunal full jurisdiction except in cases of hopeless confusion. Section 3 of the English Arbitration Act requires the parties only to subject their disputes to an arbitration panel in a particular place (arbitral seat) *or* under specific rules (procedural law).[62] Under the English law, the choice of the procedural law of arbitration would imply the country in which the arbitration has its seat,[63] and the selection of either will be sufficient to show the parties' intention to arbitrate.[64] If neither the seat nor the procedural law has been agreed to, the effect of the arbitration agreement will be determined after looking at the parties' agreement and all the relevant circumstances.[65] In a pair of recent cases, the arbitration clauses contained in the charterparties were extremely abbreviated such that they consisted of only the words "Arbitration-London".[66] Nevertheless, the courts were unwilling to deny the effect due to uncertainty; rather, they "expand" the clause in accordance with the parties' "presumed" intentions.[67]

4.015   In all instances, the "specificity to arbitral institution" has never been required as a cardinal factor for the determination of validity in international arbitration practice.[68]

---

[59]   See Norbert Horton, "The Arbitration Agreement in Light of Case Law of the UNCITRAL Model Law", [2005] *International Arbitration Law Review*, 150.

[60]   *Lucky-Goldstar International (HK) Ltd v Ng Moo Kee Engineering Ltd* [1993] 2 HKLR 73; case summary in (1995) XX *Yearbook of Commercial Arbitration* 280.

[61]   Per Kaplan J, *ibid.*, 74.

[62]   Section 3 of the English Arbitration Act, which provides that the arbitral seat is designated (a) by the parties to the arbitration agreement, or (b) by any arbitral or other institution or person vested by the parties with powers to fix the seat, or (c) by the arbitral tribunal if so authorised by the parties, or determined, in absence of any such designation, having regard to the parties' agreement and all the relevant circumstances.

[63]   *ABB Lummus Global Ltd v Keppel Fels Ltd* [1999] 2 Lloyd's Rep 24.

[64]   William Tetley, "Good Faith in Contract: Particularly in the Contracts of Arbitration", (2004) 35 *Journal of Maritime Law & Commerce*, 561.

[65]   Section 3(c) of the English Arbitration Act.

[66]   *Tritonia Shipping Inc v South Nelson Forest Products Corp* [1966] 1 Lloyd's Rep 114; *Dubai Islamic Bank PJSC v Paymentech Merchant Services Inc* [2001] 1 All ER (Comm) 514.

[67]   See Clare Ambrose and Karen Maxwell, *London Maritime Arbitration* (2nd ed.) (London: LLP, 2002), 30; see also Gu Weixia and Joshua Lindenbaum, "The NYPE 93 Arbitration Clause: Where Ends the Open-End?", (2006) 37 *Journal of Maritime Law & Commerce*, 249.

[68]   This approach has been concluded through research on the most authoritative textbooks on international commercial arbitration including Redfern and Hunter, *Practice of International Commercial Arbitration* (2004), 165–168; Lew, *Comparative International Commercial Arbitration* (2003), 165–172; Lawrence Craig, William Park and Jan Paulsson, *International Chamber of Commerce Arbitration* (3rd ed.) (New York: Oceana Publications, 2000), 85–91; Gaillard and Savage, *Fouchard Gaillard Goldman on International Commercial Arbitration* (The Hague: Kluwer Law International, 1999), 262–270.

However, difficulties might arise in an institutional arbitration jurisdiction such as China, where a stringent restriction on the party's drafting autonomy has been imposed by the creation of a requirement to designate clearly and unequivocally the name of the arbitral institution, which is rare practice among modern arbitration regimes.[69] On the one hand, the Chinese provision puts too heavy a burden on all arbitration agreements to become valid; on the other hand, it fails to provide solutions to fixing those agreements that are defective in this regard.

2. JUDICIAL EFFORT ON RELAXING THE LEGISLATIVE RIGIDITY

Because of the over-rigidity and inherent deficiency of the Arbitration Law on regulating the validity of arbitration agreements, the judiciary has stepped in to address the practical problems stemming from the stringent requirement. Since the promulgation of the Arbitration Law, approximately 30 interpretative documents have been released by the SPC regarding the handling of arbitration cases,[70] which constitutes an important source of the legal framework of Chinese arbitration. With respect to "defective" arbitration agreements, judicial replies (*pifu*) and opinions (*yijian*) have centred upon how to broaden the scope of the formal "written requirement" and liberalise the "institutional ambiguity" in substance.[71] In the meantime, although the official judicial interpretative power is vested only in the SPC, some Local Higher People's Courts (LHPCs) in economically better developed areas have also made their contributions to the regulatory development in this regard.[72] Given the remarkable numbers of the replies and opinions issued by both the central and local judiciaries, this section details the developments in a chronological order with the year 2006 as the turning point, when the SPC promulgated the very impressive "unified judicial interpretation on arbitration law" based on its accumulated experience over more than a decade.[73]

4.016

(a) The first decade: 1995 to 2005

This part of the discussion concerns the judicial interpretations on defective arbitration agreements by both the SPC and LHPCs in the period from 1995 to 2005. Moreover, it reads between the lines of these interpretative documents to explore the difference in approach of the central and local judiciaries towards the drafting autonomy of arbitration and underlying reasons for the difference.

4.017

---

[69] Articles 16, 18 of the Arbitration Law.

[70] See Appendix in CIETAC (ed.), *Selected Jurisdictional Decisions by the CIETAC (Zhongguo Guoji Jingji Maoyi Zhongcaiweiyuanhui Guanxiaquan Jueding Xuanbian)* (Beijing: China Commercial Publishing House, 2004), 601–633.

[71] See Li Hu, "Setting Aside an Arbitral Award in the People's Republic of China", (2001) 12 *American Review of International Arbitration*, 9–10.

[72] See discussions above in Chapter 1 under the heading "Sources of Regulations on Arbitration".

[73] See discussions below under the heading "Critical Turning since 2006: Unified SPC Interpretation on Arbitration".

(i) *Interpretative documents by the Supreme People's Court*

On "non-signatory third party"

Incorporation by reference

4.018   For contracts where arbitration agreements are not directly included, incorporation by referring to an existing document that contains an arbitral clause has been recognised as satisfying the "written" requirement under art.16 of the Arbitration Law.[74] This was explicitly affirmed by the 1996 SPC reply in the *Sino-Mongolian case*,[75] where the contract provided that "matters not covered in the contract shall be governed by the Joint Conditions of the Delivery Protocol between China and Mongolia[76]" in which arbitration was provided as the means of dispute resolution.[77]

Contract assignment

4.019   Prior to the promulgation of the Contract Law,[78] the judiciary and arbitration commissions were divided on how to give effect to arbitration agreements in cases of contract assignment.[79] The people's courts held that, notwithstanding the assignment, the arbitration agreement included would be binding only on the assignor and could not automatically extend to the assignee.[80] However, CIETAC generally preferred a more liberal approach of finding that once a contract had been assigned, any arbitration agreement therein contained would be assigned as well.[81] Given the conflicting views and practices, the SPC issued its judicial opinions via a reply to the Hubei Higher People's Court in 1999 (the SPC Hubei Reply).[82] The SPC pointed to art.80 of the newly promulgated Contract Law, which provides that the assignee will acquire all accessory rights related to the main contractual rights following the assignment.[83]

---

[74]   As Wang Shengchang put it, "In complex transactions involving numerous contracts based on standard terms and conditions, it is sometimes found that a standard or *borrowed* arbitration agreement has been used". This means that the parties, familiar with a provision for arbitration agreement contained in another document, *simply introduce that provision into their contract by reference to it*, as it stands". See Wang Shengchang, *Resolving Disputes in the PRC: A Practical Guide to Arbitration and Conciliation in China* (Hong Kong: FT Law & Tax Asia Pacific, 1997), 78.

[75]   SPC Reply on the Manner of Determining Jurisdiction in a Sino-Mongolian Contract that Fails to Provide for Arbitration Directly. Fa Han [1996] No. 177, issued by the SPC on 14 December 1996.

[76]   The Protocol on Mutual Joint Conditions for the Delivery of Goods Between Trade Entities of the Two Countries Agreed by MOFTEC of the People's Republic of China and the Department of International Economy and Supply of the People's Republic of Mongolia, dated 4 November 1988.

[77]   See case reference of "Sino-Mongolia Economic Contract", compiled in Tang Dehua and Sun Xiujun, *Arbitration Law and New Judicial Interpretations (Zhongcaifa ji Peitao Guiding Xinshi Xinjie)* (Beijing: People's Court Publishing, 2003), 152–153.

[78]   The Contract Law was adopted and promulgated by the NPC on 15 March 1999.

[79]   See Jingzhou Tao, *Arbitration Law and Practice in China* (2004), 40.

[80]   See SPC case comments on the SPC Reply to the Zhejiang Higher People's Court dated 19 March 1997, compiled in Tang and Sun (ed), *Arbitration Law and New Interpretations on Relevant Regulations* (2003), 202.

[81]   See CIETAC case comments on "validity of the arbitration agreement following the contract assignment", in CIETAC (ed.), *Selected Jurisdictional Decisions by the CIETAC* (2004), 116.

[82]   See case report by Wang Shengchang, "Arbitration Agreement and the Confirmation of Its Validity" (Zhongcai Xieyi ji qi Youxiaoxing Queding) in CIETAC (ed.), *Symposium Essays on Economic and Trade Arbitration across the Taiwan Straits (Haixia Liang'an Jingmao Zhongcai Yantaohui Wenji)* (Beijing: China Law Press, 2001), 18–20.

[83]   See art.80 of the Contract Law. For assignment of the rights, the assignor should notify the other contracting parties of the assignment. However, according to art.84, for assignment of the duties, apart from notifying, the assignor also needs to obtain the consent of the other contracting party.

Therefore, any arbitration agreement contained in the original contract would be binding on the assignee as part of the accessory rights transferred.[84] Eventually, it was held that the arbitration clause was equally binding on the third-party assignee, despite the lack of a separate written arbitration agreement signed by the assignee.[85] The Reply has received warm welcome by those who study international arbitration and practitioners as a significant development of the SPC in enhancing parties' arbitral wishes.[86]

Bill of lading (B/L)

In the maritime industry, arbitration is invariably triggered where the bill of lading incorporates an arbitration clause in the charterparty under which it is issued.[87] However, when a shipowner issues the bill, the holder is not required to sign on it, leaving the effect of the arbitral clause contained within it in doubt.[88] Moreover, the bills are transferable documents.[89] This raises questions with regard to the binding effect of the original arbitral clause on any subsequent holders. The SPC, in its reply to the Guangdong Higher People's Court, recognised the effect of the arbitration clause to an eventual B/L holder.[90] It pointed out that, "[a]lthough the appealing party did not sign the bill, it had expressly agreed to the arbitration clause contained therein. Hence the arbitration agreement should be valid and binding upon both the carrier and the B/L holder".[91] The affirmation engendered more confidence in the Chinese system of arbitration by maritime practitioners. However, since its effect must be conditional upon the "holder's express consent", parties are still very much wary that their intention to arbitrate could be denied absent such requirement.[92]

4.020

---

[84] This view was also shared by CIETAC and had been endorsed at the workshop on the determination of validity of arbitration agreement jointly sponsored by the SPC, the Beijing Higher People's Court, the Beijing Intermediate People's Court and CIETAC, which was held in December 1997.

[85] See the "SPC Hubei Reply". Similar case has also been found in the SPC reply to the Henan Higher People's Court (the "SPC Henan Reply"). In that case, the SPC held that the Xinquan Company (the "XC") assigned its rights to the Liaoning Company (the "LC") and had informed the Henan Company (the "HC"). Accordingly, the creditor's rights should be based on the original contract to be realised. The LC (assignee) accepted the agreement of assignment, which should include as well the arbitration clause herein with. See the case report recorded in Wang, "Arbitration Agreement and the Confirmation of Its Validity" (2001), 15.

[86] See Gu Weixia, "Thinking about the Application of Subrogation in China's Commercial Arbitration (Guanyu Daiwei Qingqiuquan zai Zhongguo Shangshi Zhongcai zhong Yingyong de Sikao)", (2004) 88 *Arbitration and Law (Zhongcai yu Falu)*, 62.

[87] For general information of the arbitration clause in the charterparties and bills of lading, *see* Y.M. Lin (ed), *Philip Yang on Shipping Practice* (Dalian: Dalian Maritime University Press, 1995), 570–571.

[88] See Peter Binder, *International Commercial Arbitration in UNCITRAL Model Law Jurisdictions* (2000), 76 (identifying unsigned arbitration clauses in bills of lading as a prominent situation).

[89] See Stasia M. Williams, "Something Old, Something New: The Bill of Lading in the Days of EDI", (1991) 1 *Transnational Law & Contemporary Problems*, 562 (defining "negotiability" of the bill of lading as "transferability").

[90] SPC Reply on the Validity of an Arbitration Clause Contained in the Bill of Lading of an International Maritime Dispute between Fu Jian Produce Co and Jin Hu Shipping Co, Fa Han [1995] No. 135, issued by the SPC on 20 October 1995.

[91] *Ibid.*

[92] See Li Hai, "Thinking about the Several Questions Regarding the Validity of the Arbitration Clause in the Bill of Lading (Guanyu Tidan Zhongcai Tiaokuan Xiaoli Ruogan Wenti de Sikao)", (2005) 94 *Arbitration and Law (Zhongcai yu Falu)*, 83.

On "unclear arbitration commission"

Selecting two arbitration commissions

4.021   In its reply to the Shandong Higher People's Court, the SPC declared that arbitration agreements were valid where the parties provided for submission of their dispute to "either the CIETAC or the Qingdao Arbitration Commission". The SPC confirmed that such an arbitration clause was certain and operative, entitling the party to initiate arbitral proceedings before either of the two agreed arbitration institutions.[93]

Selecting both arbitration and litigation

4.022   The SPC, in its reply to the Guangdong Higher People's Court, held that parties' intention to arbitrate was unclear under such arbitration agreement, and the arbitration clause shall be void under the Chinese law unless parties subsequently reached a separate agreement to submit their disputes to a specific arbitration institution.[94]

Referring to a non-existent arbitration commission

4.023   The SPC, in a pair of cases, replied to the Zhejiang and Sichuan Higher People's Courts that reference to non-existent arbitration commissions shall be invalid unless the parties reached a supplementary agreement specifying clearly the relevant arbitration institution where the disputes were to be submitted.[95]

Incorrect name of arbitration commission

4.024   The SPC held that if the name of the selected arbitration commission was erroneously recorded in the arbitration agreement, the agreement may still be valid, provided that the correct name of the commission could be readily ascertained. This opinion was applied to a CIETAC case to give effect to an agreement that incorrectly referred to CIETAC as "China International Trade Arbitration Commission" (missing the word "Economic").[96]

Specifying the place of arbitration only

4.025   The validity of such an agreement was first considered by CIETAC in 1995.[97] Since then, three relevant interpretative documents have been issued by the SPC. The judicial

---

[93]   SPC Reply to Questions Concerning the Validity of an Arbitration Clause in Which Two Arbitration Institutions Are Simultaneously Selected, Fa Han [1996] No. 176, issued by the SPC on 12 December 1996.

[94]   SPC Reply to the Validity of the Arbitration Agreement Which Agrees to Both Arbitration and Litigation, Fa Han [1996] No. 110, issued by the SPC on 18 April 1996.

[95]   SPC Reply to the Jurisdictional Dispute of a Sino-Foreign Contract between a Yiwu Hotel and a Hong Kong Co, Fa Han [1996] No. 141, issued to the Zhejiang Higher People's Court on 9 September, 1996. The SPC Reply to the Validity of the Arbitration Agreement Agreeing on an Unclear Arbitration Commission, Fa Jing Ta Zi (1996) No. 26, issued to the Sichuan Higher People's Court on 10 October 1996.

[96]   SPC Reply Regarding a Case in Which the Validity of the Arbitration Clause Remained Unaffected by the omission of Words from the Name of the Arbitration Institution Therein, Fa Jing [1998] No. 159, issued by the SPC on 2 April 1998.

[97]   The arbitration clause in the CIETAC case provided that if the parties failed to resolve a dispute arising between them, then "dispute should be referred to an arbitration institution established in the respondent's country". The respondent claimed that the above-mentioned "arbitration institution established in the respondent's country" did not expressly indicate CIETAC; and in addition, CIETAC was not the only arbitration institution existing in the PRC. It was argued that the arbitration clause was uncertain in that it failed to identify the arbitration institution and shall be void (case unreported).

opinions, however, have changed drastically. In 1997, the SPC opined that, where the parties fail to include a specific arbitration commission but have provided the place of arbitration, such arbitration agreement will be void.[98] As such, the expression that "any dispute between the parties shall be resolved by the arbitration institution in Beijing" will be regarded as a void agreement. Later, a similar scenario arose before the Hebei Higher People's Court, where the arbitration clause provided that "any dispute arising out of the contract shall be submitted to the arbitration institution in Shijiazhuang".[99] The SPC, in this case, however, relaxed their stance a bit by stating that, "although the name of the arbitral institution is not specified, since there is only one arbitration commission in the given city, i.e. the Shijiazhuang Arbitration Commission, the arbitration clause is certain in this context and therefore should be enforceable and valid".[100] It shall be noted that notwithstanding the similar wording in the two cases, the circumstances were different. In the former case, there were more than two arbitration commissions in Beijing whilst there was only one such commission at the time in Shijiazhuang.[101] Therefore, the underlying policy remains that even if the institution is not clearly spelled out, the arbitration agreement would be valid as long as the arbitral institution is ascertainable or can be inferred with some degree of certainty from the surrounding circumstances.[102] Unfortunately, the SPC stepped back from the approach of *ascertainable inference* and returned to the blanket denial approach. In its later reply to the Shandong Higher People's Court,[103] it opined that, "by specifying the place of arbitration without nominating the arbitral commission, then unless the parties can reach a supplementary agreement on the choice of the commission, their arbitration agreement shall be held void, so that the court will have jurisdiction over the disputed matter".[104]

Conclusion

Given the above illustrations, it is evident that during the period from 1995 to 2005, the SPC, through its issuance of over 20 pieces of interpretative documents, has resolved a lot of obstacles to determining the validity of defective arbitration agreements in light of both the formal and substantial defects that were unresolved by the Arbitration Law. But concerns still exist as to the SPC's shortcomings in terms of providing clarification on the means of "written form" other than "signing" in the arbitral practice, particularly written forms such as waiver of objection, and in agency relationship.[105] There are further concerns with respect to SPC's swinging attitude on the designation of "unclear arbitration commission". Significant gaps remain between

4.026

---

[98] SPC Reply on the Validity of an Arbitration Clause with Selected Arbitration Venue but No Arbitration Institution, Fa Han [1997] No. 36, issued by the SPC on 19 March 1997.

[99] SPC Reply to the Hebei Higher People's Court on the Validity of an Arbitration Agreement, Fa Jing [1998] No. 287, issued by the SPC on 6 July 1998.

[100] *Ibid.*

[101] *Ibid.*

[102] Tang and Sun, *The Arbitration Law and Its Pertaining New Judicial Interpretations by the SPC* (2003), 202.

[103] SPC Reply on Several Issues of Ascertaining the Validity of the Arbitration Agreement, Fa Shi [1998] No. 27, issued by the SPC on 21 October 1998.

[104] *Ibid.*

[105] See Joseph T. McLaughlin, "Planning for Commercial Dispute Resolution in Mainland China", (2005) 16 *American Review of International Arbitration*, 142 (providing examples as to how there is a shortage of explanations by the SPC).

the Chinese and international practice with respect to an arbitration agreement that provides for institutional arbitration without unequivocally quoting the name of the institution.[106] Lastly, there has been inconsistency among the judicial opinions where the agreements "specify the place of arbitration only", with the foregoing being one such example. In facing the challenges unsettled by the SPC, some LHPCs have developed more liberal approaches with their own local judicial opinions.

(ii) *Judicial opinions by Local Higher People's Courts*

The "Beijing Opinion" 1999

4.027   In 1999, the Economic Trial Division of the Beijing Higher People's Court (BHC) issued its opinions regarding the determination of a petition to ascertain the validity of an arbitration agreement (the Beijing Opinion).[107] The Beijing Opinion was designed to provide guidance to the intermediate and district people's courts in Beijing on handling such petitions, and comprised a series of questions and answers frequently faced by these courts.[108] Among all the opinions issued, arts.1 and 2 addressed specifically the effect of an arbitration agreement on a non-signatory third party in the agency context.[109]

4.028   Article 1 of the Opinion stipulates that where an arbitral agreement is concluded by an agent without authority or exceeding its authority, the agreement will not be binding on the principal. If, in any of the foregoing circumstances, a third party submits an application for arbitration on the basis of such an arbitration agreement, the agreement shall be voided between the principal and the third party and the arbitration commission will have no jurisdiction unless a supplementary agreement is reached.[110] Article 2 goes on to provide that in an arbitration agreement signed by a foreign agent, the agreement will not be binding upon the domestic principal and the third party.[111]

4.029   The BHC guidance, however, fails to take into account whether the third party has actual knowledge of the existence of an agency relationship as the newly promulgated

---

[106]   See Eu Jin Chua, "Legal Implications of a Rising China: The Laws of the People's Republic of China: An Introduction for International Investors", (2006) 7 *Chinese Journal of International Law*, 139.

[107]   The Beijing Opinion on Some Issues Regarding the Determination of an Application for Ascertaining the Validity of an Arbitration Agreement, and Motions to Revoke an Arbitration Award, issued by the BHC, 3 December 1999.

[108]   *Ibid.*

[109]   The Beijing Opinion provides explanations for the following issues:
   (1) validity of arbitration agreement in the agency relationship;
   (2) the effect of arbitration agreement upon investor and investee in the JV contract;
   (3) the validity of arbitration agreement when both arbitration and litigation are provided;
   (4) the validity of arbitration agreement when two arbitration commissions are provided;
   (5) independence of arbitral clause when the main contract is non-existent;
   (6) independence of arbitration agreement made under duress or undue influence;
   (7) invalidity of *ad hoc* arbitration agreement;
   (8) the scope of arbitration agreement;
   (9) the procedure of jurisdictional challenge handled by the court;
   (10) the validity of arbitration agreement in cases of "incorporation by reference".

[110]   Article 1 of the Beijing Opinion.

[111]   Article 2 of the Beijing Opinion.

Contract Law notes.[112] In accordance with arts.402 and 403 of the Contract Law, the validity of the contract signed by the agent shall be binding on the principal depending on whether the third party reasonably knows about the agency relationship between the agent and principal at the conclusion of the contract.[113] If the third party has such knowledge, the arbitration agreement shall be binding upon the principal;[114] while in cases of an undisclosed principal, the third party could invoke the arbitration agreement against either the principal or the agent.[115] In both cases, the arbitration agreement should extend to bind the principal.

In conclusion, despite its attempt to remedy the problems in arbitral practice, the Beijing Opinion fails to address the newly promulgated Contract Law with respect to the rights and obligations surrounding the agency relationship when regulating the effect of arbitration agreement. Thus, the Beijing Opinion may not be satisfactory in filling the practical gap on the relevant arbitral issues despite the fact that it parallels the positions of the local judiciary in developing the arbitration jurisprudence and practice.

4.030

The "Shanghai Opinion" 2001

Two years later, the Shanghai Higher People's Court (SHC), in light of the developments brought by the new Contract Law, promulgated its own opinions to further explore the issues unresolved in the SPC interpretations (the Shanghai Opinion).[116] The Shanghai Opinion covers a number of important issues in arbitral practice, and arts.2 and 5 particularly deal with the practical difficulties arising from defective arbitration agreements.[117]

4.031

---

[112] See Wang Liming and Xu Chuanxi, "Fundamental Principles of China's Contract Law", (1999) 13 *Columbia Journal of Asian Law*, 1.

[113] See arts.402 and 403 of the Contract Law. See also Lutz-Christian Wolff and Bing Ling, "The Risk of Mixed Laws: The Example of Indirect Agency under Chinese Contract Law", (2002) 15 *Columbia Journal of Asian Law*, 181.

[114] Article 402 of the Contract Law (regulating the agency of an unnamed principal). Although the agent signs the contract in his/her own name, the third party is made aware of such agency relationship. Therefore, if the contract contains an arbitration clause, it shall automatically bind the principal.

[115] Article 403 of the Contract Law (regulating the agency of an undisclosed principal). The circumstances need to be ramified whether it will bind the principal or the agent.

[116] The Shanghai Opinion on Some Issues Regarding the Implementation of the Arbitration Law of the People's Republic of China, issued by the SHC, 3 January 2001.

[117] The Shanghai Opinion covers the following issues:
    (1) identification of written arbitration agreements;
    (2) inaccurate reference to the name of an arbitral institution;
    (3) disputes concerning the jurisdiction of an arbitral institution;
    (4) jurisdictions of an arbitration agreement and appeals for setting aside;
    (5) the binding force of the original arbitration agreement to its legal successor after merger, split or termination of the original contractual party;
    (6) definition of "foreign-related" arbitration;
    (7) applications for effecting property protection or evidence protection measures;
    (8) submission of an arbitration agreement after court proceedings have been commenced;
    (9) service by the court of a re-arbitration notice;
    (10) awards in excess of the scope of the statement of claim;
    (11) appeals to the court for setting aside the decision of an arbitration tribunal for transferring the case to an investigation authority;
    (12) effect of an arbitration document by public announcement; and
    (13) procedures for the application of enforcement of an award.

4.032   Article 2 of the Shanghai Opinion clarifies the proper judicial approach with respect to the determination of the validity of an arbitration agreement if it makes inaccurate reference to the arbitration commission. The SHC opines that because parties usually have limited understanding of the arbitration system and arbitral institutions, it is not uncommon that they refer to an arbitration commission inaccurately in their arbitral agreements. In such cases, as long as the identity of the commission is ascertainable from the surrounding facts, the court should uphold the effect of the arbitration agreement.[118] For better understanding, the Shanghai Opinion then gives some examples of defective draftsmanship referring to arbitral institutions in Shanghai where its effect can be saved by the context. This may include agreements using the language such as "Shanghai Arbitration Institution", "Shanghai Arbitration Organization", "arbitration by the relevant department in Shanghai", "arbitration in Shanghai", etc. [119] Because there are two arbitral institutions in Shanghai, the party will be deemed to have selected both the Shanghai Arbitration Commission (SAC) and the CIETAC Shanghai sub-commission under the Shanghai Opinion.[120] Hence, according to a previous SPC reply, the arbitration agreement is certain and enforceable if parties would agree to submit their disputes to either institution.[121]

4.033   Article 5 of the Shanghai Opinion concerns whether the arbitration agreement binds its legal successor when the original party signing the agreement has been merged, divided or terminated.[122] Article 5 based its legal authority on the newly promulgated Contract Law and its provisions on legal transfer and assignment. Pursuant to art.90 of the Contract Law, the transferee shall be bound by the original contractual rights and obligations following the transfer unless otherwise agreed.[123] The SHC thus explains that where there is a valid arbitration agreement, any reorganisation of the original contracting party that leads to an assignment of the rights and obligations (including merger, division or termination) will bind the original contracting party's legal successor unless parties agreed otherwise.[124]

4.034   The Shanghai Opinion has been given a lot of commendation for its timely interacting with the development of the Contract Law.[125] Moreover, the pragmatic approach taken

---

[118]   Article 2 of the Shanghai Opinion.

[119]   Under art.2 of the Opinion, the following descriptions are regarded as having chosen the SAC:
    (1) arbitration commission of the Shanghai city;
    (2) arbitration organisation affiliated to the Shanghai Municipal Government; and
    (3) arbitration under the bureaus of Shanghai.
    The following descriptions are regarded having chosen the CIETAC Shanghai branch:
    (1) China International Economic Arbitration Commission, Shanghai branch;
    (2) Shanghai International Economic and Trade Arbitration Commission; and
    (3) Shanghai Foreign-related Economic Arbitration Commission.

[120]   CIETAC has two branches, the Shanghai Sub-commission and the Shenzhen Sub-commission. In 2004, the CIETAC Shenzhen Sub-commission was re-named to the CIETAC South-China Sub-commission.

[121]   See discussions above with respect to SPC Reply 176 [1996].

[122]   Article 5 of the Shanghai Opinion.

[123]   See art.90 of the Contract Law (determining that where a party is merged after the contract's formation that the merged party will hold the same rights and obligations of the former parties under the contract).

[124]   Article 5 of the Shanghai Opinion provides that the arbitration agreement will not be binding to the legal successor unless it reaches a new arbitration agreement or an expressive agreement to give up arbitration with the other contracting party.

[125]   See Wang and Qu, "Several Comments on the Shanghai Opinion 2001", in CIETAC (ed.), *2001 Arbitration and Law Yearbook (Zhongcai yu Falu 2001 Niankan)* (Beijing: China Law Press, 2002), 407–408.

by the SHC prioritises the parties' intention to arbitrate by referring to the surrounding circumstances of the arbitration agreement. Dr Wang Shengchang concludes that the Shanghai Opinion pioneers the efforts of the local judiciary in giving judicial preference to parties' drafting autonomy.[126]

(iii) *Reading between the lines*

As discussed previously, the provisions of the Arbitration Law fail to resolve the rigidity of the validity requirements for effective arbitration agreements. Consequently, in tackling the legislative rigidity and to fill in the practical gap, the work has been left to the courts, with the major improvements contributed by the SPC, augmented by the LHPCs.

4.035

In interpreting the requirement on form, remarkable improvements have been made to expand the "signature-based written" requirement. Besides endorsing the form of consent by "incorporation by reference", the SPC has also recognised the effect of arbitration agreements in some situations involving contract assignment and maritime bills. By doing so, the SPC has been seen as a swinging pendulum of strict textual adherence under the Arbitration Law to a more intention-based interpretation. The LHPCs go even further; they give effect to arbitration agreements where contractual parties have undergone reorganisations.

4.036

When it comes to the substantive requirement, an even longer list of judicial documents has been recorded to clarify the uncertainty of "designated arbitration commission". In this respect, the SPC seems to allow the arbitration agreement to be deemed valid even if concurrent arbitral institutions have been nominated. However, the bottom line is that the institution must be clearly ascertainable from the parties' drafting, and moreover, a supplementary agreement must be reached to appoint one institution. By comparison, the judicial approach taken by the LHPCs seems more pro-arbitration in that it not only acknowledges the validity of agreements that incorrectly refer to arbitral commissions but also lays down the solutions should there be any jurisdictional conflict due to the choice of two commissions.[127] That said, art.2 of the Shanghai Opinion has been widely regarded as a bold stride of the local judiciary to show greater respect to the parties' arbitral intention.[128]

4.037

In reading between the lines of these judicial documents, it is found that despite the fact that there is no clear legal basis for the LHPCs to exercise judicial interpretative power, they do issue judicial opinions and these opinions tend to influence arbitral jurisprudence and practice. This is because decentralisation in the course of pursuing economic reforms has fuelled local judicial efforts to develop their own practice in implementing the national rules according to their own needs.[129] As such, the lack of national guidance in certain aspects would create some room for local measures

4.038

---

[126] See Wang Shengchang, "Arbitration Agreement and the Confirmation of Its Validity" (Zhongcai Xieyi ji qi Youxiaoxing Queding), in CIETAC (ed.), *Symposium Essays on Economic and Trade Arbitration Across the Taiwan Straits* (2001), 18–20.

[127] Article 2 of the Shanghai Opinion; see discussions above.

[128] See Wang and Qu, "Comments on Shanghai Opinion 2001", 407.

[129] Hu Kangsheng, Vice-Director of the Legislative Affairs Commission of the NPCSC, "Speech at the Seminar 'Resolving Differences in China'", reprinted in CIETAC (ed.), *Arbitration and Law Yearbook 2001*, 7.

to play a role. It deserves to be noted that although judicial guidelines at both the central and local levels have shown significant progress in liberalising parties' drafting autonomy, the local judiciary has been generally more liberal and "benevolent" in the honouring of defective agreements. They strive to save the defective draftsmanship as much as possible by referring to extraneous evidence and by reading in a selection of arbitration commission for the parties even when only the place of arbitration is mentioned.[130] This may be explanatory by the fact that more pressure to liberalise has been put on the judicial front lines, i.e. the local judiciary, particularly those in economically well-developed areas where the practice of commercial arbitration has developed into a more advantageous level. The two judicial opinions issued by the BHC and SHC therefore have resulted in resounding compliments from both the judiciary and arbitration communities. The Shanghai Opinion in 2001 is particularly well received for having cleared up quite a few practical uncertainties. In CIETAC's words, "The Shanghai Opinion has made crucial contributions to the development of arbitration in China by the local judiciary and these guidelines impact the arbitral practice not only in Shanghai but also the entire country".[131]

4.039   However, gaps remain after comparing international arbitration norms. For example, judicial documents at both the central and provincial levels fail to satisfactorily reflect the relevant changes taking place in other important Chinese legislations such as the Contract Law. The inconsistencies include, for example, the effect of arbitration agreements on non-signatory third parties in the context of agency relationship.[132] In addition, from time to time, all those judicial opinions appear to be sporadic pieces of documents before the public. They may not be consistent with each other in a number of instances and perhaps conflict with each other, which make them very difficult for reference in arbitral practice. As such, a unified judicial interpretative document compiling all these opinions from various levels would better serve the practical needs before the Arbitration Law is overhauled.

(b) Critical turning since 2006: Unified Supreme People's Court interpretation on arbitration

4.040   In its latest attempt, a decade later, the SPC spearheaded the reform by issuing its unified interpretation on Chinese arbitration, the Interpretation on Several Issues Concerning the Application of the PRC Arbitration Law (the SPC Interpretation), as effective in September 2006.[133] The SPC Interpretation has been based significantly on the two Draft Provisions previously issued by itself in 2003 and 2004 respectively, namely, Several Regulations on How the People's Courts Handle Foreign-related

---

[130] See, art.2 of the Shanghai Opinion; see also discussions above.
[131] See Wang and Qu, "Comments on Shanghai Opinion 2001", 407–408.
[132] See discussions above in the comments to the Beijing Opinion in 1999.
[133] *Interpretation on Several Issues Concerning the Application of the PRC Arbitration Law*, promulgated by the SPC on 23 August 2006, and with effect on 8 September 2006, available at the people's court website, www. chinacourt.org.

Arbitration and Foreign Arbitration Cases (the Foreign-related Draft)[134] and Interpretations to Several Issues on the Application of the Arbitration Law (the Domestic Draft).[135]

As far as the regulation of arbitration agreements is concerned,[136] the newly issued SPC Interpretation appears to be a good summary of the relevant provisions contained in the Contract Law and various SPC and LHPC judicial opinions on the topic.[137] It codifies the existing arbitration rules and practices and provides further clarification to certain issues that have in the past led to technical challenges to arbitration agreements. At the same time, however, it steps backward from the pro-validity initiatives in some cases cited in the two Drafts and leaves other important issues unanswered. **4.041**

(i) *Two previous Supreme People's Court Draft Provisions*

For the purpose of the present review of the 2006 SPC Interpretation, its previous two Draft Provisions are of particular relevance and will be referred to throughout this section as a comparative base in outlining both the improvements and problems of the latest SPC approach towards arbitration. **4.042**

Broad meaning of "written agreement"

Both the Foreign-related and Domestic Drafts comprehensively deal with the increased flexibility of the traditionally strict "written" requirement for arbitration agreements. **4.043**

First, the provisions are consistent with the Contract Law in that whether an arbitration agreement is in writing will be determined in accordance with art.11 of the Contract Law,[138] which refers to "any signed form capable of tangibly representing its contents, such as written instruments, letters and electrically or electronically transmitted documents".[139] Then, as an exceptional deviation from the traditional "signature-based writing" rule, art.16 of the Foreign-related Draft provides that a valid arbitration agreement will be deemed to have been made where one party commences arbitral proceedings and the other party joins in the proceeding without jurisdictional objection and files a substantive defence. This creation of the "waiver of objection" standard is similar to the practice of "exchange of statements of claim and defence"[140] under the Model Law. **4.044**

---

[134] Several Issues on How People's Court Handle Foreign-related Arbitration and Foreign Arbitration Cases (Draft Provisions for Opinion Solicitation), issued by the SPC on 31 December 2003.

[135] Interpretations to Several Issues on the Application of the PRC Arbitration Law (Draft Provisions for Opinion Solicitation), issued by the SPC on 22 July 2004.

[136] The SPC Interpretation concerns two important aspects in arbitration: arbitration agreements and arbitral awards.

[137] See discussions about the SPC Interpretation in a Symposium on "Judicial Review of Foreign-related Arbitration", co-organised by South-China Sub-commission of the CIETAC and 4th Civil Division of the SPC, 15–16 November 2004, Shenzhen.

[138] See art.25 of the Foreign-related Draft; see also art.14 of the Domestic Draft.

[139] See art.11 of the Contract Law.

[140] See art.7(2) of the Model Law, which stipulates that the arbitration agreement shall also be considered "in writing", and therefore valid if there is "an exchange of a statement of claim and defence in which the existence of an agreement is alleged by one party and not denied by another". See also comments by Binder, *International Commercial Arbitration in UNCITRAL Model Law Jurisdictions* (2000), para 2-027.

4.045   To resolve the practical uncertainty raised by the BHC, the Foreign-related Draft, in addressing the effect of arbitration agreements in the context of agency relations, provides in art.21 that the agreement will not bind the principal if it is concluded by an agent without authorised power, ultra vires or after the power expires.[141] However, in accordance with the Contract Law, the arbitration agreement signed by the agent will be established between the principal and the third party as long as the substantive contract per se binds the principal; and this will be based on whether the third party has actual knowledge of the agency relationship at the time of concluding the arbitration agreement with the agent.[142]

4.046   Both Drafts further articulate that the succession or transfer of the legal rights and obligations of a party in a contract where the arbitration agreement forms a part would lead to the transfer of the arbitration agreement. This expansive view on "written form of consent" has been endorsed by the SPC before[143] and has now been codified in arts.28 (succession), 29 (assignment) and 31 (subrogation) of the Foreign-related Draft as well as arts.1 (succession) and 2 (assignment) of the Domestic Draft[144] unless the third party assignee or successor disagrees with or proves himself unaware of the arbitration clause at the time of assignment or succession.[145]

4.047   Finally, art.30 of the Foreign-related Draft deals with the transfer of arbitration agreements in the context of charterparties and Bs/L. It states that an arbitral clause contained in a charterparty shall be deemed to be incorporated and therefore binding on the B/L holder, provided the incorporation is expressly stated on the face of the bill and the arbitral clause is valid.[146] It is notable that over a decade, the SPC seems to soften its tone a bit as the express consent by the bill holder is no longer required. However, it might still be arguable that an express statement on the "face" of the bill appears restrictive in that it could deny maritime arbitration cases where the statement of incorporation may not be made "express" enough or made within the lines of the bill.[147]

Curable instances of "ambiguous arbitration institution"

4.048   In the beginning, both of the two Draft Provisions replace the use of the term "arbitration commission (*zhongcaiweiyuanhui*)" in the Arbitration Law with "arbitration institution (*zhongcaijigou*)".[148] It is interesting to note that except for the use of the word "commission" in China, most arbitral institutions abroad adopt different titles which imply that they are institutional arbitration service providers.[149]

---

[141]   See art.21 of the Foreign-related Draft.

[142]   See arts.402 and 403 of the Contract Law.

[143]   See discussions above, with respect to the "SPC Hubei Reply" and "SPC Henan Reply"; see also art.5 of the "Shanghai Opinion 2001".

[144]   See arts.28, 29, 31 of the Foreign-related Draft; see also arts.1 and 2 of the Domestic Draft.

[145]   See art.29(2) of the Foreign-related Draft and art.2(2) of the Domestic Draft.

[146]   See art.30 of the Foreign-related Draft.

[147]   See Li Hai, "Thinking about the Several Questions Regarding the Validity of the Arbitration Clause in the Bill of Lading" (2005), 92.

[148]   See arts.22–26 of the Foreign-related Draft and arts.5–7 of the Domestic Draft.

[149]   To name a few, in Hong Kong, the arbitration institution is called "Hong Kong International Arbitration *Centre*"; in London, the "London *Court* of International Arbitration (LCIA)"; in New York, the "American Arbitration *Association*".

Pursuant to the Contract Law, parties to a contract with foreign elements[150] are allowed to agree to submit their disputes to arbitration either within or outside China.[151] They are thus allowed to choose institutional arbitration abroad even if the governing law of their arbitration agreement is Arbitration Law.[152] As such, it is absurd to reject the validity of these agreements when strict adherence to the term "commission" is actually impossible. It may also be indicated that the SPC hopes to address to some extent the localisation concerns such as the use of the term "arbitration commission" and hence to move Chinese arbitral regulations more parallel to international arbitration terms and uses. Beyond the wording change, three main aspects of reforms are brought by the two Drafts with respect to liberalising the rigidity of "designated arbitration commission" standard under the Arbitration Law.

First, arts.22–26 of the Foreign-related Draft and arts.5–7 of the Domestic Draft detail the circumstances under which arbitration agreements should be voided under arts.16 and 18 of the Arbitration Law, yet would be curable in the arbitral practice. This may include cases such as an agreement providing for arbitration "by two or multiple arbitral institutions".[153] Further, both Drafts articulate that if an arbitration agreement provides for arbitration at a certain place but fails to designate a specific arbitral institution, the agreement is not invalidated by the fact that more than one institution exists at the place of arbitration.[154] Although it fails to clarify which institution in the circumstance should be the proper one to assume the jurisdiction, the reasonable assumption is that without any supplementary agreement specifying the exact institution, the principle of "first come, first served" will be applied so that the arbitral institution which first receives an application for arbitration seizes its jurisdiction.[155] In addition, where the parties make incorrect reference to an arbitral institution, but its proper identity can still be ascertained by reference to the surrounding context, the court should declare the agreement valid and decline its jurisdiction over the dispute.[156] Similarly, where an arbitration clause makes reference only to the rules of a specific arbitral institution, the court may refer the matter to arbitration under that institution whose rules are referred to.[157] **4.049**

The second aspect concerns the scenario where the parties opt for both arbitration and litigation. Following a previous SPC opinion, art.20(4) of the Foreign-related Draft provides that such arbitration agreements are invalid.[158] The approach in the **4.050**

---

[150] Under the judicial interpretations of the General Principles of Civil Law (1983), a dispute is "foreign-related" if either of the party is a non-Chinese citizen; or the subject-matter of the dispute is not in China; or the establishing and changing of the legal relationship takes place outside China. And this interpretation applies to the circumstances of Hong Kong, Macao and Taiwan-related disputes.

[151] See art.128 of the Contract Law.

[152] If the governing law of the arbitration agreement is not the Arbitration Law, then parties may be allowed to choose *ad hoc* arbitration in a foreign jurisdiction as well, which is widely recognised under international arbitration practice.

[153] See art.22 of the Foreign-related Draft; see also art.5 of the Domestic Draft.

[154] See art.23 of the Foreign-related Draft; see also art.5 of the Domestic Draft.

[155] See art.5 of the Shanghai Opinion in 2001; see also comments by Wang and Qu, "Comments on Shanghai Opinion 201"(2001), 407–408.

[156] See art.24 of the Foreign-related Draft; see also art.6 of the Domestic Draft.

[157] See art.6 of the Foreign-related Draft.

[158] See art.20(4) of the Foreign-related Draft.

Foreign-related Draft, however, conflicts with that of the Domestic Draft, which provides under its art.7 that such agreements will not be voided and that the case will be adjudicated in either the arbitral institution or the court whichever adjudicatory body files the application first.[159] The liberal approach in the Domestic Draft is welcomed by the practitioners as the more realistic interpretative technique and more pro-arbitration stance of the SPC.[160]

4.051   Lastly, art.20(6) of the Foreign-related Draft deals with the controversial issue of *ad hoc* arbitration agreements in China. It seems that the SPC now relaxes its traditional stance by providing an exception under art.27 of the Foreign-related Draft to allow the *ad hoc* agreement in some cases. Article 27 exception consists of two limbs: first, both parties to the arbitration agreement must be nationals of Member States to the New York Convention (NYC); second, the laws of both countries must not prohibit *ad hoc* arbitrations.[161] Since the SPC has held that *ad hoc* arbitrations are not permitted in China,[162] then pursuant to the second limb of art.27 exceptions, an *ad hoc* arbitration agreement between a Chinese party and a foreign party may nevertheless be voided. As such, on its face, the rule dramatically reduces the ability of the parties to a Sino-foreign contract to conduct *ad hoc* arbitrations. Additionally, the SPC seems to lean towards arbitration agreements that provide for *ad hoc* arbitrations outside China.[163] The potential impact of art.27 is nonetheless far-reaching as it is the threshold of possible defrosting of *ad hoc* arbitral practice in China. The Draft Provisions were expected to be formally recognised with this partial recognition of *ad hoc* arbitration agreements. However, this did not occur, leaving the status of *ad hoc* arbitration agreements still an open-ended question in the Chinese arbitration system, as the following sections will discuss.

(ii) *Unified judicial interpretation on arbitration*

4.052   The unified SPC Interpretation of 2006, on the basis of the two Drafts previously issued, is the latest attempt by the SPC to clarify its positions on a number of contentiously defective arbitration agreements. Compared with the two Drafts, the latest interpretation involves both encouraging steps of a general preference towards confirming the effect of arbitration agreements and disappointing moving away from the liberalisation efforts.

Confirming the broad meaning of "written agreement"

4.053   The 2006 Interpretation generally confirms the liberal approach of the two Drafts on the writing formality. Consistent with art.15 of the Foreign-related Draft, art.1 of the Interpretation aligns the definition of written form with art.11 of the Contract Law.[164]

---

[159]   See art.7 of the Domestic Draft.
[160]   See Jian Zhou, "Judicial Intervention in International Arbitration: A Comparative Study of the Scope of the New York Convention in U.S. and Chinese Courts", (2006) 15 *Pacific Rim Law & Policy Journal*, 454.
[161]   See art.27 of the Foreign-related Draft.
[162]   Most recently, in the case of *People's Insurance Co of China, Guangzhou Branch v Guangdong Guanghe Power Co Ltd* (2003) Ming Si Zhong Zi No. 29, the SPC confirmed the inadmissibility of *ad hoc* arbitrations in China.
[163]   See Sun Nanshen, "Jurisdictional Conflicts in the Judicial Review of Foreign-related Arbitrations", in Han Jian (ed), *Judicial Review of the Foreign-Related Arbitration* (Beijing: China Law Press, 2006), 19.
[164]   See art.1 of the SPC Interpretation; see also discussions above on the Draft Provisions.

Article 11 then confirms the form of consent by way of incorporation by reference. It provides that where a contract stipulates that an arbitration clause in another contract or document shall be applied to resolve disputes under the contract at issue, the parties shall refer the dispute to arbitration in accordance with such clause.[165] Although the wording is not entirely clear, it appears that a general reference to such contract or document will be sufficient, which is in accordance with an earlier SPC reply.[166]

With respect to the effect of arbitration agreements upon non-signatory third parties in contractual transfer (succession, assignment and subrogation), the SPC Interpretation is generally in line with the approach taken in its Draft Provisions that the arbitration agreement shall be binding on the party to whom contractual rights are assigned, transferred or subrogated.[167] However, it goes on to provide a significant exception, other than those already mentioned in the Drafts—the arbitration agreement will not be binding if the transferee is unaware of the existence of a separate arbitration agreement at the time of transfer or assignment.[168] It thus introduces a presumptive rule that the arbitration agreement will be binding on the transferee or assignee, but can be rebutted by showing a lack of knowledge, although the exact scope of "lack of awareness" is unclear. For example, to what extent is the transferee or assignee's implied or constructive knowledge of the existence of arbitration agreement relevant? The SPC fails to provide any further guidelines, leaving the practice vague on the point. Additionally, some other controversial non-signatory third party cases, in the agency and bill of lading contexts, have been omitted that had previously been addressed in the Foreign-related Draft.[169] The provisional omission may lead to greater uncertainty of the regulatory regime and causes the arbitral practice to be inconsistent on these issues.

4.054

Stepping backward on "curable arbitration institution"

The unified SPC Interpretation confirms the usage of the term "arbitration institution" in the two Drafts. With respect to guidelines for substantive validity, arts.3–7 of the Interpretation deal specifically with curable instances of a vague yet ascertainable arbitral institution as required under arts.16 and 18 of the Arbitration Law.[170] Most notably, art.4 of the Interpretation provides under its second part that "if the arbitration institution can be ascertained pursuant to the arbitration rules which have been agreed by the parties to be applicable, the arbitration agreement is valid".[171] It is clear from most institutional arbitration rules which institution the rules refer to. It thus appears sufficient that if parties in China agree on institutional arbitration rules such as those of the International Chamber of Commerce (ICC) and Hong Kong International

4.055

---

[165] See art.11 of the SPC Interpretation.
[166] See the SPC Reply on the Manner of Determining Jurisdiction in a Sino-Mongolian Contract that Fails to Provide for Arbitration in 1996, see fn 75 above.
[167] See arts.8 and 9 of the SPC Interpretation.
[168] See art.9 of the SPC Interpretation.
[169] See art.21 (agency relationship) and art.30 (bill of lading) of the Foreign-related Draft.
[170] See arts.3–7 of the SPC Interpretation.
[171] See art.4 of the SPC Interpretation.

Arbitration Centre (HKIAC) to point to arbitration under that institution.[172] Such an approach is similarly worded with art.26 of the previously issued Foreign-related Draft[173] and art.4(3) of the recently revised CIETAC rules.[174]

4.056   The Interpretation, in response to art.5 of the Domestic Draft and art.22 of the Foreign-related Draft, clarifies the scenario where two or more arbitration institutions have been concurrently nominated. To the disappointment of arbitration scholars and practitioners, it pronounces under art.5 that such agreements will be deemed invalid.[175] The SPC steps backward from the liberal attempt previously taken under both Drafts which provided that such an agreement would nonetheless be considered effective and enforceable.[176] The backward step is further reflected by art.6, which, in a similar vein to art.5, denies the effect of arbitration agreements with concurrent arbitral jurisdictions resulting from parties' stipulation to the place of arbitration only. This negates the aforementioned pro-validity approaches under both Drafts in which all possible arbitration institutions in the named place may assume jurisdictions.[177]

4.057   What is also worth noting is the provision for validity arising from those "split arbitration agreements", which refer disputes to either an arbitration institution or a court.[178] Article 7 of the Interpretation, contrary to the liberal approach previously taken under art.7 of the Domestic Draft,[179] announces the invalidity of such agreements, unless one party commences arbitration and the other party does not object prior to the tribunal's first hearing.[180] In so providing, the SPC suggests that the so-called split agreements or clauses—often favoured by foreign financial institutions—will not be enforced in China, at least to the extent that they are governed by the Chinese law.[181]

4.058   As noted above, art.4 of the Interpretation helps, to some extent, alleviate the requirement that an arbitration institution such as the ICC Court of Arbitration has to be specifically designated in an arbitral agreement.[182] However, to the great dismay of international arbitration practitioners, the new judicial explanation neither goes further to confirm the validity of *ad hoc* arbitration agreements, albeit limited, as art.27 of the Foreign-related Draft did,[183] nor has it clarified the status of foreign institutional arbitration seated in China, as the previous interpretations failed to do.[184] Pursuant to art.31, the Interpretation will supersede all regulations, notices, replies and

---

[172] The general assumption has been confirmed in the joint conference on the "SPC Interpretation on the Application of the Arbitration Law", co-held by the Civil Division of the SPC, Research Institute of the SPC, CIETAC and China Arbitration Association, 15 December 2006, Beijing, http://www.cietac.org.cn/NewsFiles/NewsDetail.asp?NewsID=540.

[173] See art.26 of the Foreign-related Draft.

[174] See art.(3) of the 2005 CIETAC Arbitration Rules.

[175] See art.5 of the SPC Interpretation.

[176] See art.22 of the Foreign-related Draft and art.5 of the Domestic Draft.

[177] See art.23 of the Foreign-related Draft and art.5 of the Domestic Draft.

[178] Craig, Park and Paulsson, *ICC Arbitration* (2000), para 3-11.

[179] See art.7 of the Domestic Draft.

[180] See art.7 of the Interpretation. See also art.20 of the Arbitration Law and discussions below in Chapter 5 with respect to the timeline for raising such objection to arbitral jurisdiction.

[181] Such "split arbitration agreements or clauses" are often favoured by foreign financial institutions in China, such as foreign banks, insurance companies.

[182] See discussions above.

[183] See art.27 of the Foreign-related Draft.

[184] See discussions above on art.27 of the Foreign-related Draft.

opinions issued by the SPC to the extent that there are any inconsistencies between provisions contained therein and in the Interpretation.[185] It is thus unlikely that parties can still refer to art.27 of the Foreign-related Draft specifically with reference to *ad hoc* arbitration. In particular, it remains questionable whether an *ad hoc* arbitration agreement in China may still be admissible where both of the art.27 exceptions under the Foreign-related Draft are satisfied.

(iii) *Comments on the latest Supreme People's Court approach*

After more than a decade of experience in interpreting defective arbitration agreements, the 2006 SPC Interpretation may be considered a systematic summary of the past sporadic judicial replies, notices, opinions and guidelines. More importantly, due to its *de facto* rule-making power in China, the SPC Interpretation has dual significance. First, it serves as quasi-legislative attempt to bridge the gap between the Arbitration Law and international arbitration norms on the topic. Second, it shows the evolving degree of judicial respect of people's courts to the parties' drafting autonomy in arbitration.

4.059

To sum up, the Interpretation attempts to unify the overlapping and even conflicting provisions in both Drafts so as to merge the two tracks.[186] Disappointingly, it moves away from the pro-validity approach taken in the two Drafts on the substantive validity requirement, although it generally conforms to the expansive understanding of "written" formality previously adopted. As illustrated before, prior to the unified Interpretation is officially promulgated, a more liberal interpretative technique has been endorsed in the Draft Provisions where surrounding circumstances are taken into account in ascertaining the parties' intent to arbitrate. As such, the two Drafts have indicated a significant preference by the judiciary for arbitration and they appear to respect the principle of party autonomy generally. However, it appears that under some provisions of the current approach, the practice of "designated arbitration institution" still adheres to the rigid textual interpretation without taking into consideration further facts to preserve the parties' arbitral wishes. In particular, arts.5, 6 and 7 of the unified Interpretation could be unduly restrictive in some cases. Compared with international arbitration norms, the general rule is to give effect to the parties' arbitral intention as far as possible. As such, even if two arbitral institutions or both arbitration and court litigation have been referred to in the arbitration agreement, that should not render the agreement *ipso facto* invalid. Instead, as some leading international arbitrators who focus on Chinese practice suggest, the latest approach by the SPC is too stringent and fails to adopt more liberal effective interpretation techniques:

4.060

"It is strange that the SPC now steps backward from its Foreign-related Draft where a principle of effective interpretation used to be adopted. However, if there is a clear desire

---

[185]   Article 31 of the SPC Interpretation.

[186]   For examples of provisional overlaps, see pairs such as art.25 (Foreign-related Draft) and art.14 (Domestic Draft); arts.28, 29 (Foreign-related Draft) and arts.1, 2 (Domestic Draft); arts.22, 23 (Foreign-related Draft) and art.5 (Domestic Draft); art.24 (Foreign-related Draft) and art.6 (Domestic Draft). For provisional contradictions inside or outside the Draft, see discussions above in Section C.3.2.1 of this Chapter.

to submit the dispute to arbitration, such a desire should, as far as possible, be given effect to, by seeking to construe the clause in such a way as to render it effective."[187]

4.061   The unexpected answer to some of the most controversial issues on the specificity of arbitral institutions may suggest a restrictive approach on the part of the SPC in accommodating the parties' drafting autonomy. However, in a recent symposium focusing on the provisional gap between the Interpretation and its previous two Drafts, an SPC official stated that, "[t]here are many different views on the two Drafts after their opening to the public for comments and the current text is the just result for balancing these views".[188] It might be arguable that the SPC is worried about liberalising this traditional legislative rigidity too quickly and going too far beyond the Arbitration Law text. Hence, a compromise has been put forward by the judiciary in treating arbitration the way it has after carefully balancing the inflexibility of the current regime and full-scale liberalisation.

4.062   There are also a few other contentious issues that the latest unified Interpretation fails to respond to its previous Drafts. Among them is whether to recognise the validity of arbitration agreements providing for *ad hoc* arbitration and foreign arbitration in China. As outlined in previous discussions, for the first time in the history of arbitration in China, *ad hoc* arbitration is provided under art.27 of the Foreign-related Draft. The provision has been seen as a revolutionary progress and was widely expected to be formally adopted as part of the SPC's agenda, so as to create a more arbitration-friendly environment for foreign business. This, however, did not occur, which leaves the practice of *ad hoc* arbitration standing at the crossroads of the SPC-led reform of Chinese arbitration. It could be argued either that the SPC has finally decided to give up recognising agreements providing for *ad hoc* arbitration in China entirely, even when the demanding exceptions under art.27 of the Foreign-related Draft have been satisfied, or that art.27 exceptions still cannot be fit into the Chinese model of arbitration. And there remains uncertainty with respect to the legal status of *ad hoc* arbitration agreements conducted outside China that the latest SPC Interpretation fails to address in its previous Foreign-related Draft. As previously mentioned, *ad hoc* awards may run the risk of being denied recognition and enforcement by the people's court if the Chinese law serves as governing law between the disputing parties. Moreover, the SPC's failure to address the effect of arbitration agreements that select the ICC arbitration in China could arguably be because the ICC Court does not sit well with the meaning of "arbitration commission" under the Arbitration Law; nor is there any clear legal mechanism for enforcing the resulting ICC (or other foreign institutional) award that has been made in China. Although the SPC may not be able to solve all these problems, Dr Moser, a lawyer at a widely known international law firm, suggests that its omission on these highly contentious issues in the latest

---

[187]   Johnson Tan, "Jones Day Commentary on the Interpretation of the Arbitration Law of the PRC by the Supreme People's Court", published by Jones, Day, Reavies and Pogue, December 2006, available at http://www.jonesday.com/search/search.aspx?qu=arbitration&limit=pubpdfs. Johnson Tan is the managing partner of the Jones Day Beijing Office and the leader of the ADR group of Jones Day China.

[188]   Speech by Mr Luo Dongchuan, Vice-Head of the Research Institute of the SPC on the joint conference on the "SPC Interpretation on the Application of the Arbitration Law", co-organised by the Civil Division and Research Institute of the SPC, CIETAC and CMAC, 15 December 2006, Beijing.

Interpretation reflects judicial concerns about the current institutional monopoly in Chinese arbitration, which will be the focus of the section below.[189]

3. *AD HOC* AND ICC ARBITRATION AGREEMENTS IN CHINA

In light of Chinese government's continued reluctance to recognise *ad hoc* arbitration, the following discussion will first analyse the fundamental reason that restrains the liberalisation process. The second part examines the success of an *ad hoc* arbitration case against the current regulatory framework before this section ends with proposals for legislative recognition and the possible political challenges entailed.   **4.063**

(a) Problems of state control

Although almost all countries permit *ad hoc* arbitration in their national arbitration legislations, in the history of commercial arbitration in China, *ad hoc* arbitration has never been ratified by the legislation or protected in practice. The regulatory obstacles have most recently involved the omission of the issue in the 2006 unified SPC Interpretation on arbitration and a case in 2003 in which the SPC struck down an arbitration clause providing for *ad hoc* arbitration in China.[190] The following part of the discussion attempts to explain the institutional monopoly from the perspective of the state's overwhelming desire to control arbitration in China. The actual impact of such a monopoly in China (both theoretically and practically) will also be addressed in this part.   **4.064**

Determined to achieve a breakthrough in the economic reform, China started to practice a "socialist market economy" since 1992.[191] The socialist market economy has been described both as a major improvement to the previous planned economy and an "inherent dichotomy" by the legal scholars.[192] On the one hand, the reform brings the prospect of greater managerial autonomy in market transactions and increases the diversity of economic actors.[193] Hence, unlike the planned economy where the driving force was government production orders, in a market economy, the market players have the freedom to make decisions for themselves.[194] On the other hand, in order to ensure that China's market develops according to the Party ideology and policy,   **4.065**

---

[189] The speech by Dr Michael J. Moser (managing partner of O'Melvany Hong Kong Office) at the symposium "Developments in the Settlement of International Commercial and Investment Disputes – Chinese and German Perspectives", co-organised by HKIAC and German Institution of Arbitration (DIS) at the HKIAC, Hong Kong, 8 December 2008.

[190] *People's Insurance Co of China, Guangzhou v Guanghope Power et al*, [Min Si Zhong Zi] No. 29 of 2003, Civil Division, SPC.

[191] The new but powerful idea that the overall objective of China's economic reform in the next few decades would be the establishment of a "socialist market economy" was quickly written into the Constitution of the PRC in early 1993.

[192] Wang Liming and Xu Chuanxi, "Fundamental Principles of China's Contract Law", (1999), 1–2.

[193] See generally, He Guanghui, "Reform of the Chinese Economic Structure (Zhongguo Jingji Tizhi Gaige)", *FBIS Daily Report of China*, 23 March 1990, 21.

[194] Zhang Wenxian, "Market Economy and the Spirit of Modern Law (Shichang Jingji yu Xiandai Fazhi Jingshen)", (1994) 6 *Chinese Legal Science (Zhongguo Faxue)*, 12; Wang Zhengbang, "The Modern Market Economy as a Rule of Law Economy (Shichang Jingji Nai Fazhi Jingji)", (1994) 25 *Studies in Law (Faxue Yanjiu)*, 26.

the establishment of a socialist market economy has been the declared objective and the focus of the Party State's efforts to boost socioeconomic development.[195] State intervention and control is therefore decisive in the regulation of the market and to maintain the Party policy of centralised censorship despite rising recognition that reform requires more freedom for economic actors and their transactions.[196] The legal implication of the transition from a planned to a socialist market economy has thus been understood as the conception of a relationship between an economic base and a social superstructure within the Party State, which is featured as a paraphrase of the "high-level institutionalised commodity economy" under the Party ideology.[197] As such, during the market transition, state agencies still wish to exercise considerable control over market activities for the sake of predictability and stability to preserve socialism, which includes the State's means of dispute resolution.

4.066   State control of arbitration has been expressed in the way of controlling the *outcome* of arbitration during the transitional period. By adopting an institutional arbitration system in China, these arbitration institutions are made state agencies subject to control by the Party leadership. For example, prior to the Arbitration Law came into effect in 1995, arbitration cases involving domestic business disputes were handled by the Economic Contract Arbitration Commissions (ECACs) within the Administrations of the Industry and Commerce around China, through a system of mandatory jurisdiction.[198] Technology disputes were heard by the Technology Contract Arbitration Commissions (TCACs) attached to the Bureau of Science and Technology of the local people's government.[199] The ECACs and TCACs were subordinate to the governmental departments at various levels, so they were subject to governmental scrutiny of their dispute resolutions. This explains the historical preference for using arbitration in China, such as the ECACs. Because these are administrative adjudication systems that are easy to control under Chinese style top-down administrative governance. Foreign-related arbitrations were then handled by the foreign-related arbitration institutions, namely CIETAC and CMAC, which, although technically called independent social organisations of foreign trade, received subsidies from the State Council for their businesses, and the way they handled disputes with foreign parties was inspected by the Central Government.[200] In the realm of pre-Arbitration Law arbitration, only specific institutions could conduct arbitration in China and thus, it is clear how China was able to control the outcome of the arbitration.

4.067   The institutional monopoly has been affirmed in the Arbitration Law, which is most obviously reflected in arts.16 and 18 as regards the rigid specificity to the arbitration

---

[195]   Zhang Wenxian, "Reflections on Macro-economic Control and its Law and Policy (Guanyu Hongguanjingji Tiaokong jiqi Falu yu Zhengce de Sikao)", (1994) 1 *Peking University Law Journal (Zhongwai Faxue)*, 3.

[196]   Wang Baoshu, "The Socialist Market Economy and Research in Economic Law (Shehuizhuyi Shichangjingji yu Minshangfa Yanjiu)", (1993) 3 *Chinese Legal Science (Zhongguo Faxue)*, 20.

[197]   Albert H.Y. Chen, "The Developing Theory of Law and Market Economy in Contemporary China", in Wang Guiguo and Wei Zhenyin (eds.), *Legal Developments in China: Market Economy and Law* (Hong Kong: Sweet & Maxwell Asia, 1996), 5–6.

[198]   Article 2 of the Regulations of the PRC on the Arbitration of Disputes Involving Economic Contracts.

[199]   Article 2 of the Provisional Regulations Concerning the Administration of Organization for Technology Contract Arbitration Institutions.

[200]   Jiang Xianming and Li Ganggui, *Study of Chinese Arbitration Law (Zhongguo Zhongcaifa Yanjiu)* (Nanjing: Southeast University Press, 1996), 28.

commission in arbitration agreements. For the purpose of regulating these Chinese arbitration commissions, Chapter 2 of the Arbitration Law makes special provisions for their establishment[201] and structure.[202] The re-organised Local Arbitration Commissions (LACs) have thus replaced the previous ECACs and TCACs and they have been set up at the prefecture level across the country in accordance with the Arbitration Law. CIETAC and CMAC retained their status as foreign-related arbitration institutions in China as separately addressed in Chapter 7 of the Arbitration Law[203] despite the subsequent merging of jurisdictions between the two types of arbitration commissions.[204]

State control has however been extended to the post-Arbitration Law stage where, through a "1995 State Council Notice",[205] the newly established LACs are required to be registered with the local Department of Justice (DOJ) and attached to the Legislative Affairs Office (LAO) of the local people's government. Hence, the dispute resolution work of the LACs is made part of the legal administration under the locality.[206] Moreover, the re-organisation of personnel and finance of these LACs is led by many governmental departments of the locality.[207] Finally, it is emphasised in the Notice that the LACs are to "help the government resolve business disputes and *to achieve socioeconomic stability in the locality* for the construction of a socialist market economy for the entire country".[208] As such, the outcome of arbitration by the LACs shall be accountable to the local political and administrative interests, given the basis of their establishment and their stated function to help with local administration and economic stability. This connection is buoyed by the local government's use of its LACs to resolve disputes to play upon a localisation sentiment in matching the outcome to the local economic interests. On the other hand, CIETAC and CMAC remain accountable to the State Council in dealing with foreign-related disputes, particularly when the disputes involve assets of State-Owned Enterprises (SOEs),[209] although in

4.068

---

[201] Articles 10 and 11 of the Arbitration Law state that the establishment of arbitration commissions shall be registered with the administrative department of justice of the relevant province, autonomous region or municipality directly under the Central Government.

[202] Article 12 of the Arbitration Law requires that an arbitration commission must be composed of one chairman, two to four vice chairmen and seven to 11 members.

[203] Article 66 of the Arbitration Law provides that foreign-related arbitration commissions may be organised by China Chamber of International Commerce, composed of one chairman, a certain number of vice chairmen and members.

[204] All arbitration commissions in China have been able to receive both domestic and foreign-related disputes as a result of the State Council Notice in 1996 and subsequent revisions to the CIETAC Rules in 1998. See discussions above in Chapter 2.

[205] Notice Concerning the Improvement of the Work on Re-organization of Arbitration Commissions, promulgated by the State Council in 1995. See also discussions above in Section A.3 of Chapter 1.

[206] See art.1 of the Notice of the General Office of the State Council Regarding Further Strengthening the Reorganization of Arbitration Institutions.

[207] *Ibid.*

[208] *Ibid.* See also, Vai Io Lo, "Resolution of Civil Disputes in China", (2001) 18 *UCLA Pacific Basin Law Journal*, 129.

[209] G. Liu and A. Lourie, "International Commercial Arbitration in China: History, New Developments and Current Practice", (1996) 13 *John Marshall Law Review*, 28; see also Jason Pien, Note, "Creditor Rights and Enforcement of International Commercial Arbitral Awards in China", (2007) 45 *Columbia Journal of Transnational Law*, 602.

general they have more foreign arbitrators and are subject to less interference by the government in their decision-making processes.[210]

4.069   According to this logic, it is easy to see how any arbitration conducted by a non-Chinese arbitral institution may invite the possibility of unexpected outcomes for the government. It will thus be considered as outside the realm of state control and hence a deviation from the socioeconomic stability. Furthermore, traditional Chinese respect for the power of office emphasises the role of institutions rather than individuals and hence pushes the government to adhere to an institutional style of arbitration.[211]

(b) Formal mediation, actual arbitration

4.070   Despite the questionable basis in law, the following case may be one of the few exceptional ones in which *ad hoc* arbitration was accomplished without changing the current legal framework.

4.071   Sinotrans Dalian Company (Sinotrans) as charterer, entered into a time charter with the shipowner Hainan Dongda Shipping Company (Dongda) on 20 October 1998. The *arbitration clause* in the contract provided that, "All disputes arising out of the contract shall be arbitrated in Beijing". Both companies are located in Dalian. The disputes arose and Dongda asked Mr Hu Zhengliang, a law professor at the Dalian Maritime University and a Beijing CMAC panel-arbitrator to assist them in resolving the dispute. Subsequently, Sinotrans also requested Mr Hu to arbitrate the dispute. On 18 May 1999, the parties agreed for the dispute to be arbitrated by Mr Hu. Mr Hu asked for both parties' submissions. He then requested Mr Wang Jianping, also a professor at the Dalian Maritime University but with a speciality in navigation technology, to give an expert report of the navigation database provided by the parties. On 10 July 1999, Mr Hu drafted and delivered to the parties his decision by way of a document entitled "An Opinion on Mediation". Both parties honoured the decision.[212]

4.072   Although it was formally titled "An Opinion on Mediation", in essence, the document was not only an arbitral award but also an *ad hoc* arbitral award. Reasons are as follows.

4.073   First, there was an intention to arbitrate rather than mediate. Apart from the original arbitration clause enclosed in the charterparty, after the dispute arose, both parties chose *ad hoc* arbitration in Dalian rather than the institutional arbitration at CMAC in Beijing. It was reasonably foreseeable that the *ad hoc* arbitration in Dalian offered the following advantages: (a) both parties were located in Dalian; it was convenient and cost-effective to conduct the arbitration in Dalian rather than in CMAC in Beijing; and (b) Mr Hu was familiar with maritime arbitration and was known to both parties.[213]

---

[210]   Cao Lijun, "Letters – CIETAC's Integrity", (2005) 168 *Far Eastern Economic Review*, 7. See more discussions below in Chapter 7.

[211]   Kang Ming, "Ad Hoc Arbitration in China", [2003] *International Arbitration Law Review*, 200.

[212]   Kang Ming, "Ad Hoc Arbitration's Status Quo and Future in China", in Wang Baoshu (ed), *Collective Essays on Commercial Law, Vol.3 (Shangshi Falu Lunwen Xuan Disan Juan)* (Beijing: China Law Press, 2001), 168.

[213]   Kang Ming, *A Study on Commercial Arbitration Service (Shangshi Zhongcai Fuwu Yanjiu)* (Beijing: China Law Press, 2004), 210–212.

Moreover, neither party considered the resolution as "mediation" at any stage. It is notable that the word "arbitration" rather than "mediation" was utilised by both parties in their correspondences. More importantly, Mr Hu is an arbitrator under the CMAC. In the process, Mr Hu made no attempt to mediate in the traditional sense such as persuading the parties to reach a mutually agreeable compromise. Rather, he relied on his professional knowledge of maritime law, expert's opinion, relevant legal provisions and shipping customs to deal with the dispute by following the arbitral procedure. The "Opinion" was independent of both parties' desires and contained orders rather than suggestions.[214]

4.074

Then why was the title "Opinion on Mediation" used? According to Kang Ming, Vice Secretary-General of the CIETAC, although it was expected that the parties would honour Mr Hu's decisions, a risk still remained that the losing party might not do so due to the lack of enforcement mechanism for *ad hoc* arbitration in China.[215] As such, if this had happened, the winning party would not have been able to enforce the award since it was the outcome of *ad hoc* arbitration. The word "mediation" was therefore used as a strategy to avoid the risk of non-enforcement of *ad hoc* arbitral award.

4.075

(c) Proposal for legislative recognition and its political challenges

Despite the encouraging case report above, it is worth noting that attempting a successful *ad hoc* arbitration—under the "pretense" of mediation—is just technical manoeuvring to circumvent legal requirements; or, more accurately, a kind of "fashioning of practical remedies without violating the current legal framework".[216] Given the fact that *ad hoc* arbitration has not yet been liberalised in China, the practice of "formal mediation, actual arbitration" might be arguably acceptable while waiting for the Arbitration Law to be amended. However, in the long run, in order to align the Chinese arbitration system with international norms, legislative recognition will be required to codify support for the practice of *ad hoc* arbitration in China. Likewise, it is highly advocated that foreign arbitration be allowed in China and be written into the amendment of the Arbitration Law. The merits for legalising *ad hoc* arbitration and foreign arbitration in China are evident. Parties are expected to enjoy more choices of arbitration providers that are facilitated by both institutional and *ad hoc* arbitrations, and conducted by both Chinese and foreign arbitral bodies. Furthermore, given the current bureaucratic practice of local arbitration commissions, the introduction of *ad hoc* arbitration seems particularly necessary, which would either provide an alternative to the administratively tainted institutional arbitration in China (providing parties a way to avoid administrative interference) or pressure the local commissions

4.076

---

[214] One of the major differences between arbitration and mediation is that the procedure of the former is independent from both parties leading to an award of final resolution as order of enforcement. However, the latter requires both parties' involvement and co-operation with the mediator assisting in reaching the final compromise and suggestions. See, for example, discussions by Wang Shengchang, "The Relation between Arbitration and Mediation", (2004) 49 *China Law*, 68; see also Jun Ge, "Mediation, Arbitration and Litigation: Dispute Resolution in the People's Republic of China", (1996) 15 *UCLA Pacific Basic Law Journal*, 28.

[215] See fn 213 above.

[216] Liu Xiaohong, *Jurisprudence and Empirical Research on International Commercial Arbitration Agreement (Guoji Shangshi Zhongcaixieyi de Fali yu Shizheng Yanjiu)* (Beijing: Commercial Publishing House, 2005), 88.

to be better qualified and more transparent in catering to market demand rather than administrative needs.

4.077   However, even after we tout the benefits of legalising the practice of *ad hoc* arbitration, one has to realise that the political problem of state control remains a much more serious challenge to its inclusion in the revised Arbitration Law. Politicians tend to avoid the inclusion by blaming Chinese economic conditions. Because in *ad hoc* arbitration, the burden is placed on the parties to organise and administer the arbitration and if problems arise, such as intentional delays by the parties or arbitrators, the assistance of an arbitration institution or an independent appointing authority will not be available.[217] *Ad hoc* arbitration thus requires the highest degree of good faith in execution.[218]

4.078   As such, the argument has been made that the fledging level of fiduciary duties in the socialist market transition is still unable to maintain the high degree of good faith required for *ad hoc* arbitration. Likewise, the argument has been made that the predictability of *ad hoc* dispute resolution will be hard to guarantee and it will thus be detrimental to socioeconomic stability and finally, be detrimental to the immature market system. These arguments have been put forth by one Chinese top legislative official responsible for the Arbitration Law. Liu Maoliang, Vice Chief of the Legislative Affairs Office of the State Council, expressed recently that "*ad hoc* arbitration should go slow in China until we have a more developed and mature market economy".[219] This argument makes the development of *ad hoc* arbitration in China a nullity, as the Chinese leadership has made it clear very recently that China will remain a developing country for the long term.[220] There is as such more political resistance than economic restraint when it comes to allowing *ad hoc* arbitration and foreign arbitration in China. The answer is political in the sense that China still wishes to maintain the "control" over the final result of arbitration through its institutional and administrative influence, so as to extend the "control" to its economic matters such as the domestic market and foreign trade and investment. Hence, any future implementation of international arbitration norms will depend on liberalisation of not only the market economy but also the political atmosphere.

---

[217]   William Tetley, "Good Faith in Contract: Particularly in the Contracts of Arbitration" (2004), 561.

[218]   These duties are derived from the application of good faith principle in general contract performance where the parties should observe various ancillary duties including the duty to cooperate with and assist each other in the performance of the contract. See Wang Liming and Xu Chuanxi, "Fundamental Principles of China's Contract Law" (1999), 12.

[219]   Liu Maoliang, Vice Chief of the Legislative Affairs Office of the State Council, "Ad Hoc Arbitration Should be Slow for Implementation in China", (2005) 54 *Arbitration in Beijing Quarterly*, 8–12.

[220]   Chinese Premier Wen Jiabao mentioned in his 2007 Lunar New Year address that "China will remain in a rather long period of time in the status of the initial period of socialist market economy (*Shehuizhuyi Chujijieduan*)". See Wen Jiabao, "Several Issues on the Historic Tasks and Foreign Policies that China Face in the Initial Period of Socialism, *Xinhua News Net*, Beijing, 26 February 2007, available at http://news.xinhuanet.com/politics/2007-02/26/content_5775212.htm.

CHAPTER 5

ARBITRAL JURISDICTION

Another aspect of the peculiarity of the regulation of arbitration agreements in China is that arbitral jurisdiction is entertained by the arbitration commission rather than the arbitral tribunal. The study in Chapter 5 attempts to examine in detail the peculiar Chinese system of determining arbitral jurisdiction. Topics will first cover the actual gap between the Arbitration Law and international arbitration norms on the point of arbitral jurisdiction, and after which the second part will elaborate on the underlying reasons for such commission-oriented arbitral jurisdiction in China. The third part will comment on the struggling development by some leading Chinese arbitration commissions in the context of restoring the tribunal's jurisdictional autonomy and aligning with international practices before this chapter ends with some evaluations on the future development trend.

Two points should be clarified before the discussion. First, the issue of arbitral jurisdiction may involve several factors such as the existence and validity of the arbitration agreement; capacity of the parties;[1] and the arbitrability of the disputes submitted,[2] etc.[3] However, the discussion in this chapter will only focus upon the existence and validity of the arbitration agreement due to its cornerstone role in the entire arbitration system. In the subsequent analysis, the ruling of arbitral jurisdiction is confined to the ruling of the existence and validity of an arbitration agreement. Secondly, the authoritative institutions which are entitled to rule on the arbitral jurisdiction include both the arbitral body and the people's court.[4] As the court's jurisdictional power is normally considered as an aspect of judicial supervision over the arbitration agreement which will be dwelled upon in Chapter 7, the following discussion will only focus upon the arbitral jurisdiction entertained by the arbitral body, i.e. the arbitration commission and arbitral tribunal in China.

1. DENYING TRIBUNAL'S JURISDICTIONAL COMPETENCE

In the Chinese arbitration system, the principle of *competence-competence* has been "painted with Chinese characteristics"[5]—the arbitral tribunal is denied ruling on its own jurisdiction; rather, it is determined by the arbitration commission and subject to judicial review by the people's court.[6] This section begins the discussion by outlining the doctrine of *competence-competence* under international arbitration norms; and

---

[1] Capacity of the parties refers to whether the parties to arbitration enjoy "proper legal standing" to attend the arbitration proceeding.

[2] Arbitrability refers to whether the disputes submitted fall into the scope of the arbitration agreement and the national arbitration statute.

[3] Liu Xiaohong, *Jurisprudence and Empirical Studies of International Commercial Arbitration Agreement (Guoji Shangshi Zhongcaixieye de Fali yu Shizheng)* (Beijing: Commercial Publishing House, 2005), 66.

[4] Generally, the arbitral body and court enjoy concurrent jurisdictions over the existence and validity of the arbitration agreement before or during the arbitral proceeding. Apart from that, the court also has the judicial review over the arbitration agreement after the end of the proceeding, i.e. until the stage of recourse against arbitral awards. For example, see arts.8(1), 16(3) and 34(2) of the Model Law.

[5] Zhang Yulin, "Towards the UNCITRAL Model Law: A Chinese Perspective", (1994) 11 *Journal of International Arbitration*, 129.

[6] Article 20 of the Arbitration Law.

then identifies the legislative gap and practical difficulties under the Chinese regulation by comparison with international practices.

(a) Doctrine of *competence-competence*

5.004   The doctrine of *competence-competence*, literally "jurisdiction to decide jurisdiction", means that an arbitral tribunal can rule on its own jurisdiction, including any challenges regarding the existence or validity of the arbitration agreement, subject to the final decision by the court.[7] The doctrine has been widely accepted in modern arbitration laws and rules, including the UNCITRAL Model Law, English Arbitration Act 1996, UNCITRAL Arbitration Rules and the ICC Rules of Arbitration. Indeed, as one international arbitrator has stated recently, "If there is one thing over which modern writers on arbitration seems to agree, it is that arbitrators must be allowed to rule on their own jurisdiction".[8]

5.005   This doctrine is clearly provided under art.16 of the Model Law, which states that an arbitral tribunal is entitled to rule on its own jurisdiction and jurisdictional challenge.[9] Under the jurisprudence of art.16, the rationale underlying the tribunal's jurisdictional competence is the principle of party autonomy—by referring the relevant dispute to the jurisdiction of the tribunal, the parties impliedly vest to the tribunal all disputes under their agreement, including "any objections with respect to the existence or validity of the arbitration agreement".[10] The counterpart provisions can be found under art.21 of the UNCITRAL Arbitration Rules.[11] Thus, an arbitral tribunal can independently rule on its own jurisdiction without having to apply to a court or an arbitration institution for authorisation.[12] According to the UNCITRAL Working Group, "The arbitration tribunal may rule on its jurisdiction not only in the absence of a valid agreement to arbitrate, but may *proprio motu* decide it has no jurisdiciton even when the dispute is not arbitrable".[13] Based on the critical importance of art.16, all 50 adopting countries included the *competence-competence* principle in their arbitration statutes in securing the tribunal's jurisdiction.[14] Moreover, a country adopting the Model Law without the text of tribunal's *competence* could not rightfully advertise its arbitration system as being in conformity with the Model Law.[15] In the Model Law-adopting jurisdictions such as Hong Kong, this doctrine is expressly endorsed under ss.6(1) and 34C of the Arbitration Ordinance

---

[7]   Alan Redfern and Martin Hunter, *Law and Practice of International Arbitration* (London: Sweet & Maxwell, 2004), 9; Emmanual Gaillard and John Savage (eds), *Fouchard Gaillard Goldman on International Commercial Arbitration* (The Hague: Kluwer Law International, 1999), 395.

[8]   Professor Dr Alan Uzelac, "Jurisdiction of the Arbitral Tribunal: Current Jurisprudence and Problem Areas under the UNCITRAL Model Law", [2005] *International Arbitration Law Review*, 153.

[9]   Article 16 of the Model Law.

[10]   See UN Document, A/40/17, para 150. See also, comments by Chen Zhidong, *International Commercial Arbitration Law (Guoji Shangshi Zhongcai Faxue)* (Beijing: China Law Press, 1998), 145.

[11]   Article 21 of the UNCITRAL Arbitration Rules.

[12]   Peter Binder, *International Commercial Arbitration in UNCITRAL Model Law Jurisdictions* (London: Sweet & Maxwell, 2000), para 4-006.

[13]   Professor Pieter Sanders, *The Work of UNCITRAL on Arbitration and Conciliation* (The Hague: Kluwer Law International, 2004), 15.

[14]   See Annotations on art.16 of the Model Law, UN Document A/40/17.

[15]   Binder, *International Commercial Arbitration in UNCITRAL Model Law Jurisdictions* (2000), para 4-008.

(Cap.341) in both domestic and international arbitrations.[16] In a recent case held by the High Court, *Nanhai West Shipping Co v Hong Kong United Dockyards Ltd,* the tribunal has even been granted broad discretion to rule on the scope of their jurisdictional power.[17]

The similar approach can be found in the English Arbitration Act which makes the power to rule on its own jurisdiction a default authority for arbitral tribunals unless there is evidence that parties did not intend to bestow that power. Under s.30 of the English Arbitration Act, unless otherwise agreed by the parties, an arbitral tribunal can rule on its own substantive jurisdiction, including whether there is an arbitration agreement, whether it is valid, what matters have been submitted to arbitration, etc.[18]

5.006

For the institutional arbitration rules, the ICC Court goes even further by stating under art.6(2) of its 1998 Rules that if any party raises one or more pleas concerning the existence, validity or scope of the arbitration agreement, the arbitration shall proceed if it is *prima facie* satisfied by the Court that an arbitration agreement under the Rules may exist. In such a case, any decision as to the jurisdiction of the Arbitral Tribunal shall be taken by the Arbitral Tribunal itself".[19] According to the authoritative guide to ICC arbitration, the only mandate of the Court under art.6(2) is to reach *"prima facie"* decision on the existence of an agreement; and the *"prima facie* test" under the Rules requires the Court always to allow an arbitration to proceed, unless it is so obvious that there is no ICC arbitration agreement between the parties.[20] In recent years, a more liberal approach has been taken within the Court which normally prefers to allow contested issues of fact or law to be presented to the arbitral tribunal "whenever there has appeared to be a reasonable possibility that an ICC arbitration agreement might be found to exist on the basis of a greater airing of the facts and the law before the Court".[21]

5.007

Thus, in dealing with the issue of arbitral jurisdiction, the prevailing practice is that both the jurisdictional and adjudicatory powers have been conferred upon the tribunal which is selected by the parties and which finally issues the award. The practical effect of asserting the tribunal' jurisdictional competence is crucial. On one hand, it largely prevents the tactical delay of the arbitration proceeding by the respondent should he intend to stifle the claim by going to the court;[22] on the other hand, the tribunal's jurisdictional and adjudicatory powers are combined to ensure the consistency of the ruling on the case.[23] Even in institutional arbitrations where the institution usually takes an important role in moving the arbitral process forward, as the experience of the

5.008

---

[16]   Section 6(1) applies the doctrine in domestic arbitration, while s.34C in international arbitration.
[17]   *Nanhai West Shipping Co v Hong Kong United Dockyards Ltd* [1996] 2 HKC 639. See also summary in Alvarez, Kaplan and Rivkin (eds), *Model Law Decisions: Cases Applying the UNCITRAL Model Law on International Commercial Arbitration (1985–2001)* (The Hague, Kluwer Law International, 2001), 174.
[18]   Section 30 of the English Arbitration Act.
[19]   Article 6(2) of the ICC Arbitration Rules.
[20]   Lawrence Craig, William Park and Jan Paulsson, *International Chamber of Commerce Arbitration* (3rd ed.) (New York: Oceana Publishing, 2000), 257.
[21]   Yves Derains and Eric Schwartz, *A Guide to the ICC Rules of Arbitration* (2nd ed.) (The Hague: Kluwer Law International, 2005), 80.
[22]   See discussions with respect to arbitral efficiency by Gu Weixia, "Security for Costs in International Commercial Arbitration", (2005) 22 *Journal of International Arbitration*, 194-4, 201–202.
[23]   See Martin Hunter, "International Commercial Dispute Resolution: The Challenge of the 21st Century", (2000) 16 *Arbitration International*, 379–382.

ICC Rules shows, the institution (the ICC Court) generally continues the proceeding if it is *prima facie* satisfied that an arbitration agreement may exist, saving the power to rule on jurisdictional objections to the ICC arbitral tribunal. As such, both the parties' autonomy and arbitral efficiency are well preserved.

(b) Regulation of the Arbitration Law and its serious defects

5.009   In China, under the Arbitration Law, there are two articles concerning arbitral jurisdiction. First, art.19(2) provides, "The arbitral tribunal shall have the power to affirm the validity of a contract".[24] In the recently published guide to Chinese arbitral practice, the provision shall be understood as allowing the tribunal to have both the jurisdictional power to decide the effectiveness of the arbitration agreement and substantive power to adjudicate the merits of the case.[25] More references are found under the annotations to the Arbitration Law, "For the second paragraph of art.19, the Arbitration Law provides in explicit terms that the arbitral tribunal has the power to determine the validity of a contract so that the tribunal may deal with the dispute *more efficiently* and make an arbitral award accordingly."[26] (Emphasis added.)

5.010   Several questions are raised with respect to this legislative interpretation. First, whether the contract refers to the principal contract alone or it involves the arbitration agreement as well.[27] In other words, whether the tribunal has the power to decide upon the validity of the arbitration agreement and jurisdiction of the dispute. As understood by the author, it may not be convincing that the tribunal's jurisdictional and adjudicating powers be separated only on the basis of the separability of the arbitration agreement from the principal contract. Secondly, given the clear legislative aim to realise the efficiency of the arbitral proceeding, it may thus be argued that the jurisdictional power should belong to the tribunal for the sake of time and human resource.[28] If this is the right answer, then more problematic situations may arise out of the forthcoming stipulation.

5.011   Article 20 further provides: "If a party challenges the validity of the arbitration agreement, it may request the arbitration commission to make a decision or apply to the people's court for a ruling. If one party requests the arbitration commission to make a decision and the other party applies to the people's court for a ruling, the people's court *shall* give a ruling."[29] As observed by Mo, the article shows clearly three aspects on how to determine the arbitral jurisdiction in China. First, either the

---

[24]   Article 19 of the Arbitration Law.

[25]   Denis Brock and Kathryn Sanger, "The Arbitration Agreement and Arbitrators" in Daniel Fung and Wang Shengchang (eds), *Arbitration in China: A Practical Guide* (Hong Kong: Sweet & Maxwell, 2004), para 8-91.

[26]   Legislative Affairs of the NPCSC of the PRC, *Arbitration Laws of China* (Hong Kong: Sweet & Maxwell, 1997), 62.

[27]   Simply, arbitration agreement is in essence a procedural contract for resolving dispute between the parties. More often than not, the arbitration agreement is adopted as an arbitration clause inside the main contract.

[28]   Zhang Ye, "On Preventing the Delaying and Disruption of the Arbitral Proceedings (Lun Fangzhi Zhongcai Chengxu de Tuoyan he Pohuai) in CIETAC (ed), *Arbitration and Law Yearbook 2001 (Zhongcai yu Falu 2001 Niankan)* (Beijing: China Law Press, 2002), 205–206.

[29]   Article 20 of the Arbitration Law.

arbitration commission or the people's court has the power to rule on the validity of the arbitration agreement. Secondly, the arbitral tribunal is not entitled to rule on such issues. Thirdly, should there exist a jurisdictional conflict between the arbitration commission and the people's court, the court prevails over the commission on determining the jurisdictional matter.[30]

The stipulation leaves many ambiguities. To begin with, it only considers the challenge to the validity of the arbitration agreement, but fails to mention the jurisdictional disputes arising from the existence of the agreement. The Chinese legislature used to share a similar ignorance on the issue of separability where the separable effect under a non-existent main contract is excluded.[31] By analogy, it might be argued that drafters had not thought carefully about the scope of the jurisdictional issue. Moreover, it fails to explain the jurisdictional challenge in cases of document-only arbitration.[32] Pursuant to art.39 of the Arbitration Law, arbitration cases could be processed on basis of the written submissions by the parties without the hearing held.[33] The silence of the law leaves jurisdictional practice defective, until it was recently picked up by the Rules of the China International Economic and Trade Arbitration Commission (CIETAC) that where a case is to be decided on the basis of document only, such an objection shall be raised before the submission of the first substantive defense.[34] Most controversially, the provision empowers the arbitration commission rather than the arbitral tribunal to rule on the validity of an arbitration agreement. This obviously contradicts the underlying meaning of art.19 which seems to empower the tribunal to rule on the validity of the entire contract including the arbitration agreement.[35] The logical conclusion of art.20 is that where an objection to the jurisdiction is submitted before the tribunal, the tribunal must report that to the arbitration commission and wait for the commission's decision on the jurisdiction before it can rule on the substance. As commented by Song, the splitting workload of jurisdiction-ruling and merit-adjudicating between the commission and tribunal unduly delays the proceeding and moreover, makes the tribunal subject to the commission.[36] Wide criticisms have drawn upon the legislation's departing substantially from the doctrine of *competence-competence*, depriving the Chinese tribunals of the arbitral autonomy to rule on its own jurisdiction.[37]

5.012

---

[30] John Mo, *Arbitration Law in China* (Hong Kong: Sweet & Maxwell Asia, 2001), 104–105.

[31] See art.19(2) of the Arbitration Law.

[32] The document-only arbitration refers to those simple arbitration cases where the arbitration hearing can take place on basis of the documents submitted and without the participation of the parties.

[33] Article 39 of the Arbitration Law.

[34] Article 6 of the 2005 CIETAC Rules.

[35] See discussions above in art.19.

[36] Song Lianbin, "On the Principle of *Competence-Competence* in International Commercial Arbitration (Lun Guoji Shangshi Zhongcai zhong de Guanxiaquan Yuanze)", (2000) 2 *Jurisprudence Review (Faxue Pinglun)*, 12.

[37] See comments such as Wang Shengchang, "The Chinese Characteristic System of Arbitral Jurisdiction Determination (Zhongguo Tese de Zhongcai Guanxiaquan Jueding Zhidu)", (2003) 75 *Arbitration and Law (Zhongcai yu Falu)*, 26; Qiao Xin, *Research on Arbitral Power (Zhongcaiquan Yanjiu)* (Beijing: China Law Press, 2001), 191–192; Xie Shisong, *Commercial Arbitration Law (Shangshi Zhongcai Faxue)* (Beijing: Higher Education Press, 2003), 212–213; Song Lianbin, *Research on Jurisdictional Power in International Commercial Arbitration (Guoji Shangshi Zhongcai Guanxiaquan Yanjiu)* (Beijing: China Law Press, 2000), 94–95.

(c) Significant gaps with international arbitration norms

5.013   The following discussion delves into comparative analyses between the Arbitration Law and international arbitration norms in identifying the regulatory gap on the issue of arbitral jurisdiction.

5.014   First, international norms provide broader scope than the Arbitration Law in entertaining the arbitral jurisdiction wherever the arbitration agreement has been effectively concluded, in existence or not. Secondly, as accepted worldwide, it is the individual arbitral tribunal rather than the arbitration institution to determine the jurisdictional challenge. If the first gap could be easily remediable with China's more experienced draftsmanship, more problems arise out of the second gap. The Chinese legislation contrasts drastically against the international practice and is "unique" in that the jurisdictional power is exercised by the relevant arbitration commission rather than the arbitral tribunal.[38] It is the arbitration commission which is the only authoritative arbitral body for jurisdictional ruling in China, both primarily and finally.[39] In consequence, one practical gap is that the arbitral proceedings may be detrimentally affected because the tribunal has to wait for the commission's decision on the jurisdictional challenge before it can rule on the substance; the other is that if the arbitration commission involves itself on substantive merits review in determining the jurisdictional ruling, its decision might conflict with the later findings by the tribunal. The concerns are well demonstrated by the following CIETAC case.

5.015   A contract for the sale of equipment was signed by a Hong Kong company and a Shenzhen company. In performing the contract, the dispute arose. One party applied to CIETAC for arbitration on 15 December 1995. At the beginning of the arbitral proceeding in January 1996, the respondent raised jurisdictional objection. The tribunal therefore submitted the jurisdictional challenge to the commission. The commission did not reply until 1 August 1996 (six months later) when it declared that the arbitral jurisdiction should be held on the case because the contract had been actually performed. However, after more than two years' hearing, the tribunal gave its final finding in the arbitral award where the contract was held not to have been actually performed by the parties.[40]

5.016   It is clear that the arbitration commission is not the adjudicating body to deal with the substantive claims. However, in order to make a correct decision, its jurisdictional

---

[38]   China is the only country in the world where the jurisdictional competence belongs to the arbitration institution rather than the arbitral tribunal. See Wang Shengchang, "The Chinese Characteristic System of Arbitral Jurisdiction Determination—Achievement and Problems (Zhongguotese de Zhongcai Guanxiaquan Jueding Zhidu—Chengjiu he Wenti)" in CIETAC (ed), *Selected Decisions on Jurisdiction by the CIETAC (Zhongguo Guoji Jingji Maoyi Zhongcai Weiyuanhui Guanxiaquan Jueding Xuanbian)* (Beijing: China Commercial Press, 2004), 2.

[39]   According to Wang Shengchang, for accepting the arbitral case, only the arbitration commission can make the preliminary ruling whether it has jurisdiction or not. Then, if the respondent raises the challenge, it is as well the arbitration commission who makes the final determination. *Ibid.*

[40]   The case sources from Qiu Shi, "Arbitration: Why is Self-contradictory—A Perspective of an Arbitration Case on a Dispute Arising from a Purchase Contract (Zhongcai Zixiang Maodun Wei Na Ban—Yiqi Gouxiao Hetong Jiufen'an Toushi)", *Legal Daily (Fazhi Ribao)*, 30 May 1998, 6. See also, Zhao Jian, *Research on Judicial Supervision over International Commercial Arbitration (Guoji Shangshi Zhongcai de Sifa Jiandu)* (Beijing: China Law Press, 2000), 103.

ruling may inevitably invite a preliminary evaluation of the merits of the case; and such pre-judgment may likely conflict with the subsequent findings of the tribunal as the CIETAC case above shows. Thus, art.20 of the Arbitration Law may place the arbitration commission in a dilemma. If the tribunal's ruling is respected, the commission has to revise its decision; or the tribunal needs to follow the commission's "wrong" decision and give up its own ruling. If the commission revises its jurisdictional ruling in accordance with the tribunal, the rendering of self-contradictory decisions within the arbitration body not only obstructs the arbitral efficiency but also ruins the parties' confidence in selecting arbitration. If the tribunal follows the commission's ruling, the tribunal's independence and autonomy in China is thrown into question. This deviates from the value of arbitration, which is reputed as an expedient and independent way of commercial dispute resolution.

In considering the gap between the commission-oriented and tribunal-oriented **5.017** arbitral jurisdiction, a further issue may deserve attention. As noted, both types of institutional and *ad hoc* arbitrations are allowed in international arbitration practices. In the circumstance of *ad hoc* arbitration, the *ad hoc* tribunal is the only arbitral body,[41] and there is no controversy with regards to whom the jurisdictional power belongs. However, in cases of institutional arbitration, as the study of the ICC Court of Arbitration above shows, the permanent institution (the ICC Court) and the tribunal are two different concepts and perform different functions. According to the ICC Rules, the ICC Court, assisted by its Secretariat,[42] is to ensure the application of the ICC Rules and mainly responsible for managing the institutional operation and administering the case flow.[43] In initial periods, the Court will accept the arbitral case and process it to the tribunal as long as the *prima facie* evidence[44] shows that an arbitration agreement was reached between the disputant parties.[45] Once the tribunal is constituted, the Court will no longer involve itself in the arbitral proceeding but only provide administrative service and logistic support to the tribunal's merit adjudicating and award rendering.[46] The tribunal is the only real authority entrusted and empowered by the parties' agreement. Should a jurisdictional challenge be raised with respect to the ICC arbitration, "the tribunal is privileged to determine the jurisdiction which can overrule that previously made by the institution".[47] This is also commonly accepted

---

[41] This is one of the most notable differences between the institutional and *ad hoc* arbitration. For analysis on this point, see Julian D.M. Lew, *Comparative International Commercial Arbitration* (The Hague: Kluwer Law International, 2003), 33, 36.

[42] In the ICC arbitrations, the Secretariat within the ICC Court is comprised of numerous members, who on a day to day basis, are responsible for the administration of a caseload of arbitrations which an established organic structure for administering the case. See, Craig, Park and Paulsson, *International Chamber of Commerce Arbitration* (2000), 21.

[43] According to the ICC Rules, the ICC Court, assisted by its Secretariat, has powers to (1) determine the existence of a *prima facie* arbitration agreement (art.6(2)); (2) appoint arbitrators (art.9); (3) determine the place of arbitration (art.14(1)); (4) determine fees and expenses of arbitration (art.31).

[44] Article 6(2) of the ICC Rules. The *prima facie* evidence may include, *inter alia*, whether the arbitration agreement exists is in writing.

[45] Craig, Park and Paulsson, *International Chamber of Commerce Arbitration* (2000), 21–24; see also Yang Lin, "On the Legal Status of Arbitration Institution—Revisiting the Arbitration Law of Our Country", (2005) 98 *Arbitration and Law (Zhongcai yu Falu)*, 42–43.

[46] *Ibid.*

[47] Yves Derains and Eric A. Schwartz, *A Guide to the ICC Rules of Arbitration* (2nd ed.) (The Hague: Kluwer Law International, 2005), 77.

in the Model Law-adopting jurisdictions to ensure the principle of party autonomy and arbitral autonomy so that the tribunal (arbitrators) can tailor the proceeding. For example, the Hong Kong International Arbitration Center (HKIAC) orients itself to the "assistant" for the tribunal appointment and procedural administration.[48] By doing so, jurisdictional autonomy is well reserved to the party-appointed tribunal.

5.018   Thus far, China is an absolute institutional-arbitration country. However, the Arbitration Law fails to resolve the allocation of arbitral power between the arbitration commission and individual tribunal regarding jurisdictional management and determination. The "commission-dominant theory" is prevailing in Chinese arbitration, which has possibly led to an improper enlargement of the power of the commissions.[49] Notwithstanding the strong demand for revision of tribunals' *competence-competence* by academics, it is said that the tribunals' competence (autonomy) is "shadowed under the Chinese arbitration commissions".[50] The following study therefore tries to explore in detail, such institutional "shadow" so as to explore the underlying difficulties and practical constraints along the reform process.

2. Tribunal's Competence in the Shadow of Arbitration Commission

5.019   This part of the discussion will address the practical constraints to the tribunal's jurisdictional competence caused by the Chinese state control on arbitration, which has been expressed by a macro-level prevalence of the "institution" in China, both economically and administratively; and a micro-level administrative infrastructure of most of the arbitration commissions, both before and after the Arbitration Law took effect.

(a) Historic prevalence of the "institution" in China

5.020   There are two outstanding reasons accumulating to the historic prevalence of the "institution", in this context, the arbitration commission in China. They are the transitional nature of the social, economic and legal conditions and preserved administrative dominance under political control.

(i) *Transitional socialist market economy*

5.021   Modern commercial arbitration is the natural product of the development of a market economy. The liberal market system requires the corresponding dispute resolution,

---

[48]   For the details of the administrative and logistic assistance offered by the HKIAC, see the HKIAC link http://www.hkiac.org/HKIAC/pdf/Rules/HKIAC%20Procedures%20for%20International%20Arbitration.pdf; and Christopher Wing To, "Developments of the Hong Kong International Arbitration Center", (2000) 12 *International Business Lawyer*, 506.

[49]   Song Lianbin, Zhao Jian and Li Hong, "Approaches to the Revision of the 1994 Arbitration Act of the People's Republic of China", (2003) 3 *Journal of International Arbitration*, 178–179.

[50]   Feng Kefei, "The Theory of Competence-Competence and Its Practical Application in Our Country (Guanxiaquan/Guanxiaquan Lilun jiqi zai Woguo de Shijian)", (2002) 71 *Arbitration and Law (Zhongcai yu Falu)*, 103.

such as arbitration, to respect freedom of contract and party autonomy; moreover, to be independent of state administration and judiciary. One Chinese writer has made an insightful comment:

> "Modern commercial arbitration, in essence, refers to the market entities—by making use of the modern market resources and with minimum interferences from the public power—to privately resolve the dispute by parties' autonomy."[51]

The arbitration system of China, however, was born and brought up in the environment of the planned economy. Before the economic reform, there were no market operations and no independent market subjects. Enterprises were either owned by the people as a whole (*quanmin suoyouzhi*) or by collectives (*jiti suoyouzhi*).[52] They had no rights to freely dispose of their property since the property belonged to either the State or the community; the means of production were allocated and distributed according to the State plan.[53] Consequently, all economic activities were handled by the highly centralised state authorities.   **5.022**

For example, in 1961, the Central Government issued the Regulations Governing State-owned Industrial Enterprises. Among the provisions, it stipulated that "disputes arising from domestic economic contracts should be arbitrated by the specialised organs set up within the local economic commission at each level".[54] Further, the People's Bank of China at each municipal level was authorised to execute decisions of the economic commissions by withholding or paying the price of the goods involved.[55] The economic commissions and banks were described as functioning in a manner "analogous to that power of Western tribunals and courts".[56] CIETAC was then established as an official institution for arbitrating disputes pertaining to foreign trade; while disputes concerning domestic trade were under the exclusive control of relevant state economic commissions.[57] The private sector was not in existence at that time. The role of the "institutional public" was strengthened, while that of the "individual private" was neglected. The government-appointed institution was the only authoritative power for arbitration. The arbitral tribunal was considered to be   **5.023**

---

[51]   Zhao Jian, "Positioning and Behaving of the Arbitration System of Our Country in New Era (Xinshiqi Woguo Zhongcai Zhidu de Dingwei yu Zuowei)", *Brief Newsletter of the CIETAC Arbitration Research Institute (Zhongcai Yanjiusuo Jianbao)*, 13 November 2004, 6.

[52]   Since the establishment of PRC in 1949, the Chinese government implemented a centrally controlled economic system by abolishing free markets and nationalizing the private companies as state-owned enterprises. Enterprises were natured as "socialist public ownership (*shehuizhuyi gongyouzhi*)".

[53]   For an in-depth discussion of the allocation and distribution structure of the enterprises during the period of planned economy, see Shen Hong, *Transitional Economics of China (Zhongguo Zhuanxing Jingjixue)* (Shanghai: Shanghai Sanlian Press & Shanghai People's Press, 1995).

[54]   The Legislative Affairs Commission of the NPCSC of the PRC, *Arbitration Laws of China* (1997), 18.

[55]   SPC (ed), *Notice of the Central Committee of the Chinese Communist Party and State Council Relating to Strict Adherence to the Procedures for Capital Construction and to the Strict Performance of Economic Contract* in *Compilation of Laws and Regulations of the Central People's Government (Zhongyang Renmin Zhengfu Faling Huibian)* (1962–1963, Vol.13) (Beijing: China Law Press, 1964), 62–63.

[56]   Stanley B. Lubman, *Bird in a Cage: Legal Reform in China after Mao* (California: Stanford University Press, 1999), 96.

[57]   See also discussions below.

formed temporarily for handling individual cases. It therefore could not be entitled to rule on such fundamental issues of arbitration as the arbitral jurisdiction.[58]

5.024   In the 1980s, suffering from the stifling economy, the country embarked on the economic transformation from the purely planned to a "socialist market economy".[59] Arbitration, which was then regarded as a method of attracting foreign investment,[60] began to play more important roles in the "socialist market system".[61] The transition from a planned to a market economy has required new infrastructures and processes for resolving disputes between increasingly autonomous market players. With respect to arbitration, international norms of private law are increasingly seen by Chinese commentators as necessary components of China's transition to a market economy.[62]

5.025   Thus, development of the notions of free will and contract theory as the basis for commercial arbitration has paved the way for respect for private sector and individual autonomy.[63] However, the fledging economy did not seem to support the State's liberalising its means of arbitration. This has been seen in the country's over-emphasis on the system of institutional arbitration in the Arbitration Law. Because of the institutional character, there is no *ad hoc* arbitration. Even in cases of institutional arbitration, the arbitral jurisdiction has been considered the jurisdiction of the commission instead of the tribunal. As such, the Chinese logic of *competence-competence* has been formed—the commission shall have the final say in its own jurisdiction. It is noteworthy that although some basic concepts such as contractual freedom have been recognised by the Arbitration Law, arbitration is still largely entrusted to the institutional control rather than parties' autonomy, such that parties may just agree to submit their disputes to CIETAC or other State-recognised arbitration commissions. According to Professor Pitman Potter, such distrust of the tribunal (party's autonomy), at its root, mirrors China's struggling exploration of the "socialist market economy".[64] On this point, some Chinese authors have shared a similar view: on one hand, the State needs to legally establish recognition and authorisation of the "private rights" for promoting a market-oriented economy; on the other hand, the embedded ideologies of the "centralised plan" and "socialist public" thwart the

---

[58]   This bears the analogy to the jurisdictional determination system in the Chinese court system. In the Chinese judicial system, it is the court but not the judge that enjoys the judicial jurisdiction; and it is the court rather than the judge that has the power to finally determine the judicial jurisdiction.

[59]   The concept of "socialist market economy" was officially written into the PRC Constitution in 1993.

[60]   Arbitration was thought as an effective and efficient means to resolve transnational commercial disputes, and more importantly, the use of arbitration could help to circumvent the drawbacks of the Chinese judicial system. See also discussions above in Chapter 1.

[61]   Arbitration began to appear on the Chinese laws as a preferable dispute resolution in foreign-related disputes, e.g. the Law on Sino-Foreign Joint Ventures in 1980. More and more foreign-related legislations contained provisions of arbitration since then. See also discussions above in Chapters 1 and 4.

[62]   See Zhang Yulin, "Towards the UNICTRAL Model Law: A Chinese Perspective", (1993) 13 *Journal of International Arbitration*, 87.

[63]   See generally, Michael J. Moser, "China's New International Arbitration Rules", (1994) 11 *Journal of International Arbitration*, 5; Shen M., "New Developments in Our Country's Arbitration System (Lun Woguo Zhongcai Zhidu de Xin Fazhan)", (1995) 4 *Wuhan University Law Review (Faxue Pinglun)*, 40; Ge Liu and Alex Lourie, "International Commercial Arbitration in China: History, New Developments and Current Practice", (1995) 28 *John Marshall Law Review*, 539.

[64]   Pitman B. Potter, *The Chinese Legal System: Globalization and Local Legal Culture* (London, New York: Routledge Pressing, 2001), 11.

country's steps, so that institutions are reluctant to share their previous monopolies with private autonomies.[65] As such, the liberalisation of legal institutions, not only the arbitration commission but also the court, has developed in the context of China's deepening marketisation.

(ii) *Preserved administrative dominance under political ideology*

In China, cultural percepts concerning political centrality and historically derived imperatives of the administrative hierarchy constitute the most unique elements of the Chinese legal culture, while the former has contributed to the latter.[66] Such cultural heritage had been well observed in the days of planned economy until it was recently challenged by the wave of economic reform and liberal legal ideas in the 1990s. In the first place, only government-appointed institutions were considered to have authoritative powers for arbitration where administrative control could be exercised on all economic activities, including dispute resolution.[67] In the second place, the institution was hierarchical, under which the higher-level authorities closely supervised the lower-level so that "superiors" could crucially decide the fate of "inferiors" in order to maintain centrality, unity and stability. For example, if the enterprises had disputes in carrying out a contract, then their superiors in the municipality of state industry, economic commissions and probably the bank would get involved in finding a compromise. Dispute resolution is not an impartial adjudication; rather, it is a politically biased decision.[68] Besides, traditional Chinese respect for power of office, to which some people in the field of arbitration subscribe, also contributes to administrative dominance in arbitration.[69] Consequently, the arbitral competence also foreshadows a strong sentiment of administrative influence.

5.026

However, the practice of handling arbitration by administrative institutions has seriously hindered the development of Chinese arbitration. Along with economic reform and China's increasing involvement in the global market, the political and administrative impact has been constrained. Most notably, the Arbitration Law provides that arbitration shall be carried out independently without administrative interference[70] and in addition, arbitration commissions shall be liberalised to be independent from administrative bodies and there shall be no subordinate relationships.[71] Such liberal norms did accord with the principle of party autonomy and arbitral autonomy. Notwithstanding the foregoing, however, the Arbitration Law further mandates that the Chinese arbitration commissions be organised and established under the administrative

5.027

---

[65] Zhao Chengbi, "Rethinking the Nature and Feature of Arbitration in Our Country (Dui Woguo Zhongcai de Xingzhi ji Tedian de Zaitantao)", (2005) 95 *Arbitration and Law (Zhongcai yu Falu)*, 6–7.

[66] Lubman, *Bird in a Cage: Legal Reform in China after Mao* (1999), 96.

[67] See discussions above on the Regulations Governing State-owned Industrial Enterprises, where the economic commissions and people's banks were empowered for arbitrating domestic trade disputes and enforcing arbitral awards.

[68] Lubman, *Bird in a Cage: Legal Reform in China after Mao* (1999), 97.

[69] For example, in Chinese history, magistrates discharged all governmental functions, both administration and dispute resolution. See, Song, Zhao and Li, "Approaches to Revision of the 1994 Arbitration Act of the PRC" (2003), 179.

[70] Article 8 of the Arbitration Law.

[71] Article 14 of the Arbitration Law.

agencies where administrative concerns arise.[72] The suspending dilemma is more evident since the "1996 Notice" when local arbitration commissions could accept foreign-related cases.[73] Most local arbitration commissions then find themselves at conflicting crossroads. On one hand, these commissions are newly organised under the Chinese government and are staffed and led by government-appointed officials whose education and training draw almost exclusively on political and administrative experience.[74] On the other hand, they have been undergoing increasing exposure to liberal international commercial arbitration norms through the participation by foreign parties and foreign arbitrators in their hearing processes. These international factors exercise a strong impact, prompting Chinese arbitration to increasingly peel away from the administrative bodies.[75]

5.028   As Potter analyses it, there are social and political difficulties in accepting arbitration commissions as independent and autonomous dispute resolution institutions in the context of China.[76] The dilemma between the increasing pursuit of autonomous arbitration commissions and long established traditions of bureaucratic institutions reflects more or less the uncertainties and tensions as to the permissible parameters that the administrative bodies can accommodate with liberal legal values. This may also help to answer the Chinese distinctive commission-oriented arbitral competence. Whilst individual tribunals (arbitrators) are fully autonomous under the parties' free appointment and their ruling results hard to predict, the adjudication results by the commissions might be easier to control given their administrative origin and background of establishment and organisation.

(b) Problems of the arbitration commission infrastructure

5.029   If arbitration is agreed to be a facilitator of economic development and propelled by the government, the question of to what extent the government should get involved needs to be well defined. As analysed above, Chinese arbitration entails reform hurdles both economically and administratively. Moreover, there are still substantive organic hurdles that the administrative power has inserted into the infrastructure of the arbitration commissions, both before and after the Arbitration Law took effect.

5.030   Before the discussion, one aspect needs to be clarified. CIETAC and China Maritime Arbitration Commission (CMAC) have been historically stated to be more autonomous arbitration bodies organising and acting independently of both the China Council for Promotion of International Trade (CCPIT)[77] and the Chinese government, albeit they

---

[72]   Article 10 of the Arbitration Law.
[73]   See more detailed discussions, above at Chapters 1 and 2.
[74]   See more detailed discussions about the organic infrastructure of the local arbitration commissions, below at Chapter 6.
[75]   See S. Huang, "Several Problems in Need of Resolution in China by Legislation on Foreign Affairs Arbitration", (1993) 10 *Journal of International Arbitration*, 95. For case examples of the international exposure of local arbitration commissions, see Guo Xiaowen, *Case Studies of China Economic Contract Arbitration Commission* (Hong Kong: Sweet & Maxwell, 1996).
[76]   Potter, *The Chinese Legal System: Globalization and Local Legal Culture* (2001), 33–34.
[77]   CCPIT also acts as the China Chamber of International Commerce.

are subject to financial scrutiny from the State.[78] Particularly, in a recent international conference, CIETAC was claimed to rely completely on income earned from its arbitration fees[79] instead of receiving funds from the government, demonstrating its independence.[80] It might be arguable whether such a statement is true or not. But given the more serious administrative taints of the majority of local arbitration commissions which greatly restrict Chinese arbitration development, the following discussions will concentrate upon those local arbitration commissions.

(i) *Pre-Arbitration Law: Purely administrative agency*

Before the era of the Arbitration Law, domestic arbitration commissions shared some main organic features. First, commissions were established within the administrative bodies and the structure followed the administrative organic rules.[81] Contract disputes involving Chinese parties were arbitrated under the Economic Contract Arbitration Commission (ECAC), which was established within the State Administration for Industry and Commerce (SAIC) at different levels.[82] The ECAC served as a subordinate department to the SAIC for dealing with domestic contract dispute resolution. Secondly, there were close personnel affiliations between the leaders of the arbitration commissions and those of the relevant administrative bodies. The chairmen and vice-chairmen of the ECACs were appointed by the directors or deputy directors of the SAIC and its local officials.[83] The arbitrators were also assumed by cardres from the relevant governmental departments and even enjoyed administrative ranks.[84] Last but most importantly, the relationship between the arbitration commissions was hierarchical, so that the commissions established within the SAIC at the national level could supervise the hearings and awards of the lower level.[85] By analogy, the relationship between the arbitral tribunal and arbitration commission was also hierarchical, such that the chairman and vice-chairmen of a commission had power to directly handle a case or order the tribunal to rehear a case if the leaders considered the arbitral award erroneous even if the award was a legally effective one.[86]

5.031

---

[78] Interview with Mr. Wan Jifei, Chairman of the China International Chamber of Commerce (30 May 2003). Wan mentions it as the main reason why foreign parties are attracted by and satisfied with the arbitration service provided by CIETAC and CMAC.

[79] Arbitration fees handed to CIETAC includes both the administrative fees to the commission and remunerations of arbitrator(s).

[80] Michael J. Moser, "Roundtable on Arbitration and Conciliation Concerning China: Commentary", 17th ICCA Conference, 16–18 May 2004, Beijing.

[81] The forms of the organization of the ECAC were decided according to the Organic Rules of Economic Contract Arbitration Commissions, issued by the State Administration for Industry and Commerce on 23 December 1983.

[82] Regulations of PRC on the Arbitration of Disputes Involving Economic Contracts, promulgated by the State Council on 22 August 1983, Guo Fa [1983] No. 119. See, "Arbitration Committees to Handle Contract Disputes", Beijing Xinhua Domestic Service, 1 September 1983, reprinted in *FBIS Daily Report: China*, 2 September 1983, K3-K4; see also Wu Tong, "Where is Our Arbitration of Domestic Economic Contracts Going (Woguo Guonei Jingji Hetong Zhongcai xiang Hechu Zou)", (1991) 2 Chinese Jurisprudence (Zhongguo Faxue), 82–84.

[83] Article 5 of the Organic Rules of Economic Contract Arbitration Commissions, issued by the State Administration for Industry and Commerce on 23 December 1983.

[84] Article 16 of the Organic Rules of Economic Contract Arbitration Commissions. The arbitrators were divided into different ranks, i.e. section (*gu ji*), division (*ke ji*), office (*chu ji*) and department (*si ju ji*) respectively, depending on the hierarchical level of the Administration and the relevant qualification of the arbitrator himself.

[85] Article 38 of the Rules for Handling of Cases by Economic Contract Arbitration Commission, issued by the State Administration for Industry and Commerce on 23 December 1983.

[86] The Legislative Affairs Commission of the NPCSC of the PRC , *Arbitration Laws of China* (1997), 21.

5.032   Strictly speaking, before 1995, domestic arbitration was not arbitration at all but a
system of administrative adjudicature. The arbitration commissions were purely
administrative agencies, and further, affiliated and subordinate to their relevant
governmental superiors. This was partly because of the highly centralised planned
economy where the administrative powers dominated all economic activities, and
partly owing to the legislative blank of arbitration at that time. As Professor Stanley
Lubman has put it, in the then context of China, the administrative nature of arbitration
is mostly expressed as regards the "administrative and hierarchical commands"[87]
that the tribunal received from the commission, which it must obey. However, this
has left the autonomy and credibility of Chinese local arbitration commissions in
great doubt and has implied a checkered road towards embracing the autonomous
institutionalisation of Chinese arbitration.

(ii) *Post-Arbitration Law: Administrative taints unresolved*

5.033   The Chinese legislature realised the thorny problem of administrative encroachment
and began to implement reform of the arbitration commissions. Thus, one of the most
significant objectives of the Arbitration Law has been concentrated upon establishing
an independent arbitration institution system so that the parties' autonomy will not
be interfered with by the administrative powers.[88] In theory, parties should now enjoy
more freedom for resolving their disputes through arbitration. However, in practice,
because of the lack of any detailed implementing rules under the Arbitration Law
and the conflicting ancillary administrative documents issued,[89] the restructure of
arbitration commissions is still in the hands of the administrative bodies.

5.034   The personnel constituents became the first hurdle where the Arbitration Law requires
that an arbitration commission shall be composed of chairman, vice-chairmen
and members;[90] but it fails to designate how these personnel shall be selected. By
referring to the *Scheme for Reorganising Domestic Arbitration Institutions* (the
Scheme), the members of the first secretariat of an arbitration commission should
be appointed by the local people's government from "consultative recommendation"
by the government departments of legislative affairs, economic and trade affairs,
system restructuring, legal affairs, industry and commerce, science and technology,
etc. and the CCPIT.[91] As with the internal operation custom of the governmental
departments, such "consultative recommendation", in essence, makes the arbitration
commission a "joint office" of representatives from the consultative departments.[92]
Thus, in the initial periods until 2000, 83.1 per cent of the leadership (chairman,
vice-chair, secretary-general) of local arbitration commissions were assumed by local

---

[87]   Lubman, *Bird in Cage: Legal Reform in China after Mao* (1999), 94.
[88]   See arts.10, 14 of the Arbitration Law; see also comments by Wang Wenying, "Distinctive Features of Arbitration
in China: A Historic Perspective", (2006) 23 *Journal of International Arbitration*, 66.
[89]   See also discussions above at Chapter 1, under the title, "Inconsistent Ancillary Rules".
[90]   Articles 11, 12 and 66 of the Arbitration Law.
[91]   *Scheme for Reorganizing Arbitration Institutions,* Guo Ban Fa (1995) No. 44, issued by the General Office of the
State Council. The *Scheme* was mainly for the purpose of resolving the new arbitration commissions' problems
relating to the staff, funds, housing, rank and affiliations to the local people's government.
[92]   Wang Hongsong, "Existing Problems of the Arbitration Law and Its Reform Suggestions (Zhongcaifa Cunzai de
Wenti ji qi Xiugai Jianyi)", (2005) 52 *Arbitration in Beijing (Beijing Zhongcai)*, 21.

government officials.[93] The concern is that if the Scheme was to ensure the smooth transition of the commissions by way of administrative assistance in the initial period, there should be no need to continue now. However, the Scheme further provided that when the terms of the commission members are running out, the new members should be once again nominated and appointed through consultation between the old members and "relevant government departments".[94] This might be understood as to regularise and stabilise the administrative impact upon the commission composition, which undoubtedly goes against the "non-governmental and independent" ideologies under the Arbitration Law.

Secondly, on legal status, pursuant to the *Notice on Further the Work of Restructuring the Arbitration Institutions* (the Notice), the establishment and operation of the arbitration commissions shall be "led (*qiantou*)" by the legislative affairs office (*fazhiban*)[95] under relevant level of the people's government.[96] However, once the commissions were established, these "leading departments (*qiantou jiguan*)" eventually became the "departments-in-charge (*yewu zhuguan jiguan*)" of the corresponding arbitration commission such that they decide upon the personnel constituents and other important developing issues of the commission.[97] Accordingly, administrative approval by the legislative affairs office has become necessary even regarding those trifling matters such as the remuneration of the commission members. In context, it is hard to argue that the administrative hierarchical relationships have been eradicated. However, as most of the local commissions are presently characterised as "institutions with ownership by the whole people (*quanmin suoyouzhi shiye danwei*)" whose operational funds come from the state treasury,[98] it might be plausible to introduce the governmental hands for "guidance (*zhidao*)".[99] Nevertheless, such "guidance" should be well regulated and restricted in assisting the commissions to an independent status rather than making them subordinate to the administrative powers. Furthermore, if we turn to art.10(2) of the Arbitration Law, it seems that the non-administrative chamber of commerce in a given city may also be empowered to establish and organise

5.035

---

[93] Department of Coordination of the Legislative Affairs Office of the State Council (ed), *An Overview of the Chinese Arbitration Institution* (Beijing: China Pricing Press, 2001). The survey was sent to 156 arbitration commissions, among which 136 responded. According to the figures listed by the survey result, 96 chairship are assumed by the city mayors and vice mayors; 29 assumed by the secretary-general of the municipal government of the city; 1 assumed by the former chief justice of the local higher people's court; 3 assumed by the chairman of the CCPIT; only 2 assumed by the law school professor and 4 professional arbitrators.

[94] The "relevant departments" refer to those government departments of legislative affairs, economic and trade affairs, system restructuring, judicial affairs, industry and commerce, science and technology, and the CCPIT, the same as consulted in the initial period of establishment.

[95] The legislative affairs office is defined as one of the directly subordinated agencies under the relevant government to be responsible for the legislative and other legal affairs of the government. For example, see, http://www.chinalaw.gov.cn/jsp/contentpub/browser/contentproe.jsp?contentid=co1865792191, which is the Legislative Affairs Office of the Central Government (State Council).

[96] *Notice on Further the Work of Restructuring the Arbitration Institutions*, issued by the General Office of the State Council, 22 May 1995.

[97] Wang Hongsong, "Existing Problems of the Arbitration Law and Its Reform Suggestions" (2005), 21.

[98] Wang Yongqing, "Several Issues on Re-organizing the Arbitration Commissions (Chongxin Zujian Zhongcai Jigou de Ruogan Wenti)", in Department of Coordination of the Legislative Affairs Office of the State Council, *An Overview of Chinese Arbitration Institutions* (2001), 25–35.

[99] Wang Hongsong, "Existing Problems of the Arbitration Law and Its Reform Suggestions" (2005), 22.

arbitration commissions.[100] However, influenced by the inertia of the planned economy and administrative dominance, the immature system of the chamber of commerce in China makes the chambers incapable of playing the role and therefore throwing the ball back to the government.[101] Essentially, against such a structural background, whether an arbitration commission can operate independently is largely an issue of administrative attitude towards arbitration in the given locality. To put it more directly, if the local government respects the contractual autonomy and takes on arbitration as an independent dispute resolution, the arbitration commission may have more chances to escape from the administrative shadows. In this respect, the Beijing Arbitration Commission (BAC) benefits greatly from the liberal "non-interference" approach by the Beijing People's Government[102] which helps to put forward BAC as one of the hottest destinations for arbitration among business people.[103]

5.036   Lastly, on the financial source, as discussed above, arbitration commissions under the cap of "institutions (*shiye danwei*)"[104] are financially sponsored by the state treasury. However, the present institution system is set up on the basis of the planned economy with their financial source and development controlled directly by the relevant department-in-chief.[105] The author thus describes two problematic situations that underlie the system. First, if the local commission could run itself well and make profits from its satisfactory arbitral service charges, such a profit might still need to undergo administrative scrutiny, whether strict or flexible. Then the arbitration commission might be justified as financially independent, for example, CIETAC.[106] More problems rest with the second situation. Since the promulgation

---

[100]   Article 10(2) of the Arbitration Law provides that either the relevant department of the municipal governments or the chamber of commerce shall arrange to organize the arbitration commission.

[101]   As a matter of fact, many chambers of commerce in China are also administrative in nature. The true independent chambers of commerce with functions that are played in those developed countries have not been set up completely in China. See Wang Yongqing, "Several Issues on Re-organizing the Arbitration Commissions" (2001), 24.

[102]   As the Head of the Beijing Municipality of Justice shared with the media, "The biggest support of government to arbitration commissions is non-interference." See news report in the *Shanghai Justice Daily*, 12 December 2004, 4.

[103]   Wang Hongsong, Secretary-General of BAC, "Decade Review of Beijing Arbitration Commission", available at the BAC website, http://www.bjac.com.cn/introduce/2007.htm. BAC's independent status will be further dwelled upon in subsequent discussions under the heading "Reform suggestions and administrative challenges".

[104]   There are different ways of classifying institutions. For example, profitable and non-profitable institutions; administrative and non-administrative institutions. See, art.2 of the *Provisional Regulations of the State Administration for Institutional Registration,* issued by the State Council on 25 October 1998.

[105]   Cheng Furong and Su Shunmin, "Several Counter-measures for Reforming the System of Institutions during the Period of Transition (Zhuangui Shiqi Shiye Danwei Tizhi Gaige de Jidian Duice)", (2002) 3 *Hangzhou College of Commerce Review*, 17 (Hangzhou College of Commerce is now renamed as Zhejiang University of Industry and Commerce).

[106]   The financial independence of CIETAC, however, has been lately challenged due to the fact that Wang Shengchang (the then Vice-Chair and Secretary-General of CIETAC) has been arrested and detained on charges of financial irregularity and *illegally distributing state assets to staff*. Wang was arrested on 24 April 2006 when he arrived at the offices of CCPIT in Beijing for a meeting and on the same day, the Audit Bureau and Ministry of Finance ordered that the commission turn over its funds to the government. If CIETAC is truly financially independent and runs itself through the intake of arbitration service fees, how can the judiciary charge Wang on the basis of "illegal distribution of state assets". As the *South China Morning Post* commented on the issue, "Wang was a scapegoat for a problem that had arisen due to the commission's ambiguous status as a semi-governmental entity, the miniscule fees earned by mainland arbitrators and the hundreds of millions of Yuan the commission earned for its services".

See *Mealey's Publication on International Legal News,* available at http://www.mealeys.com/legalnews/international.html.

of the Arbitration Law, local commissions have been widespread in accordance with art.10(1) wherever the administrative level is sufficient.[107] It is noteworthy that such establishment caters for administrative needs[108] rather than market demand for dispute resolution.[109] Hence, some arbitration commissions are facing the problem of "looking for rice to cook",[110] especially those in the vast hinterland, who rely on the financial support of local governments for survival.[111] Consequently, such "poverty" has further strengthened their reliance on administrative power, making the "survival of the best" rule a sacrifice under financial control.

Through an extensive examination (personnel constituents, legal status and financial source) of the existing local arbitration commissions, it would appear that they are still largely restricted by governmental hands. It is regrettable that although the Arbitration Law does cherish "independent" wishes, its implementing gap has left most local commissions prone to administrative interference. In this context, similarly, it is easy to infer that the arbitral tribunal is vulnerable to administrative and institutional interferences, and the deprivation of its jurisdictional autonomy thus becomes a logical result.

5.037

(c) Political and administrative interventions to arbitral autonomy

Since the 1990s, China has been evolving through an extraordinary period of economic and social change. The rejection of the highly centralised planned economy and monopoly of office power, and the search for free markets, contractual autonomy and administrative liberalisation include many clashes with traditional institutions along the progressive road which affects all aspects of Chinese social life. In this regard, the transformation of arbitration institutions and their interaction with the economic and administrative transition provide an opportunity for investigating the evolving structure of these institutions—primarily, the vast numbers of local arbitration commissions that have sprung up in the past decade.

5.038

---

[107] According to art.10(1) of the Arbitration Law, arbitration commissions may be established in each administrative level of cities that can be divided into districts. By December 2010, there have been over 200 local arbitration commissions in China. See discussions above at Chapter 1.

[108] For example, before Li Shui (Zhejiang Province, southeast China) becomes a city that can be divided into districts in May 2000, it used to be a county of the city of Hangzhou (Capital of Zhejiang Province), where a branch office of the Hangzhou Arbitration Commission was established. Then a Li Shui Arbitration Commission was founded right after in September 2003. See report in Kang Ming, *A Study on Commercial Arbitration Service* (Beijing: China Law Press), 153–154.

[109] The common practice of other developed arbitration jurisdictions is that the arbitral institution is set corresponding to the market needs of dispute resolution, e.g. the HKIAC, SIAC, and LCIA. Even in UK which has kept an established tradition of commercial arbitration, there are only two arbitration institutions within the country, the LCIA and LMAA.

[110] Lu Yunhua (Head of the Legislative Affairs of the State Council), *Speech in the Symposium on the Development of Nationwide Arbitration Works,* held in CIETAC, 2003, unpublished.

[111] The transitional economy in China and the vast territory lead to the unbalanced development of the regional economy with rapid progress in some areas and slow progress elsewhere. See, generally, World Bank, *China 2020: Development Challenges in the New Century* (Washington D.C.: World Bank, 1997). According to the survey by CIETAC, more than three-fourths of local arbitration commissions are facing "grim" difficulties in balancing itself. (Source: *Interview with Wang Wenying,* Director of Arbitration Research Institute of the CIETAC, 22 December 2006).

5.039   Through this investigation, it is concluded that although legislative rhetoric has claimed to diminish the administrative impact upon arbitration institutions, the reality is discouraging: most of the commissions are still dependant on the local people's government for survival, both in operational funds and arbitration caseload.[112] Besides the self-blamed implementing gap by the Arbitration Law, it at least reflects the fact that the administrative power remains a strong influence on Chinese arbitration institutions. This implies the administrative undermining of the arbitral jurisdiction as well. First, by analogy to the hierarchical relationship between the arbitration commission and its department-in-chief, the arbitral tribunal is also structurally inferior and functionally subordinate to the commission. Thus, the determining of the arbitral jurisdiction as one of the key functions of the arbitral tribunal is understood as executing the "administrative hierarchical commands" from the commission so that it can be easily deprived. Secondly, owing to the governmental control permeating every aspect of the institutional infrastructure, it is convincing that the commissions are prone to administrative interference. Therefore, the logical conclusion could be drawn that administratively-dominated commissions may in turn administratively overshadow the jurisdictional competence and arbitral autonomy of its lower-level tribunals. Thirdly, given the country's distinctive unitary institutional arbitration system where *ad hoc* arbitration practice is not recognised in China, no individual tribunal could be lucky enough to escape from the administrative impact.

5.040   Elaborate discussions may provide insights into the reform hurdles of the arbitration institutions and, further, one of the major reform hurdles facing the development of Chinese arbitration. In this regard, it might be more understandable why reforming the tribunal's *competence-competence* is such a difficult issue, as it depends not only upon the legislative recognition as most of the modern arbitration jurisdictions do, but also upon the political environment to allow further independence of the arbitration institutions which should provide strong institutional support for the tribunal's independence. Infrastructure deficiency has thwarted arbitral autonomy where the tribunal should have complete freedom to rule on its own jurisdiction. Reform is therefore urged upon the arbitration commissions for respecting the tribunal's *competence-competence* as they should have been. However, because the institutional independence of arbitration commissions is essentially a problem intertwined with political and administrative liberalisation in China, its development may not be an easy task.

3. CIETAC's STRUGGLING DEVELOPMENT

5.041   On the regulatory drawbacks, unfortunately, thus far, no subsequent legislation or any judicial interpretations have filled in the gap of *competence-competence*. The regulatory

---

[112] In addition to personnel and financial dependence, most local arbitration commissions are still reliant on local people's government in developing business. The main administrative "support" in this regard is to require the enterprises to include the arbitration commission in the given locality in the arbitration agreement. Song Lianbin called it as another kind of "local protectionism" of Chinese arbitration; see Song Lianbin, "From Ideologies to Rules—Several Issues of Attention for Amending the Arbitration Law (Linian Zouxiang Guize—Zhongcaifa Xiuding ying Zhuyi de Jige Wenti)", (2005) 52 *Arbitration in Beijing (Beijing Zhongcai)*, 2.

failure may be reflected most recently by the SPC Interpretation on arbitration in 2006 where the arbitral jurisdictional power was confirmed to be enjoyed by the arbitration commission rather than the arbitral tribunal.[113] In these circumstances, regulatory change to the tribunal's jurisdictional autonomy has to take place along with the initial reform of the institutional rules of the arbitration commissions. Such change has witessed a "struggling" process through the following two phases: in the first phase, before the change of the rules, the development of institutional practice to allow the commission to share part of the jurisdictional competence with the tribunal; and in the second phase, institutional reform for tribunal's jurisdictional autonomy to be recognised by the commission rules.

(a) "Commission-dominated" to "commission-tribunal-shared"

Among Chinese arbitration commissions, CIETAC was the first to openly criticise the defective practice of "commission-dominated" arbitral jurisdiction and embarked on the reform in 2001.[114] The reform was acclaimed as a series of "technically remedial measures".[115] These internal measures are designed to introduce the jurisdictional competence of the tribunal into practice although it is supposed to be within the legislative authority to rule only on the merits of the case.[116] As such, the remedies represent a breakthrough of the restriction of the Arbitration Law under which jurisdictional power belongs just to commissions.[117]

5.042

The CIETAC measure follows a three-step formula: (1) if the jurisdictional challenge is straightforward, the commission will rule on the jurisdiction directly. If the commission considers the jurisdictional dispute complicated or the surrounding facts yet to be ascertained, then (2) before the composition of the tribunal, the commission will render a "preliminary ruling" of the jurisdiction based on the *prima facie* evidence[118] and wait for the tribunal's further ruling after it has examined the case details; (3) if the tribunal has been established, the commission will consult with the tribunal before it renders the "preliminary ruling". In either case of (2) or (3), should the tribunal find after its substantive hearing that no jurisdiction should be entertained, the tribunal shall then report its findings and opinions in writing to the commission. The commission will "confirm, revise or reverse" the preliminary ruling, and to render

5.043

---

[113] See arts.7 and 13 of the SPC Interpretation on Arbitration (2006). See also, previously, arts.5–8 of the Domestic Draft (2004) and arts.22–26 of the Foreign-related Draft (2003). See discussions above under the heading "Critical Turning since 2006: Unified SPC Interpretation on Arbitration" of Chapter 4.

[114] Wang Shengchang, "The Chinese Characteristic System of Competence-Competence in Arbitration: Achievements and Problems" (2004), 236–237.

[115] *Ibid.*

[116] Article 19, paragraph 2 of the Arbitration Law. See discussions above under the heading "Regulation of Arbitration Law and its Serious Defects".

[117] Article 20 of the Arbitration Law. See discussions above under the heading "Regulation of the Arbitration Law and its Serious Defects".

[118] Pursuant to art.14 of the then Arbitration Rules of the CIETAC (Rules 2000), the applicants need to submit the arbitration agreement and evidentiary documents for substantive claims. Thus, no matter the evidence is true or not, CIETAC could accept the case should these documents exist.

a new jurisdictional decision in accordance with the opinions of the tribunal.[119] The following case illustrates the measure.

5.044   On 20 September 2000, a Hong Kong company (claimant) reached a plastics sales contract with a Chinese company (respondent) where the CIETAC arbitration was agreed. The respondent objected to the arbitral jurisdiction on 19 February 2002, arguing the non-existence of Clauses (15) to (24) of the contract under which the CIETAC arbitration was named. On 24 June, before the tribunal was established, the commission made a preliminary ruling on basis of the *prima facie* evidence that the arbitration clause existed and therefore it had jurisdiction over the case. On 2 July, the respondent challenged the jurisdiction again, arguing its representative had never signed the clauses. Then, CIETAC replied to the respondent that the existence and validity of the signature would be ruled by the tribunal. On 20 January 2003, the oral hearing was held in the CIETAC headquarter in Beijing when the tribunal investigated and verified the signature of the clauses.

5.045   After a hearing and investigation, the *tribunal* made the ruling as follows:

> "In summary, the tribunal held that the signatures on the pages from Clauses (15) to (24) were true. They were signed by the representative of the respondent. The arbitration clause was validly reached between the disputing parties selecting the CIETAC and therefore the arbitral jurisdiction was satisfied. The tribunal would go on to examine the other facts of the case relating to the substantive claim ..."

5.046   The *commission*, after receiving the factual findings and jurisdictional opinions by the tribunal, confirmed its jurisdictional decision on 27 June 2003, that there was "a valid arbitration agreement between the claimant and respondent and the arbitration commission had jurisdiction over the case".[120]

5.047   The above CIETAC case shows how the jurisdictional decision is issued by the combined efforts of the commission and tribunal. While the commission needs to determine the jurisdictional challenge without pre-judgment of the merits, the tribunal exercises its power to delve into the evidence and return to the commission with its opinions on the validity of the arbitration agreement. As such, CIETAC successfully saves itself from the "embarrassing" conflict between the jurisdictional pre-judgment by the commission and the actual adjudication by the subsequent tribunal. The development is encouraging in the sense that jurisdictional competence has been developed from the previous "commission-dominated" to the current "commission-tribunal-shared" model where individual tribunals may also enjoy part of the jurisdictional autonomy should the complexity of the case warrant it.

5.048   Against the backdrop where both the Arbitration Law and the then CIETAC Rules[121] empowered only the commission to rule on the arbitral jurisdiction, these adaptive

---

[119]   Wang Shengchang, "The Chinese Characteristic System of Competence-Competence in Arbitration: Achievements and Problems" (2004), 236–237.

[120]   CIETAC (ed), *Selected Jurisdictional Decision by the CIETAC (Zhongguo Guoji Jingji Maoyi Zhongcai Weiyuanhui Guanxiaquan Jueding Xuanbian)* (Beijing: China Commercial Publishing, 2004), 244–246.

[121]   The then CIETAC Rules (Rules 2000), stipulated under art.4 that should the parties raise jurisdictional challenge, only CIETAC or the people's court has the power to rule on the jurisdiction.

measures were "struggling" because such technical bypassing of the laws may run into the risk of violating the laws in practice. That explains the "struggling" costs for promoting the parties' and tribunal's autonomy in the transitional period (before the change of the Law and Rules). Although the CIETAC practice might bring the Chinese practice closer to international norms, the measures were both rudimentary and costly because the tribunal's competence had to be conducted "underground"— avoiding the knowledge of the publications—until it was recently recognised officially by the Rules.

(b) Tribunal's competence recognised by commission rules

In 2005, CIETAC officially introduced jurisdictional autonomy of the arbitral tribunals through art.6 of the amendment to its rules:[122]   **5.049**

> "The CIETAC shall have the power to determine the existence and validity of an arbitration agreement and its jurisdiction over an arbitration case. *The CIETAC may, if necessary, delegate such power to the arbitral tribunal.*
>
> Where CIETAC is satisfied by *prima facie* evidence that an arbitration agreement providing for arbitration by the CIETAC exists, it may make a decision based on such evidence that it has jurisdiction over the arbitration case. *Such a decision shall not prevent the CIETAC from making a new decision on jurisdiction based on facts and/or evidence found by the tribunal during the proceedings that are inconsistent with the prima facie evidence.*"[123]

The author, by use of emphasis, highlights the main development of the regulation with respect to arbitral jurisdiction under the new CIETAC Rules. To begin with, the commission may now delegate jurisdictional power to the individual tribunal. This shows CIETAC's determination in advancing the tribunal's *competence-competence*. In addition, the new Rules officially affirm the long-established "underground" practice of "joint" ruling on arbitral jurisdiction. Thus, the commission may make a decision allowing the tribunal to assume jurisdiction if the *prima facie* evidence so suggests; and may ultimately make a new decision should later evidence suggest inconsistency based on the tribunal's findings.   **5.050**

But the new CIETAC rules are not exempt from problems. The controversy is first related to a theoretical issue, i.e. whether art.6 of the Rules sits well with art.20 of the Arbitration Law. Under the PRC Legislation Law, internal institutional rules do not carry the force of law and they must accord with national law provisions.[124] However, with the development of the market economy, some common practices within the institution have been reduced to rules to make up for the outdated laws. Then, if the state legislative and judiciary do not expressly object to such practices, the rules   **5.051**

---

[122]   The Rules 2005 was revised and adopted on 11 January 2005 and effective from 1 May 2005.

[123]   Article 6 of the CIETAC Rules 2005. The 2005 Rules are available at http://www.cietac.org.cn/english/rules/rules.htm.

[124]   According to art.2 of the Legislation Law, only national laws promulgated by the NPC and NPCSC; administrative regulations, rules, decrees by the central or local people's government or governmental departments carry the force of law in China.

shall not be "violating" the law. On the other hand, if we set aside the theoretical problem and turn to practical aspects, the CIETAC move has been warmly welcomed by parties and legal practitioners in light of its move towards a higher degree of party autonomy and arbitral autonomy. Among its heralds, it is praised as the "most pragmatic method conceivable to achieve the arbitral autonomy under the current legislation".[125] Unfortunately, the liberalisation is still short of necessary details, i.e. under what circumstances the jurisdictional competence may be delegated. If it is a "necessity" test,[126] then to what extent could the discretionary power be exercised by the commission, particularly in complex cases.[127] The new jurisdictional rules are silent on the crucial implementation part where tribunals are still pushing for a move towards arbitral autonomy. Some writers suggest that CIETAC may need more time to accumulate practical experience for supplementing the newly-introduced rules;[128] more argue that CIETAC's "intentional" omission may be justified as a "cautious approach for self-protection and not offending the legislative mandates".[129] The latter opinion may serve as a footnote to the "struggling" efforts by the top Chinese arbitration institution in aligning itself with international practice.

5.052 In the author's view, compared with its previous "underground measures", the new rules, though "struggling", mark a braver stride in recognising the tribunal's *competence-competence*. The rules may help to avoid the legal deficiencies through the commission's internal jurisdictional authorisation to the tribunal. By doing so, jurisdictional authority still remains with the commission in a strict sense, which is still in accordance with the current Chinese arbitration jurisprudence. Most importantly, the CIETAC liberal reform encourages the reform efforts of the Chinese local arbitration commissions.

(c) Ring the bell of party and tribunal autonomy

5.053 The above discussion demonstrates the institutional endeavors for developing the tribunal's jurisdictional autonomy in China. As analysed, before the legislative change, the reform was preceded by the change in the arbitration rules of the commissions. This is most notably evidenced by the CIETAC move from its informal technical measures to formal recognition in its Rules of 2005, where CIETAC tribunals can now rule on both their arbitral jurisdiction and jurisdictional challenge if the commission so delegates. It is true that such liberal arbitration rules can help to expand the parties' autonomy and arbitral autonomy. In the context of China, the rules play a particularly important role in promoting arbitration practice given the country's

---

[125] Wang Shengchang and Cao Lijun, "Towards a Higher Degree of Party Autonomy and Transparency: The CIETAC Introduces Its 2005 New Rules", [2005] *International Arbitration Law Review*, 118.

[126] Tao Jingzhou and Zhao Jing, "CIETAC: Revising Its Arbitration Rules", (2005) 10 *Arbitration Newsletter of the International Bar Association*, 17.

[127] See discussions above about CIETAC's "technical measures" in 2001.

[128] This view is expressed most recently by the current CIETAC Secretary General, Mr. Yu Jianlong, in his talk on the "Managing Business Disputes in China" Conference, held on 26 March 2007 in Harvard Club, New York.

[129] See Lian Lirong, "The Latest Developments in CIETAC's Arbitration Rules", available at www.european-arbitrators.org/europeanarbitratorsfiles/ content/papers.html.

unitary institutional arbitration system. However, as aforementioned, institutional rules do not carry the force of law in China. Thus, in revolutionising the arbitral jurisdiction, the change in the rules might be seen as an institutional effort to expect a positive response from the state legislation—either to revise the Arbitration Law or to issue judicial interpretations by the SPC. After all, development of the rules indicates the developing trend of Chinese arbitration, especially when the reform is initiated by CIETAC as the institutional leader of the Chinese arbitration commissions.[130] The hope is that the vast local commissions would follow the CIETAC move in liberalising their arbitration rules so that the progress might be hastened through the distinctive Chinese way of reforming institutional rules before the law is officially revised. If smoothly processed, then China would be closer to the goal of integrating itself with international arbitration norms and practices. This is encouraging, though the author has to point out some underlying problems in China that may cause the reform process to be slow and checkered.

To begin with, local commissions may be reluctant to reform the rules. This is because they are subject to strong administrative influences where "consultative approval" from the relevant "department-in-chief" might be necessary before the rules could be changed.[131] In addition, different from CIETAC which has an established history of international exposure, local commissions are more accustomed to catering for local parties and local administrative needs.[132] Therefore, they may be more afraid of not complying with the Arbitration Law provisions. However, if local rules do not change, the jurisdictional autonomy will still be monopolised by the administrative-dominated commissions. Thus far, only BAC has liberalised its institutional rules in allowing the tribunals to rule on the jurisdiction via the commission's delegation.[133] Nevertheless, only one or two odd changes (CIETAC and BAC) will not be enough to prompt the reform wheels forward.

5.054

Moreover, even if local commissions followed the CIETAC move and were willing to embrace adaptive updates, the process could be quite a "struggle" owing to the impediment of their administrative infrastructures. At a macro level, given the unbalanced development among these commissions, the degree of liberalisation may vary tremendously depending on how the local people's government concerned takes arbitration. At a micro level, since the CIETAC approach does not specify the conditions with respect to how the jurisdictional authority can be delegated, it is hence a discretionary power by the commission and its leadership. As presented above, most of the local arbitration commissions in China are still financially dependent and functionally subordinate to the local administrative power. Then the optimistic move of arbitral autonomy may not necessarily end up with desirable effects unless the institutional independence of the arbitration commission is first realised.

5.055

---

[130] As the oldest, largest and most reputable arbitration institution in China, the CIETAC move is considered to lead the development of the other Chinese arbitration commissions.

[131] See discussions above under the heading "Post-Arbitration Law: Administrative taints unresolved".

[132] Local commissions are exposed to international cases and parties only after the "Notice 1996". See discussions above under the heading "System of Dual-track Arbitration" of Chapter 2.

[133] See art.6(4) of the Rules of the BAC, revised in 2006.

5.056   In essence, the problems embedded in the reform of the tribunal's jurisdictional autonomy reflect the institutional challenge to the administrative regime. On one hand, the Chinese arbitration commissions have been tolerated so far under administrative control and have been expecting legislative change. The desire has become particularly strong since the two rounds of SPC Drafts were promulgated. However, neither the Drafts nor their subsequent unified Interpretation has brought about the long-waited legislative change on recognising the tribunal's *competence-competence*. On the other hand, discouraging news of the further delay to the Arbitration Law revision[134] has pushed some front-line commissions to struggle along the development path by reforming rules themselves. But reform of the rules itself could not overcome all of the deficiencies in the legal framework which is based on China's economic and administrative conditions. These factors suggest the adaptive process of Chinese arbitration is both informal and checkered under administrative powers. In conclusion, although reform of the institutional rules encouraged the development of tribunal's jurisdictional competence in China, given the prevailing role of the commission in the Chinese arbitration system, the informal adaptation requires institutional support, in the sense that both institutional independence and liberal rules are necessary. The following discussions thus explore the feasibility of developing such institutional support by studying the example of BAC.

(d) Reform suggestions and administrative challenges

5.057   With the deepening economic integration and administration liberalisation, one can witness attempts by local arbitration commissions in advancing *competence-competence* by way of institutional support. The author thus discusses one of such successful examples, the BAC, in order to assess its future impact upon Chinese local arbitration commissions.

(i) *Institutional independence plus liberal rules*

5.058   Established in 1995 under the Beijing People's Government (BPG), the management infrastructure of the BAC (the Committee) comprised one chairman, four vice-Chairmen and several members. In September 2007, the Committee was passed to the fifth session which pursued the reform goals of making BAC into an independent

---

[134]   The Arbitration Law was thought to be revised in 2004, as a decade of its promulgation, reflected in Song, Zhao and Li's article in 2003. (See, Song, Zhao and Li, "Approaches to the Revision of the 1994 Arbitration Act of the People's Republic of China" (2003)). However, the legislative change did not occur. Legal academics further considered the Arbitration Law amendment to take place after the SPC introducing its two rounds of interpretations (two Draft Provisions in 2003 and 2004) and placed high expectations on the long-waited legislative reform to occur after the SPC Unified Interpretation in 2006. The legislative breakthrough was still unseen, which comes to the conclusion of "further delay" to the revision of the Arbitration Law. See, a cluster of discussions by famous Chinese arbitration academics in Issue 60 of the journal *Arbitration in Beijing (Beijing Zhongcai)* in 2007, including Song Lianbin, "Comments on the SPC Interpretation on Several Issues in Applying the PRC Arbitration Law (*Ping Zuigao Renmin Fayuan guanyu Shiyong Zhonghua Renmin Gongheguo Zhongcaifa Ruogan Wenti de Jieshi*)"; Qiao Xin, "Supporting Arbitration and Developing Arbitration (*Zhichi Zhongcai, Fazhan Zhongcai*); Lin Yifei, "Understanding the New Judicial Interpretation on the Arbitration Law (*Zhongcaifa Xin Sifajieshi Jiedu*)".

arbitration institution.[135] The reform is achieved through a dual-level effort, institutional independence and the application of liberal rules.

The efforts for institutional independence are reflected through the following three aspects. First, on the personnel constituents, BAC pays great attention to the personnel independence and expert characteristic of its leadership. The Chairman of the Committee is Professor Jiang Ping, former President of the China University of Political Science and Law and one of the most renowned jurists in China. The Vice-Chairmen and other Committee members are either renowned law professors or experienced legal practitioners.[136] BAC goes on to require under its internal regulations that the chairmen and staff members of the Committee cannot act as arbitrators unless otherwise jointly appointed by both parties.[137] Because the Committee is the decision-maker of the development of BAC, the prevention of its members from serving as arbitrators is to guarantee the independence and impartiality of the tribunal.[138] Secondly, on the legal status, BAC is an institution in name yet is reported to operate and be administered in the way of an enterprise to be independent from the influences of the legal affairs office of BPG.[139] The Committee is the management body of BAC, under which the BAC Secretariat (the Secretariat) works as the general office, administering the institutional operation (human, financial resources) and providing logistic support for parties in arbitral proceedings.[140] As aforementioned, this has mainly benefited from the enlightened "non-interference" approach by BPG towards arbitration. Indeed, the "non-interference" approach has been emphasised by all the past and present officials of the legislative affairs office of BPG, laying a solid foundation for BAC's institutional independence.[141] Lastly, concerning financial sources, after more than a decade of development, BAC is reported to have been able to maintain its operation on a self-sufficient basis through the income of arbitration fees.[142]

5.059

BAC further reformed its arbitration rules in 2007. Among the other changes, it officially liberalised the arbitral jurisdiction under art.6(4) of its Rules:

5.060

---

[135] See http://www.bjac.org.cn/organise/index.htm.

[136] A detailed description of the BAC 5th Committee members is available thorough the webpage of the BAC, http://www.bjac.com.cn/en/organise/index.htm.

[137] See arts.7, 8 and 11 of the Administrative Measures for the Engagement of Arbitrators of the BAC, available at http://www.bjac.com.cn/en/arbiter/aptitude.htm.

[138] See discussions on this topic below under the heading "Hidden Obstacles to Tribunal Formation" of Chapter 6.

[139] See, Wang Hongsong (Secretary-General of the BAC), "Speech on the 2005 Spring Tea Reception for the BAC Arbitrators (Zai 2005 Nian Zhongcaiyuan Chunjie Chahuahui Shang de Jianghua)", (2005) 54 *Arbitration in Beijing (Beijing Zhongcai)*, 76.

[140] Wang Hongsong, "Decade Review of Beijing Arbitration Commission" (Chinese New Year speech, January 2006), available at http://www.bjac.org.cn/organise/report.htm.

[141] The Legislative Affairs Office of the BPG states that the best support to the arbitration is not to interfere into arbitration, reported as well in the "Decade Review", *ibid*.

[142] Jiang Ping, "2006 Working Report of the BAC", available at http://www.bjac.com.cn/introduce/2006.htm. Jiang mentions in the speech that other than paying a considerable amount of tax to the government, BAC also owns more than 3000 square meters of office space and 59 parking lots in China Merchant Tower, which is located in the CBD in Beijing, and modern office equipment and facilities.

"The BAC, *or if authorized by the BAC*, the Arbitral Tribunal, shall have the power to rule on the jurisdictional objections and objections to the validity of an arbitration agreement. The Arbitral Tribunal can deliver its decision in the form of either an interim award or a final award".[143]

5.061   As such, BAC tribunals may now rule on their own jurisdiction if the commission so authorises. Even if jurisdictional power is not delegated, given the institutional support by the commission at a micro level and administrative support by BPG at a macro level, party autonomy and arbitral autonomy may be guaranteed. BAC's rule update is considered the first breakthrough among the vast local Chinese arbitration commissions.[144] More importantly, owing to its high awareness of and swift response to the issue of *competence-competence* in China, the arbitral quality is greatly improved. BAC is then acclaimed as willing to adjust its procedures to accommodate party autonomy and arbitral efficiency, and is therefore favored by parties both at home and abroad.[145]

5.062   BAC's success is reflected as a good combination of both an independent arbitration institution and a liberal rule promoter. Given that *competence-competence* of the tribunal has not yet been recognised in China, such transitional mode of dual-level institutional efforts might serve the adaptation purpose before the Arbitration Law is amended. However, in the long run, it is strongly advocated that the Arbitration Law should learn the experience of international arbitration norms to fully incorporate the doctrine of *competence-competence* in its legislative revisions.

5.063   The above discussions show the success of the institutional effort on the part of BAC which is regarded as the "pioneer" for reforms of vast local arbitration commissions in developing *competence-competence* in China. As shown from BAC experience, the reform requires the administrative support from the local people's government, or at least non-interference by the government. BAC is fortunate on this point in being the forerunner owing to the enlightened attitude of BPG towards arbitration. However, the administrative attitude may vary substantially across the country. After all, BAC and BPG set a good example for other local commissions. Before the revision of the Arbitration Law when tribunals' jurisdictional competence is expected to be officially recognised, the transitional mode of "dual-level" institutional efforts may be the best practical way to satisfy the adaptation needs. This is mainly due to the country's deepening economic and administrative transformation where parties (market entities) require more freedom and higher autonomies in arbitration. As such, there have been increasing calls for BAC's practice to be further encouraged among local arbitration commissions. During the process, it might be more feasible to achieve institutional independence before embarking on reforming the rules so that possible administrative interference in rule changing procedures could be prevented. In the end, the remarkable

---

[143]   Article 6(4) of the BAC Rules 2007, available at http://www.bjac.com.cn/en/program/rule.htm.
[144]   See, comments by Wang Wenying, "Comparative Research on Arbitration Rules and Revision of the CIETAC Rules (Zhongcai Guize Bijiao Yanjiu ji Maozhong Guize de Xiugai)", (2006) 94 *Arbitration and Law (Zhongcai yu Falu)*, 22.
[145]   Jerome A. Cohen and Adam Kearney, "Domestic Arbitration: The New Beijing Arbitration Commission", in Freshfields (ed), *Doing Business in China* (The Hague: Kluwer Law International, 2005), s.3.02, IV-3.2.

number of institutional rule liberalisations and their positive feedback from practice will lead to the legislative change in officially recognising the tribunal's jurisdictional autonomy.

(ii) *Administrative challenges*

The adaptation of *competence-competence* in China is concluded to be a chequered process. Over the past decade, gigantic gaps remain between international arbitration norms as the Chinese arbitral jurisdiction is still monopolised by the arbitration commission. However, official legislative efforts in liberalising the tribunal's arbitral autonomy are not encouraging thus far. This legislative discouragement may involve, most recently, the resuming emphasis of the arbitration commission in jurisdictional determination by the most recent SPC Interpretation in 2006. The analysis shows that the transitional market economy and historic administrative prevalence are the two primary reasons leading to the denial of tribunals' jurisdictional competence (albeit they are the real authority for merit adjudication). Such peculiar commission-oriented arbitral jurisdiction has seriously undermined the parties' confidence in arbitration as an autonomous and efficient dispute resolution. Even Chinese arbitration commissions, after long-tolerated administrative control, are disappointed at the delay in the revision of the Arbitration Law. Institutional efforts by some more developed commissions thus arise in the context of the struggle to restore part of the jurisdictional competence from the commission to individual tribunals by reforming the rules. The reform is inaugurated by CIETAC, and subsequently followed by BAC which is regarded as the "pilot project" for reforms of vast local arbitration commissions in developing *competence-competence* in China. The evolution is described as "struggling" for the following reasons. First, the update of the rules builds upon the local experience of the arbitral practice. Secondly, the change deviates from traditional ideologies of arbitral jurisdiction in China. In the end, the lack of official legislative support leaves the institutional efforts with many uncertainties. This represents the informal Chinese way of adaptation.

5.064

On the other hand, despite the fact that commission rules do not carry the force of law, they do promote the practice of arbitration, facilitate the legislative process and imply the adaptive trend. It is thus hoped that the Chinese adaptation process might be propelled and hastened by such a distinctive change of institutional rules. However, except for CIETAC and BAC, there have been significantly few reports of local arbitration commissions following suit. It is possible to deduce that the problem of such slow process is mainly due to the administrative-tainted infrastructure of the vast local arbitration commissions. Their financial and functional reliance on the local people's government foreshadows the reform of institutional independence, and finally hinders the development of institutional rules. This accords with the country's purely institutional arbitration distinction. The development of the parties' autonomy will therefore, in its practical application, be prone to institutional influence such as administrative influence over jurisdiction discussed in the present chapter. BAC's adaptive story tests the feasibility of liberalisation of local arbitration commissions under the current economic and administrative scenario. As shown from BAC experience, realisation of the independence of commissions depends largely on administrative support, or at least on non-interference from the local people's government. Only if institutional independence is realised can the liberal

5.065

rules really support the adaptation. Given the scarce report of the change of the local commissions, it may thus be concluded that the local people's governments may not have been adequately equipped to treat arbitration commissions independently and the vast commissions may not be prepared yet to turn themselves into independent institutions serving the parties' autonomy rather than administrative purposes. This may also help to explain that the desperately slow legislative adaptation of the tribunal's jurisdictional autonomy might arise from legislative concerns about too radical a change from the one to which Chinese arbitration institutions have been accustomed.

5.066   The above concerns emphasise the fact that the development of jurisdictional autonomy (an extension of party autonomy) is not an easy task in China. This is because adaptation depends not only on the progress of the law itself but also on the economic and legal culture and behavior of those involved in relations regulated by the law: in this respect of arbitral jurisdiction, the arbitration commission and related administrative powers surrounding the Chinese social settings. It is thus possible to argue that, in China, the goal of the tribunal's complete independence (an extension of the parties' full autonomy) to rule on its own jurisdiction in line with the international practice still has a long and challenging way to go. To this end, it is noteworthy that the reform represents an institutional challenge to the administrative regime. Institutional reform encourages the development of *competence-competence* and enhances parties' trust in arbitration. The adaptation process is slow and chequered and the degree of adaptation may not be satisfactory thus far. However, the respect for parties' autonomy still progresses, with the aim of achieving an optimal balance where the public could accommodate with the private sector, and the administrative powers with the market.

CHAPTER 6

PANEL ARBITRATOR SYSTEM AND TRIBUNAL FORMATION

Freedom of tribunal formation is critical to party autonomy in any given arbitration system. In China, however, the practice has been controlled under a closed panel system where parties can only appoint arbitrators listed on the panel of the relevant arbitration commission. The past couple of years have seen some leading Chinese arbitration commissions adapting their rules to align with international standards. Chapter 6 will first review the peculiar Chinese closed panel arbitrator system of tribunal formation by critically comparing it with international arbitration norms and practices. The second part will discuss some thorny issues threatening parties' autonomy and interest under the existing closed panel system and as such shed light on some of the practical constraints facing the arbitration system in China today. The final part will comment on institutional initiatives in reforming the situation and their administrative challenges entailed before this chapter ends with some proposals for change.

6.001

1. PANEL ARBITRATOR SYSTEM

One of the most attractive advantages of arbitration is that parties can choose their own adjudicators—the arbitrators. Under international arbitration norms, it is agreed that parties should enjoy full freedom in deciding upon both the criteria for and rules of appointment of their prospective arbitrators.[1] In the Chinese context, however, the practice of appointment is controlled under a panel system whereby parties are restricted to appoint arbitrators on the panel of the relevant arbitration commission.

6.002

(a) Legislative deficiency under the Arbitration Law

The following study attempts to show that the Arbitration Law is deficient in that it fails to provide adequate autonomy to arbitral parties on both the criteria (qualifications) and rules (procedure) for appointing arbitrators. Legislation stipulates the criteria for appointing arbitrators of both Chinese and foreign nationality without specifying the rules of appointment, leaving that to the discretion of arbitration commissions.

6.003

(i) *Controlled criteria for appointment*

Generally, the qualifications for being an arbitrator in China are strict and detailed. However, different qualifications apply in relation to arbitrators sitting on different "tracks" with more relaxed standards applying to arbitrators in foreign-related cases.

6.004

Strict qualifications required in general

Article 13 of the Arbitration Law specifies the key legal requirements for qualification as an arbitrator in China. An arbitrator in China must be righteous and upright, and moreover, meet one of the following conditions:

6.005

---

[1] Arthur L. Marriot, "Some Brief Observations on the Constitution of the Arbitral Tribunal" in Albert Jan van den Berg (ed), *Improving the Efficiency of Arbitration Agreements and Awards: 40 Years of Application of the New York Convention: ICCA Series No. 9* (The Hague: Kluwer Law International, 1999), 324–325.

(1)   have been engaged in arbitration work for at least eight years;

(2)   have worked as a lawyer for at least eight years;

(3)   have served as a judge for at least eight years;

(4)   have been engaged in legal research or legal education, possessing a senior professional title; or

(5)   have acquired knowledge of law, engaged in professional work in the field of economics and trade, possessing a senior professional title or having attained an equivalent professional level.[2]

6.006   Accordingly, art.13 sets forth both the moral and professional qualifications for an arbitrator in China:[3] (a) an arbitrator must be a morally impeachable person who is regarded as upright and impartial by the public; (b) he/she must have sufficient years of expertise in some special areas such as law, trade and economics.[4]

6.007   In other parts of the world, an arbitrator's qualifications are regulated in two ways: first, the legislation defines professional conditions that a person must possess to become an arbitrator (strict qualification); secondly, the legislation allows the parties to freely choose arbitrators subject only to morality requirements and general principles of law (common qualification).[5] It is rare practice for a country to decide upon the professional competence of arbitrators on behalf of the parties.[6] As Song observes, most developed arbitration states have adopted the "common" approach to qualifying arbitrators, with China and Taiwan being the only two exceptions.[7] Based on his research, China sets particularly high and strict professional conditions in qualifying arbitrators as compared with those of their counterpart—judges.[8] Articles 9 and 12 of the Judges' Law of the PRC state the professional conditions to be qualified as a Chinese judge:

---

[2]   Article 13 of the Arbitration Law.

[3]   Legislative Affairs Commission of the NPCSC of the PRC (ed), *Arbitration Laws of China* (Hong Kong: Sweet & Maxwell Asia, 1997), 49.

[4]   *Ibid.*, 49–50.

[5]   Song Lianbin, "From Ideology to Rules: Several Issues that should be Noted for the Amendment of Arbitration Law (Linian Zouxiang Guize: Zhongcaifa Xiuding ying Zhuyi de Jige Wenti)", (2005) 52 *Arbitration in Beijing (Beijing Zhongcai)*, 5.

[6]   For example, the Arbitration Ordinance (Cap.341) does not include specific provisions regulating the professional qualifications for arbitrators, but the Ordinance does require that arbitrators should act fairly and impartially. See s.2GA of the Arbitration Ordinance.

[7]   Song, "From Ideology to Rules: Several Issues that should be Noted for the Amendment of Arbitration Law" (2005), 4–5. For example, the Taiwan Arbitration Act stipulates strict qualifications: (a) have served as a judge or a prosecutor; or (b) have practiced as a lawyer, accountant, architect, engineer or as a professional in other commercial fields for at least five years; or (c) have been appointed as arbitrators in arbitration cases of domestic or foreign arbitration institutions; or (d) have taken a position of assistant professor or above for at least five years in domestic or foreign colleges or universities that are recognised by Taiwan Department of Educations; or (e) have specialised knowledge or technology relating to a specialised field and have worked in the field for at least five years.

[8]   Song, "From Ideology to Rules: Several Issues that should be Noted for the Amendment of Arbitration Law" (2005), 6.

(1)   to pass the national judicial examination;[9] and

(2)   to have two to three years experience engaged in legal work after graduating
       from university or college; or three to four years of legal work for qualifying
       in a provincial higher people's court or the Supreme People's Court.[10]

There is thus an eye-catching difference in the legal qualifications for arbitrators   **6.008**
and judges. While an arbitrator is required to have eight years of legal or judicial
experience or of a senior professional title in the field of trade and economics, a judge
may be admitted as long as he/she engages in legal work for two years after passing
the judicial exam.[11] The legislative provisions further state that university graduates
have to work for about ten years before they can obtain a senior professional title.[12]
Thus, while the work of judges is quite similar to that of arbitrators and arbitrators
are required to apply the same laws in the adjudication of cases, the professional
qualifications required by the Arbitration Law for arbitrators are far more stringent
than those required for judges.

Separate qualifications for dual tracks

On the other hand, Chapter 7 of the Arbitration Law, which deals specifically   **6.009**
with foreign-related arbitrations, contains a stipulation in art.67 dedicated to the
appointment of foreign arbitrators:

> "A foreign-related arbitration commission may appoint arbitrators from among foreigners
> with special knowledge in the fields of law, economics and trade, science and technology,
> etc."[13]

It is noteworthy that art.67 does not make reference to the requirements under art.13.   **6.010**
The appointment of foreign arbitrators is thus not subject to art.13 restrictions and
there are no specific qualifications required of foreigners (including residents of Hong
Kong, Macao and Taiwan)[14] to serve as arbitrators. The "specialist in a particular
field" requirement does not contain specific implementation rules such as established
years of experience or the like. The criteria for foreign arbitrators thus appear more
discretionary and more relaxed than the criteria for domestic arbitrators. Further, only
foreign-related arbitration commissions (i.e. China International Economic and Trade
Arbitration Commission (CIETAC) and China Maritime Arbitration Commission
(CMAC)) were entitled to appoint foreign arbitrators until the later blurring of the
jurisdictions. As noted previously, there is no longer any bifurcation between the two
types of arbitration commissions since the promulgation of the "1996 Notice" by the
State Council, pursuant to which CIETAC and CMAC are no longer privileged to handle

---

[9]   Article 9 of the Judges' Law, effective from 28 February 1995.
[10]   Article 12 of the Judges' Law.
[11]   The National Judicial Exam is a uniform exam for qualifying not only the judges but also lawyers and prosecutors
       as well. See art.2 of the Implementing Measure on National Judicial Examination, effective from 1 January 2002.
[12]   Legislative Affairs Commission of the NPCSC of the PRC, *Arbitration Laws of China* (1997), 50.
[13]   Article 67 of the Arbitration Law.
[14]   Hong Kong, Macao and Taiwan-based arbitrators are considered as foreign arbitrators, and cases involving
       elements from these three jurisdictions are considered as foreign-related cases.

exclusively foreign-related cases. As such, local commissions may have jurisdiction over international disputes and they can now appoint foreign arbitrators to their panels for settling international disputes. By the same token, and subsequent to their rules update in 1998, CIETAC and CMAC may also have domestic panel lists to satisfy domestic needs. Over the past decade, however, the Arbitration Law has neither been updated nor have the controversies between the legislation and practice been resolved.

6.011   The overwhelming impression therefore is that preferential treatment has been reserved for parties in foreign-related arbitration. By reference to the legislative annotations, the dual-track criteria for arbitrators' appointments, or more precisely, the more relaxed criteria for foreign arbitrators, were aimed at internationalisation of China's foreign-related arbitrations and expediting and expanding China's economic and trade relations with other countries.[15] This is understandable in the initial period when the Arbitration Law was put into effect. However, with the convergence of the two types of arbitration commissions, is maintaining the separate qualifications for arbitrators still justifiable? The failure of the Arbitration Law updates brings about many implementation problems and causes discriminative treatment among both the parties and the arbitrators as will be looked into in the following discussions.

(ii) *Controlled rules of appointment*

6.012   The legislative control over the parties' autonomy in tribunal formation is further extended to the procedural rules of appointment. Such control is exercised under a dual-tier mechanism: (a) the Arbitration Law authorises the arbitration commissions to appoint the arbitrators through a panel system; (b) should the parties fail to appoint from the panel list, the chairman of the arbitration commission will step in as the default appointing authority.

Appointment from the arbitration commission panel list

6.013   At the first stage, institutional control is not apparent as the Arbitration Law does not expressly provide for a panel system. However, upon close examination, the panel system may be inferred from arts.11 and 13.

6.014   The last paragraph of art.13 states that an arbitration commission must have a registered panel list of arbitrators.[16] This corresponds to s.4 of art.11, which requires that a Chinese arbitration commission must have its own appointed arbitrators listed on the panels to be formulated.[17] Pursuant to these provisions, arbitrators are selected from among qualified persons and appointed by the arbitration commission.[18] The names on the panel lists thus become a pool for the parties' appointment of arbitrators when forming tribunals in an individual case. Therefore, even if some person satisfies the legislative qualifications under art.13 (or art.67 for foreign nationals), he/she still cannot be appointed by parties, subject to further institutional control under the Arbitration Law jurisprudence. This indicates the country's institutional adherence

---

[15]   Legislative Affairs Commission of the NPCSC of the PRC, *Arbitration Laws of China* (1997), 90.
[16]   Article 13 of the Arbitration Law.
[17]   Article 11 of the Arbitration Law.
[18]   Legislative Affairs Commission of the NPCSC of the PRC, *Arbitration Laws of China* (1997), 47.

in arbitration. In one respect, the panel arbitrator system is adopted to satisfy the institutional establishment of the arbitration commissions; whilst in another respect, China, through these institution panel lists, enables the commissions to oversee the channels under which a certain person may or may not be appointed.

Default appointment by the arbitration commission chairman

At the second stage, the fact that an arbitration commission's chairman will act as the defaulting appointment authority is further indicative of the level of institutional control. Pursuant to arts.31 and 32 of the Arbitration Law, if the tribunal is composed of three arbitrators, then each of the two parties will appoint one arbitrator from the commission panel list, and the third presiding arbitrator will be jointly appointed by the two parties. However, should the parties fail to exercise the appointment within the time limit or fail to reach an agreement on the appointment of the presiding arbitrator, they will jointly entrust the chairman of the arbitration commission to make the appointment.[19]

6.015

Accordingly, the chairman of the commission becomes particularly important due to its power of direct appointment of arbitrators when the parties fail to appoint them.[20] Although it is not uncommon for the sake of procedural efficiency to have a default appointing authority provided by legislation, the key emphasis is whether the authority is independent and impartial in making the decision. Unfortunately, as observed by Professor Jerome Cohen,[21] such independence and impartiality may hardly be attained in China in view of the administrative structure of Chinese arbitration commissions[22] which would more often than not be compelled to appoint local officials as arbitrators in domestic cases and Chinese nationals as arbitrators in international cases.[23] This critique is shared by an active arbitration commentator, Tao Jingzhou,[24] who has raised serious concerns regarding the default power of the commission chairman to appoint a presiding arbitrator in international cases. Based on his experience as an arbitrator in CIETAC cases over a decade, Tao remarked that "the chairman usually, with very few exceptions, appoints Chinese nationals as presiding arbitrator".[25] This provides an opportunity for the Chinese presiding arbitrator to impose his/her ruling in the final award[26] and the foreign party may consider him/herself disadvantaged, if not prejudiced, under a somewhat alien environment. These practical concerns will be addressed in more detail in a comparison with international arbitration norms and practices.

6.016

---

[19] Articles 31 and 32 of the Arbitration Law.

[20] Legislative Affairs Commission of the NPCSC of the PRC, *Arbitration Laws of China* (1997), 70.

[21] Jerome A. Cohen is Professor of Law at New York University Law School, and one of the earliest and most renowned foreign arbitrators appointed by CIETAC.

[22] See discussions above on the administrative infrastructure of the arbitration commissions, the personnel constituents in particular, under the heading "Problems of the Arbitration Commission Infrastructure" in Chapter 5.

[23] Jerome A. Cohen, "Time to Fix China's Arbitration", (2005) 168 *Far Eastern Economic Review*, January 2005, 31. See also, discussions below under the heading "Hidden Obstacles to Tribunal Formation".

[24] Tao Jingzhou is recognised as an expert in international trade, arbitration and serves as the Chair of the Commission on International Commercial Arbitration of ICC China and the listed arbitrator of both CIETAC and the Hong Kong International Arbitration Centre.

[25] Jingzhou Tao, *Arbitration Law and Practice in China* (The Hague: Kluwer Law International, 2004), para 294.

[26] Article 53 of the Arbitration Law provides that, when the tribunal is unable to reach a majority opinion, the arbitral award shall be made in accordance with the opinion of the presiding arbitrator.

(iii) *Legislative intent on the controlled approach*

6.017   It may be recalled that during the drafting of the Arbitration Law, there was heated debate as to whether the State should control the criteria and rules of the appointment of an arbitrator. The arguments were primarily divided into two groups. The first group opined that the strict qualifications and appointment channels were aimed at guaranteeing the quality of arbitrators.[27] To the extent that the quality of arbitration depends largely on the quality of arbitrators, it may be justifiable for the conditions to be as detailed as possible. However, such justifications were soon overhauled by the second group of opinions which focused upon the stability and continuity of existing arbitrators within arbitration commissions during the transitional period. They argued that "the new appointment must solve the problem of those arbitrators who had been working for the commissions prior to the implementation of the Arbitration Law".[28] Thus, in accordance with the practical situation existing at the time and to maintain the stability of arbitration work in the post-Arbitration Law period, the criteria were incorporated into art.13 of the new law.[29] The legislative intent to preserve the existing pool of arbitrators is particularly evident from art.13(1) which allows any person with eight years' of work experience in the area of arbitration to be admitted.[30] Apparently, many ex-arbitrators prior to the adoption of the Arbitration Law have been saved by this provision.

6.018   On the procedural rules of appointment, Dr Qiao Xin revealed in her study of arbitral power that due to the inertia of planned economy where the State controlled all economic activities, the Chinese legislature did not entrust parties in an arbitration to appoint their adjudicators because dispute resolution relates to social order and is somewhat "public"; therefore the legislature authorised the commissions to do so on behalf of the parties.[31] This comment is helpful in that it reflects the controlling ideologies embedded in the Arbitration Law. Fundamentally, research shows that the legislature is inclined towards the notion of control over arbitration.

(b) Distinctive features of the commission panel

6.019   The commission panel has three salient features. First, arbitration commissions have discretion in qualifying arbitrators to their panel lists. Secondly, following the dual-track legislative distinction under the Arbitration Law, separate panels are maintained for the appointment of arbitrators from domestic and foreign nationals. Thirdly, and most controversially, parties have to appoint arbitrators from the particular panel list of the relevant commission to which their case belongs (i.e. either domestic or foreign-related). This part of the discussions intends to illustrate in depth the peculiar

---

[27] Wang Shengming and Xu Xiuchun, "Several Issues on the Arbitration Law (Guanyu Zhongcaifa de Ruogan Wenti)" in the Research Office of the Legislative Affairs Office of the State Council (ed.), *Handbook on Reorganizing Arbitration Institutions (Chongxin Zujian Zhongcai Jigou Shouce)* (Beijing: China Legal System Publishing, 1995), 17–53.

[28] Wang and Xu, "Several Issues on the Arbitration Law", *ibid.,* 28.

[29] Legislative Affairs Commission of the NPCSC of the PRC, *Arbitration Laws of China* (1997), 50.

[30] Article 13(1) of the Arbitration Law.

[31] Qiao Xin, *The Studies on Arbitral Power—Procedural Justice and Right Protection of Arbitration (Zhongcai Quan Yanjiu—Zhongcai zhi Chengxu Gongzheng yu Quanli Baozhang)* (Beijing: China Law Press, 2001), Chapter 3.

institutional closed panel system of the tribunal formation in China in preparing for the comparative analyses with international arbitration norms and practices in the forthcoming section.

(i) *Institutional discretion for qualifications*

Under Chapter 4 of the Model Constitution of Arbitration Commissions (the Model Constitution) issued by the State Council in 1995,[32] each commission is allowed to interpret the requirements of art.13 of the Arbitration Law as they see fit.[33] Accordingly, there are no uniform standards for the enlisting of arbitrators among different arbitration commissions across the country; the Arbitration Law merely provides the minimum standard,[34] on which basis each commission then develops its own qualifications for appointing arbitrators to the particular panels.

6.020

For instance, in addition to art.13 requirements, CIETAC and CMAC have jointly promulgated the Stipulations for the Appointment of Arbitrators (the Stipulations).[35] In its most recent version of 2005, the Stipulations require three more professional conditions for being a Chinese arbitrator on the panels of CIETAC and CMAC; that he/she:

6.021

(1)   is willing to observe the Rules, including the Ethical Rules for Arbitrators[36] and other relevant regulations of CIETAC and CMAC;[37]

(2)   has a good grasp of a foreign language and can adopt it as a working language; and

(3)   can guarantee the time to handle the cases under the Rules.[38]

On the other hand, following the dual-track criteria for foreign and domestic arbitrators under the Arbitration Law,[39] the Stipulations provide for different qualifications for the appointment of foreign arbitrators. In addition to art.67 conditions, foreign nationals are

6.022

---

[32]   The Model Constitution of Arbitration Commission, issued by the State Council on 28 July 1995.

[33]   See Chapter 4 of the Model Constitution entitled "Arbitrator". This chapter sets out the guiding procedural rules applicable to the panel appointment by an arbitration commission:
(1)   The appointment should be recommended by the Chairman's meeting of the arbitration commission, and be endorsed by the general meeting of the arbitration commission concerned.
(2)   The term of an appointed arbitrator is three years and is renewable at the end of the term.
(3)   An arbitration commission could maintain panels of arbitrators according to their professions.
(4)   The names of the panel arbitrators should be reported to the Arbitration Association of China for filing purposes.

[34]   Tao, *Arbitration Law and Practice in China* (2004), para 255.

[35]   Stipulations for the Appointment of Arbitrators, jointly promulgated by CIETAC and CMAC on 1 September 1995, revised on 1 September 2000 and 24 January 2005, respectively.

[36]   The Ethical Rules for Arbitrators provide details regarding the conduct and behaviour expected of an arbitrator in undertaking an arbitration. It reiterates the duty of an arbitrator to remain independent and impartial in conducting the arbitration, to thoroughly and meticulously examine all the evidence, and to be both fair and reasonable in assessing and determining the merits of the arguments presented by the disputing parties. The Ethical Rules are available at http://www.cietac.org.cn/index_english.asp.

[37]   Once appointed, arbitrators must carry out their functions in accordance with the law and the Ethical Rules for Arbitrators to regulate the conduct of arbitrators.

[38]   Article 2(1) of the Stipulations (2005), at http://www.cietac.org.cn/shiwu/zhongcaishiwu.asp?type=sw4.

[39]   See discussions above under the heading "Legislative Deficiency Under the Arbitration Law".

asked "to observe the rules and regulations of the arbitration commission and to have some knowledge of Chinese".[40] These conditions provide some comparable requirements to the appointment of Chinese arbitrators so that discriminative impressions may be alleviated.[41] However, "the appointing terms can be loosened appropriately"[42] and such discretionary "loosening of the terms" may nevertheless imply discriminations. Moreover, it is evident that the requirements for the appointment of foreign arbitrators are less restrictive than those applicable to their Chinese counterparts.

6.023   Local arbitration commissions have also formulated their own sets of standards in arbitrator appointment. Among them, the most prominent local commission, the Beijing Arbitration Commission (BAC), issued its own Administrative Measures for the Engagement of Arbitrators (the Administrative Measures).[43] According to the most updated Measures in 2006,[44] to qualify as a Chinese arbitrator of BAC, an individual must satisfy all the following conditions, including:

(1)   comply with the relevant Rules[45] of BAC;

(2)   act independently and handle cases effectively and efficiently;

(3)   have the record of service, knowledge and experience in a specialised field as required by art.3 of the Administrative Measures;[46] and

---

[40]   Article 2(2)(5) of the Stipulations, see fn 35 above.

[41]   Wang Wenying, "Comparative Studies on Arbitration Rules and the Amendment of the CIETAC Rules (Zhongcai Guize Bijiao Yanjiu ji Maozhong Guize de Xiugai)", (2005) 94 *Arbitration and Law (Zhongcai yu Falu)*, 26.

[42]   Article 2(2)(5) of the Stipulations, see fn 35 above.

[43]   Administrative Measures for the Engagement of Arbitrators of BAC, formulated by BAC in October 1999, and revised in 2001, 2004, 2006, respectively. The 2006 Administrative Measures are available at the BAC webpage: http://www.bjac.com.cn/arbiter/aptitude.htm.

[44]   The current Measures were passed by BAC on 14 August and effective from 1 September 2006.

[45]   The relevant rules of BAC include the Arbitration Rules, the Ethical Standards for Arbitrators, the Several Provisions on Raising Arbitration Efficiency and the Administrative Measures.

[46]   BAC prescribes in art.3 special conditions for persons from different professional fields. These specific-field-related qualifications are as follows:
(1)   For those engaged in legal education or research, they must have possessed a senior professional title of professor, research fellow, etc., or of associate professor, associate research fellow with doctor's degree and outstanding competence in the case handling with abundant education or research experience in civil or commercial law.
(2)   For those who are lawyers, they must have obtained a master's or higher degree; or, to have obtained a bachelor's degree but have acted as a presiding/sole arbitrator on many occasions, with outstanding competence and abundant experience in the case handling. Further, he or she shall have a higher level of speciality and good reputation in the Bar, without any violation of disciplines or ill fame.
(3)   For those engaged in economic and trade activities, they must have possessed a senior title of the technical post in his/her own profession; or to have possessed associate senior title with a master's or higher degree. Further he or she shall have been engaged in economic and trade activity or in the professional and technical work for at least eight years with relevant knowledge of law and abundant experience.
(4)   For those who are retired or resigned judges, they must have a bachelor's degree above in law and have been engaged in the trying of civil or economic disputes consecutively over a long period of time, then within two years, they could be appointed. The conditions can be loosened for those prestige judges such as chief justice or deputy presiding judge or other higher than those with good reputation in the speciality and outstanding competence in the case handling.
(5)   For those dealing with other legal affairs, they must have obtained a bachelor's degree above in law, and to have obtained the senior title such as senior economist, senior engineer, or to have taken office of leadership post such as a division chief or a higher officer in an organ of legislation, law enforcement or other legal affairs, or to have taken office of the deputy chief and yet handled arbitration or litigation cases for many times with outstanding competence.

(4)   be less than 66 years of age; as to those having served as a presiding/sole arbitrator numerous times, being very experienced, the above age requirement can be relaxed but must not exceed the age of 75 in principle.[47]

On the other hand, a person from Hong Kong, Macao, Taiwan or other countries who wishes to qualify as an arbitrator of BAC only needs to have abundant experience in arbitration practice and be able to devote adequate time and attention to handling cases.[48] As with the legislative traditions of giving preferential treatment to the foreign-related regime, these conditions are also more relaxed compared to those applicable to the domestic regime.[49]   **6.024**

Two points may be observed after comparing the appointment criteria of CIETAC with that of BAC. First, in qualifying Chinese arbitrators, BAC sets stricter and higher standards than CIETAC. Secondly, both CIETAC and BAC set different standards for Chinese and foreign arbitrators, with the requirements for foreigners being more discretionary. Arbitration commissions therefore exercise considerable power in the appointment of arbitrators. The requirements in the Arbitration Law are just preliminary qualifications, leaving the final criteria of appointment for arbitration commissions to decide. The actual parameters for arbitrators to become qualified and listed hence essentially depend on the discretion of the particular commission, and the qualifications could vary from commission to commission as the CIETAC and BAC cases above show.[50] However, within a commission, as with the country's dual-track arbitration tradition, different sets of qualifications are established on the basis of nationality with foreigners enjoying fewer constraints in getting listed.   **6.025**

(ii) *Separate panels for dual tracks*

The separate qualifications have resulted in separate panels within a commission. For example, CIETAC has prepared both a Panel List of Arbitrators for Domestic Cases (*Guonei Zhengyi Zhongcaiyuan Mingce*) (the Domestic Panel) and a Panel List of Arbitrators for International Cases (*Guoji/Shewai Zhengyi Zhongcaiyuan Mingce*) (the International Panel). The Domestic Panel includes only Chinese arbitrators whilst both Chinese and foreign nationals are on the International Panel.[51] So far, the CIETAC International Panel list is comprised of some 700 arbitrators, among whom over 500 are Chinese nationals.[52]   **6.026**

A comparison of the two panel lists reveals some key defects of the system. To begin with, the names of the same Chinese arbitrators appear on both the Domestic and International Panel lists. To that extent, it might be arguable that CIETAC discriminates against foreign nationals in arbitrating domestic cases.   **6.027**

---

[47]   Article 2 of the Administrative Measures (2006).
[48]   Article 4 of the Administrative Measures.
[49]   *Ibid*.
[50]   The control of the qualifications of arbitrators by arbitration commission may be further reflected by their control on the rules of removal of arbitrators who may breach the stipulated code of conduct formulated under the discretion of each arbitration commission.
[51]   See the Domestic and International Panels of Arbitrators, promulgated by CIETAC, effective from 1 May 2005.
[52]   *Ibid*.

6.028   Of the remaining 200 foreign arbitrators sitting on the International Panel, 40 were drawn from Hong Kong, Macao and Taiwan and the remaining 160 were drawn from other countries and regions. However, some of the foreign countries are represented by a very limited number of arbitrators. In other words, if the parties from those countries opt for CIETAC arbitration, there would be hardly any favourable arbitrator candidates for choice. The imbalance of nationalities on the fixed panel seriously challenges the impartiality of CIETAC tribunals. Most importantly, pursuant to the CIETAC Instructions on the Application of the Panels of Arbitrators (the Instructions), a particular panel is only applicable to a particular type of arbitration cases, i.e. parties are obliged to select and appoint arbitrators only from the panel list relevant to the nature of their case (domestic or foreign-related).[53] Thus, parties to foreign-related cases generally have more options than parties to domestic cases because they can appoint both Chinese arbitrators and arbitrators from Hong Kong, Macao, Taiwan and other foreign countries. Concerns have been raised with respect to Chinese foreign investment enterprises, which are deemed to be domestic entities under PRC Law and may therefore lose the opportunity to appoint foreign arbitrators from the CIETAC International Panel.[54]

6.029   However, local arbitration commissions may now draw on international experts when compiling their panels of arbitrators for foreign-related disputes. For example, the current BAC Panel (*Beizhong Mingce*) has 309 arbitrators listed, 49 of whom have a foreign nationality background.[55] The Shenzhen Arbitration Commission (SZAC) and Shanghai Arbitration Commission (SAC), however, have only 28 and 26 foreign nationals appointed to their 409-arbitrator SZAC Panel (*Shengzhong Mingce*)[56] and 436-arbitrator SAC Panel (*Shangzhong Mingce*),[57] respectively.

6.030   There are a couple of observations on the local commission panels as well. In the first place, the composition of foreign arbitrators within the local panels varies from commission to commission. It is interesting to note that whilst BAC enjoys a higher share of international arbitrators (15 per cent) on its entire panel list, the figures in SZAC and SAC are far lower. On the other hand, SZAC and SAC have a larger pool of arbitrators in general. It is fair to argue that the more the number of arbitrators listed, the more choices parties can enjoy; and the more internationalised the arbitrators that are listed, the more internationalised the local commission will be, as the parties' choices of arbitrators could be more diversified. Secondly, rather than following the dual-track practice of CIETAC, some local commissions have maintained a unified panel list for the appointment of both domestic and international arbitrators notwithstanding the different qualifications imposed on them. Dr Lin Yifei of the CIETAC South-China Sub-Commission Secretariat praises such practice in his recently published studies

---

[53]   Articles 1 and 2 of the Instructions on the Application of the Panels of Arbitrators, promulgated by CIETAC and with effect from 1 May 2005.
[54]   Denis Brock and Kathryn Sanger, "The Arbitration Agreement and Arbitrators" in Daniel R. Fung and Wang Shengchang (eds), *Arbitration in China: A Practical Guide* (Hong Kong: Sweet & Maxwell Asia, 2004), para 8-63.
[55]   See the Panel List of Arbitrators of BAC, accessible at: http://www.bjac.com.cn/arbiter/roster.htm.
[56]   See the Panel List of Arbitrators of SZAC, accessible at: http://www.szac.org/mien_01.asp?currentpage=30&by mode=&Cate=&Name=.
[57]   See the Panel List of Arbitrators of SAC, accessible at: http://www.accsh.org/accsh/node8/node36/index.html.

on arbitrators, analysing some possible reasons that might have led to the merging of the Domestic and International Panel lists. In a positive respect, some local commissions unify the separate lists to make the system of appointment more user-friendly. And the practice tends to serve as one of the selling points in the arbitration market versus CIETAC or other local commissions that are still using separate lists. On a negative note, local commissions do not have as many international arbitrators as CIETAC. The small number of foreign arbitrators may explain why it has not been worthwhile for separate lists to be maintained.[58] He points out, in particular, that unifying dual-track panels could help multiply parties' options and thus contribute to more autonomous arbitrations in China.[59] Dr Lin fails to take into account, however, that although commissions such as BAC, SZAC and SAC do not separate the panels, parties to domestic disputes are nevertheless restricted to appointing arbitrators with Chinese nationality.[60] In this sense, a unified panel system in these local arbitration commissions seems superficial as the bifurcations and the restrictions on the parties' choices nevertheless exist.

(iii) *Compulsory appointment under the closed panels*

Although the Arbitration Law does not provide explicitly that arbitrators must be appointed from the listed panels of the particular commissions,[61] commission rules in China generally only permit persons listed with a particular commission to act as arbitrators in the arbitral proceedings conducted by that particular commission.[62] The CIETAC Rules, before the 2005 update, required parties to choose arbitrators from the panel list relevant to the nature of the case.[63] For local commissions, the same closed-panel approach has also been unanimously taken under the current rules of BAC, SAC and SZAC.[64]   **6.031**

Dr Wang Wenying of the CIETAC Research Institute studied arbitral power and concluded that there are adequate reasons for the implementation of the closed panel   **6.032**

---

[58] Lin Yifei, "The Multiple Arbitration Institutions – Proposition to the Development Mode of the Chinese Arbitration Institutions (Duomen Zhongcai Jigou – Zhongguo Zhongcai Jigou Fazhan Moshi Shexiang)", (2005) 55 *Arbitration in Beijing (Beijing Zhongcai)*, 1–11.

[59] *Ibid.,* 10.

[60] For example, see art.1 of the Regulations of the Appointment of Arbitrators of BAC *(Beijing Zhongcai Weiyuanhui Zhongcaiyuan Pingren Guifan)*, available at: http://www.bjac.cn/arbiter/guifan.htm; see also art.1 of the Instructions of the Panel of Arbitrators of the SAC *(Shanghai Zhongcai Weiyuanhui "Zhongcaiyuan Mingce" Shiyong Xuzhi)*, available at: http://www.accsh.org/accsh/node8/node37/index.html; SZAC has no such regulations or instructions as to the usage of the panel list.

[61] Legislative Affairs Commission of the NPCSC of the PRC, *Arbitration Laws of China* (1997), 50.

[62] John Mo, *Arbitration Law in China* (Hong Kong: Sweet & Maxwell, 2001), para 5.03.

[63] See art.24 of the 2000 CIETAC Rules, accessible at http://www.cietac.org.cn/shiwu/zhongcaishiwu.asp?type=sw3. In the latest update of its 2005 Rules, the CIETAC has relaxed its hands in allowing parties choices off the list under certain conditions; see discussions below under the heading "Specific Reform for Widening Parties' Choices in Tribunal Formation".

[64] See art.17 of the 2006 BAC Rules, accessible at www.bjac.com/cn/program/rule.htm; art.24 of the 2005 SAC Rules, accessible at www.accsh.org/accsh/rode5/index.htm; and art.32 of the 2001 SZAC Rules, accessible at www.szac.org/guide_003.asp.

system in China.[65] She emphasised the fact that since China is far from being a mature arbitration community, parties may not be able to make "rational" decisions regarding appointment on the one hand and arbitrators may not conscientiously observe professional ethics on the other hand.[66] As such, the closed panel system under which compulsory appointment has developed might help to guarantee the high quality of arbitration via the commission's strict examination of arbitrator qualifications.[67] Dr Song Lianbin later analysed the possible causes of the parties' lack of "rationality" in making the appointment of an arbitrator.[68] According to him, relationships (*guanxi*) could lead people to appoint persons with good relations with them rather than with strong qualifications.[69] This analysis might provide some hints regarding why the rules of Chinese arbitration commissions unanimously require the parties to appoint arbitrators from among their own panels of arbitrators.[70]

6.033   Despite the foregoing, having a closed and compulsory panel system invites questions regarding both party autonomy and arbitral impartiality. The situation could be aggravated by the parties' limited access to arbitrators' information. Panel information put on commission websites and brochures, in most cases, only includes the name, profession, specialities and city or country of residence of each panel member.[71] How can parties rely on the "thin" information to make a "rational" appointment? The limited or inadequate information on arbitrators on the panel list is one serious problem in Chinese arbitration that hinders the parties' procedural autonomy.[72] Aware of the problem, some commissions have since enhanced the information available about arbitrators on the panel list. Among them, BAC has supplemented information with respect to the "nationality" and "working language" of the arbitrators,[73] whilst CIETAC has just commenced uploading the resumes of the panel-listed arbitrators on their website if the arbitrators themselves do not object.[74] Notwithstanding these efforts, information regarding arbitrators' background and independence remains insufficient. As observed by Professor Cohen, the network of *guanxi* could be very wide within the relatively small group of practitioners from which legal counsels,

---

[65]   Wang Wenying, Director of the CIETAC Research Institute, *Arbitral Power in the People's Republic of China: Reality and Reform* (Thesis for the degree of SJD at the University of Hong Kong, 2004), 235–237, available in the Law Library of the University of Hong Kong. The author is grateful to Dr Wang for her permission of the access to her first-hand research materials during the author's studies.

[66]   *Ibid.*, 236.

[67]   *Ibid.*

[68]   Song, "From Ideology to Rules – Several Issues Worthy of Attention in Revising the Arbitration Law" (2005), 6.

[69]   In Chinese culture, relations (*guanxi*) seem to be more important than professional qualities. This traditional culture still influences the behaviours of Chinese people today. Lawyers who have good relations with judges of courts may have more opportunities to be chosen as counsels than those with high level in legal qualifications. Similarly, parties may prefer to appoint arbitrators with good relations to them than those with high qualifications.

[70]   Mo, *Arbitration Law in China* (2001), para 5.03.

[71]   As the author learned from Professor Liu Xiaohong, a panelled arbitrator of the SAC, more often than not, she is appointed by the friends' recommendations of their own experience of personal affiliations, etc. rather than by the parties' mere utilisation of the panel information.

[72]   Chen Luming, "International Commercial Arbitration in China", (1996) 13 *Journal of International Arbitration*, 145.

[73]   See Panel List of BAC, at: http://www.bjac.com.cn/en/images/Arbitrators.pdf.

[74]   See Panel List of CIETAC, the resume can be accessed via clicking on the section of "Details", available at http://www.cietac.org.cn/Query/zhongcaiyuannew.asp?type=sy.

arbitrators and arbitration administrators (commission staff members) are drawn.[75] It is not uncommon in CIETAC practice to have a law professor to serve as the legal counsel of one party who happens to be supervising the doctoral thesis of the arbitrator or even the CIETAC administrator.[76] The closed panel system and its associated problems have seriously restricted parties' autonomy and diminished their confidence in the impartiality of Chinese arbitration.[77]

(iv) *Comments on commission practice*

In summary, the Chinese practice of arbitrator appointment gives a strong impression of state control. It is noteworthy that state control has been extended and stressed through the practice of institutional control by arbitration commissions—the Arbitration Law legally supports the commissions' discretion in not only controlling the qualifications but also the procedure of appointment of arbitrators. Specifically, each individual commission formulates its own set of qualifying criteria and these criteria vary from commission to commission. For the rules of appointment, institutional control has been deployed in a dual-layer manner: the compulsory requirement for arbitrators to be qualified onto a commission's listing panel; and the compulsory selection from the fixed panel in the formation of the individual tribunals. In international commercial arbitration, few institutional rules require that the arbitrator must appear on a list maintained by the institution to become qualified.[78] China is perhaps one of the few jurisdictions in the world that restricts parties' choice of arbitrators to a fixed panel maintained by the arbitration institutions.[79]

6.034

Many have argued for abolishing the closed panel system. Among the advocates, some foreign practitioners have expressed disappointment when their clients had to appoint arbitrator(s) who may not have been fit for the case in terms of either nationality or qualifications. The situation could be even more serious as parties' access to the information about potential arbitrators is generally quite limited. As Johnson Tan (managing partner of Jones Day[80] Beijing Office) expressed recently, "sometimes, to appoint an arbitrator from the CIETAC panel list is just like a game of finding a worse candidate by kicking off the worst. And the people chosen never represent the best as

6.035

---

[75] Cohen, "Time to Fix China's Arbitration" (2005), 31–37.

[76] Professor Cohen presents one another example which he experience himself as cases of conflicts of interest. He discovered that the advocate for the respondent had, without public announcement, become a Vice Chairman of CIETAC shortly before the hearing. That meant the presiding arbitrator was the subordinate of the other side's advocate. Nevertheless, at the outset of the hearing, when the presiding arbitrator asked whether the parties wished to disqualify any arbitrator, neither the presiding arbitrator nor the advocate thought it necessary to reveal this crucial fact. Professor Cohen commented in his article that CIETAC should be at fault due to its negligent or intentional failure of its personnel to make necessary disclosure. *Ibid.*, 34.

[77] See discussions further on this topic below under the heading "General Reform in Respecting Parties' Procedural Autonomy".

[78] Julian D.M. Lew, *Comparative International Commercial Arbitration* (The Hague: Kluwer Law International, 2003), para 10-43.

[79] See Ramon J. Alvins and Victorino J. Tejera-Prerez, *The International Comparative Legal Guide to: International Arbitration* (London: Global Legal Group, 2004), Chapter 41.

[80] Jones Day (Jones Day, Reavis & Pogue LLP) is one of the earliest international law firms that open Chinese business. Jones Day currently has Beijing, Shanghai, Hong Kong and Taipei Offices in conducting the legal services to foreign customers.

we do not know and are not allowed to know the potentials at all".[81] Chinese academics have also argued vigorously that the system restricts the right of the parties to have complete autonomy regarding who should determine the dispute between them.[82] Against this backdrop, international arbitration norms and practices still serve the best guidance to identify the practical gaps and encourage future reforms in China's arbitration system.

(c) Gap with international arbitration norms and practices

(i) *Qualifications for appointment: Strict vs liberal*

6.036   First, international arbitration norms relax the conditions for a person to be qualified as an arbitrator in that any person should enjoy the right to be selected and appointed. For example, the Model Law allows the parties to choose arbitrators freely subject only to morality requirements. Thus, the Model Law does not specify explicit restrictions on arbitrators' qualifications as long as the parties are satisfied with the appointee's impartiality and independence.[83] The states that have adopted the Model Law generally follow the more relaxed traditions of the Model Law and require only minimum qualifications for arbitrators, such as having the civil capacity to be appointed.[84]

6.037   By the same token, the Rules of the International Chamber of Commerce Court of Arbitration (ICC) provide that parties should enjoy complete freedom in agreeing on the criteria of arbitrators. As opposed to the defining of the arbitrators' qualifications and appointment of them, under art.9(1) of the Rules, the ICC Court is only tasked with "confirming" the parties' free appointment (i.e. acting upon nominations made by the parties) in order to ensure the tribunal appointed satisfies the Rules' requirement of independence and impartiality.[85] According to the authoritative commentary on ICC arbitration by Craig, Park and Paulsson, it is unlikely that the Court will refuse to confirm the appointment under art.9(1) unless it is so obvious that the proposed arbitrator would be unsuitable for the arbitration in terms of neutrality.[86] Indeed, in the more recent published guide to the ICC Rules, the ICC Court considers the assessment of arbitrators' qualifications an "inherently hazardous exercise", as it has generally wished to allow the parties the "widest possible freedom" in selecting arbitrators.[87]

6.038   Therefore, under international arbitration norms, parties enjoy broad freedom and full autonomy in appointing their preferred arbitrators. As Lew emphasises that:

---

[81]   Johnson Tan, "The Panel System in Chinese Arbitration", Speech at the *Dispute Resolution Forum* co-held by the Jones Day, Reavies & Pogue, Freshfields Bruckhaus Deringer and Lovell's, Shanghai, 15–16 February 2006.

[82]   Song, "From Ideology to Rules – Several Issues Worthy of Attention in Revising the Arbitration Law" (2005), 6. See also Zhao Xiuwen, "Reforming Chinese Arbitration Law and Practices in the Global Economy (1)", available at the *China Civil Law Website*: www.civillaw.com.cn/en/article.asp?id=797.

[83]   See art.11(5) of the ML when it requires that in the cases of defaulting appointment, the court or other authorities shall secure the arbitrator's independence and impartiality.

[84]   See generally, Pieter Sanders, *The Work of UNCITRAL on Arbitration and Conciliation: Second and Expanded Edition* (The Hague: Kluwer Law International, 2000), 91–92.

[85]   Article 9(1) of the ICC Rules. And the "confirmation" system has become a distinctive feature of the ICC arbitration system.

[86]   Lawrence Craig, William Park and Jan Paulsson, *International Chamber of Commerce Arbitration* (3rd ed.) (New York: Oceana Publishing, 2000), 187.

[87]   Yves Derains and Eric Schwartz, *A Guide to the ICC Rules of Arbitration* (2nd ed.) (The Hague: Kluwer Law International, 2005), 158.

"It is a major advantage of international commercial arbitration that the parties can submit the dispute to a tribunal of their own choice. They can appoint persons in whom they have confidence, and who have the necessary legal and technical expertise they consider necessary for the determination of their particular dispute."[88]

The obvious difference between the Arbitration Law and international arbitration norms lies in the fact that parties in China are denied the autonomy to define the qualifications of their own adjudicators. Under international arbitration community, both institutional and *ad hoc* arbitration are practiced. In the context of *ad hoc* arbitration, parties are afforded a maximum degree of procedural flexibility in that they can specify every detail of their arbitrators' qualifications.[89] China, on the other hand, still does not "believe" that parties have the ability to choose their arbitrators. Limitations on who may be appointed as an arbitrator in China correspond with the exclusion of *ad hoc* arbitration practices in China, as the state does not trust the parties to manage the arbitration process themselves. In another respect, while arbitration institutions in Model Law countries may impose some general professional conditions of their panel arbitrators to supplement any "gaps" in the Model Law, these conditions are no more stringent than those required of judges in their respective jurisdictions.[90] Taking the case of China, however, where the national arbitration legislation has already imposed very strict criteria on arbitrators' qualifications, the arbitration institutions impose even stricter requirements, which could prevent a person who is competent to be a Chinese judge from becoming admitted as a Chinese arbitrator.[91] The constraints on party autonomy in China are far tighter than in international practice, which suggests a strong degree of state control by the Chinese government over private dispute resolution mechanisms. A positive explanation may be that due to the immaturity of the Chinese arbitration system, the degree of arbitrator professionalism is far from being satisfactory in serving the market. It thus makes China different from countries with well-developed arbitrator professionalism.[92] As such, state control over arbitrator's qualifications may, to a certain extent, be justified.

6.039

One last point worth noting in this context is that while Chinese arbitration practice treats Chinese and foreign nationals differently with respect to being qualified as arbitrators, the international trend endeavours to eliminate such restrictions on arbitrators' qualifications based on nationality. One good example in this regard is art.11(1) of the Model Law, which requires that "no person shall be excluded from acting as an arbitrator by virtue of his nationality".[93] The report of the Model Law Working Group concluded that this provision "takes the Model Law's goal of harmonising international trade law a step further by stipulating that any person of any nationality may be appointed as an arbitrator on the equal footing by the parties' preference".[94] China is certainly lagging behind in this respect.

6.040

---

[88] Lew, *Comparative International Commercial Arbitration* (2003), para 10-4.
[89] *Ibid.*, para 3-10.
[90] See discussions below on the criteria for being a panel-listed arbitrator in HKIAC.
[91] See discussions above under the heading "Controlled criteria for appointment".
[92] Mo, *Arbitration in China* (2001), para 5.03.
[93] Article 11(1) of the Model Law.
[94] UN Document, A/CN.9/264 and 265, art.11, para 1.

(ii) *Procedure of appointment: Panel list vs party agreement*

6.041   Secondly, international arbitration norms provide parties with full autonomy to agree on the procedure for appointing arbitrators. Article 11(2) of the Model Law stipulates that the parties should enjoy complete freedom in agreeing on the procedure on how the tribunal is appointed and formed.[95] Similarly worded under art.7(1) of the UNCITRAL Rules, party-favoured arbitrators can be appointed directly by the parties without any control by any institutions.[96] Even for those arbitration institutions in Model Law jurisdictions where panel lists of arbitrators are provided, parties may still be permitted to appoint arbitrators directly from outside the panel list. Indeed, direct appointment may be used in either *ad hoc* arbitration facilitated by the arbitration institution[97] or institutional arbitration administered by the arbitration institutions.[98] Under arts.11(3)–11(5) of the Model Law and arts.6(2)–6(3) of the UNCITRAL Rules, the appointment of the presiding arbitrator is also subject to the parties' agreement.[99]

6.042   In a similar vein, the ICC Rules and English Arbitration Act both provide that parties are free to agree on the procedure for appointing the arbitrator(s), including the procedure of appointing any chairman or umpire.[100] Under the ICC Rules of appointment, the only task of the ICC Court is to confirm the parties' free appointment as long as the arbitrators' independence and neutrality appears sufficient.[101] Pursuant to s.18(1) of the English Arbitration Act, parties are even free to agree on what is to happen in the event of a failure of the procedure of appointment of the tribunal.[102] Thus, the international practice purports to increase the probability of a good working relationship within the tribunal and give the parties direct influence on the appointment process.[103]

6.043   It is further provided that, to ensure efficiency, where appointment by the parties is impossible or parties fail to exercise the right of appointment within a certain time limit, the default appointing authority will appoint the tribunal.[104] The Model Law and the UNCITRAL Rules articulate that in making a default appointment, "the appointing authority shall have due regard to any qualifications required of the arbitrator by the agreement of the parties and to such considerations" for securing the independence and impartiality of appointment.[105] Among the adopting jurisdictions, for example, in Hong Kong, the Hong Kong International Arbitration Center (HKIAC) is empowered to make such default appointment subject to further approval by the Chief Judge of

---

[95]   Article 11(2) of the Model Law.

[96]   Article 7 of the UNCITRAL Arbitration Rules.

[97]   The arbitration institution may provide the space, equipment and other logistic services to facilitate the appointment of the arbitrators and formation of the tribunal. However, the parties select otherwise the *ad hoc* arbitration rules such as the UNCITRAL Rules rather than the rules of the institution in carrying on the arbitration.

[98]   By comparison to the above note, the parties still abide by the arbitration rules of that particular institution but may directly appoint arbitrators off the panel list administered by the institution.

[99]   Articles 11(3), 11(4), 11(5) of the Model Law and arts.6(2), 6(3) of the UNCITRAL Arbitration Rules.

[100] Section 9 of the ICC Rules; s.6(1) of the English Arbitration Act.

[101] Article 9 of the ICC Rules.

[102] Section 18(1) of the English Arbitration Act.

[103] Lew, *Comparative International Commercial Arbitration* (2003), para 10-94.

[104] Article 11(4) and 11(5) of the Model Law.

[105] Article 32 of the Model Law and art.6(4) of the UNCITRAL Rules.

the High Court.[106] In Singapore, similarly, the back-up functions are exercised by the Chairman of the Singapore International Arbitration Center (SIAC) subject to endorsement by the Chief Justice of the High Court.[107] In any case, legislations in both jurisdictions provide sufficient detail on the independence of the default appointing authority in order to secure arbitral independence and impartiality.[108]

Under the English Arbitration Act and ICC Rules, it is as well observed that unless to **6.044** the extent that there is no such agreement at all on the procedure of appointment by the parties will the default appointment mechanism step in to apply.[109] The English Arbitration Act default mechanism, under s.18, empowers the English courts to act as the independent appointing authority.[110] In considering how to exercise the powers in relation to the appointment procedure, in a similar approach to the Model Law and the UNCITRAL Rules, English courts are required to take into account any agreement of the parties as to the prospective arbitrator's qualification and competence.[111] Guidance as to the exercise of the court's default power of arbitrators' appointment was also given in the English Court of Appeal case in *The Lapad*, where Justice Moore-Bick observed that respect for the principle of party autonomy and the desirability of holding the parties to their arbitration agreement provided strong grounds for exercising the default power of appointment unless the court was satisfied that the resulting tribunal would not be impartial.[112] The ICC Rules go even further by requiring under its art.9(1) that in making the default appointment, the ICC Court shall have due regard to the prospective arbitrators' "nationality, residence, availability and ability",[113] and the chairman of the tribunal shall be of a nationality "other than both disputant parties unless the parties do not otherwise object".[114] Although the ICC Rules do not subject the default appointment decision made by the ICC Court to any judicial considerations, in securing arbitral independence, the prospective arbitrators appointed are required to declare their neutrality and impartiality and shall disclose in writing to the Secretariat any facts or circumstances that might call into question their independence, failing which will lead to them being challenged and removed later under the Rules.[115] In both cases of United Kingdom and ICC, a two-step safeguard net for the balance of both party autonomy and arbitral independence and efficiency has been established.

---

[106] See s.12 of the Arbitration Ordinance.

[107] See art.13 of the Singapore Arbitration Act. In Malaysia and New Zealand, the court exercise the power of the appointing authority of arbitrators in the arbitral proceeding. Source: Pieter Sanders and Albert Jan van den Berg (eds), *International Handbook on Commercial Arbitration: National Reports/Basic Legal Texts* (The Hague: Kluwer Law International, 2002).

[108] See s.12 of the Arbitration Ordinance and art.13(6) of the Singapore Arbitration Act.

[109] Section 16(2) of the English Arbitration Act; art.8(4) of the ICC Rules.

[110] Section 18(1) of the English Arbitration Act.

[111] Section 19 of the English Arbitration Act.

[112] *The Lapad* [2004] 2 Lloyd's Rep 109.

[113] Article 9(1) of the ICC Rules. Indeed, according to Derains and Schwartz, the so-called "ability" may include factors such as language, legal qualifications, expertise in the commercial or technical field that is the subject of arbitration, expertise in arbitration, age, physical and material resources. See Derains and Schwartz, *A Guide to the ICC Rules of Arbitration* (2005), 158–163.

[114] Derains and Schwartz, *A Guide to the ICC Rules of Arbitration* (2005), 155.

[115] Article 7(2) of the ICC Rules. See also comments by Stephen Bond (a former Secretary General of the ICC Court) in connection with the Rules, "The Experience of the ICC in the Confirmation/Appointment Stage of an Arbitration", in ICC (ed.), *The Arbitral Process and the Independence of Arbitrators* (Paris: ICC Publishing, 1991), 9–11.

6.045   China is different from international practices in several aspects. In the beginning, parties cannot directly appoint arbitrators as the channel of appointment is controlled by arbitration commissions. Foreign commentators have discussed various aspects of Chinese arbitration procedure that hinder the principle of party autonomy, criticising in particular the procedure of arbitrator appointment from a panel list rather than on the basis of parties' direct arbitration agreement.[116] Further, an arbitral tribunal formed through the Chinese default appointment mechanism may cast serious doubt on the integrity of the arbitration process. Since the appointment decision is based on the commission chairman's discretion,[117] his/her independence and impartiality are critical. However, as the previous studies on the structure of the arbitration commissions show, personnel constituents are to a large extent tainted by local government shadows where political and administrative interventions are hardly avoidable.[118] Specifically, the independence of an arbitrator appointed under such mechanism may well be susceptible to the influence of the chairman of the commission. Dr Wang mentions one such example in her studies of arbitral independence:

> "Supposing that the chairman of an arbitration commission has appointed an arbitrator and he just says to that arbitrator, 'The case is important and you shall deal with it carefully'. Those words by themselves suggest nothing about intervention. However, the arbitrator appointed may think in this way, 'Why does the chairman show particular concern for this case? Why does he consider the case important? How much attention shall I pay to the case?'"[119]

6.046   Any such thought represents a hidden intervention that is not easy to avoid under the Chinese network (*guanxi*) psychology. It may subsequently influence the arbitrator's decisions in handling the case. Further, an arbitrator is paid to serve on a tribunal. The panelled arbitrators have economic incentives to be appointed and are thus eager to follow the chairman's "orders". This, on the other hand, may help to explain the much criticised phenomenon of the chairman selecting a Chinese national as presiding arbitrator because the *process* and *outcome* could be much easier to "control".[120] Another explanation may be found in the controlled pricing policy in Chinese arbitral practice. Under art. 76 of the Arbitration Law, the measures for charging arbitration fees are subject to examination and approval by the price control authorities of the Chinese government rather than being decided by the parties' agreement.[121] The provision, however, is faced with challenges under the economic globalisation which requires

---

[116]   Sarah Catherine Peck, "Playing By a New Set of Rules – Will China's New Arbitration Laws and Recent Membership in the ICC Improve Trade With China?", (1995) 12 *Journal of International Arbitration*, 51–64.

[117]   Articles 31 and 32 of the Arbitration Law.

[118]   See discussion above under the heading "Problems of the Arbitration Commission Infrastructure" in Chapter 5.

[119]   Wang Wenying, "Studies on the Arbitral Independence in China (Zhongguo Zhongcai Dulixing Wenti Yanjiu)", (2004) 89 *Arbitration and Law (Zhongcai yu Falu)*, 68.

[120]   Song, "From Ideology to Rules: Several Issues Worthy of Attention for the Revision of the Arbitration Law" (2005), 6; see also Tao, *Arbitration Law and Practice in China* (2004), para 294.

[121]   Article 76 of the Arbitration Law provides that the parties shall pay the arbitration fees according to regulations of the Chinese government.

service prices to be oriented by the market.[122] As such, the Chinese arbitration charge system fails to meet international standards where some foreign nationals nominated by the chairman of the commission have been known to decline appointment due to financial considerations.[123] For a foreign party conducting an arbitration in China, there are legitimate concerns about the equality and integrity of the arbitration.[124]

(iii) *Panel appointment: Closed vs open*

Thirdly, international arbitration norms entitle parties the complete freedom to choose any person of any nationality and without limitation to any panels. In Model Law jurisdictions, while it is not uncommon for an arbitration institution to form its own standards for arbitrators and appoint qualified persons as members of its own panels, panel members are only listed on a basis of suggestion and thus parties are free to select other arbitrators. Thus, parties are encouraged to appoint persons whom they think are most appropriate in handling their cases.[125] The HKIAC, for example, has established a panel of arbitrators each of whose members are selected for high expertise and professionalism.[126] Besides panel members published on its website,[127] the HKIAC also maintains a database of other arbitrators who, although not meeting the Panel Selection Committee's criteria[128] for inclusion on the panel may yet be suggested to parties in suitable cases requiring specialist expertise. As such, parties may have a larger pool from which they can draw their prospective arbitrators. Most significantly, however, the parties are allowed to appoint arbitrators from outside the institutional panels and databases.[129] The principle of party autonomy is both well observed and balanced against an institutional culture of maintaining a pool of high-standard arbitrators available for the parties to select from. The SIAC shares

6.047

---

[122] Annex 4 of the Protocol on the Accession of the People's Republic of China to the WTO. During negotiations, some WTO members stated that China should allow prices of trade goods and services in every sector to be determined by market forces; and pricing practices based on government guidance should be eliminated.

[123] Tao, *Arbitration Law and Practice in China* (2004), para 294.

[124] The then CIETAC secretary-general Wang Shengchang points out that the current pricing policy in Chinese arbitral practice is obviously not favourable and attractive enough to support and promote international arbitration as the parties may simply decide to engage in forum-shopping. See Wang Shengchang and Sarah Hilmer, "China Arbitration Law v UNCITRAL Model Law" [2006] *International Arbitration Law Review*, 7.

[125] Peter Binder, *International Commercial Arbitration in UNCITRAL Model Law Jurisdictions* (London: Sweet & Maxwell, 2000), paras 3-021 and 3-022.

[126] See s.A of the Guidelines on Inclusion on the HKIAC Panel of Arbitrators, accessible at the HKIAC website: http://www.hkiac.org/HKIAC/HKIAC_English/main.html.

[127] HKIAC published the details of its panel arbitrators, including the location, name, title and means of contact. Among the 263 arbitrators on the panel, 164 have given permission to HKIAC to put their CVs on the website.

[128] HKIAC requires that persons who want to be included into the panel of arbitrators must demonstrate the following criteria, (1) have substantial arbitration experience; (2) have substantial connection with East Asia; (3) not having been found guilty by a Court or misconduct by a disciplinary tribunal which calls into question his/her ability to act as arbitrator; and (4) be under 75 years of age.
For certainty in the appointment practice, HKIAC provides further clarifications on the "substantial arbitration experience" by stating that, "A Hong Kong resident candidate can qualify to join the Panel on the basis of having acted as arbitrator on domestic or international cases. A non-Hong Kong resident candidate can qualify to join the Panel on the basis of having acted as arbitrator on international cases". See also, s.B in the Guidelines on Inclusion as the HKIAC Panel of Arbitrators, see fn 129 above.

[129] Article 3.4 of the HKIAC Domestic Rules requires that the appointment of arbitrators is based on parties' agreement, http://www.hkiac.org/HKIAC/pdf/Rules/e_domestic.pdf. The HKIAC International Rules follows the UNCITRAL Arbitration Rules.

a similar open panel style in the arbitrator appointment. As Warren Koo, the ex-Chairman of the SIAC notes:

> "The panel of arbitrators run by the SIAC is not to shrink but to swell parties' choices and thus to provide some references should the parties wish; however, never will the parties be restricted to the panel names."[130]

6.048   Although not providing a panel system, the ICC Court, in making its default appointment of arbitrators, however, generally requests a proposal from the ICC National Committees,[131] which maintain a wide international network closely tied to the business and legal communities in more than 90 countries which they represent.[132] The National Committees are in a far better position than the Court's Secretariat in Paris to identify locally prominent professionals who may be qualified to act as arbitrators in ICC cases and, in particular, to assist the Court in expanding the pool of potential arbitrators beyond those who are already well-known internationally.[133]

6.049   By contrast, the Arbitration Law authorises the commission to have a closed panel list and restrict parties' choices to the list. The legislative authorisation has been read between the lines of arts.11 and 13 and the rules of each arbitration commission have required the parties to select only those persons listed on the particular panel of the commission to which their disputes belong.[134] If the panel system is adopted for the sake of the quality of arbitration, it may not be convincing that a closed panel guarantees quality. Further, because the parties legitimately expect the widest latitude in their choice of arbitrators, a system that limits parties to picking arbitrators from a fixed panel will restrict the freedom of the parties to select the most appropriate arbitrators; and may even place parties arbitrating in China at a disadvantage because parties will find themselves better off under other jurisdictions where they are allowed free access to candidates outside the institutional panels.

6.050   As noted, many critics have pointed out that in order for CIETAC to operate as a truly international body, the disputing parties should have more freedom in choosing their arbitrators.[135] Therefore, in the 1994, 1998, 2000 and 2005 amendments of the Rules, CIETAC responded to the growing concerns of the closed panel system by increasing the number of available arbitrators on the international list from 89 to over 700.[136] The expanded panel list is clearly an improvement. However, a mere increase in the number of arbitrators on the panel can neither exhaust expertise in every technical field nor represent nationalities from each jurisdiction. Until recently

---

[130] Email interview with Warren Koo by the author as regards the arbitrator appointment in the SIAC (done on 12 May 2006).

[131] Articles 9(3)–9(5) of the ICC Rules.

[132] See the list of the ICC's National Committees at *Appendix 3*, in Derains and Schwartz, *A Guide to ICC Rules of Arbitration* (2005).

[133] Craig, Park and Paulsson, *International Chamber of Commerce Arbitration* (2000), 197.

[134] See discussions above under the heading "Compulsory appointment under the closed panels".

[135] See discussions above.

[136] See the updated Panel of Arbitrators of the CIETAC, effective from 1 May 2005, available at the CIETAC website, http://www.cietac.org.cn/index_english.asp.

(Rules of 2005),[137] CIETAC has never allowed parties' arbitrator appointment any departure from its panels. Local arbitration commissions such as BAC, SAC and SZAC, on the other hand, have been adhering to the closed panel system[138] despite a trend of on-going recruitment of more arbitrators to their panels.[139] It may be arguable that Chinese arbitration commissions fail to recognise a key lesson from international arbitration norms that parties should be allowed to choose and appoint arbitrators from beyond the realm of the mandatory list. According to Philip Yang, the ex-Chairman of HKIAC, although the qualifications of getting appointed as an arbitrator in China are inflexible, the practice will never restrict the freedom of parties if the panel is adopted in an open fashion, like the practice of HKIAC.[140] Tao and Kang have also made similar arguments that the panel lists could still be maintained but may remain available for reference purposes where parties should be able to appoint arbitrators off the list.[141] Therefore, rather than the previous enlargement of the pools, opening up of the panel list would be a more meaningful reform towards party autonomy.

(d) Conclusion: State control vs party autonomy

As comparative study of international arbitration norms and practices shows, parties have broad freedom in choosing arbitrators, including the freedom to define qualifications and prescribe appointment procedures. It is further noted that free appointment by the parties has particular meanings in a developed commercial society because this will increase the likelihood of commercial cooperation during the proceedings as well as the voluntary enforcement of the award subsequently rendered.[142] However, modern arbitration in China was born and brought up as part of the administrative system under the planned economy for resolving social and economic disputes. State control over arbitrators thus bears a special meaning for ensuring socioeconomic stability.[143] Based on this fact, the notion of state intervention on arbitrators' qualifications is formed to ensure the quality of arbitration particularly in the context of market

6.051

---

[137] In the newly updated Rules in 2005, CIETAC may allow parties to choose arbitrators outside the compulsory panel list. See discussions below under the heading "Remedial Measures by CIETAC".

[138] See art.17 of the Arbitration Rules of the BAC (latest rules being effective from 1 April 2008), accessible at www. bjac.com/cn/program/rule.htm; art.24 of the Rules of the SAC (latest rules being effective from 1 May 2005), accessible at www.accsh.org/accsh/rode5/index.htm; and art.27 of the Rules of the SZAC (latest rules being effective from 1 May 2011), accessible at www.szac.org/guide_003.asp.

[139] The local arbitration commissions have been witnessed expanding its panels of arbitrator by not only increasing the number but also detailing the classifications of the panels in accordance with the specialities and case natures. This is what is taken as another step to facilitate the competition in the arbitration market. On this topic, see generally, Kang Ming, *A Study on Commercial Arbitration Service (Shangshi Zhongcai Fuwu Yanjiu)* (Beijing: China Law Press, 2005), 168–172.

[140] Philip Yang Liangyi, opening address entitled "The Current Development of the Chinese Arbitration" in the Symposium jointly held by the HKIAC and City University of Hong Kong in March 2004, at the HKIAC.

[141] Kang, *A Study on Commercial Arbitration Service* (2005), 133; see also Tao, *Arbitration Law and Practice in China* (2004), para 288.

[142] Song, "From Ideology to Rules: Several Issues Worthy of Attention for Revising the Arbitration Law" (2005), 5–6.

[143] Mo, *Arbitration Law in China* (2001), para 5.04.

transitions.[144] Further, under the institutional arbitration distinction in China and against the background of their administrative infrastructure, institutional control by arbitration commissions has developed as a natural stretch of administrative control.[145] Thus, controlling arbitrators has become an important task of each commission. This is mostly evident where the Arbitration Law has, through authorisation to the arbitration commission, *controlled* both the criteria and procedure of appointment— the commission first appoints the arbitrators to their panel lists, and the parties must then appoint from those listed arbitrators. Through the commission's obliging parties to appoint arbitrators only from its fixed panels, qualifications of the members have been filtered in accordance with specific needs of the particular commission. The overwhelming institutional control has raised serious concerns regarding the integrity of the tribunal. Moreover, the present system, closed and unique to each individual arbitration commission, substantially restricts the parties' procedural autonomy in arbitration. In the global context, in particular, parties may well shop the forum and they may choose a jurisdiction where procedural autonomy is more friendly.[146] As such, China is very likely to lose in the institutional competition of the arbitration market if rigid control over tribunal formation continues to be maintained. An alarm for reform has been called by arbitration academics and practitioners. However, as will be subsequently dealt with in this chapter, the commission panels display certain features that may have led to "improper incentives" for the continuation of the closed panel system. The following discussion thus attempts to identify such "improper incentives" so as to shed light on some of the practical constraints facing the arbitration system in China.

2. HIDDEN OBSTACLES TO TRIBUNAL FORMATION

6.052   In examining whether parties' autonomy and interest have been endangered by institutional control, this part of the discussion will concentrate on the status quo of the closed panels among the Chinese arbitration commissions—its distinctions and problems.

6.053   The closed panel system of Chinese tribunals has three marked features. First, arbitration commissions tend to appoint their own staff members as arbitrators, and these arbitrators have formed a special group called the "staff panel" swapping between administrative and professional roles. Secondly, a considerable number of the administrative officials are appointed as arbitrators. Lastly, most arbitrators listed on

---

[144]   Shen Sibao and Xue Yuan, "On the Positioning and Reform of the Chinese Commercial Arbitration System (Lun Woguo Shangshi Zhongcai Zhidu de Dingwei jiqi Gaige)", (2006) 4 *Legal Science Monthly (Faxue Yuekan)*, 70–71. See also Geoffrey Chan and Terence Tung, "Chapter 9: Commencement of Arbitration and Arbitration Proceedings" in Fung and Wang (eds), *Arbitration in China: A Practical Guide* (2004), para 9-93.

[145]   Zhao Xiuwen, "Reforming Chinese Arbitration Law and Practices in the Global Economy (1)", available at the *China Civil Law Website*: www.civillaw.com.cn/en/article.asp?id=797 (last visited 28 July 2011).

[146]   Recent amendments to national arbitration laws reveal a trend towards increased autonomy granted to arbitration. The market driven nature of the international arbitration business makes it hard for states to insist upon control because arbitration simply will not be held in unaccommodating states. See, Katherine Lynch, *The Forces of Economic Globalization: Challenges to the Regime of International Commercial Arbitration* (The Hague: Kluwer Law International, 2003), 187.

the panels of the local commissions are drawn from the local community where the commission is located.

(a) Perils of institutional bias: Staff panel

To begin with, presently in China, many panel-listed arbitrators are selected from internal staff members of the arbitration commission. Such practice originates from art.13(1) of the Arbitration Law which, as mentioned above, stipulates that having previous experience in arbitration work can be a basis for qualifying as an arbitrator in China.[147] Accordingly, if a staff member has been working for over eight years, the person may be appointed if the commission thinks fit. As a matter of practice, Mo observes arbitration commissions are more willing to appoint their own staff members as these persons are familiar with the arbitral procedure. Indeed, such appointment is regarded as an effective means to ensure the standard of arbitrators as well as useful to control the quality of arbitration within the arbitration commission concerned.[148] Currently, most senior staff members of the commission, including the chairman, vice-chairman, secretary-general and other departmental heads have been included into the panel list.[149]

6.054

Criticisms have been voiced against such a practice. Notably, these staff arbitrators are usually the power-holders and decision-makers within an arbitration commission. They have powers to appoint persons to the panel list as well as make default appointment of arbitrators should the parties fail to do so within the time limit.[150] Additionally, some senior staff members control jurisdictional issues and decide on the procedural management of arbitration cases.[151] Hence, considering the powerful role of these staff arbitrators and their special relationship with the arbitration commission, non-staff arbitrators may be hesitant to dissent from the opinions of their staff counterparts to avoid breaking the harmonious relationship within the tribunal.[152] If they dissent, there is a risk that they will not be appointed the next time. Meanwhile, the party who did not appoint a staff arbitrator might suspect bias should the arbitral award be favourable to the other side who appointed a staff arbitrator. As the leading arbitration commission in China, CIETAC has been under considerable criticism by Professor Cohen, who pointed out that one of the biggest defects of CIETAC arbitration is its persistent selection of its own personnel as arbitrators, especially the presiding arbitrators, which arguably allows for the exercise of institutional influence and even

6.055

---

[147] See s.(1) of art.13 of the Arbitration Law; see also discussions above.

[148] Mo, *Arbitration Law in China* (2001), para 5.10.

[149] For example, in CIETAC, there are a number of departments under the Secretariat, including the Domestic Business Department, Foreign-related Business Department, Legal Supervision Department and *etc*. The organic structure under the CIETAC Secretariat is available at: http://www.cietac.org.cn/jieshao/luetu.asp?type=js7.

[150] Articles 31 and 32 of the Arbitration Law.

[151] Some staff arbitrators, in particular, the secretary-general and deputy secretary-general, are in charge of the administration of the arbitral procedure. Due to the fact that under the current context of China, only the commissions are empowered to render the decision on arbitral jurisdiction, these arbitrators may well discuss and decide internally whether to accept the case or not. See also discussions above on the commission-oriented arbitral jurisdiction in Chapter 5.

[152] Kang Ming, "Existing Problems of the Internal Arbitrators within the Arbitration Institutions (Zhongcai Jigou Neibu Zhongcaiyuan Wenti)", in Kang, *A Study on Commercial Arbitration Service* (2005), 144.

control over the panel's decisions.[153] Song shares a similar concern in this respect, since most staff members have become full-time professional arbitrators within the commission, their fixed positions are more like judges sitting in the court where the parties do not have much opportunity to choose their preferred adjudicators and finally have to yield their arbitration autonomy to the decision of the institution.[154]

6.056 Whilst many commentators criticise such a practice, the handling of arbitration cases by staff arbitrators is not considered a conflict of interests under the Arbitration Law nor under the rules of the arbitration commissions in China. In fact, a substantial part of the income of many staff of the arbitration commissions is derived from their arbitrator fees.[155] Ironically, some local commissions even consider being listed as an arbitrator on the commission panel as a condition for internal staff promotion.[156]

6.057 It appears, however, that the criticism has been heeded, as Cao Lijun, a CIETAC staff arbitrator, maintains that CIETAC now requires that "all staff members should decline the appointment *by parties* unless it is a joint appointment as a sole arbitrator or presiding arbitrator".[157] However, it does not prevent CIETAC from continuing the practice of allowing its staff members to be appointed *by the chairman* of CIETAC when the parties have defaulted in making the appointment.[158] Yet, what is the difference between the staff arbitrators appointed by the parties and by the chairman? Either way of appointment would have no bearing upon an arbitrator's level of morality and professionalism. The dilemma still seems to engulf CIETAC, which is seeking to eliminate the institutional impact on the parties' interest and arbitral independence.[159]

(b) Perils of government bias: Official panel

6.058 Besides staff arbitrators, many of the panel members are government officials or retired officials from administrative organs. Based on the previous study regarding the administrative infrastructure of most arbitration commissions, the commissions usually appoint officials to the panel in order to establish good relations with the administrative departments to better carry out their work. Owing to the institutionalised system of Chinese arbitration, arbitrators in China receive some sort of institutional or official recognition.[160] Officials bearing the title of "arbitrators" take it as an honour of status[161] as well as an extra opportunity to earn income. Thus, an elusive

---

[153] Professor Jerome A. Cohen, "International Commercial Arbitration in China: Some Thoughts from Experience", paper presentation at the *International Economic Law and China in Its Economic Transition Joint Conference*, held in Xiamen, 4–5 November 2004.

[154] Song Lianbin, "Comments on the Judicialization Trend of the Arbitration (Zhongcai Susonghua Qushi zhi Pingxi)", (2005) 55 *Arbitration in Beijing (Beijing Zhongcai)*, 46.

[155] Ellen Reinstein, "Finding A Happy Ending for Foreign Investors: The Enforcement of Arbitration Awards in the People's Republic of China", (2005) 16 *Indiana International and Comparative Law Review*, 39.

[156] Cohen, "International Commercial Arbitration in China: Some Thoughts from Experience" (2004), 46.

[157] Cao Lijun, "Letters – CIETAC's Integrity", (2005) 168 *Far Eastern Economic Review*, 4–5.

[158] *Ibid.*

[159] See discussions below under the heading "Remedial Measures by CIETAC".

[160] This is mostly due to the official privilege granted to the institution which has been extended to the arbitrators on that institutional list. See Mo, *Arbitration Law in China* (2001), para 5.03.

[161] Interestingly, officials would more often than not, print the title of "arbitrator" of a particular arbitration commission on their name cards as a kind of honour.

interdependent relationship is established between the arbitration commission and the official arbitrators appointed to the commission's panel list.[162] For these reasons, it might lead to a similar conclusion on the risk of parties' autonomy and interest being endangered by the administrative powers as concerned in previous chapters.

In particular, Kang Ming, vice-secretary-general of CIETAC, analyses two main situations associated with the selection of official arbitrators.[163] First, if the dispute is concerned with state assets or one of the parties is a government-related entity such as a state-owned enterprise (SOE), the sitting of official arbitrators in the tribunal, whether appointed by a party or default, may give rise to a perception that the other side will be disadvantaged at the cost of state interests.[164] Secondly, suppose neither the parties nor the dispute relates to the government business, three more scenarios may be deduced: (1) if the entire tribunal is composed of official arbitrators, then the senior official would influence junior colleagues due to the Chinese tradition of respecting hierarchy; or (2) if the majority of the tribunal is represented by the official arbitrators, then very likely, their opinions will be influential upon the third non-official arbitrator as a result of the esteem to the power of office;[165] or (3) if only one official arbitrator sits in the tribunal, the official's influence could still be significant.[166]

6.059

Kang concludes his analyses from the perspective of a commission leader, where he is concerned about the possible pressures on the impartiality and independence of the arbitrators.[167] Although it is arguable whether the official status of the arbitrators would bring about biased results, it is hard to dispel the psychological influence upon non-official arbitrators under the administrative ritual and thus hard to dispel the misunderstandings upon the parties over the decision-making within the tribunal. Even if there is no actual bias, the Chinese traditional culture of "respect for power of office" will make it difficult to shake off the perception because such influence may exist inherently, unconsciously, potentially and elusively.[168] This is what worries some foreign parties, who know of cases where the presiding official arbitrator has rendered a decision which could not be justified by their professional arbitrator appointed.[169] Otherwise, as they are restricted to the fixed panel, if one party appoints an official arbitrator, the other party may also feel compelled to appoint another official from the

6.060

---

[162] After all, arbitration commissions need the administrative support to be established in China. They cannot be established nor survive without the support of the Party Committee, the People's Congress, the Government, the Court and all social circles.

[163] Kang, *A Study on Commercial Arbitration Service* (2005), 158–166.

[164] *Ibid.*, 164; see also Johnson Tan, "Main Features of Arbitration in China", in Fung and Wang (eds), *Arbitration in China: A Practical Guide* (2004), para 4-11.

[165] The official arbitrators enjoy the "upper hand" because they are perceived to understand the law and policies and therefore "persuasive" to the other arbitrators sitting in the same panel.

[166] For example, if one arbitrator is a senior official of the Lawyers' Department of the Justice Bureau which oversees the lawyers of that city, and the other two arbitrators are lawyers under his administration, then it is hard to say the lawyer arbitrators would not be influenced by the official arbitrator.

[167] Kang, *A Study on commercial Arbitration Service* (2005), 166.

[168] Wen Jie, "Status Quo and Reform: Chinese Arbitrator System (Zhongguo Zhongcaiyuan Zhidu de Xianzhuang ji Gailiang)", available at the China Arbitration Website: http://www.china-arbitration.com/3a1.asp?id=951&name=仲裁研究.

[169] Cohen, "International Commercial Arbitration in China: Some Thoughts from Experience" (2004).

panel with a similar hierarchical rank to the opponent's appointee so as to win an equal footing in the arbitration.[170]

(c) Perils of localisation bias: Localised panel

6.061   Localisation of arbitrators is yet another serious problem compromising the parties' interests in the arbitral procedure in China. As noted, local arbitration commissions share a common practice in appointing persons within the local region where the commission resides. Such practice can be traced back to the administrative notice of the State Council in 1995, which requires the panel composition to be geographically near to the place of the commission.[171] Although there is no restriction on the appointment of non-local arbitrators, for the sake of arbitral efficiency, the availability of local arbitrators may save time and costs.

6.062   Local parties are often delighted to resort to a local commission given their acquaintance with the community. This, however, may not be a wise choice for the non-local parties, including foreign parties as well as domestic parties from outside the region. As noted in the previous chapter, most local commissions receive some form of protection, and therefore are subject to administrative interference, from the local people's government.[172] Moreover, these commissions close their panels and require parties to select arbitrators from the rosters of localised arbitrators instead of allowing them a free and wide choice. Non-local parties are thus unlikely to prevent the local government from interfering with the decision-making of the localised tribunals.[173] Such practice of localisation may involve further instances where, if the parties fail to agree on the choice of presiding arbitrator, local commissions might appoint a local person to chair the tribunal. Under these circumstances, it is therefore very likely that the local arbitrators will show bias in favour of the local parties. Then non-local parties may be hesitant to choose the arbitration commission of the region as the forum for dispute resolution unless they can find arbitrators coming from their home regions as well. Indeed, many local commissions have difficulties in attracting foreign-related cases particularly because of the lack of sufficient competent arbitrators from outside

---

[170] One lawyer from the Lovell's Shanghai Office shared with the author that she would be willing to appoint an official arbitrator for the interests of her client in arbitration in both CIETAC Shanghai Sub-Commission and SAC. She further shared with the author that, such appointment could well bring benefits to the case as the official arbitrators appointed, due to his/her high ranking, may be respected very much within the tribunal and his/her opinion could be very persuasive to the other fellow arbitrators. She admitted, however, that such appointment could be unfair to the other party who did not appoint an official arbitrator. Therefore, she suggested to her fellow lawyers that, "Knowing the other party had appointed an official arbitrator, you might as well follow suit to secure the interests of your own client".

[171] Article 3(2) of the Scheme for Reorganizing Arbitration Commissions (issued by the State Council on 26 May 1995) requires that the arbitration commissions should appoint arbitrators mainly from within the local province, local autonomous region or local municipality directly under the Central Government where the arbitration commission is located.

[172] See discussions above under the heading "Problems of the Arbitration Commission Infrastructure" in Chapter 5. The local protectionism may involve interplay of *guanxi* coming from the local government, local communist party committee, business and personal influences that interfere with the decision-making of the arbitration panel.

[173] Jerome A. Cohen, "The Delicate Art of Arbitration", *Financial Times (Asian Edition)*, 30 November 2005.

the local area.[174] Accordingly, the localisation of panel arbitrators not only restricts party autonomy but also impacts adversely on the quality and integrity of the Chinese arbitration.

(d) Conclusion: Various controls in interplay on party and tribunal autonomy

It is important to note that, under the Chinese closed panel system, various influences are at play. A delicate relationship exists between the arbitration commission and its panel arbitrators in that the commission issues the panel arbitrator status in exchange for retaining internal talents (staff arbitrators); obtaining administrative support for institutional survival and development (official arbitrators); as well as protecting the interests of the local parties (localised arbitrators). These distinctive features of tribunal formation within the Chinese arbitration practice have thus led to improper incentives for the "closing" of the panels by commissions, which may then exert influence on party autonomy from various sources and channels. Indeed, the main reason for the underlying problem still lies in the lack of institutional integrity of the Chinese arbitration commissions as they suffer from seriously distorting influences from other governmental departments, political organisations, and businesses.[175]

6.063

In view of the fact that appointing staff arbitrators is common practice in Chinese arbitration, at present, it may be impossible to abolish the system given the long established institutional prevalence. It is encouraging to note that, however, BAC has lately rejected such practice in a bold manner.[176] In its most recently amended Administrative Measures of the Appointment of Arbitrators in 2006, BAC requires the staff members not to accept appointment either *from the parties or the commission chairman* unless both parties jointly agreed.[177] CIETAC and other local commissions should refrain as well from appointing members of its own staff as arbitrators, in order to reduce institutional influence over the tribunal. Today there is no shortage of capable arbitrators in China, both Chinese and foreign, and CIETAC should allow parties more choices beyond the panel list.

6.064

For appointment of official arbitrators, given the delicate inter-relations between the administrative departments and arbitration commissions, the commissions may be reluctant to give up the administrative "support" and thus slow to abandon the official panels. Where the practice of official arbitrators may not be entirely eradicated, in any event, administrative influence should be diminished where party autonomy and interest shall never be harmed. An open-styled panel system where parties could select arbitrators off the list thus becomes particularly important in reducing the administrative impact.

6.065

---

[174] Taroh Inoue, "Introduction to International Commercial Arbitration in China", (2006) 36 *Hong Kong Law Journal*, 154.

[175] See discussions above under the heading "Tribunal's Competence in the Shadow of Arbitration Commission" in Chapter 5.

[176] Wang Hongsong, "Keep abreast the Spirit of Arbitration Law, Establish the Modern Arbitration Institution (Linghui Zhongcaifa Jingshen, Jianshe Xiandaihua de Zhongcai Jigou)", (2005) 57 *Beijing Arbitration (Beijing Zhongcai)*, 3–4.

[177] Article 3 of the Administrative Measures of the Appointment of Arbitrators of BAC, revised in August 2006 and put into effect from September 2006.

6.066   Lastly, the localisation of arbitrators poses potential dangers to both the autonomy of the parties as well as the independence of the tribunal. Any commission that hopes to attract customers in the arbitration market needs to open the panel list to embrace more non-local experts. This is essential for local commissions because they are now being allowed to receive foreign-related cases, while most of them may not be able to assemble a roster as ample and distinguished as CIETAC in including a large number of foreign experts. Difficulties might persist, nevertheless, due to long-established "protections" most local commissions enjoy under the local administrative "shelter".

6.067   To summarise, the practices of appointing staff and localised arbitrators to panels were intended only as a transitional arrangement in the initial period of implementation of the Arbitration Law;[178] so was the practice of appointing official arbitrators in the then context of China's fledging arbitration system. It is high time, in the interest of China's economic and legal development, that these issues be brought out of their historic shadows and aligned with international norms and practices. The subsequent discussions attempt to reflect efforts by the leading arbitration institution in China, CIETAC, to respond to the international trend of increasing party autonomy.

3. REMEDIAL MEASURES BY CIETAC

6.068   CIETAC, in an effort to respond to international pressure of increasing party autonomy, recently updated its Rules. The changes involve both a general empowerment of the parties to vary the rules of the institution and a small widening of the parties' choices of arbitrators.

(a) General reform in respecting parties' procedural autonomy

6.069   Previously, when parties opt for CIETAC arbitration, the Rules issued by CIETAC govern the proceedings. Variations made by the parties to CIETAC Rules have to some extent been allowed since 2000.[179] Such procedural autonomy, however, has an important limitation, which is that the variation must first be approved by CIETAC's chairman.[180] Such a requirement has been abolished under the updated Rules in 2005 where the parties can now agree to apply other arbitration rules or to amend CIETAC Rules except when such agreement is inoperative or in conflict with the mandatory provisions of the law of the seat of arbitration.[181] The removal of the commission chairman's official endorsement largely liberalises the parties' ability to decide upon the arbitral procedures. The new rule is therefore a remarkable achievement towards

---

[178] Article 13(1) of the Arbitration Law regarding the staff arbitrator and art.3(2) of the Scheme for Reorganizing Arbitration Commissions, see discussions above.

[179] Article 7 of the 2000 CIETAC Arbitration Rules, effective from 1 October 2000.

[180] *Ibid.*

[181] Article 4, para 2 of the 2005 CIETAC Arbitration Rules, effective from 1 May 2005.

liberalisation of institutional influence on the conduct of arbitration proceedings.[182]
As such, parties can now select other arbitration rules to govern their procedure,[183]
including the rules on the appointment of arbitrators to form their tribunals.

(b) Specific reform for widening parties' choices in tribunal formation

The 2005 Rules set forth a new mechanism for appointing arbitrators. For the first   **6.070**
time, CIETAC permits parties to appoint arbitrators off the panel list; and the presiding
arbitrator may now be chosen from the match found in the parties' list of preferential
names.

(i) *Appointing arbitrators off the panel list*

Parties can now agree to appoint arbitrators from outside the compulsory panel list.[184]   **6.071**
Although a non-panelist will still need to meet the same criteria as those applicable
to admission to the CIETAC panel,[185] this largely opens up the scope of choice,
as CIETAC's panel predominately consists of Chinese nationals, with a majority
coming from its staff and those with government background living locally with
acquaintances. The loosening of the CIETAC panel will increase dramatically the
pool of experts and foreigners available to serve on a CIETAC tribunal and hence
has significant practical impacts on increasing the parties' procedural autonomy.[186]
However, such off-the-list appointment does not enjoy complete freedom, as it can
only be done with confirmation by CIETAC's chairman.[187] Yet no implementation
rules have been laid down to guide the chairman's decision-making. The silence as
to under what circumstances the approval could be obtained has shared a similar
vagueness to that happened in the commission's delegation of jurisdictional power
concerned by the previous chapter,[188] the opaque practice of which may dim earlier
optimism.

---

[182] Jingzhou Tao, "Challenges and Trends of Arbitration in China" in Albert Jan van den Berg (ed), *New Horizons in International Commercial Arbitration and Beyond: ICCA Congress Series No. 12* (The Hague: Kluwer Law International, 2005), 84. In the article, Tao mentioned that increasingly autonomous market economy would call for increasing roles of the parties played in the market; thus, the institutions of arbitration would be in future acting no more than administering facilitators.

[183] It seems possible from the updated CIETAC Rules that parties can now select other arbitral rules to govern arbitral proceeding including the UNCITRAL Rules. This appears to reflect CIETAC's evolving willingness to administer arbitration under rules other than its own, and it may further expresses somewhat a leaning towards allowing *ad hoc* arbitration in China.

[184] Article 21, para 2 of the CIETAC Rules 2005.

[185] The appointee or nominee shall possess the minimum requirements provided in art.13 of the Arbitration Law (for Chinese nationals), or art.67 (for foreign nationals). It is arguable whether the appointee must obtain the same qualifications of the CIETAC panel-listed arbitrators. In a recent conference (*Managing Business Disputes in China*, 26 March 2007 at the Harvard Club, New York), the current CIETAC secretary-general, Mr Yu Jianlong, replied that the criteria under which the off-listed arbitrators will get approved will be analogous to those qualifications required under the 2005 CIETAC Rules, despite there has been no such case so far. Darren Fitzgerald seems to endorse such higher qualification requirement for non-panel arbitrators. See Darren Fitzgerald, "CIETAC's New Arbitration Rules: Do the Reform Go Far Enough?" [2005] *Asian Dispute Review*, 5.

[186] Fitzgerald, "CIETAC's New Arbitration Rules: Do the Reform Go Far Enough?", *ibid*.

[187] Article 21(2) of the CIETAC Rules 2005.

[188] See discussions above under the heading "Tribunal's Competence Recognised by Commission Rules" in Chapter 5.

(ii) *Appointing presiding arbitrator by matches*

6.072   The updated Rules have also enabled parties to agree on the presiding arbitrator[189] by requiring each party to submit a list of up to three candidates for matches.[190] This purports to increase the chances of "meeting of minds" by the parties.[191] If there is one common candidate in the lists, then he/she will be the presiding arbitrator; where there is more than one common candidate, the chairman of CIETAC will choose one from them; should no name match, the chairman will make his own appointment, which may result in an appointee other than any of the names on the lists provided by the parties.[192] Apparently, allowing parties' involvement in selecting the most appropriate person to chair the tribunal can be very helpful in diminishing the institutional role of the commission in this important procedural decision.

(c) Inherent defects under the institutional framework

6.073   CIETAC currently honours the parties' agreement in selecting their own arbitrators. The new Rules endeavour to give parties more freedom in managing tribunal composition, in the sense of adopting both an open-styled panel system for appointing arbitrators and a "mind-meeting" mechanism for finding the presiding arbitrator. By and large, as the most influential arbitration institution in China, these efforts have been hailed as an active response to the parties' desire for freer choices under a more liberal economy.[193] While the panel system is still fundamental to Chinese arbitration under the country's institutional arbitration tradition, the opening of the panel list is indeed a courageous step and perhaps the boldest reform the institution can make under the current legislative mandate. The new Rules have received positive feedback from both academics and practitioners for respecting more parties' procedural autonomy. However, do the improvements go far enough to realise party autonomy?

6.074   In particular, as we recall the lessons from previous chapters, due to the existing administrative infrastructure, the discretionary approval from the chairman of CIETAC may actually defeat the parties' original intention of selecting arbitrators from off the list.[194] The conditional permission on the parties' wider choices thus could become an awkward compromise on party autonomy within the context of institutional control. Indeed, parties are still very cautious and even reluctant to exercise their right to make an off-the-list appointment. Such an appointment has barely been reported since the

---

[189]   As a matter of fact, it is highly unlikely that disputants will reach a consensus on the appointment of the presiding arbitrator, or in the case of a one-member tribunal, the sole arbitrator.

[190]   Article 22(3) of the 2005 CIETAC Rules. It is understood that, following art.21 of the Rules, the proposing of the prospective presiding arbitrator, if CIETAC agrees, need not be from the CIETAC panels as well.

[191]   Chua Eu Jin, "Arbitration in the People's Republic of China", (2005) 1 *Asian International Arbitration Journal*, 23.

[192]   Article 22(4) of the 2005 CIETAC Rules. Under art.23 of the Rules, the appointment of the sole arbitrator shall follow the same procedure.

[193]   Cohen, "The Delicate Art of Arbitration" (2005).

[194]   See discussions above under the heading "Tribunal's Competence Recognised by Commission Rules" in Chapter 5, where the author commented that the discretionary approval of the CIETAC chairman in allowing the tribunal's jurisdictional autonomy could very likely end up with undesirable results.

promulgation of the new Rules.[195] This could be due to a concern that the subsequent enforcement of the award may be problematic owing to uncertainty over the proper "qualifications" of the off-listed arbitrators.

Nevertheless, key challenges faced by the reform remain the way in which arbitration commissions work. In this regard, CIETAC's continuing practice of requiring the commission chairman to scrutinise the choices beyond the list clearly gives the institution leverage over parties' autonomy and compromises parties' interests. However, the many intertwined political and administrative pressures operating behind CIETAC make its reform appear competent yet hesitant, which continues to be one of the major hurdles to its internationalisation. This is the dilemma that CIETAC needs to resolve in balancing party autonomy and institutional influence. The enthusiastic pursuit of an unconditional open-panel system therefore becomes the urgent task of developed commissions, such as CIETAC, which stands at the forefront of Chinese arbitration practice and which needs to compete on the arbitration market internationally.   6.075

(d) Proposals for change

Studies on the Chinese closed panel system reveal a dual layer of *control* on private tribunal formation: legislative control through the Arbitration Law in adopting commission panels and institutional control under the arbitration commission rules requiring parties to appoint arbitrators from commission panel lists. Such control amounts to a serious constraint on party autonomy, standing in sharp contrast against international arbitration norms. The situation becomes worse with the commission's staff members and government officials dominating the mandatory panel list among most, if not all, arbitration commissions. Moreover, the majority of the staff and official arbitrators come from a common local background. In view of delicate local connections (*guanxi*), the arbitrators are susceptible to influences from various sources and aspects, further compromising the parties' autonomy and interests. This analysis further shows that just as the reluctance to accept *ad hoc* and *competence-competence*, the primary reasons contributing to the closed panel practices are China's political and administrative dominance in its economic and social life. Accordingly, parties' expectation of an autonomous and fair dispute resolution mechanism of Chinese arbitration might be gradually losing.   6.076

Institutional efforts have thus been made within this context. Adaptive endeavours were first seen from CIETAC, which as the leading arbitration institution in China, has many times pioneered reforms in line with international norms and practices. Lately, CIETAC has taken an important step forward in allowing the parties to choose their arbitrators from beyond the panel lists. However, it is submitted that such permission should *not* attach any discretionary conditions such as the need for approval by the chairman of the commission, as the potential for administrative and political interference may result in deviation from reform objectives. On the appointment of   6.077

---

[195] According to the statistics of the CIETAC Research Institute, since the promulgation of the updated CIETAC Rules, only three cases have adopted the arbitrators chosen from beyond the panel list. (Email interview with Dr Wang Wenying, Head of the CIETAC Research Institute, 28 February 2008).

presiding arbitrators, the new "match-up" scheme appears another praiseworthy effort to respect the parties' meeting of minds. It is good to note, as well, that some more developed local commissions, such as BAC, preceded CIETAC in embarking on such scheme.[196]

6.078 Both reforms have *failed* to resolve, however, concerns about the imbalance of nationalities within the tribunal and the resulting Chinese biases where the foreign parties may still worry about the impartiality of dispute resolution. Yet the inside story shows that even if the nationality requirement is to be liberalised, foreign arbitrators may nevertheless decline appointment due to unreasonably low fees paid to arbitrators in the Chinese arbitration system. Compensation for arbitrators will thus need to be duly increased to attract qualified foreign specialists; this, in turn, will require appropriate adjustments to the commission's fee structure,[197] which may also come down to whether the arbitration commissions are willing to step out of the shadows of administrative and political control. However, apart from the commission's financial constraints, there are further concerns with respect to the affordability to engage in such foreign arbitrator service by the Chinese parties. There have been more and more reports on big Chinese companies adopting foreign arbitral institutions in resolving their transnational disputes in recent years.[198] It is thus expected that Chinese parties will gradually engage in appointing foreign arbitrators as a result of the ever-booming Chinese economy.

6.079 Is it likely that China's arbitration commissions will be ready, willing and able to adopt these recommendations in the foreseeable future? CIETAC's recent Rules update suggests that it may be possible to do so, although the discretionary approval of the chairman is expected to stay for a certain period of time to maintain the institutional influence. It may also be possible for the local commissions in the major cities such as BAC to reform along CIETAC lines, thereby offering the parties considerable freedom in managing the arbitral procedure. However, local commissions themselves may have difficulties abandoning their compulsory roster of arbitrators without the active support of the local people's government which supervises the development of the relevant local commission. The lack of institutional integrity of the majority of local arbitration commissions could therefore subject their reform endeavours to interferences from various sources. All these factors reflect practical constraints on the development of arbitration in China. In addition, without formal recognition by state legislations, informal changes by update of institutional rules may be fraught with risks. Thus far, the newly issued SPC Interpretations in 2006 also fail to touch upon these issues,[199] and a revision to the Arbitration Law is urgently called for to incorporate the above proposals and accomplish these reform endeavours.

---

[196] See art.18(2) of the BAC Rules 2004 (effective from 1 March 2004) available at http://www.bjac.com.cn/program/rule.htm.

[197] Zhao, "Reforming Chinese Arbitration Law and Practices in the Global Economy (1)", fn 145 above.

[198] For example, in 2001, Sino-Petro adopted ICC arbitration for resolving a major transnational dispute. In 2003, Lenovo went to AAA for arbitration. There are as well a large number of Chinese companies choosing HKIAC and SIAC for arbitrations each year.

[199] SPC Interpretations on Several Issues out of the Application of the Arbitration Law of the People's Republic of China, see discussions above under the heading "Critical Turning since 2006: Unified SPC Interpretation on Arbitration" in Chapter 4. The interpretations, however, failed to touch upon the regulations of the appointment of arbitrators.

JUDICIAL INTERVENTION AND ENFORCEMENT

As studied in Chapter 5, in China, the final say over arbitral jurisdiction, such as ruling on the existence and validity of an arbitration agreement,[1] belongs to the national court, which is deemed as one of the two limbs of supervisory powers of courts versus arbitration.[2] However, the real exercise of judicial supervision depends on how the court treats arbitration, which is largely influenced by the status quo of its judicial system in a given jurisdiction. Chapter 7 attempts to explore the answers to three key questions. First, whether there is any shortage in the legislative approach of judicial review over arbitral jurisdiction under the current Arbitration Law and its ancillary rules after comparison with international arbitration norms. Secondly, to what extent recently the Supreme People's Court (SPC) has made efforts to live up to international standards for prevention of excessive judicial intervention in arbitral jurisdiction. Thirdly, whether these regulatory remedies are sufficient, particularly whether enforcement difficulties still exist despite the rigorous SPC pro-arbitration move in the past decade.

7.001

1. CONCERNS ABOUT EXCESSIVE JUDICIAL INTERVENTION

(a) Prioritised judicial review under the Arbitration Law and Supreme People's Court interpretations

The "parallel reviewing power over the arbitration agreement between the arbitral body and national court" underlying art.5 of the Arbitration Law seems to conflict with the "prioritised judicial review" subsequently prescribed under arts.20 and 26 where legislative ambiguity arises.

7.002

(i) *Legislative ambiguity among the provisions*

Under the Arbitration Law, judicial review over the arbitration agreement is addressed through the provisions of arts.5, 20, and 26. In the beginning, art.5 mandates the conditions to invoke such review:

7.003

> "If the parties have concluded an arbitration agreement and one party initiates an action in a people's court, the people's court shall not accept the case and shall refer that to the arbitration commission, unless the arbitration agreement is null and void. The decision by the arbitration commission is final."[3]

According to the legislative annotations, art.5 has been formulated to respect the original intention of the parties to arbitrate. Further, the provision intends to strike a balance between party autonomy and judicial intervention in that the people's court will not intervene in the arbitration process *unless* its basis, the arbitration agreement,

7.004

---

[1] As previously explained in Chapter 5, for the purpose of this book, the judicial supervision over the arbitral jurisdiction is used interchangeably with that over the existence and validity of the arbitration agreement. See the "Introduction" part of Chapter 5.

[2] The court's supervisory power over arbitration is exercised in two ways: (1) to examine the effectiveness of the arbitration agreement; (2) to review the arbitral award.

[3] Article 5 of the Arbitration Law.

is non-existent or invalid.[4] Article 5, thus, appears to accord with modern arbitration norms.[5]

7.005   In addition, art.20 addresses the procedure with respect to the exercise of judicial review by dealing with the competing jurisdiction between a court and an arbitration commission, where the party challenges the validity of an arbitration agreement. Pursuant to art.20:

> "If a party challenges the validity of an arbitration agreement, it may request the arbitration commission to make a decision or apply to the people's court for a ruling. If one party requests the commission to make a decision and the other party applies to the court for a ruling, the court *shall* give a ruling. A party's challenge of the effect of the arbitration agreement shall be raised prior to the arbitral tribunal's first hearing."[6]

7.006   This jurisdictional challenge provision has two aspects of meanings: (1) if the parties separately apply to the arbitration commission and the people's court for a ruling on the effect of the arbitration agreement, the decision of the court will prevail; and (2) the request for judicial review (raising the jurisdictional challenge) should be made before the first hearing of the tribunal.[7] It follows from art.20 that judicial power to review the effect of arbitration agreements trumps the arbitration commission. This, however, contradicts the underlying ideology of art.5 and may lead to internal conflict about the understanding of the provisions.[8]

7.007   In further dealing with the condition and procedure prescribed under arts.5 and 20, art.26 goes on to provide that:

> "If the parties have concluded an arbitration agreement and one party has initiated an action in a people's court without declaring the existence of the arbitration agreement and, after the people's court has accepted the case, the other party submits the arbitration agreement prior to the first hearing of the court, the people's court shall dismiss the case unless the arbitration agreement is null and void. If, prior to the first hearing, the other party has not raised an objection, it shall be deemed to have renounced the arbitration agreement and the people's court shall continue to try the case."[9]

7.008   Subject to the time-limit under art.20, art.26 provides that the failure to submit the jurisdictional challenge to the court within the statutory period (before the first hearing) will be treated as a waiver of the arbitration agreement.[10] Yet, art.26 fails to clarify the confusion between arts.5 and 20 as to whether judicial review over the effect of an arbitration agreement is superior to its arbitral counterpart.

---

[4]   Legislative Affairs Commission of the NPCSC of the PRC (ed), *Arbitration Laws of China* (Hong Kong: Sweet & Maxwell, 1997), 36–37.

[5]   John Shijian Mo, *Arbitration Law in China* (Hong Kong: Sweet & Maxwell, 2001), 105.

[6]   Article 20 of the Arbitration Law.

[7]   The Legislative Affairs Commission of the NPCSC of the PRC, *Arbitration Laws of China* (1997), 62–63.

[8]   Mo, *Arbitration Law in China* (2001), 106.

[9]   Article 26 of the Arbitration Law.

[10]   Legislative Affairs Commission of the NPCSC of the PRC, *Arbitration Laws of China* (1997), 66.

The legislative ambiguity under the Arbitration Law was addressed, in 1998, by the **7.009**
SPC Reply to Several Issues of Ascertaining the Validity of Arbitration Agreements
(the SPC Reply).[11] Under art.3(1) of the SPC Reply, if an arbitration commission
has accepted the jurisdictional challenge and has rendered a decision *prior to* the
same motion being filed to the people's court, the court *must* dismiss the application.
However, if the arbitration commission has not made its decision before the party raises
jurisdictional challenge to the court, the court *shall* accept the application of challenge
and notify the commission to terminate the arbitral proceeding.[12] In 1998, the Xiamen
Intermediate People's Court applied this article of the SPC judicial interpretation in
Re Xingda Co (Xiamen) Ltd.[13]

According to the SPC Reply, under art.3(2), the following could occur: (1) if one party   **7.010**
files a dispute arising from contract or other property issues for arbitration, while the
other party challenges the validity of the arbitration agreement before the people's
court, and (2) initiates the lawsuit in respect of the same dispute, then, (3) once the
case has been accepted by the people's court, the court *must* instruct the arbitration
commission to terminate the arbitral proceeding. Article 4 further provides that after
the court decides the arbitration agreement to be either valid or invalid, it *shall* send
a copy of its ruling to the arbitration commission, which must then decide either to
resume the proceeding or withdraw the case according to the court's instructions.[14]
In 1999, these rules were applied in *Hongji Real Estate Development Co Ltd v
Communication Bank (Chongqing).*[15] The case relates to a contract for the sale of
a commercial residence concluded in December 1998. The contract contained an
arbitration clause to the "arbitration institution of Chongqing Municipality". Since the
Hongji Company did not wish to pursue arbitration for resolving disputes, in 1999,
it applied to the Chongqing Higher People's Court for a ruling that the arbitration
clause was invalid and asked the court to try the case instead. The court notified the
Chongqing Arbitration Commission to suspend the arbitral proceeding. In ruling
on the validity, the court held that the arbitration clause was reasonably clear as the
Chongqing Arbitration Commission was established in accordance with the Arbitration
Law. The court dismissed the application and the arbitration commission resumed the
arbitral proceeding.[16]

---

[11] Reply on Several Issues of Ascertaining the Validity of the Arbitration Agreement, Fa Shi [1998] No. 27, issued
by the SPC on 26 October 1998.

[12] Article 3(1) of the SPC Reply.

[13] In the *Re Xingda* case, there was a contract for the sale of steel between a Xiamen Company (A) and a Hong
Kong Company (B). The contract of sale had two versions: a printed English version providing for arbitration in
CIETAC and a handwritten Chinese version providing for arbitration in US. In 1998, A submitted the dispute to
CIETAC, but B challenged the CIETAC's jurisdiction to the Xiamen Intermediate People's Court on the ground
of the hand-written arbitration clause. The Xiamen Court, while the CIETAC proceedings were still ongoing to
reach the determination on the effect of the arbitration clause, accepted the case and notified the CIETAC to stop
the proceeding pursuant to art.3(1) of the "SPC Reply 1998". (State Information Center, *Database of Chinese
Law*, CD, in Chinese).

[14] Article 3(2) of the SPC Reply.

[15] *Selected Cases on Chinese Arbitration*, available at China Arbitration Website, http://www.china-arbitration.com.

[16] *Ibid.*

7.011   There are several points worth noting in understanding art.3 of the SPC Reply. To begin with, under Chinese jurisprudence, judicial interpretations must be qualified by the primary law to be interpreted.[17] Pursuant to art.20 of the Arbitration Law, the jurisdictional challenge to arbitration must be raised prior to the first hearing of the arbitral tribunal. Therefore, the SPC rules apply only when a party brings the jurisdictional challenge before the first hearing of the arbitral tribunal. In addition, within the timeline, the judiciary may intervene whenever the arbitration commission's decision on the effect of arbitration agreement is pending, and the arbitral proceeding must be stopped once the court accepts the case. In accordance with art.3(2), the arbitral tribunal can only resume the proceeding if the court instructs it to do so. As such, the rules may provide the chance for the opposing party to use dilatory tactics to request judicial review. It is thus submitted that such judicially-oriented review procedures defeat the efficiency of arbitration. Moreover, the SPC rules confirm the primacy of judicial power in determining the arbitral jurisdiction versus the arbitration commission.[18]

7.012   While there is a rising trend to minimise judicial intervention in arbitral proceeding in the international arbitration community, the comparative research discussed below shows that the gap between the Chinese regulatory approach and international norms is still large.

(ii) *Gap with international arbitration norms and practices*

7.013   This section will discuss two major defects of judicial review over arbitral jurisdiction in China in comparison with international arbitration norms: (1) the prioritised judicial review in procedure, and (2) the wider scope of judicial scrutiny in reviewing defective arbitration agreements.

Procedure of Review

7.014   While international arbitration norms recognise national courts as the final authority to determine arbitral jurisdiction, the grant of a stay in cases of jurisdictional challenge will never stop the arbitral proceeding from moving forward. Instead, there are parallel proceedings before the tribunal and court.

7.015   Largely modeled on the basis of art.21 of the UNCITRAL Rules which deals with jurisdiction pleas in the arbitral tribunal,[19] under the UNCITRAL Model Law, judicial review of the arbitration agreement can be exercised in three different stages—before, during or after arbitral proceedings. Pursuant to the Model Law:

---

[17]   According to the Legislation Law and People's Court Organization Law, the SPC judicial interpretation can not violate the provisions of the basic law it interprets.

[18]   Some authors comment such "priority" as one aspect of Chinese distinctive "court-decisive" theory in arbitration. See Zhao Xiuwen, *Studies on the International Commercial Arbitration and Its Applicable Law (Guoji Shangshi Zhongcai jiqi Shiyong Falu Yanjiu)* (Beijing: Beijing University Press, 2002), 43.

[19]   Articles 21(3)–21(4) of the UNCITRAL Rules provides that in general, the arbitral tribunal should rule on the plea as a preliminary question. However, the tribunal may also proceed with the arbitration and rule on the plea in its final award which will only happen when it considers that the plea is obviously unfounded.

(1)   The court may decide, *before the tribunal has been formed*, whether a valid arbitration agreement exists. Arbitral proceedings may nevertheless be commenced or continued and an award may be made, while the issue is pending before the court.[20]

(2)   *During the arbitral proceeding*, if the tribunal decides as a preliminary ruling of the validity of the arbitration agreement,[21] within 30 days upon the receipt of the ruling of the tribunal, any party may request the court to decide the matter, which decision is subject to no appeal.[22]

(3)   If the tribunal decides to rule on the validity of an arbitration agreement in the arbitral award which is usually the circumstance when it is convinced it has jurisdiction,[23] then, the court's review must wait till *after the arbitral proceeding ends* and be exercised during the proceeding of recourse against the award.[24]

In dealing with the jurisdictional challenge, the Model Law acknowledges that the tribunal's ruling on arbitral jurisdiction is subject to a final ruling of the court.[25] However, after the tribunal has been formed and the arbitral proceeding has been commenced, a party intending to make a jurisdictional challenge must first exhaust available arbitral procedures in accordance with art.16(3) of the Model Law. For example, recently, in *Netsys Technology Group AB v Open Text Corp*, the Ontario Supreme Court in Canada granted a stay and held that it would not be appropriate for the court, at this stage [during the arbitral proceeding], to rule before the tribunal has spoken on the effect of arbitration agreements. Thus, the court deferred to the arbitrator to be the first to interpret the arbitration clause.[26]   **7.016**

Moreover, the Model Law requires that any challenge to the tribunal's jurisdiction should not affect the arbitral hearing of the case. The purpose of such "concurrent or parallel proceedings", in the words of Professor Peter Binder,[27] is to avoid the dilatory tactics and disruption to the proceedings by unfounded challenges to the jurisdiction of the tribunal.[28] Particularly, the tribunal is allowed to continue with the arbitral hearing and even render an award while the jurisdictional challenge is pending before the   **7.017**

---

[20] Article 8(2) of the Model Law.
[21] According to art.16 of the Model Law, the arbitral tribunal has discretion to choose whether to decide a jurisdiction problem in the manner of preliminary question or in an award of merits.
[22] Article 16(3) of the Model Law.
[23] Article 16(3) of the Model Law.
[24] Article 34(2)(A) of the Model Law.
[25] Article 16(3) of the Model Law.
[26] *Netsys Technology Group AB v Open Text Corp* (Stinson J, unpublished), 29 July 1999, CLOUT No. 3134.
[27] See Peter Binder, *International Commercial Arbitration in UNCITRAL Model Law Jurisdictions* (London: Sweet & Maxwell, 2000), para 2-047.
[28] See the *Analytical Commentary of the Model Law*, "to reduce the risk and effects of dilatory tactics of a party reneging on his commitment to arbitration", UN Document A/CN.9/264, Art.8, para 5. For example, the tribunal can "assess in each case whether the risk of dilatory tactics is greater than the danger of wasting money and time in a useless arbitration", and decide accordingly a jurisdiction question preliminarily or in the final award. See also Howard Holtzman and Joseph Neuhaus, *A guide to the UNCITRAL Model Law on International Commercial Arbitration: Legislative History and Commentary* (Deventer: Kluwer Law and Taxation, 1989), 486.

court. As such, two proceedings are allowed at the same time, one before the national court concerning the jurisdictional matters and the other before the arbitral tribunal on the merits of the case.

7.018   The United Kingdom takes a similar "concurrent/parallel" approach regarding the procedure of judicial review over arbitration agreements. First, the English court will only rule on the effect unless it is satisfied that the arbitration agreement is null and void, inoperative or incapable of being performed.[29] Secondly, whilst different standards apply to the judicial review of different types of arbitral awards (domestic and international),[30] the regime for reviewing arbitral jurisdiction as to the condition and procedure are applicable to both domestic and international arbitration.[31] Thirdly and most importantly, by virtue of s.67(2) of the English Arbitration Act, the arbitral tribunal may continue the arbitral proceeding and make an award *while* an application to the court challenging arbitral jurisdiction is pending; and the tribunal can move to render the jurisdictional determination in the form of either a preliminary ruling or a final award.[32]

7.019   Based on the authoritative commentary on the English Arbitration Act forwarded by Lord Justice Bingham in association with the Chartered Institute of Arbitrators, the purpose of s.67(2) is to avoid unnecessary delay in arbitral proceedings, and to "let the arbitrators who used to be timid about proceeding in such circumstances have clear authority to do so".[33] In *The Joanna V,* the English Commercial Court struck down a motion by the respondent who attempted to halt the arbitral proceeding by challenging the jurisdiction of the arbitral tribunal.[34]

7.020   Chinese regulations have addressed the issue of judicial supervision over arbitration agreements by dividing the jurisdictional power between the court and arbitration commission. The overwhelming impression of the Arbitration Law and SPC Reply is that procedurally, the court has been equipped with greater authority in reviewing the arbitration agreement. Therefore, rather than the "concurrent or parallel proceedings" approach under the Model Law and English Arbitration Act, where judicial "intervention" should follow the tribunal's ruling on arbitral jurisdiction,[35] the people's courts in China are authorised to exercise jurisdictional power even prior to that of the arbitral tribunal (*youxian guanxiaquan*). This peculiar procedural mechanism allows judges in China to intervene in the arbitral proceedings too early and may improperly subject arbitration to the courts in practice. Some Chinese commentators argue that the procedural priority of the people's court in reviewing arbitration agreements allows for excessive judicial intervention or even a negation of the doctrine of

[29]   Section 9(4) of the English Arbitration Act.
[30]   Parties can appeal on a question of law of domestic arbitral awards, while this is not available to international awards. See s.69 of the English Arbitration Act. This is similarly worded under s.23 of the Arbitration Ordinance (Cap.341).
[31]   Section 9(4) of the English Arbitration Act.
[32]   Section 67(2) of the English Arbitration Act.
[33]   Bruce Harris, Rowan Planterose and Jonathan Tecks, *The Arbitration Act 1996: A Commentary* (4th ed.) *(Forwarded by Senior Law Lord Bingham and Published in Association with the Chartered Institute of Arbitrators* (London: Blackwell Publishing, 2007), 309.
[34]   *The Joanna V* [2003] 2 Lloyd's Rep 617.
[35]   The tribunal's jurisdictional power derives from the doctrine of *competence-competence*.

competence-competence.[36] In addition, unless the tribunal has accepted the case and has made a ruling on the effect of arbitration agreement before the court's action, all arbitral proceedings will be stayed until the court has announced its decision.[37] Hence, the objecting party may take advantage of the procedural loophole and delay the dispute resolution process.

More controversially, art.58 of the Arbitration Law stipulates that the people's courts can revoke or refuse to enforce an arbitration award on the basis of a "non-existent" arbitration agreement.[38] Pursuant to art.20 of the Arbitration Law, Chinese judicial review with respect to arbitral jurisdiction may only be exercised before the commencement of arbitral proceedings.[39] It is therefore contentious whether "invalidity" could be a ground for invoking judicial review in the award enforcement stage or whether the judicial supervisory power regarding arbitration agreements can be extended to post-award stage. The Arbitration Law failed to address the issue and the subsequent SPC Reply did not clarify this point.   **7.021**

Scope of Review

Prevailing international norms provide a broader scope than the Arbitration Law in saving defective arbitration agreements by national courts. As such, in practice, courts have openly shown their tendency to respect the parties' intention to arbitrate except in cases of extreme vagueness of arbitral agreements.   **7.022**

Pursuant to art.8(1) of the Model Law, the court is bound to honor the arbitration agreement, "unless the agreement is null and void, inoperative or incapable of being performed".[40] Under art.8(1), which is modeled on art.II(3) of the New York Convention (NYC), the court of a contracting state, when challenged by one party with respect to the effect of the arbitration agreement between the parties, shall at the request of one of the parties, refer the parties to arbitration, "unless it finds the said agreement is null and void, inoperative or incapable of being performed".[41] Section 9(4) of the English Arbitration Act has adopted similar wordings to the Model Law and NYC with respect to a mandatory stay by the English courts even if there is only a slim chance for "operativeness or effectiveness" of arbitration agreements.[42] This is natural as most of the jurisdictional challenges that come before the court relate to ambiguous arbitration agreements resulting from defective draftsmanship—defectiveness often borders on the verge of enforceability and unenforceability.[43] Thus, it is important that to what   **7.023**

---

[36]   Xie Shisong, *Studies on Commercial Arbitration (Shangshi Zhongcai Faxue)* (Beijing: Higher Education Press, 2003), 209–210.

[37]   See art.3 of the SPC Reply.

[38]   Article 58 of the Arbitration Law and art.260 of the Civil Procedure Law both provide grounds for the refusal of the recognition and enforcement of arbitral awards, among which, the first ground refers to "the non-existence of an arbitration agreement". Neither of the two provisions involves the "invalidity of the arbitration agreement" as one of the grounds to exercise judicial supervision.

[39]   See the wordings "prior to the first hearing" provided in art.20 of the Arbitration Law.

[40]   Article 8(1) of the Model Law.

[41]   Article II(3) of the NYC.

[42]   Section 9(4) of the English Arbitration Act.

[43]   See ICCA, "Resolutions of the Working Group II: Arbitration and Courts", in *Proceedings of the Sixth International Arbitration Congress*, Mexico City, 13–16 March 1978, recorded in (1979) IV *Yearbook of Commercial Arbitration* xxii, para 2.

extent national courts accommodate these drafting defects and consequent pathologies. In this regard, both English courts and courts under Model Law jurisdictions have been found to give broad interpretation to arbitration agreements, favoring arbitral authority. This happens even in some extreme pathological cases, such as the famous *Lucky Goldstar* ruling rendered by Justice Kaplan in Hong Kong.[44] Based on Professor Pieter Sander's observation of international commercial arbitration, this broader scope of judicial respect for arbitration prevalent in the international context has become a general trend where courts are increasingly willing to "recognise the preference of parties to have their commercial disputes decided in arbitration".[45]

7.024   In China, however, the court has been vested with more judicial discretion in reviewing arbitration agreements. The obvious difference between the Chinese regulations and international norms is that the Arbitration Law lacks a transitional area of "operativeness/inoperativeness" through which the court's mandatory stay has been restricted to circumstances of either nullity or invalidity of arbitration agreements.[46] The omission of "inoperativeness" as the critical ground to opt-in/out-of the court's jurisdiction surely enlarges the scope of judicial scrutiny. As such, it restricts the room for judicial "support" whereby the court can take into account the surrounding circumstances to "imply" the parties' intent to arbitrate.[47] Given the rigid validity requirements of the arbitration agreement under the Arbitration Law,[48] this may provide an excuse for the Chinese court to reject arbitral jurisdiction by adopting a strict textual interpretation of the arbitration agreement and consequently stay the arbitral proceedings in cases of "pathological yet operative" arbitral clauses. The legislative deficiency with regard to judicial power over arbitral jurisdiction raises the concern of excessive judicial intervention into arbitration.[49] This also helps to explain why the SPC has been busy issuing judicial interpretations regarding pathological arbitration agreements and why it has been so vigorous in leading the reform of aligning Chinese arbitration with international standards.[50]

(b) Supreme People's Court initiatives to limit judicial intervention: Alignment with international arbitration norms

7.025   In response to the international trend of giving more judicial respect to arbitration, the SPC, over the past decade, has issued a long list of clarifications as regards how to exercise judicial supervision over arbitration agreements. Basically, these clarifications

---

[44] *Lucky-Goldstar International (HK) Ltd v Ng Moo Kee Engineering Ltd* [1993] 2 HKLR 73: reference to "arbitration in a third country under the rules of International Commercial Arbitration Association" was also saved by the Hong Kong High Court—the court held that "the arbitration clause was poorly drafted, yet sufficiently indicated the parties' intention to arbitrate and therefore operative and capable of being performed".

[45] Julian D.M. Lew, *Comparative International Commercial Arbitration* (The Hague: Kluwer Law International, 2003), 73.

[46] See the wordings "null and void" in arts.5 and 26(1) of the Arbitration Law.

[47] See Gao Fei, "Support and Supervision towards Arbitration by Chinese Courts (Zhongguo Fayuan dui Zhongcai de Zhichi yu Jiandu)", (2001) 66 *Arbitration in China (Zhongguo Zhongcai)*, 7.

[48] See art.16 of the Arbitration Law; see also discussions above in Chapter 4.

[49] Chen Zhidong, *International Commercial Arbitration Law (Guoji Shangshi Zhongcai Fa)* (Beijing: China Law Press, 1998), 144.

[50] See discussions above in Chapter 4.

have been introducing reforms such as more cautious procedures and more liberal scopes in exercising the review power.

(i) *More cautious procedure*

The reform to implement more cautious procedure with respect to arbitration includes the introduction of the following schemes: (1) the pre-reporting system, (2) an intermediate-level-above and collegiate-panel system, and finally (3) a review-waiving system.   **7.026**

Pre-reporting system

The SPC, through issuing a series of notices in 1995 and 1998 (the SPC Notices), established the "pre-reporting" system (*youxian baogao*) among the people's courts in reviewing the effect of foreign-related arbitration agreements and arbitral awards.[51] In accordance with these notices, the "pre-reporting" system can be sub-divided into three scenarios in arbitral cases involving foreign elements: (1) before the SPC replies officially, the lower people's courts shall not announce the arbitration agreement to be null or void; (2) until the SPC replies officially, the lower people's court shall not rule to refuse the recognition and enforcement of award; and (3) only after the SPC replies officially can the lower people's courts rule to deny the effect of arbitration agreements or arbitral awards.[52]   **7.027**

The origin of the "pre-reporting" system arises from the damaging case of *Revpower* in 1993 where the Shanghai Intermediate People's Court refused to recognise and enforce a foreign arbitral award due to the bankruptcy of a Shanghai factory.[53] Other reasons may be attributed to the dual-track approach adopted by the Arbitration Law where preferential treatment has been reserved to foreign-related arbitration.[54] Based on this tradition, grounds for enforcing foreign-related awards are aligned with international standards and restricted to procedural review; however, domestic arbitral awards need to be subject to substantive as well as procedural checks.[55] Under   **7.028**

---

[51] See the SPC Notice on Some Issues Concerning Foreign Arbitration and Arbitration in Foreign Countries, Fa Fa (1995) No. 18; Notice on Regulations on the Fee and Time Limit of Recognition and Enforcement of Foreign Arbitration Awards, Fa Shi (1998) No. 28; and Notice on Some Issues Concerning Setting Aside Arbitration Awards Related to Foreign Elements by the People's Court, Fa Fa (1998) No. 40.

[52] *Ibid*.

[53] In order to deny the legal effect of the arbitral award made by a tribunal in the Arbitration Institute of the Stockholm Chamber of Commerce (SCC) against a Shanghai factory in 1993, the Shanghai Intermediate Court accepted a separate lawsuit filed by the factory on the same subject matter after the date of the final hearing of the arbitration was set. The Court did not correct its mistake until after the Supreme People's Court exerted pressure and the Shanghai factory was declared bankrupt in 1996. The *Revpower* case even triggered a political motion against China's admission to the WTO in the US Congress. For the details of the case, see Alberto More, "The Revpower Dispute: China's Breach of the New York Convention?", in Chris Hunter (ed), *Dispute Resolution in the PRC—A Practical Guide to Litigation and Arbitration in China* (Hong Kong: Asia Law & Practice Ltd, 1995), 151–158; see also Zhang Xian Chu, "The Agreement between China and the Hong Kong SAR on Mutual Enforcement of Arbitral Awards: Problems and Prospects", (1999) 29 *Hong Kong Law Journal*, 468.

[54] Zhao Xiuwen, "On the Principles of Arbitration Jurisdiction from Perspective of the Revpower Case (Cong Ruifudongli An Kan Zhongcai Guanxiaquan Yuanze)", (1998) 3 *Jurists' Review (Faxuejia)*, 78–87.

[55] Domestic awards in China will be checked on the grounds of "errors of law", "insufficiency of evidence", and "arbitrator misconduct"; see art.63 of the Arbitration Law and art.217 of the Civil Procedure Law. The grounds of foreign-related awards are limited to procedural irregularities; see arts. 70, 71 of the Arbitration Law and art.260 of the Civil Procedure Law.

these circumstances, because ineffective agreements are one of the grounds leading to the denial of enforcement of foreign-related awards,[56] a separate and preferential treatment regarding the judicial review over foreign-related arbitral agreements has thus been formed.

7.029 The "pre-reporting" system has an interesting feature, which is to control the negative ruling of the lower people's courts. If the foreign-related arbitration agreement has been upheld and the arbitral award enforced at the lower level judiciary, then reporting is not at all necessary. With respect to arbitration agreements, the "report" is mandatory only when the lower level people's courts tend to *negate* the effect of the agreement. Since there is no appellate procedure for rulings on matters of arbitral jurisdiction, the key importance of the "pre-reporting" is to prevent undue local influences over arbitration[57] and to improve the enforceability of arbitral jurisdictions by setting up a "pyramidal internal supervisory mechanism within the judiciary" where the SPC can control the final result of review.[58] As Tao concludes it, the system reflects the prudential attitude of the SPC towards arbitration agreements and is seen as a positive trend by the SPC in leading the lower level people's courts in China to support arbitration.[59]

7.030 The scheme, however, is not free from defects. Obviously, it is only applicable to the foreign-related regime. The quality of judicial review over domestic agreements is not subject to the same examination. Thus, vast numbers of domestic arbitration agreements are still risky ventures subject to the discretionary power of local judges. Moreover, the timeline is unclear for such "report". In the three notices issued by the SPC, there are only time limits provided for the judicial review of awards, whereby the intermediate people's court shall report to the higher people's court its decision to revoke or set aside within 30 days of the party's enforcement period; the higher people's court shall, by the same token, report to the SPC within 15 days of its decision.[60] However, none of the SPC notices issued have mentioned time limits for the review of arbitration agreements. Imagine that no timelines have been set for reporting and pre-reporting (of judicial review of arbitral agreements), parties whose agreements have been turned down at lower level courts will have endless waits before they get answered from higher level courts. That certainly runs contrary to the efficiency argument of arbitration.

Intermediate-level-above and collegial-panel system

7.031 Subsequent to the introduction of the "pre-reporting" system, in 2000, in a reply to the Shandong Higher People's Court, the SPC pronounced that any motion challenging the effect of foreign-related arbitration agreements must be made before the people's

---

[56] Article 260(1) of the Civil Procedural Law.
[57] For the local administrative influence over arbitration, see discussions above in Chapters 5 and 6. For the local judicial influence over arbitration, see discussions below under the heading "Enforcement Analysis and Practical Application of the SPC Initiatives".
[58] Wang Shengchang, "Arbitration Agreement and Its Validity Determination (Zhongcai Xieyi jiqi Xiaoli Queding)" in CIETAC (ed), *Symposium Essays on Economic and Trade Arbitration between the Taiwan Straits (Haixia Liang'an Jingmao Zhongcai Yantaohui Wenji)* (Beijing: China Law Press, 2001), 39.
[59] Jingzhou Tao, *Arbitration Law and Practice in China* (The Hague: Kluwer Law, 2004), 58.
[60] See the SPC Notices in 1995 and 1998.

court at the intermediate level or above.[61] Furthermore, the SPC now mandates under art.12 of its 2006 Interpretation (the SPC Interpretation) that any jurisdictional challenge on the basis of a non-existent or invalid arbitration agreement, irrespective of it being foreign-related or domestic, will be received by the intermediate people's court.[62] Generally, intermediate courts are equipped with better qualified and more experienced judges as compared with basic level courts (district courts).[63] The upgrade of the handling level for jurisdictional review could thus help downplay the local influences and better protect the quality of judicial review.[64] In the long run, however, district courts may also be entitled to hear foreign-related cases with their quality gradually improved.

In addition, a collegiate-panel mechanism has now been introduced under art.15 of the SPC Interpretation which requires the people's court to form a collegiate panel to conduct the examination of arbitration agreements.[65] This provision[66] adds further "caution" to the procedure of judicial review over arbitration agreements. For the first time in the Chinese arbitration history, arbitration cases, albeit very simple ones with small amounts of money involved, may be considered by the collective wisdom of three judges. Although the provision may be questioned with respect to the allocation of judicial resources, generally, this is seen as a welcomed development as it may increase the likelihood of parties' arbitral wishes being upheld.

7.032

Review-waiving system

In an attempt to further address the concerns of prioritised judicial review under the Arbitration Law and the SPC Reply, art.13 of the SPC Interpretation, on basis of art.8 of its previous Domestic Draft,[67] restates the relationship between the arbitration commission and people's court in the case of a competing jurisdiction:

7.033

"Pursuant to art.20 of the AL, where a party does not object to the validity of an arbitration agreement prior to the tribunal commences the first hearing of the case, but later applies to the people's court for announcing the invalidity of the agreement, the people's court shall not accept the case.

If an arbitration commission has made its ruling on the effect of an arbitration agreement, any application made by a party to the people's court for setting aside the decision of the commission shall not be entertained by the people's court."[68]

---

[61] SPC Reply to the Shandong Higher People's Court on "Which Level of People's Court Shall Handle the Jurisdictional Challenge of the Validity of Arbitration Agreements", Fa Shi [2000] No. 25.

[62] It should be noted that whilst art.10 of the Domestic Draft still bifurcates the court level system in reviewing the arbitration agreement, art.12 of the 2006 SPC Interpretation appears to take matters to a broader horizon.

[63] Article 9, para (6) of the Judges' Law of the PRC; see also discussions below under the heading "Analysis of enforcement divergences and difficulties".

[64] Tao, *Arbitration Law and Practice in China* (2004), 38.

[65] Article 15 of the SPC Interpretation.

[66] There have been no counterpart provisions in either Foreign-related or Domestic Draft to address the number of the judges in exercising the judicial review.

[67] See, para 2, art.8 of the Domestic Draft.

[68] Article 13 of the SPC Interpretation.

7.034   The most recent SPC Interpretation re-emphasises the stage when judicial review could be exercised upon the arbitration agreement, i.e. before the first hearing of the arbitral tribunal,[69] and where the arbitration commission has not ruled on the effect of the agreement.[70] This SPC arrangement is called a "review-waiving" system and is acclaimed as a contribution to international arbitration jurisprudence on the finality of the jurisdictional determination by the arbitral body.[71] That is, the people's court would waive its supervisory power once the effect of the arbitral agreement has been decided by the arbitration commission and such a decision is considered "final" with no further chance of review. The "review-waiving" system, cited by Professor Liu Xiaohong of East China University of Political Science and Law, is an extreme case of the SPC's approach to minimise judicial intervention with regard to the ruling of arbitral jurisdiction.[72] Other commentators, however, argue that it deprives the parties the right of judicial recourse on the issue of arbitral jurisdiction, and therefore it is not compatible with the international stipulations.[73] Generally, it should be a welcomed development. Once the arbitration commission has ruled on the validity of the arbitral agreement, it will bring certainty and finality to its effect. However, it is not clear whether arbitral proceedings could continue, pending the jurisdictional challenge before the court, prior to the tribunal rules on the jurisdiction (as the previous comparative study concerns). The latest SPC Interpretation fails to address the point. Therefore, it may be argued that "prioritised" judicial review still exists in some stage of the arbitral proceeding.

(ii) *More liberal scope*

Remediable pathologies

7.035   As elaborated in previous chapters, over the past decade, great progress has been made in liberalising the scope of validity of arbitration agreements via SPC's issuing judicial interpretations with respect to defective arbitration agreements.[74]

---

[69]   Article 20 of the Arbitration Law.

[70]   Article 3(1) of the SPC Reply.

[71]   Ge Xingjun (Head of Enforcement Division of the SPC), "Brief Comments on the Judicial Supervision over Arbitration and Improvement of Arbitration System (Jianshu Zhongcai Sifa Jiandu yu Zhongcai Zhidu de Wanshan)", in CIETAC South-China Sub-commission (ed), *Judicial Review of the Foreign-related Arbitration* (Beijing: China Law Press, 2006), 16–17.

[72]   Liu, *Jurisprudence and Empirical Research on International Commercial Arbitration Agreements* (2005), 79.

[73]   Under international arbitration norms, parties can still resort to the court for reviewing the arbitral jurisdiction even after the arbitral tribunal renders the decision. In China, since neither art.58 of the Arbitration Law nor art.260 of the Civil Procedure Law provides for "invalidity of the arbitration agreement" as one ground to revoke the arbitral award, Zhao considers that if the court waives the judicial supervision after the tribunal rules on the validity of the arbitration agreement, then it is equal to the court's depriving the parties of the right of judicial resort on the point of jurisdictional challenge on the basis of an invalid arbitration agreement determined by the commission. See Zhao Xiuwen, "Arbitral Seat and Judicial Supervision (Zhongcai Didian yu Sifa Jiandu)", in CIETAC South-China Sub-commission (ed), *Judicial Review of the Foreign-related Arbitration* (2006), 51.

[74]   See, e.g. a list of SPC replies (*pifu*), notices (*tongzhi*), and opinions (*yijian*) issued by the SPC regarding the interpretation of defective arbitration agreements, above under the heading "Judicial Efforts on Relaxing the Legislative Rigidity" of Chapter 4.

On one hand, the SPC now no longer adheres to the signature-based writing, and **7.036** a more expansive scope of the "written agreement" has been introduced.[75] Besides "incorporation by reference",[76] the SPC, corresponding with the recently published Contract Law, also recognised the effect of arbitration agreements in circumstances of contract transfer and as such can extend its effect to non-signatory third parties.[77] On the other hand, many drafting defects with respect to "clear and unequivocal arbitration commission or institution" have been stated as remediable and operative. For example, most recently, by virtue of its Interpretation in 2006, the SPC mandates that prescribing the institutional rules will be sufficient to indicate the choice of the arbitral institution which administers the rules.[78] Moreover, unclear drafting in respect of the "arbitral institution" may be held valid so long as the institutional identity can be reasonably ascertainable from the surrounding context.[79]

The interpretations by China's highest judiciary have shown more respect to parties' **7.037** drafting autonomy in arbitration and help to bridge the gap between the Arbitration Law and international arbitration norms. The practical reality of the SPC-led reform, such as the enforcement of defective arbitration agreements, will be examined in Section 2 of this chapter.

Freedom of choice in applicable law

In international commercial arbitration, finding the law applicable to an arbitration **7.038** agreement is the pre-condition in determining its validity.[80] However, in many cases, parties may forget to spell out the governing law of their arbitration agreements. Where the jurisdictional challenge is brought before the people's court, Chinese judges used to apply universally the *lex fori* (law of the reviewing court) in determining the effect of the arbitration agreement.[81] Hence, the arbitral jurisdiction may easily be turned down due to the rigid requirements imposed on the validity of the agreement by the Arbitration Law. According to art.145 of the Contract Law, parties can choose

---

[75] SPC Interpretation (2006), art.1. See discussions, above, under the heading "Unified judicial interpretation on arbitration" of Chapter 4.

[76] *Ibid,* art.11.

[77] *Ibid.,* arts. 8 and 9.

[78] *Ibid.,* art.4.

[79] *Ibid.,* art.3.

[80] Generally, entering into an international commercial contract with a provision for arbitration may, and often does involve the interplay of several different legal systems, vis.: the law governing the substantive contract (substantive rights and obligations of the parties); the law governing the arbitration agreement (validity of arbitration agreement); the law governing the arbitral procedure (institutional or *ad hoc* arbitration rules) and the law governing the recognition and enforcement of the arbitral awards (e.g. NYC). For discussions on applicable laws in international commercial arbitration, see Lew, *Comparative International Commercial Arbitration* (2003), 99–134. For example, whilst a contract may contain a clause providing for English governing law, it may also contain an arbitration agreement specifying French law to govern the interpretation of the arbitration agreement but holding arbitration before the ICC Court of Arbitration. In such cases, the arbitral procedure will be subject to the ICC Arbitration Rules whist the validity of the arbitration agreement determined in accordance with the French law. Finally, the substantive issues in the case will be judged pursuant to the English law.

[81] Adam Li and George Wang, "Conflict of Law Issues in Ascertaining Validity of An Arbitration Agreement" in Fung and Wang (eds), *Arbitration in China: A Practical Guide* (2004), para 6-21.

foreign law as the governing law only if the contract involves foreign elements.[82] The Arbitration Law fails to provide a conflict of law rule such as which law should be used to determine the validity of foreign-related arbitration agreements and the SPC tries to fill in the regulatory gap.[83]

7.039   In 1999, the SPC first announced its opinion in a rather informal way that absent the parties' choice of law applicable to their arbitration agreements, the validity should be determined according to the *lex arbitri* (law of the place of arbitration).[84] Later, in a more formal manner, art.17 of the Foreign-related Draft provided a detailed roadmap of the applicable law in determining the validity of an arbitration agreement that the people's court shall apply:

(1)   the "law" agreed upon by the parties; or

(2)   if the parties have not agreed on the "applicable law" of the arbitration agreement but have agreed on the place of arbitration (arbitral seat),[85] the law of the arbitral seat, the *lex arbitri*; or

(3)   if the parties have not agreed on the arbitral seat or the arbitral seat is not made clear from the arbitration agreement, the law of the court that received the application of jurisdictional review, the *lex fori*.[86]

7.040   In the most recent SPC Interpretations in 2006, art.16 confirms the three-step formula taken under the Foreign-related Draft.[87] The clarification accords with the general principle of party autonomy espoused under arts.19 and 28 of the Model Law, which permits the parties to freely select and determine both the substantial law and procedural rules to be followed during the arbitral proceedings.[88]

(c) Unresolved judicial intervention: Dual-track concerns

7.041   In concluding this section, in the initial stage, the Arbitration Law authorises people's courts prioritised right of review in procedure (*youxian guanxiaquan*) and more stringent review in scope with respect to arbitration agreements. This deviates from international arbitration norms and raises the issue of excessive judicial intervention

---

[82]   Therefore, in the domestic setting, there is no issue of applicability where the Arbitration Law will apply to all the arbitration agreements in determining the validity. On the other hand, whist the Arbitration Law did not mention the conflict of law rules for determining the validity of the arbitration agreement. Article 126 of the Contract Law provides for the conflict of law rules for the general contract, "the governing law will be determined according to the choice of the parties; absent the choice, the law that has the closest connection to the contract is the applicable law".

[83]   See discussions below under the heading "Unified judicial interpretation on arbitration".

[84]   *Mitsubishi Co Ltd (HK) v Sanxia Investment Co Ltd and Hubei Mechanical Engineering Co Ltd* Zui Gao Fa Fa Jing Han [1999] No. 143; reprinted in Zhu Jianlin, *Comments and Analyses on International Commercial Arbitration Cases (Guoji Shangshi Zhongcai Anli Pingxi)* (Beijing: Citic Publishing, 2002), 375–377.

[85]   Sometimes the arbitral seat is called *arbitral situs,* which is the Latin expression of arbitral seat where the arbitral proceedings are held.

[86]   Article 17 of the SPC Foreign-related Draft.

[87]   Article 16 of the SPC Interpretation.

[88]   Article 19 of the Model Law gives the parties' full freedom in choosing the procedural rules. Article 28 of the Model Law permits the parties full autonomy in selecting the law applicable to their substantive dispute.

in Chinese arbitration. The SPC, therefore, has taken a series of measures in bridging the gap. On the one hand, a more cautious judicial approach has been adopted in the procedure of review where in some extreme circumstances, people's courts may even waive their supervisory power if the arbitration commission has made a ruling on the validity of the arbitral agreement. On the other hand, more liberal interpretations on the scope of validity have been introduced for the more liberal exercise of judicial supervision.

Despite the impressive regulatory progress made by the SPC in minimising judicial interventions, it should be noted that the degree of judicial caution varies substantially between the two tracks. Preferential treatment has been reserved for the foreign-related track. Particularly, judicial review over the foreign-related regime will be extra-protected under the "pre-reporting" system. Although the handling court has been merged between the two tracks and is now upgraded to the intermediate level, foreign-related cases must be reported to the higher level people's court for approval if the lower court negates the effect of arbitration agreements or arbitral awards. As analysed, the "pre-reporting" system, by centralising the review power, would be important to prevent rampant local protectionism found in Chinese judicial practice.[89]   **7.042**

However, the "pre-reporting" system has serious shortcomings. First, the system consists of a purely internal supervision method. The parties are neither notified about the "report" nor have a chance to participate in the hearing held by the higher level people's court. Therefore, the decision-making process lacks transparency. Without the parties' right of access to the judicial proceeding, it could lead to due process concerns. In addition, allowing one case to go through limitless reviews may be an inefficient use of judicial resources. More importantly, the "pre-reporting" works like the referral system (*qingshi*) within the hierarchy of the Chinese judiciary where higher level people's courts can influence the decision of the lower levels. Thus, it harms judicial independence. Lastly and most controversially, the system is not available to the domestic regime with respect to both arbitration agreements and arbitral awards.   **7.043**

The fact that the standards for enforcing domestic awards are stricter than foreign-related awards suggests that the domestic regime is more difficult to enforce. Specifically, in an empirical study conducted by Professor Randall Peerenboom, among the sixty-three domestic awards handled by one court in a large city in Jiangsu Province, two were refused and thirty-five listed as pending.[90] Hence, the domestic regime needs careful judicial handling as well, at least no less than its foreign-related counterpart. The different treatment by the SPC raises serious concerns regarding the dual-track system. Disparate treatment could potentially lead to discrimination by people's courts from the beginning (arbitration agreement) to the end (arbitral award) with respect to the rights and autonomy of parties seeking domestic arbitration.   **7.044**

---

[89]   See discussions below under the heading "Analysis of Enforcement Divergences and Difficulties".

[90]   Randall Peerenboom, "Seek Truth from Facts: An Empirical Study of Enforcement of Arbitral Awards in the PRC", (2001) 49 *American Journal of Comparative Law*, 249.

2. ENFORCEMENT ANALYSIS AND PRACTICAL APPLICATION OF THE SUPREME PEOPLE'S COURT INITIATIVES

7.045   This section will analyse the enforcement reports of the SPC's pro-arbitration initiatives by seeking truth from facts. The enforcement samples collected in this section have been divided into two groups according to the different types of defectiveness: (1) those of "non-signatory third party"; and (2) those of "ambiguous arbitration commission". Reports by people's courts at different levels and different localities will be examined pertaining to both groups.

7.046   Before the analysis, a couple of issues must be born in mind. In China, judicial review over arbitral jurisdiction has been restricted to the pre-award stage. Thus, enforcement reports with respect to arbitration agreements are generally unavailable to the public. However, because of the "pre-reporting" system in the foreign-related regime, some negative rulings on arbitral agreements by the local people's courts become accessible through the SPC's publication of its "replies of jurisdiction" in the Gazette. The following discussion is, hence, only examining "negative" cases and limited to the "foreign-related regime". Nevertheless, it sheds light on the rulings of the domestic regime and may highlight practical constraints in the enforcement of arbitral agreements in both domestic and foreign cases.[91]

7.047   Moreover, during the transition from a planned to a market economy and in the process of developing the rule of law in China, the entire judiciary is faced with many challenges. The lack of judicial integrity and quality and the unbalanced development among the people's courts in different areas of the country may all contribute to the divergent enforcement records both in court judgments and arbitral awards. These problems are also reflected in the area of enforcement of arbitration agreements as concerned by the study below.

(a) Enforcement of "non-signatory third party"

7.048   The SPC has articulated on many occasions that transfer of legal rights and obligations of a party under an arbitration agreement should not invalidate the effect of the agreement such that it will still bind the non-signatory transferee.[92] Misunderstanding and mishandling have nevertheless been found in the local judicial application.

(i) *Longhai case: Misapplication of separability*

7.049   In 1993, the Hong Kong Longhai Company (Longhai) and Wuhan Donghu Import and Export Company (Donghu) signed an equity joint venture (EJV) contract in which a CIETAC arbitration clause was included. In December, Donghu assigned all its equities to Wuhan Zhongyuan Scientific Company (Zhongyuan) and left the EJV. Then Longhai and Zhongyuan signed a new EJV contract where Zhongyuan agreed to take

---

[91]   This is based on the fact that the court system enforcing both the domestic and foreign-related awards is the same.

[92]   The judicial guidance has been endorsed by the SPC early in its replies to the Hubei and Henan Higher People's Courts in 1997 and has been confirmed in the SPC Interpretation in 2006. See discussions above under the heading "Judicial Efforts on Relaxing the Legislative Rigidity" of Chapter 4.

over all the rights and obligations of Donghu in the original EJV contract. In 1998, a dispute arose out of the investment share between Longhai and Zhongyuan. Longhai applied to CIETAC arbitration in Beijing when Zhongyuan challenged the arbitral jurisdiction before the Wuhan Intermediate People's Court.

The Wuhan Intermediate People's Court ruled that the arbitration clause was not   **7.050** binding upon Zhongyuan on the basis that, "the arbitration clause has independent character so that the clause in the original contract has no legal force upon the new assignee". Therefore the CIETAC jurisdiction is rejected".[93] Upon reporting, the Hubei Higher People's Court replied that the arbitration agreement should survive the contract assignment and the CIETAC jurisdiction was affirmed.[94]

This case reflects how a local people's court misapplied the separability rules. The   **7.051** doctrine of separability of arbitration agreements refers to separation of arbitration clauses from the "effect" of main contracts so that the non-existence or invalidity of the main contract will not affect that of the arbitration clause.[95] Textually, however, the arbitral clause is part of the main contract such that transfer of the main contract will include transfer of the arbitral clause unless otherwise provided. Therefore, although the arbitration clause and main contract are deemed as two separate agreements in validity consideration, the former is textually attached to the latter as part.[96] As such, the arbitration clause shall be valid and binding on the non-signatory third party if it has been deemed valid before the transfer. In the case above, the new investor (Zhongyuan) has succeeded all of the rights and obligations from the original investor (Longhai) where a valid CIETAC arbitral clause forms a part. The intermediate court wrongfully applied the separability doctrine between "textual composition" and "validity effect" with respect to the relationship between the arbitral clause and its main contract and hence, this led to the denial of the arbitral jurisdiction. The *Longhai* case raises concerns with respect to the correct understanding of modern arbitration norms at the lower level people's courts.

(ii) *Huaxiang case: Scope of judicial discretions*

In July 1997, Qingdao Huaqiang International Trade Company (A), Japan Beitiaoli   **7.052** Chemical Research Institute and Japan Zhuneitiegong Company invested together in establishing the Qingdao Huaxiang Joint Venture (BJV). Article 38 of the JV contract provided that "any dispute among the three investing parties regarding the investment contract shall be resolved by CIETAC according to its rules". In September 2001, upon the agreement by the three investing parties, Huaqiang assigned its entire 35 per cent share in the JV to the Qingdao Huaqiangda Technical Company (C). Later, C withdrew all its investment from the BJV. B sued C for violating the investment obligations under

---

[93] Wuhan Intermediate People's Court Civil Adjudication (1998) No. 0277.

[94] Hubei Higher People's Court (1999) E Fa Shen Jian Jing Zai Zi.

[95] Pierre Mayer, "The Limits of Severability of the Arbitration Clause" in Albert Jan van den Berg (ed), *Improving the Efficiency of Arbitration Awards: 40 Years of Application of the New York Convention: ICCA Congress Series No. 9* (The Hague: Kluwer Law International, 1999), 68.

[96] Qu Guangqing, Chen Xiaoyun and Xing Lei, "Thinking of the Effect of the Arbitration Clause under the Contract Transfer – Comments on the *Hong Kong Longhai Co v Wuhan Zhongyuan Co*", in Song Yaowu (ed), *International Commercial Dispute Resolution Review (Guoji Shangshi Zhengyi Jiejue Luncong)* (Harrbin: Harrbin Industrial University Press, 2004), 90.

the original JV contract. Before the first statement on defence, C raised jurisdictional challenge to the Qingdao Intermediate People's Court. The challenge was based on the arbitration clause found in the original JV contract which stated that CIETAC should be the proper venue for dispute resolution.

7.053   In September 2003, in ruling on the validity of the arbitration clause between B and C, the opinions were divided within Qingdao Intermediate Court. The first group opined that "the rights and obligations of dispute resolution should accompany the general transfer of the rights and obligations of the investment contract so that the arbitration clause should be enforceable upon C and B". The second group was of the opinion that "the arbitration clause had independent nature and thus the share transfer could not necessarily lead to the transfer of dispute resolution clause unless it was expressly agreed by the transferee".[97] The Intermediate Court finally referred to the "Beijing Opinion 1999" in resolving the dilemma. Article 3 of the "Beijing Opinion 1999" provided that: "If there is an arbitration agreement among the investing parties for resolving the dispute(s) arising out of the investment, that arbitration agreement will not be binding between the investor and JV investee."[98] Hence, the CIETAC jurisdiction was denied. The Shandong Higher People's Court,[99] on the basis of the "Beijing Opinion 1999", confirmed the ruling of the Qingdao Intermediate Court through the reporting system.[100]

7.054   In the final stage of the reporting, in its reply to the Shandong Higher People's Court, the SPC confirmed the court jurisdiction and held that, "Since the BJV has not taken part in the negotiations of the JV investment contract where the arbitration clause forms a part, the arbitration agreement within the JV contract will not carry effect upon the non-investing party who did not involve in the performance of the JV contract".[101]

7.055   Several points may be observed from the *Huaxiang* case. First, like the *Longhai* case in the Wuhan Intermediate People's Court, misunderstanding as to the principle of separability also existed in the Qingdao Intermediate Court.[102] The coincidence may, to some extent, reflect the poor knowledge of modern arbitration by lower level courts. Since Wuhan and Qingdao are upper mid-level Chinese cities, their judicial quality with respect to handling of arbitration cases indicates the average quality of local Chinese judges with respect to understanding arbitration norms. In addition, when the SPC criterion is unclear, the enforcement could be subject to the discretionary interpretative power by the local judges themselves. According to the facts, the arbitration clause was agreed to resolve disputes among the investors. The transfer of

[97]   Qingdao Intermediate People's Court Civil Adjudication (2004) No. 068.
[98]   Shandong Higher People's Court, Petition to the SPC in Determining the Validity of the Arbitration Agreement in a JV Contract, Lu Gao Fa [2004] No. 203.
[99]   The Shandong Higher People's Court is the highest judicial authority in the Shandong Province where the Qingdao city resides.
[100] Article 3 of the "Beijing Opinion 1999", see discussions above under the heading "Judicial opinions by the LHPCs" of Chapter 4.
[101] SPC Reply to the Shandong Higher People's Court Concerning the Validity of the Arbitration Agreement in a JV Contract, Zui Gao Fa [2004] Min Si Ta Zi No. 41, reprinted in Wan Erxiang (ed), *China Trial Guide – Guide on Foreign-related Commercial and Maritime Trial (Zhongguo Shewai Shangshi Haishi Shenpan Zhidao)* (Beijing: People's Court Publishing, 2005), 82–83.
[102] The second group of opinion within the Qingdao Intermediate People's Court, see fn 97 above.

the share may thus justify C's arbitral *locus standi* should a dispute arise between C and the other two Japanese investors, in accordance with the then SPC guidelines.[103] However, the SPC failed to provide whether such an arbitration clause could extend its effect to the investee—the JV—which is a non-signatory third party to the original investment contract when the arbitration clause was included.

Two further issues arise within this context. First, quoting the views of the second group in the Qingdao Intermediate Court, it seems that in order for the arbitration clause to survive the contractual assignment and be effective upon the investor assignee, it must be *expressly agreed* to by the assignee.[104] If we recall the then SPC judicial interpretations, the arbitration clause shall be enforceable upon the assignee as long as the assignee is aware of the arbitral clause during the contract assignment.[105] International arbitration norms have also suggested a similar approach in determining the validity of arbitration clauses undergoing the contractual assignment or subrogation.[106] This raises the issue of compatibility of judicial opinions between the local judiciary and the SPC. Apart from the issue of justice, such as whether the share assignment in this case would involve transfer of some onerous obligations, it seems that the Qingdao Intermediate Court sets a higher burden of proof upon the assignee than the SPC does in invoking the arbitration agreement. Since most parties would not bother to specifically agree to the dispute resolution clause during the contractual transfer, the Qingdao approach may constitute an undue burden on the assignee to resort to arbitration. As such, despite the SPC's pro-arbitration guideline, it might in its practical application be subject to local understandings as the aforementioned case demonstrates.

7.056

Second, based on the holding history, both the Qingdao Intermediate and Shandong Higher People's Courts have referred to the "Beijing Opinion 1999" for authority in determining the enforceability of the arbitration clause upon the investee JV. However, the controversy arises regarding whether local judicial opinions could be applicable to judicial practices outside the issuing jurisdiction, although there are no restrictions under the Chinese jurisprudence to not do so. As outlined in previous chapters, in China, only the SPC has *de facto* rule-making power where its judicial interpretations carry the force of law.[107] The underlying rationale is to supervise and unify the judicial behavior across the country via the hierarchical arrangement of the judiciary.[108] Hence, the applicability of the local judicial opinion outside its issuing jurisdiction may still be a lingering issue not only in the area of arbitration but also in the general Chinese judicial practice. In essence, it is important to note that the two issues discussed above reflect the problem created by the uncertain scope of local judicial discretions in enforcing the arbitration agreement. The uncertain scope could be wider or narrower,

7.057

---

[103] Articles 27 and 28 of the SPC Foreign-related Draft; arts.1 and 2 of the SPC Domestic Draft. See also discussions above under the heading "Critical turning since 2006: Unified SPC Interpretation on arbitration" of Chapter 4.

[104] *Ibid.*

[105] *Ibid.*

[106] See discussions above under the heading "Significant gap with international arbitration norms" of Chapter 4.

[107] See discussions above, under the heading "Judicial interpretations" of Chapter 1.

[108] Nanping Liu, *Judicial Interpretations in China: Opinions of the Supreme People's Court* (Hong Kong: Sweet & Maxwell Asia, 1997), 21–25.

depending on how the local court perceives arbitration and whether the SPC guideline is clear enough for reference.

(iii) *Baotou case: Local interests as real consideration*

7.058   In September 2005, A Building Company (A) and B Commercial Company (B) signed a building contract where A agreed to construct a three-storey commercial building for B in Baotou city, Neimenggu Autonomous Region. Both parties further agreed that "any dispute relating to the performance of this contract will be resolved by the arbitration commission in the place of construction". Later, B refused to pay A because of the unsatisfactory quality of the building constructed. A resorted to the Baotou Arbitration Commission for dealing with the contractual dispute. In January 2006, after holding several hearings, the arbitration commission ruled in favor of A and therefore B was asked to pay the money. In February 2006, in enforcing the arbitral award, Company C (C) challenged the award to the Baotou Intermediate People's Court on the ground that the arbitration clause should be voided. C argued that B had dissolved and merged into C at the time of concluding the arbitration agreement. Since C had never signed any arbitration agreement with A, C should not be bound by the award between A and B.

7.059   In March 2006, in verifying whether the merger was true or not, the Baotou Intermediate People's Court examined the commercial background of both B and C. During the examination, the court found that C was conducting the key government-supported business (*zhengfu zhongdian fuchi chanye*),[109] and the award enforcement could affect C's working capital and lead to its cash flow problem. The Baotou Intermediate Court finally declared the arbitration agreement invalid and denied the award accordingly on the basis that:

> "The arbitration agreement could not extend to the third party. Due to the dissolution of B, a contractual relationship existed only between A and C. However, since A and C had not reached a new arbitration agreement, the original arbitration clause without C's participation would not be enforceable against C".[110]

7.060   The negative ruling was reported all the way to the SPC where it finally reversed the rulings of both the Baotou Intermediate and Neimenggu Higher People's Courts,[111] holding that the arbitration clause should succeed the merger and be effective upon the successor.[112]

---

[109] The local government, in developing the commercial economy in the given locality, will promote a series of preferential policies to support some businesses so as to attract investment and talents. For example, many of the central provinces in China have taken the information technology enterprises as the supporting objects.

[110] Baotou Intermediate Court Civil Adjudication (2006) No. 024.

[111] The Neimenggu Higher People's Court is the highest judicial authority in the Neimenggu Autonomous Region where the Baotou city resides.

[112] SPC Reply to the Neimenggu Higher People's Court, Fa Jing (2006) No. 19 Han; see also compilation in the online comments by Xu Zhiqing and Daishu, "Merger of the Company, Is the Original Arbitration Clause Still Effective (Gongsi bei Jianbin, Yuan Zhongcai Tiaokuan Shifou Renran Youxiao)", in *China Arbitration Website*: http://www.china-arbitration.com.

A pair of issues may be observed from the *Baotou* enforcement report. First, in **7.061** China, it is still doubtful whether an invalid arbitration agreement can be a ground to revoke the arbitral award. As illustrated before, people's courts can review arbitration agreements only before the arbitral tribunal has its first hearing on the proceeding.[113] Accordingly, the judicial review conducted in the current case may have arguably exceeded the timeframe required by the Arbitration Law and SPC interpretations.[114] In another respect, as the Arbitration Law and SPC interpretations have never expressly objected to judicial review taking place during or after the arbitral proceeding, there may be room for judicial discretions.

The second and more contentious issue relates to how the local judiciary exercises **7.062** their judicial discretion, i.e. the actual factors they consider in allowing or denying the arbitral jurisdiction. Based on the facts, the Baotou Intermediate Court took into account the merits of the case, particularly the economic status of the arbitral party, in determining the effect of the arbitration agreement and its subsequent arbitral award. Given that C is a key local enterprise receiving government support, it is highly probable that C's business is associated with local economic interests. If it lost the case, the government would have to pay the debt.[115] While it is not uncommon for the court to check the merits of the case in ascertaining arbitral jurisdiction, it is rare that the court gives weight to the party's economic status or its relationship with the government. It might therefore be argued that, if the party is a very important company in the given region, the arbitration agreement could be checked because being involved in a claim would harm the company's business reputation and be detrimental to the local economic interests. By controlling arbitration agreements, the local court may indirectly *control* the result of arbitration and thereby help to protect local interests and save state-owned enterprises.[116] These issues, however, raise the concern of fair play in the actual enforcement of arbitration in China. The local people's courts have the discretion to extend the period of judicial review, and in addition, they can take local interests into consideration as a ground for denying arbitral jurisdiction and outcome of arbitration. This results in low enforcement rates of arbitration agreements and subsequent arbitral awards in some parts of the country.

(iv) *Case summary*

The cases above, to some extent, reflect the difficulties in enforcing arbitration **7.063** agreements with respect to the change of arbitral parties. But for the pre-reporting system, all these agreements could have been voided under the local judicial examinations.

---

[113] See arts.20 and 26 of the Arbitration Law; see also discussions above under the heading "Concerns About Excessive Judicial Intervention".

[114] Even if the official SPC Interpretation did not come out when the case occurred, the Domestic Draft also required the exercise of judicial review be restricted to the stage before the first hearing of the arbitral tribunal; see discussions above.

[115] Xia Zhong and Chen Gang, "On the Contribution of the Government-supported Industries to the Local Economy (Lun Zhengfu Zhongdian Fuchi Chanye dui Dangdi Jingji de Gongxian)", *China Economy Times (Zhongguo Jingji Shibao)*, 12 May 2005.

[116] Gu Weixia, "Recourse against Arbitral Awards: How Far Can a Court Go? Supportive and Supervisory Role of Hong Kong Courts as Lessons to Mainland China Arbitration", (2005) 2 *Chinese Journal of International Law*, 499–500.

7.064   Several conclusions can be drawn from the case discussions. First, as is shown from both the *Longhai* and *Huaxiang* case, notwithstanding the liberal approach developed by the SPC in the past decade, local judges lack knowledge of modern arbitration theories and this practice results in a misunderstanding of the doctrine of separability. Secondly, when the SPC guideline is not clear enough, there is uncertainty regarding the scope of judicial supervision in which case the extent of the supervision depends largely on how the local judiciary understands arbitration. This was reflected in the *Huaxiang* case where the local people's court adopted a rigid interpretation of the effect of the arbitration agreement when the arbitral parties had undergone mergers. The same applies to the *Baotou* case, where the procedural timeframe of review was extended by local judicial discretion. Thirdly, the judicial check may involve examination into some merit details and even economic standing of the arbitral parties. As demonstrated by the *Baotou* case, although it is highly doubtful whether local economic interests could be applied as a determining factor in exercising the judicial scrutiny, in practice, the court had included this factor when assessing the case. Other problems may also be relevant within the context of these judicial enforcement reports, such as the interplay between local judicial opinions and SPC's judicial interpretations, and the consistency among local judicial practices in different parts of China. The Arbitration Law fails to set out any rules to deal with these issues, and the subsequent SPC Interpretations fail to improve the situation.

(b) Enforcement of "ambiguous arbitration commission"

7.065   The second group of case reports is concerned with defective arbitration agreements without including a "definite arbitration commission". Therefore, this part of the chapter will examine the extent to which local people's courts have enforced these agreements pursuant to the SPC's liberal instruction on "ascertainable arbitration commission".

(i) *Weige case: Interpretative techniques*

7.066   In 1994, the Taiwan Fuyuan Company (Fuyuan) made a timber purchase contract with the Xiamen Weige Wood Production Company (Weige). Within the contract, there was a clause providing that "both parties should refer to ICC arbitration for dispute resolution relating to the performance of the contract". Later on, a dispute arose and Fuyuan filed a claim at Xiamen Intermediate People's Court against Weige for breach of contract. Weige, before submitting its statement of defense, alleged jurisdictional objection on the basis that a valid arbitration agreement existing between the two parties.

7.067   In 1996, the Xiamen Intermediate People's Court ruled against the jurisdictional challenge on two grounds: (1) the arbitral institution was not specified by the contracting parties, and (2) the parties failed to reach a supplementary arbitration agreement clarifying the arbitral body and institutional rules. Therefore, according to arts.16 and 18 of the Arbitration Law, the arbitral clause was voided.[117]

---

[117] Sun Nanshen, "Jurisdictional Conflict Issues in the Judicial Review of the Foreign-related Arbitration", in CIETAC South-China Sub-commission (ed), *Judicial Review of the Foreign-related Arbitration* (2006), 23–24.

The Xiamen Intermediate People's Court then reported its negative rulings to the Fujian Higher People's Court. In late 1996, the Fujian Higher Court[118] opined that both the arbitral body and institutional rules could be ascertained based on parties' intention to arbitrate in the ICC Court of Arbitration: (1) both parties had agreed to the ICC arbitration; (2) pursuant to art.8 of the ICC Arbitration Rules, "when both parties submit disputes to arbitration under the ICC, it shall be deemed that both parties have selected the ICC Arbitration Rules";[119] (3) under art.1 of the ICC Arbitration Rules, "the only arbitral body attached to the ICC is the ICC Court of Arbitration, which is the only institution within the ICC that could apply the ICC Arbitration Rules".[120] Therefore, the parties shall be deemed to have selected the ICC Court of Arbitration as their arbitral body, which complied with the validity requirements under art.16 of the Arbitration Law.[121]

7.068

In this case, the key reason leading to the different enforcement results by the two levels of people's courts[122] was the different interpretative technique adopted.[123] During the judicial review, the Xiamen Intermediate People's Court adopted the textual interpretation where the prescription for the ICC itself was not taken as an arbitral institution and hence the institutional ambiguity must void the arbitration agreement. However, the Fujian Higher People's Court interpreted the arbitral agreement according to the objective of the contract. Given the textual uncertainty of the clause, the court looked into the parties' arbitral intention rather than mere text of the arbitration clause in ascertaining the identity of the institution. Therefore, the word "ICC" was interpreted as to refer to the parties' implied selection of the "ICC Court of Arbitration" for dispute resolution.[124] This judicial approach accords with art.125 of the Contract Law, which provides that when there is controversy in understanding contractual clauses, the interpretation shall follow the objective of the contract rather than its mere text.[125] The Fujian Higher People's Court gave an important indication as to how drafting defects with respect to institutional uncertainty should be dealt with

7.069

---

[118] The Fujian Higher People's Court is the highest judicial authority in the Fujian Province where the Xiamen city sits.

[119] Article 8 of the ICC Rules.

[120] Article 1 of the ICC Rules.

[121] SPC Reply to the Fujian Higher People's Court in Ascertaining the Validity of An Arbitration Clause for ICC Arbitration, Zui Gao Fa Fa Jing Han [1996] No. 449.

[122] Both the factual basis and review criteria remained the same in the first and second trial. The criteria of the judicial review in this case are arts.16 and 18 of the Arbitration Law, which prescribes a certain arbitral body is a must in validating an arbitration agreement.

[123] Cui Xuemei and Xu Peiyang, "On the Expansive Interpretation of the Arbitration Agreement and the Implied Arbitration Agreement (Lun Zhongcai Xieyi de Kuoda Jieshi—Jianyi Moshi Zhongcai Xieyi)"; available at China Court website: http://www.chinacourt.org/public/detail.php?id=187389. On the point, see also discussions of the "implied terms" in GU Weixia, "Confidentiality Revisited: Blessing or Curse in International Commercial Arbitration", (2004) 15 *American Review of International Arbitration*, 613.

[124] Professor Sun Nanshen also considered that the judicial interpretation of the Fujian Higher People's Court had referred to the international arbitration custom where the selection of the "ICC Court of Arbitration for arbitration" was always abbreviated to "ICC arbitration", see fn 117 above.

[125] According to art.125 of the Contract Law, "If a dispute arises between the parties concerning the understanding of a clause of the contract, they shall determine the true intention of that clause by making reference to words and sentences used in the contract, the relevant clauses of the contract, *objective of the contract,* trading practice and the principle of good faith". Then, as one kind of the contract, the interpretation of the arbitration agreement should follow the same rules as applied to the other contractual clauses.

in the future. The court found that the "objective-oriented" interpretative technique would show more judicial respect to party autonomy.

(ii) *Singapore case: Relevance of applicable law*

7.070   In 1998, a Shanghai Corporation (A) signed a sales contract with a Singapore Company (B) within which an arbitration clause was agreed upon as a mode for dispute resolution. However, the clause only provided that arbitration proceedings shall be held in Singapore without further specifying the arbitral institution to conduct the arbitration. Later, A brought a breach of contract action in the Shanghai Second Intermediate People's Court (Second Intermediate Court). B challenged the court's jurisdiction by relying on the arbitration clause within the contract. A argued that the arbitral clause should be voided because the arbitral institution was not articulated.

7.071   In June 1999, the Second Intermediate Court of Shanghai ruled against the validity on the ground of an unspecific arbitration institution in the arbitration agreement by referring to arts.16 and 18 of the Arbitration Law.[126]

7.072   In August 1999, in receiving the report, the Shanghai Higher People's Court (Higher Court) first examined the governing law of the arbitration agreement. Since the parties did not expressly provide for the governing law, the Court referred to the applicable law rules under the NYC under which both China and Singapore are member states. Then pursuant to art.V(1) of the NYC, "absent the parties' choice, the law of the place of arbitration will be deemed as the parties' implied choice of applicable law".[127] Accordingly, the Singaporean law was adopted to determine the validity. Because a specific arbitral institution was not required under the Singaporean arbitration legislation for validity,[128] the arbitration agreement was held valid and the arbitral jurisdiction was therefore supported.[129]

7.073   In this case, the primary reason that the courts diverged with respect to enforcement is that they applied different legal rules in interpreting the effect of the arbitration agreement. Although the law governing the arbitration agreement was not mentioned in the ruling of the Second Intermediate Court, the reference to arts.16 and 18 of the Arbitration Law indicated that the court applied *lex fori* (Chinese law) in determining the validity. The approach by the Intermediate Court reflects the often-quoted "judicial ignorance of the applicable law rules" in the review of foreign-related arbitration agreements among Chinese lower level judiciary before 2006.[130] Hence, the general application of Chinese arbitration legislation could easily deny the arbitral jurisdiction for an unclearly specified arbitral institution. The Higher Court paid more attention to

---

[126]   Sun, "Jurisdictional Conflict Issues in the Judicial Review of the Foreign-related Arbitration", see fn 117 above, 21.

[127]   Article V(1)(1) of the NYC.

[128]   Singapore adopted the Model Law in 1993; following Model Law jurisprudence, the arbitral institution is only a relevant consideration rather than an essential ingredient in determining the validity of the arbitration agreement.

[129]   The judicial analyses by the Shanghai Higher People's Court were compiled in the *China Foreign-related Commercial and Maritime Trial Web*: http://www.ccmt.org.cn.

[130]   Sun, "Jurisdictional Conflict Issues in the Judicial Review of the Foreign-related Arbitration", see fn 117 above, 24.

the importance of governing law and the Singapore Arbitration Act (*lex arbitri*) was applied. This approach was consistent with the subsequent SPC Reply to the Hubei Higher People's Court discussed previously.[131] In the *Singapore* case, before the SPC officially announced guidelines with respect to applicable legal rules in foreign-related arbitration, the Shanghai Higher People's Court had searched for Chinese legislations, including the international treaties that China had acceded to, i.e. the NYC, to save the effect of foreign-related arbitral agreements. As Professor Liu Xiaohong analyses the case, Shanghai is a leading city in the country's economic development and its judicial attitude towards arbitration could well influence the parties' confidence in Chinese commercial dispute resolution environment as a whole.[132] To that end, the affirmative decision by the Shanghai Higher People's Court may be seen as an example of the provincial effort to support arbitration.[133]

(iii) *Xiangyu case: Initial test of the Supreme People's Court Drafts*

In March 2004, the China Xiamen Xiangyu Corporation (buyer, "Xiangyu") and the Swiss Mechel Trading AG Company (seller, "Mechel") signed a steel sales contract. They agreed that, "the conducting of contractual rights and obligations shall be referring to 'CISG 1980'[134] and 'UNIDROIT PICC 1994'".[135] They further agreed that, "[f]or any dispute arising out of the contract, the parties shall arbitrate in Beijing according to the ICC Rules of Arbitration and the language of arbitration in either Chinese or English". In August 2004, the ICC Court of Arbitration in Paris accepted the complaint filed by Mechel as the Claimant with Xiangyu as the Respondent. In September 2004, Xiangyu challenged the ICC's jurisdiction to the Xiamen Intermediate People's Court for an invalid arbitration clause. Xiangyu alleged that the parties had agreed that the arbitration would be held in Beijing, and according to China's arbitration legislation, an arbitration agreement must be void if the arbitral institution is unspecified.

7.074

On November 23, 2004, the Xiamen Intermediate Court divided the examination of the arbitral clause into two stages. The first stage related to the applicable law. The court considered that, due to the separability doctrine, both the CISG and PICC should be the laws governing substantive rights and obligations of the contract rather than validity of the arbitral clause. Thus, in accordance with the SPC's judicial opinion, absent the parties' choice, the law of the agreed place of arbitration (Beijing) shall be applied to govern the validity of the arbitral clause.[136] The second stage concerns whether the arbitration institution was clearly provided so as to comply with the validity requirements under the applicable law (Chinese law).

7.075

---

[131] *Mitsubishi Co Ltd (HK) v Sanxia Investment Co Ltd and Hubei Mechanical Engineering Co Ltd*, see fn 84.

[132] Liu, *Theoretical and Empirical Research of International Arbitration Agreement* (2005), 210.

[133] See also discussions below under the heading "Analysis of enforcement divergences and difficulties".

[134] CISG is the short for the Convention on International Sales of Goods of the UN Commission on International Trade Law, available at the UNCITRAL website, www.uncitral.org/english.index.

[135] UNIDROIT PICC is the short for the Principles of International Commercial Contract of the International Institute for the Unification of Private Law, available at www.lexmercatoria.org.

[136] *Mitsubishi Co Ltd (HK) v Sanxia Investment Co Ltd and Hubei Mechanical Engineering Co Ltd*, see fn 84 above.

7.076   In the judicial examination, the court first referred to the Arbitration Law and SPC interpretations where an arbitral institution was required to be reasonably ascertainable.[137] The court then opined:

> "[G]iven the parties have adopted the arbitral clause recommended by the ICC and given further the ICC Court of Arbitration is the only institution that could conduct the ICC Arbitration Rules, there is no ambiguity in identifying the institution under the SPC interpretative jurisprudence and the parties' intention to arbitrate in ICC Court of Arbitration could be ascertained".

7.077   In giving the ruling, the court finally quoted the SPC Foreign-related Draft as the authority in supporting the judicial reasoning, art.26 of which provided that the agreement on the institutional arbitration rules should be interpreted to mean the parties' having selected the relevant institution to which the rules were attached.[138] The Xiamen Court concluded that, although the Draft had not gone into effect, it reflected the latest arbitration jurisprudence and practice of China. On 14 December 2004, the Court held that the arbitration clause was valid under the Chinese law and the ICC jurisdiction was confirmed.[139]

7.078   Several important points can be drawn from the *Xiangyu* case. To begin with, in reviewing the arbitration agreement, the Xiamen Intermediate Court had not only prioritised the rules of applicable law but also clearly understood the doctrine of separability. The application of *lex arbitri* supported the parties' intention at the time of concluding the arbitration agreement.[140] Moreover, in ruling on the effect of the arbitral clause under the Chinese law, the Court, on its own discretion, relied on the SPC interpretative jurisprudence in ascertaining the identity of the arbitral institution. This may reflect that the Court, in respecting parties' arbitral wishes, was *eager* to follow the more liberal SPC approach despite the risk that the award rendered by foreign arbitration conducted in China may not be recognised and enforced finally.[141] However, when it comes to the final stage of adjudication, it seems that the absence of specific SPC guidance and a shortage of relevant judicial precedents forced the local court to look for support outside the existing judicial interpretations. This may explain the reference to SPC Draft Provisions for legal authority despite their not having entered into force at the time of jurisdictional ruling. Overall, as the initial test

---

[137] See discussions above under the heading "Critical turning since 2006: Unified SPC Interpretation on arbitration"of Chapter 4.

[138] Article 26 of the Foreign-related Draft provides that, "if the parties agreed to some institutional rules but failed to agree to arbitration under the institution, the people's court should support the arbitration clause by allowing the institution of which the rules were attached to decide the arbitral case".

[139] Case Report of "Xiamen Intermediate People's Court Rejected the Petition to Invalidate the Arbitral Clause by the Xiamen Xiangyu Group (Xiamen Zhongyuan Caiding Xiamen Xiangyu Jituan Youxiangongsi Shenqing Hetong Zhongcai Tiaokuan Wuxiao)", compiled by the Hangzhou Arbitration Commission, 14 December 2005, available at http://www.hzac.gov.cn/alfx/al8.htm.

[140] Gu Weixia and Joshua Lindenbaum, "The NYPE 93 Arbitration Clause: Where Ends the Open-end?", (2007) 2 *Journal of Maritime Law and Commerce*, 37.

[141] See discussions above under the heading "Problems of state control"of Chapter 4.

of the SPC Foreign-related Draft,[142] the *Xiangyu* case is, undoubtedly, important to an appreciation of the increased judicial acceptance by the Chinese lower level people's courts towards arbitration.

(iv) *Case summary*

As shown by the three cases above, where the arbitral institution is not clearly provided, it is generally observed that the Chinese local people's courts tend to uphold the arbitration agreement by respecting the parties' arbitral wishes. The supportive judicial approach is mirrored through the courts' flexible interpretative technique (*Weige* and *Xiangyu*) as well as their paying attention to the rules of applicable law (*Singapore* and *Xiangyu*). The pro-arbitration approach has been most obviously reflected in the *Xiangyu* Case where the Xiamen Intermediate Court liberally exercised its discretion to refer to the yet-to-be-promulgated SPC Draft Provisions.

7.079

In *Weige* and *Singapore*, the different rulings of the first and second instances may still reflect the difficulties with enforcement at the lower and intermediate level of the judiciary. In China, generally, provincial higher people's courts are equipped with more experienced judges who are better able to draw on the principles from the national legislation and judicial interpretations in an effort to address the lack of sufficient applicable legal rules. In enforcing defective arbitration agreements regarding "ambiguous arbitration commission", because the *prima facie* wording of the agreement could satisfy the examination, the judicial check may not need to extend to case substance and there are fewer concerns about local protectionism.[143] As such, the rejection by the intermediate courts in *Weige* and *Singapore* might mostly be due to the lack of knowledge on arbitration by local judges.[144] Thanks to the pre-reporting system, the higher level judiciary could have a chance to redress the flawed adjudications of the lower level. But, whether the redress actually takes place may largely depend upon the judicial quality of the higher level court. In *Weige* and *Singapore*, both the Fujian and Shanghai Higher People's Courts understood and correctly applied the pro-arbitration approach of the SPC guidelines, so that parties' arbitral wishes had been confirmed at the provincial level rather than headed all the way up to the SPC. Given that the timelines for the "report" and "reply" under the "pre-reporting" system are unclear from the SPC Notices, the more courts involved could mean the more time costs in realising the parties' arbitral interest.[145] In addition, the different rulings on the effect of arbitration agreements in *Weige* and *Xiangyu* by the Xiamen Intermediate People's Court reflect the increasing judicial deference to the principle of party autonomy with the passage of time. Finally, it may still be doubtful

7.080

---

[142] As the judicial clerk in the Fujian Higher People's Court announced, given that the Xiangyu jurisdictional ruling (November 2004) was given just after the SPC Drafts closed its solicitation of opinions (August 2004), it was among those initial cases for judicial test. (Source: Judiciary Research Institute of the Fujian Higher People's Court).

[143] In determining the validity of the arbitration agreement in cases of "non-signatory third party", however, the judicial check may need to extend to the case substance to verify the change of the arbitral party. The substantial review could involve the knowledge of the financial standing of the relevant company such that the local protectionism concerns might arise. See discussions above under the heading "Enforcement of "non-signatory third party".

[144] See discussions below under the heading "Analysis of enforcement divergences and difficulties".

[145] Gu Weixia and Robert Morgan, "Improving Commercial Dispute Resolution in China", [2005] *Asia Dispute Review*, 6–7.

whether the then soliciting SPC Draft Provisions could be justified as legal authority in the judicial ruling. As the *Xiangyu* case indicates, though the intermediate court was eager to affirm the parties' intention to arbitrate, the SPC jurisprudence may not be clear enough to make the judges reach the decision. Luckily, the situation has now been remedied by art.4 of the most recently promulgated SPC Interpretation.[146] The reasoning report by the Xiamen Intermediate Court, however, to some extent, reflects the local judicial reluctance in exercising the pro-arbitration discretion absent SPC's specific guidelines.

(c) Analysis of enforcement divergences and difficulties

7.081   The enforcement reports above reflect the inadequate Chinese judicial system in the area of arbitration. The local people's courts lack judicial independence and integrity, and are short of knowledge and experience in handling arbitration cases.

(i) *Lack of judicial independence and integrity*

7.082   The striking ruling in the *Baotou* case indicates that some local people's courts tend to intervene into arbitration where local businesses are involved, particularly where the business affects the local economy. Local protectionism is intertwined with a general lack of independence of the court system. In China, judicial intervention in arbitration actually comes from local political and administrative pressures. Professor Randall Peerenboom has explained the issue of judicial independence by creating two categories, *collective independence* of the judiciary as a whole and *independent decision-making* by individual judges.[147] The collective independence requires the courts to be adequately funded so that they function free from governmental influences; while independent decision-making requires the judges' terms of office to be secured and their appointment depoliced so that judges can perform impartially.[148]

7.083   In China, the PRC Constitution and Organic Law of the People's Courts provide that Chinese courts have the right to be free from external interferences in their work.[149] However, the laws further require that individual courts at different levels must be administratively and institutionally accountable to the corresponding level of people's congresses.[150] In addition, courts in China are subject to the dual leadership. They receive political supervision from the Party Committee (*dangwei*) within the court, and the Party Political and Legal Affairs Committee (*zhengfawei*) outside the court (the horizontal supervision).[151] At the same time, their decisions and court judgments are scrutinised professionally by higher-level people's courts on the basis of judiciary hierarchy (the vertical scrutiny).[152] This stands in sharp contrast with the understanding

---

[146]   See, second paragraph of art.4 of the SPC Interpretation 2006; see also, discussions above under the heading "Critical turning since 2006: Unified SPC Interpretation on arbitration" of Chapter 4.

[147]   Randall Peerenboom, *China's Long March Towards Rule of Law* (Cambridge University Press, 2002), 288–290.

[148]   *Ibid.*

[149]   Article 126 of the PRC Constitution. Article 4 of the Organic Law of the People's Court.

[150]   Article 128 of the PRC Constitution.

[151]   Peerenboom, *China's Long March Towards Rule of Law* (2002), 298.

[152]   *Ibid.*

of collective independence in the Western ideologies where all individual courts enjoy functional independence. As such, based on Professor Peerenboom's observation, the Chinese courts as a whole appear to enjoy institutional independence, although individual courts do not.[153]

The independence of local people's courts is further undermined by the way in which they are funded. Courts in China are financed by governments at their corresponding levels. Therefore, local courts are subsidised by the relevant local people's government. It is unfortunate that while the SPC supervises the adjudicative work of all lower level people's courts, it has no power over their budgets.[154] Local judiciaries are thus dependent on local governments for even basic necessities such as salaries and housing allowances. However, since local governments need to support themselves and local courts through local taxes, fees and charges collected from local businesses, an incentive for the court to lean on local businesses has formed.[155] By the same token, a locally subsidised court may be subject to accusation if the ruling hampers the local economic interests and the court itself might be financially disadvantaged. Particularly, where the state-owned enterprise (SOE, *guoyouqiye*) or government-supported business (GSB, *zhengfufuchichanye*) is at issue, and where the arbitration agreement provides for arbitration outside the locality,[156] the local court is more likely to seize its jurisdiction and refuse to refer parties to arbitration outside the local jurisdiction.[157] Moreover, since Chinese local governments have a political responsibility to maintain the social stability in the locality, they might interfere in the judicial ruling if the enforcement could hamper a major local business. From the perspective of government authorities, strict implementation of independent courts and judges may lead to the loss of *control* on the final outcome of commercial dispute resolution and thus exert an adverse impact on the SOE and GSB as a political, economic and social safety net in China. Thus, the possible cash flow problems of the GSB would trigger the exercise of judicial umbrella as the *Baotou* case above illustrates. Some commentators, however, argue that, in such cases, both the court ordering enforcement and the SOE receiving the order are governmental organs. Hence, local protectionism must be prevalent unless the court can relieve itself from the budget constraints.[158]

7.084

The courts' financial reliance on the local government has allowed local political and administrative powers to encourage local protectionism. It has further led to the unbalanced development of local people's courts across the country. Former Dean Wang Chenguang of the Tsinghua University Law School notes that, the court system in the coastal areas are better developed than their hinterland counterpart as the economy in

7.085

---

[153] *Ibid.*

[154] Article 127 of the PRC Constitution.

[155] Laifan Lin, "Judicial Independence in Japan: A Re-investigation for China", (1999) 13 *Columbia Journal of Asian Law*, 199.

[156] If it is a local arbitration agreement pointing to dispute resolution under the local arbitration commission, then there is already leverage for exercise of local government control given the administrative infrastructure of these commissions.

[157] In China, SOEs are thought to promote economic development and maintain social stability in that they produce jobs and provide various forms of social welfare to their workers, retirees and their family members.

[158] See Arthur Anyuan Yuan, "Enforcing and Collecting Money Judgments in China from a U.S. Creditor's Perspective", (2004) 36 *George Washington International Law Review*.

coastal areas has been better off and administrations more liberalised.[159] By contrast, rural areas often suffer a budget constraint due to the under-developed economy. As a result, the court system there may suffer more administrative interferences. This helps to explain the difference of judicial attitudes taken by the *Baotou* and *Xiamen* Intermediate Courts albeit the former is a more recent case.[160]

7.086　　With respect to independent decision-making, in Western ideology, judicial independence includes independent decision-making by individual judges. However, it is a different story in China.[161] In the Chinese context, individual judges, by and large, do not have the right to decide cases on their own. Judges at all levels of people's courts are divided into different administrative ranks; i.e. the President of the Court (*yuanzhang*), Vice President (*fuyuanzhang*), and Division Heads of the Chambers (*tingzhang*).[162] The people's congresses at different levels decide on the appointment of the court presidents and the presidents then decide on the appointment of the vice presidents and division heads.[163] Most cases are heard by a collegiate panel of three judges and the presidents or division heads will determine which judge will act as the chair of the panel, and they may further review the panel's decisions if they think necessary.[164] In turn, collegiate panels are often required under the court's internal rules to obtain the approval of the division heads, vice presidents, president and the court's Adjudicative Committee (*shenpanweiyuanhui*)[165] before they render their judgments. Thus, the administrative rank of the judges is important in determining the final outcome of the case. The decision-making of the individual judges is controlled indirectly through these administrative means.[166]

7.087　　Outside the court, local governments and the Chinese Communist Party (CCP) Committee (*dangwei*) may further influence judicial decisions of significant cases, and on the appointment, promotion, and removal of local judges.[167] Judges rely on salaries and housing benefits provided by the municipal government. Moreover, when appointing and promoting judges, the local political and administrative regime

---

[159]　Interview notes of Wang Chenguang, Former Dean of the Tsinghua University Law School on 2 November 2004, reprinted in Ellen Reinstein, "Finding a Happy Ending for Foreign Investors: The Enforcement of Arbitration Awards in the People's Republic of China", (2005) 16 *Indiana Journal of International Law*, 37.

[160]　The Baotou Intermediate Court adjudicated the case in 2006, where the Xiamen Intermediate Court adjudicated the *Xiangyu* case two years earlier in 2004. See discussions above.

[161]　Peerenboom, *China's Long March Towards Rule of Law* (2002), 286.

[162]　Articles 19, 24, 27 and 31 of the Organic Law of the People's Court.

[163]　*Ibid.*

[164]　Article 10 of the Organic Law of the People's Court.

[165]　The Adjudicative Committee (or Judicial Committee) is the highest adjudicative body inside the court, the establishment of which functions to guide the handling of difficult cases received by the court. The committee is composed of the Party Secretary, President, Vice-Presidents and Division Heads of the court concerned. See art.11 of the Organic Law of the People's Courts.

[166]　Dean Professor Wang Liming of the People's University is one of the many scholars who have called for an end to the system of administrative ranking of judges.

[167]　The CCP Committee exerts tremendous influence at all levels of the court system. According to art.101 of the PRC Constitution, it should be the local people's congress that appoints chief judges of the provincial court and the chief judge nominate the other lower level of judges. However, in reality, the local CCP Committee often selects judges, and the people's congress ratifies its choices. These judges serve on the Adjudication Committee (*shenpan weiyuanhui*) of each court, wielding considerable power in determining the outcome of controversial cases. Most of the judges are also CCP members the leader of which discuss cases involving difficult legal issues with the Political-Legal Committee (*zhengfa weiyuanhui*) and accept general policies set by the CCP.

evaluates them in terms of obedience to its policy.[168] Hence, local judges may have to intervene in the case in order to render a favorable judgment when the local business is at stake. This is required in order to safeguard the local financial needs of the court and to allow the judge to continue to be promoted. As Professor Stanley Lubman comments on the issue, the personal dependence has resulted from the institutional dependence of the individual local people's courts, the combination of which have subjected the Chinese local judiciary to local politics and administration. Judicial interventions in arbitral enforcement follow as a natural result.[169] In this regard, the unpredictability in enforcing arbitration agreements corresponds to the past notorious records of the enforcement of arbitral awards by the Chinese local judiciaries.[170] In extreme cases, judges even helped local companies with fraudulent transfer of assets as a way of evading enforcement.[171]

The SPC has become aware of the issue and has openly criticised the detrimental practices of local protectionism in the Chinese social legal system.[172] There have been some improvements in the general enforcement records, including those taking place in the area of arbitration.[173] However, remarkable improvements have not been seen if we separate the judicial enforcement records by localities. The problem here lies in the fact that despite China is a highly-centralised system where the SPC supervises its lower level courts, local judicial powers may deviate from their central controllers in pursuing local economic interests. One author explains that local government needs to supply its own social welfare, to promote industries in its locality, and to finance itself in order to implement its plans.[174] According to the observation by Professor Pitman Potter, Chinese courts could be more dependent upon the local government due to a gradual administrative decentralisation that will be taking place alongside China's

7.088

---

[168] Yuwen Li, "Court Reformation in China: Problems, Progress and Prospects", in Jianfu Chen, Yuwen Li and Jan Michiel Otto (ed), *Implementation of Law in the People's Republic of China* (The Hague: Kluwer Law International, 2002), 55, 58–59. See also, Robb M. LaKritz, "Taming a 5,000 Year-old Dragon: Toward a Theory of Legal Development in Post-Mao China", (1997) 11 *Emory International Law Review*, 262.

[169] Stanley Lubman, *Bird in a Cage: Legal Reform in China after Mao* (California: Stanford University Press, 1999), 252, 279.

[170] According to Cheng, Moser and Wang, intermediate people's courts where respondent was domiciled or their property was located had repeatedly refused to enforce a number of arbitral awards because the enforcement might have impaired the local interests to which the courts attached significance. See, Cheng Dejun, Michael J. Moser and Wang Shengchang, *International Arbitration in the People's Republic of China: Commentary, Cases and Materials* (Hong Kong: Butterworths, 2nd ed., 2000), 76.

[171] See the *Revpower* case where the Chinese company appeared to be insolvent under the arrangement of the local people's court so that the enforcement was delayed, reported by Fredrick Brown and Catherine A. Rogers, "The Role of Arbitration in Resolving Transnational Disputes: A Survey of Trends in the People's Republic of China", (1997) 15 *Berkeley Journal of International Law*, 341–342.

[172] Ren Jianxin, the then Chief Justice of the SPC, proposed at the National Conference on Politics and Law held in December 1992 "five prohibitions" for the removal of local protectionism. Those proposals were that (1) local CPC cadres should be prohibited from interfering with the judicial process; (2) governmental officials should be prohibited from making threats against judges carrying out enforcement of court orders; (3) judicial organs should be prohibited from making unfair ruling in favor of local parties; (4) officials of the public security and procuratorial organization should be prohibited from interfering with the adjudication of commercial cases; and (5) any organ or individual should be prohibited from hindering enforcement of orders of courts.

[173] See discussions below.

[174] Inoue, "Introduction to International Commercial Arbitration in China" (2006), 180.

WTO membership.[175] The decentralisation in the course of pursuing economic reforms may then fuel the local judicial efforts to develop their own practices in implementing the national rules according to their own needs. Thus, even though local judges might understand the SPC's pro-arbitration approach correctly, they may not be able to implement it when a local interest must be protected.

(ii) *Lack of judicial competence on arbitration*

7.089   With respect to the judicial *quality* in handling arbitration cases, as reflected by a line of cases discussed previously (*Longhai*, *Huaxiang*, *Baotou*, *Weige*, and *Singapore*), there is an apparent lack of proper understanding and experience regarding standard arbitration norms and practices among local Chinese judges.

7.090   In the early 1980s, approximately two-thirds of Chinese judges did not have a law degree, and one-third were demobilised military personnel.[176] This has changed to a large extent in the early twenty-first century when new judges are required to pass the National Judicial Exam.[177] Existing judges without a law degree will be trained under the central or local judges' colleges.[178] However, education for judges on commercial law practices is still insufficient. They have limited knowledge of modern standards of arbitration, let alone the generally practised pro-validity approach in determining the effect of arbitration agreements. Accordingly, local judges sometimes mistakenly apply the doctrine of separability, as happened in the *Longhai* and *Huaxiang* cases. In addition, local judges ignore the applicable laws when determining the validity of foreign-related arbitration agreements, as seen in the *Singapore* case. This general shortage of judicial expertise on arbitration has also caused some arbitral awards to be unduly set aside or denied enforcement.[179]

7.091   The lack of a tenure system and decent salaries (as compared to lawyers) has also exacerbated the shortage of skilled commercial judges. Some judges have committed corruption, while others have abandoned their posts for the more lucrative practice in large law firms.[180] The qualifications of local judges are economic-driven.[181]

---

[175]   Pitman Potter, "Legal Reform in China: Institutions, Culture and Selective Adaptation", (2004) 29 *Law & Social Inquiry,* 465, 473.

[176]   In the reconstruction of the court system that commenced immediately after the Cultural Revolution, demobilized soldiers became judges, since they were considered good candidates owing to their propensity to promote proletarian ideologies. Thus, many of their decisions were based not on law but on communist ideologies. See Li, "Court Reformation in China: Problems, Progress and Prospects" (2002), 63; see also Lubman, *Bird in a Cage* (1999), 253–254.

[177]   Article 37 of the Judges' Law.

[178]   Report by Xiao Yang, President of the SPC of the PRC, at the 4th Session of the 9th National People's Congress in Beijing, 10 March 2001.

[179]   For example, the ground for setting aside the award where an arbitral tribunal exceeds the scope of an arbitration agreement in its award was tested in an arguable manner in *Shanghai Medical Equipment Factory for Tooth v Hu Zhunren*, which was decided by Beijing 2nd Intermediate People's Court in 1996. In the comments by Mo, judges in that case did not understand what "scope of arbitration agreement" refers to. See, Mo, *Arbitration Law in China* (2001), para 10.40.

[180]   One SPC judge commented that in 1998-1999 alone, approximately 15 per cent of all people's court judges left their positions for positions in law firms. See Interview Notes of Zhao Shiyan, former SPC judge and now attorney at the Beijing Jingtian & Gongcheng Law Firm, reprinted in Reinstein, "Finding a Happy Ending for Foreign Investors: The Enforcement of Arbitration Awards in the People's Republic of China" (2005), 37.

[181]   Dean Wang Chenguang, "Resolving Business Disputes in China", guest lecture at the NYU Law School, 18 March 2007.

Economically well developed areas attract more judicial talents and these talents are more apt to foreign cases and international arbitration norms. Therefore, judges in costal areas (such as Shanghai, Xiamen) are more competent and they take a more liberal approach towards arbitration agreements.[182] Rural areas (such as Baotou), on the other hand, are ill equipped to handle arbitration cases.[183] The unbalanced qualifications of judges bring about the uncertainty of judicial attitude and approach towards arbitration in different areas of China. This is also the reason why Hong Kong was reluctant to subject its arbitral awards to review by people's courts in all Chinese places when Hong Kong signed an agreement with China in 2000 with respect to mutual recognition and enforcement of arbitral awards across the border. Evidently, some of the intermediate courts have never taken up any Hong Kong or foreign-related cases, nor do they have qualified judicial personnel in dealing with such cases.[184]

Moreover, there are perceptions that rapid development of arbitration may disadvantage court's caseloads. This has fostered a judicial hostility towards arbitration. Such judicial hostility tends to make local people's courts compete for cases with local arbitration commissions in that local judges use their review power to turn down arbitration agreements in order to "win" the jurisdiction.[185]   **7.092**

All these different factors could affect the quality of judicial review over arbitration. Eventually, excessive judicial interventions resulting from the misunderstanding of local judges will undermine the quality of enforcement of arbitration (both agreements and awards).[186]   **7.093**

(iii) *Conclusion: Judicial constraints*

It is important to note that under the Chinese judicial review system over arbitration, a couple of defects are evident. First, most local people's courts suffer institutional deficiency in terms of both finance and function. Hence, within the current Chinese context where local protectionism and corruption are still pervasive, the local court may not be able to refrain from local Party and governmental pressures which seriously influence their decision making such as the ruling on enforcement. Second, local judges are not equipped to deal with arbitration cases. This has led to arbitrary interpretation of arbitration agreements and awards and their being unfairly denied. Under the circumstances, parties may find it difficult to proceed to arbitration at the lower level judiciary.   **7.094**

While the SPC has been working hard to pay more judicial respect to parties' autonomy and interest in arbitration by issuing a long list of liberal guidelines, the efforts are found to have been mitigated downstream, thereby negating any advantages gained by the SPC's pro-validity initiatives. Accordingly, although the SPC is pro-arbitration, lower level people's courts may not be. Their institutional incapacity (including   **7.095**

---

[182] See case analyses above in *Weige*, *Singapore* and *Xiangyu* of the Xiamen and Shanghai People's Courts.

[183] See case analyses above in *Baotou* of the Baotou Court.

[184] Zhang Xianchu, "Several Thoughts on Mutual Recognition and Enforcement Agreements on Arbitral Awards between Hong Kong and the Mainland", (2004) 17 *Arbitration and Law Journal (Zhongcai yu Falu)*, 87.

[185] Gu, "Recourse against Arbitral Awards: How Far Can a Court Go?" (2005), 497.

[186] Zhong Jianhua and Yu Guanghua, "Establishing the Truth on Facts: Has the Chinese Civil Process Achieved This Goal", (2003) 13 *Journal of Transnational Law & Policy*, 393, 429–433.

incapacity of the judicial personnel) has thus subjected the enforcement ruling, i.e. *outcome* of arbitration, to political and administrative hands. As stated previously, arbitration has been one of the areas reflecting the general enforcement problems faced with the Chinese courts. In particular, it reflects the uncertainty of enforcement by the Chinese local level courts. In light of such uncertainty, foreign investors, suspicious about the biased local judges, and in order to avoid the unpredictable and sometimes corrupted Chinese court system, often add an arbitration clause outlining a strategy for pursuing a more impartial outcome of commercial disputes. However, given that both arbitration agreements and arbitral awards must undergo review by the Chinese courts for enforcement, foreign parties may yet find themselves forced into the situation that they tried to avoid.

7.096   Domestic parties may even worry about their autonomy and interest in arbitration being denied without the procedural remedy such as the "pre-reporting" system available to their foreign-related counterparts. As aforementioned, the "pre-reporting" system applies only to foreign-related arbitration agreements and arbitral awards as a way for higher people's courts to counteract local protectionism and local judicial malpractices. It must be pointed out, however, that local protectionism attacks not only foreign parties but domestic parties from outside the region as well. Therefore, it remains uncertain how to protect the lawful arbitral interests of large numbers of domestic "alien" parties. The dual-track system and the foreign-party-favored treatment have been warmly welcomed by foreign investors as centralised review will prompt better enforcement results.[187] Nevertheless, it may not be welcomed by domestic investors and this practice has been criticised for having overlooked domestic interests. Moreover, it has been increasingly challenged that, by hierarchical reporting, the higher level judiciary can interfere into jurisdictional rulings of the lower level, which patently violates due process and independent judicial decision-making.[188] Serious measures are thus urgently needed to officially address the inadequate lower level court system in China and to significantly improve their quality in handling arbitration cases.

3. JUDICIAL REFORMS AND THEIR RESTRICTIONS

7.097   There have been wide international concerns by academics and practitioners about the enforcement problems of Chinese arbitration.[189] To redress the situation, the SPC has introduced a series of measures to enhance the infrastructure of the judiciary. Furthermore, there have been efforts at the provincial level to pay equally close attention to judicial review over arbitration on both tracks.

---

[187]   Li Hu, "Setting aside an Arbitral Award in the People's Republic of China", (2001) 12 *American Review of International Arbitration*, 36–37.

[188]   Ye Dan, "On the Reasonability of the Judicial Power in Arbitration from the Perspective of Modern Judicial Ideologies" in CIETAC South-China Sub-commission (ed), *Judicial Review of the Foreign-related Arbitration* (2006), 98.

[189]   For example, Li, "Setting aside an Arbitral Award in the People's Republic of China" (2001); Gu, "Recourse against Arbitral Awards" (2005); Reinstein, "Finding a Happy Ending for Foreign Investors" (2005); Inoue, "Introduction to International Commercial Arbitration in China" (2005).

(a) Supreme People's Court efforts in enhancing the infrastructure of the judiciary

In the past decade, the SPC has initiated reforms and measures to improve the judicial infrastructure. One of the key reforms is the *Five-Year Reform Plan of the People's Court* (1999–2003) (the First-Five-Year-Reform-Plan)[190] which focuses on promoting the quality of judges through a more depoliticised judge selection system.[191] Subsequent to that, in October 2004, the SPC promulgated the *Outline of the Second-Five-Year Reform Plan of the People's Court* (2004-2008) (the Second-Five-Year-Reform-Outline).[192]   **7.098**

The Second-Five-Year-Reform-Outline appears particularly bold in setting out no fewer than 50 objectives for upgrading the Chinese court system. As a whole, the provisions demonstrate a cautious awareness of the importance of greater professionalism, independence and integrity of the judiciary, reducing local protectionism, and stamping out corruption, while acknowledging the leadership by the Party and supervision by people's congresses at each level.[193] On collective independence, the SPC seeks to enhance the autonomy of local people's courts, and begins to explore the establishment of a *guaranteed financing* for local courts by inserting provisions in central and provincial government budgets.[194] Perhaps the program's boldest proposal is loosening the grip of local power holders over local courts. The SPC calls for "within a certain geographic area, the implementation of a system of *uniform recruitment* and *uniform assignment* of local judges in basic and intermediate courts by the upper level people's courts".[195]   **7.099**

Furthermore, under the First-Five-Year-Reform-Plan, judicial personnel must pass the National Judicial Examinations to get qualified. Under the more recent Outline, judges now need to participate in annual judicial training to keep up-to-date with professional knowledge so that they can deal with cases.[196] Some other legal education opportunities in the area of international commercial practice have also begun in China in an attempt to respond to the country's accession to the WTO. For example, since 1999, more than 240 provincial and intermediate-court-level judges have graduated from the Tsinghua-Temple International Business Law LLM program sponsored by the SPC in which an intensive course on "international commercial arbitration" is involved.[197]   **7.100**

---

[190] *Five-Year People's Courts Reform Plan* (Renmin Fayuan Wunian Gaige Gangyao 1999–2003), enclosed in the *Gazette of the SPC (Zhonghuarenmingongheguo Zuigaorenminfayuan Gonggao)* [1999] No. 6, 182–190, available at China Judge Website, http://china.judge.com/fnsx/fnsx386.htm.

[191] In the next five years, all people's courts must adopt a selection system which requires higher court judges be selected from the most-qualified judges of lower courts, or high-performance lawyers, or other high-level legal professionals. Judges who are newly recruited from the recruitment examination should first work for the intermediate people's courts and basic people's courts.

[192] *Outline of the Second-Five-Year People's Court Reform Plan* (Renmin Fayuan Di'erge Wunian Gaige Gangyao 2004–2008), available at http://www.law-lib.com/law/law_view.asp?id=120832.

[193] For the reassertion of the leadership under the Party and people's congress, see Part Seven of the Outline, *ibid.*

[194] Article 48 of the Outline, *ibid.*

[195] Article 37 of the Outline, *ibid.*

[196] Article 39 of the Outline, *ibid.* The SPC has trained the LHPC judges at the National Judge Institute, and those judges are responsible for training other judges.

[197] Source: Ms. Huang Ying, a judge from the Shanghai Higher People's Court who has participated in the Tsinghua-Temple LLM program in 2001.

Local judges from the coastal area courts may have more chances to study abroad due to the more developed economy and more liberal administration.[198] This supports the findings of pro-validity enforcement in the *Singapore* and *Xiangyu* cases by the Shanghai and Xiamen Intermediate Courts discussed previously.[199] These measures are seen as important steps to improve the understanding of modern commercial laws and arbitration norms among the Chinese judges.

7.101 The SPC, in March 2009, published its *Third-Five-Year Reform Plan of the People's Court* (2009–2013).[200] As compared with the first two reform plans, the SPC places more emphasis on the so-called "adjudication for the people".[201] Because the new reform plan stresses the socialist direction and mass line, it has been noted by commentators as moving away from its previous professionalism-building tones.[202]

(b) Local judicial efforts in merging the dual tracks

7.102 Before the official promulgation of the 2006 SPC Interpretation, many academics proposed that "pre-reporting" be clearly written into the Interpretation to keep with the more relaxed judicial supervision over the foreign regime.[203] The Beijing Higher People's Court, however, argued that the protection shall be applied equally to both sides. As such, an "internal pre-reporting" scheme has been established within the Beijing people's courts.[204]

7.103 Pursuant to the scheme, where the first instance court attempts to turn down the jurisdiction in domestic arbitration, it must report directly to the Beijing Higher People's Court. Lower level courts in Beijing cannot deny the effect of either domestic arbitration agreements or arbitral awards until they get it affirmed by the highest court in the Municipality.[205] Having done so, the gap in "pre-reporting" with respect to the previously overlooked domestic arbitral regime can now be closed in Beijing. As Judge Tian Yuxi, Head of Enforcement Division of the Beijing Higher People's Court, introduces it, "[t]he creation of the 'internal pre-reporting' system shows the determination of the Beijing judiciary to provide a pro-arbitration environment for investment both at home and abroad".[206] Beyond that, it may represent local judicial

---

[198] For example, the Shenzhen Intermediate People's Court provides western legal training program to its own judges. Each year since 1998, around 15 judges will be sent to the University of Hong Kong Law Faculty to study the Master of Common Law (MCL) program.

[199] Mei Ying Gechlik, "Judicial Reform in China: Lessons from Shanghai", (2005) 19 *Columbia Journal of Asian Law*, 122–132.

[200] *The Third-Five-Year People's Court Reform Plan* (Renmin Fayuan Di'sange Wunian Gaige Gangyao 2009–2013), available at http://www.pkulaw.cn/fulltext_form.aspx?Db=chl&Gid=114912&EncodingName=big5.

[201] *Ibid.*, s.(3).

[202] *Ibid.*

[203] See a series of academic essays commenting on the lack of incorporating "pre-reporting" system in the SPC Interpretation by Wang Shengchang, Lu Xiaolong, Zhou Chengxin, Zhang Jinqian and Song Lianbin, in CIETAC South-China Sub-Commission (ed), *Judicial Review of Foreign-related Arbitration* (2006), 127–183.

[204] Speech of Tian Yuxi, Head of Enforcement Division of the Beijing Higher People's Court, at the Forum *Protection of International Investment and Financing*, *Financing* (co-organized by the BAC, Singapore International Arbitration Centre and China Society of International Law), Beijing, 16 July 2005, available at http://www.hzac.gov.cn/zclt/lt0508012.htm.

[205] *Ibid.*

[206] Speech of Justice Tian Yuxi, *ibid.*

efforts to merge the two tracks where other provincial courts may follow the footsteps. Perhaps, rather than applying the "pre-reporting" to both foreign and domestic regimes, the system could be abolished altogether because "pre-reporting" is an inefficient use of judicial resources. In addition, it influences the independent judicial thinking of lower level judges.

(c) Restrictions under state control

The enforcement study reveals that there has been distorted state control over the judiciary in China, which has indirectly *controlled* the *outcome* of arbitration such as enforcement of both arbitral agreements and arbitral awards. Born of the dependent status of local people's courts on local governments for survival and development, they are seriously pressured by local political and administrative powers in their decision-making process. It is also observed that the Chinese local courts are not sufficiently equipped both infrastructurally and professionally to keep up with the pro-validity and pro-enforcement arbitration reforms initiated by the SPC. Thus, lack of cooperation by the local judiciary has been shown a frequent occurrence in the enforcement of arbitration agreements, thereby possibly negating any advantages gained by the SPC's pro-arbitration initiatives. It is advocated that the sooner local people's courts can realise their institutional independence and improve their quality, the better China's enforcement records can develop.

7.104

To address the enforcement difficulties pervasive among the lower level judiciary (especially the hinterland), the SPC has introduced quite a few directives aimed at the independence and integrity of the judiciary, including the very recent Second-Five-Year-Reform-Outline (2004–2008). It has also attempted to provide education opportunities on arbitration norms for lower level judges. The improved independence and education is expected to bring along the increased judicial respect to parties' autonomy in arbitration. Although an optimistic view has been taken towards the implementation of this ambitious Second-Five-Year-Outline, so far, except for Shanghai, neither the practice of "guaranteed financing" nor "uniform recruitment" of lower level judges has been reported in other places of China.[207] The most recent Third-Five-Year Reform Plan (2009–2013) has failed to touch upon the implementation issue either. As such, the real extent to which these reforms are actually implemented are yet to be seen. Based on the observation by Professor Jerome Cohen, the political status quo in China does not allow the rapid expansion of its judicial power as the Party government may not wish to make quick changes, especially those that might threaten the primacy of administrative power.[208] This, seen from another perspective, explains the checkered development of the Chinese judiciary, which is largely subject to state control such as the country's political and administrative encroachment. Therefore, more breakthrough changes need to take place to *empower* the courts and individual judges in decision-making process. Finally, the success of reform will always be tested according to its actual degree of implementation in practice.

7.105

---

[207] Mei Ying Gechlik, "Judicial Reform in China: Lessons from Shanghai", (2006), 87.
[208] Jerome A. Cohen, "China's Legal Reform at the Crossroads" (2006) 2 *Far Eastern Economic Review*, 26.

CONCLUSION AND DIRECTION FOR FUTURE REFORM

Chapter 8 will first summarise the main findings of the study, namely practical **8.001** constraints of the Chinese arbitration system. The second part then lists some proposals for prospective arbitration reforms in China. Specific reforms for tackling the practical constraints will be featured in this part, particularly with respect to the restructuring of Chinese arbitration commissions, emphasising China Arbitration Association in regulating arbitrators and, finally, empowering people's courts for effective judicial review over arbitration. Given the common cultural background and close economic ties between Hong Kong and China, Hong Kong's arbitration experience will also be discussed to draw immediate lessons to the improvement of the Chinese arbitration system. The third part ends the discussion with a general observation of the Chinese arbitration development in the future.

1. PRACTICAL CONSTRAINTS TO CHINESE ARBITRATION

Diagram 1: *Practical constraints of Chinese arbitration system*

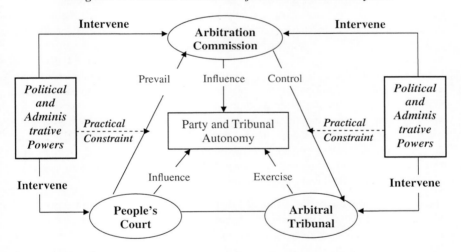

The author has argued earlier (in Chapter 3) that claims with respect to restricted **8.002** party and tribunal autonomy in Chinese arbitration on the mere basis of its regulatory deficiency might be premature, particularly because a significant gap exists between the written law and law in practice in China during its market transitions.[1] Verification into this argument has now been reflected in the diagram above (Diagram 1) regarding the *practical constraints* of the Chinese arbitration system by political and administrative powers intervening into the functioning and development of the key role players (arbitration commission, arbitral tribunal, and people's court).

---

[1] See discussions above under the heading "Pervasive state control over arbitration" of Chapter 3.

(a) Political and administrative interventions

8.003   As the major argument of this book, the fundamental problem of the Chinese arbitration system is that state control over arbitration is still very pervasive. Formally, the Arbitration Law is overly rigid. Empirically, state control has been expressed in the way of controlling the *outcome* of arbitration, by way of political and administrative powers intervening with respect to the formation of the arbitral tribunal, and infrastructure of both arbitration commissions and people's courts. Hence, the state continues to significantly affect decision-making processes of arbitral tribunals, arbitration commissions, and people's courts.

8.004   "State control" has constituted a hidden but serious obstacle to the *functioning* of the entire Chinese arbitration system. If we put the Chinese arbitration system into a triangular relationship with three legs, and each leg represents one of its key role players (as shown in Diagram 1), it is observed that, in China, however, the leg of "arbitration commission" has been too long. The arbitration commission has controlled almost all the arbitral matters covering jurisdiction, arbitrator qualification, tribunal formation, procedural details and, probably, final outcome of arbitration. As has been explained, doing so is consistent with the interest of Chinese administrative governance whereby most arbitration commissions in China are indeed administrative institutions under the shadow of local people's governments.[2] It therefore curbs the functioning and development of the second leg, the "arbitral tribunal", which should be the core leg in the modern arbitration system ensuring party autonomy and exercising arbitral autonomy. The third leg, the "people's court", although claimed to be very powerful for enjoying prioritised jurisdictional review and deciding upon arbitration enforcement,[3] is practically very weak in decision-making of individual cases under the current Chinese political ideology and administrative framework.[4] This triangular relationship thus shows an unstable and even "dangerous" chair of the Chinese arbitration system which is subject to the threat of political and administrative interventions.

8.005   Likewise, the argument can be made that "state control" has handicapped the *development* of Chinese arbitration generally. Support for this argument can be derived from the finding of insufficient protection of party and tribunal autonomy despite the vigorous progress of arbitral regulations issued by the China International Economic and Trade Arbitration Commission (CIETAC) and Supreme People's Court (SPC) over the past couple of years. First, the new rules introduced by CIETAC in 2005 have not been followed by corresponding changes in most local arbitration commissions (LACs). As has been demonstrated, the reluctance of the reform of LACs is because many of them suffer distorting reliance on the local people's governments for survival and development which have left the institutional endeavors many political challenges.[5] Secondly, while there is validity in the argument that the SPC has been working hard to pay more judicial respect to parties' autonomy and interest in arbitration, one can see that people's courts at the lower level may not be.

---

[2]   See discussions above under the heading "Problems of the arbitration commission infrastructure" of Chapters 5.

[3]   See discussions above under the heading "Prioritised judicial review under the Arbitration Law and Supreme People's Court interpretations" of Chapter 7.

[4]   See discussions above under the heading "Analysis of enforcement divergences and difficulties" of Chapter 7.

[5]   See discussions above under the heading "Reform suggestions and administrative challenges" of Chapter 5 and "Inherent defects under the institutional framework" of Chapter 6.

Due to uncertainty at the local level (i.e. local protectionism and lack of competence in handling arbitration case), the level of cooperation by the local judiciary has not been encouraging, thereby possibly negating the advantages gained by the SPC's pro-arbitration initiatives.[6] This could be explained by the fact that most of the local judiciary suffers local political and administrative pressures in decision-making processes.[7] Their institutional incapacity (including incapacity of judicial personnel) has thus subjected the enforcement, i.e. outcome of arbitration, to political and administrative interferences. The Chinese *guanxi* culture influence only aggravates political and administrative interventions from a "software" perspective, because the Party, government, judiciary, and finally, arbitration commissions, all belong to the same family under the top-down administrative governance, exerting cross impacts with intertwining relationships.

The Chinese system of "state control", however, contrasts drastically with that of the modern Western arbitration model. The Western model first recognises the effective and efficient arbitral tribunal as the core of modern arbitration. Western governments support the authority of arbitral tribunals by providing a liberal modern arbitration law. Then, the Western government maintains its influence over arbitration through effective judicial review as exercised by the powerful judiciary if the arbitral process fails to follow the law.[8] As such, the Western style of "state control" on arbitration works in a legal system whereby the court takes the real checks and balances. **8.006**

It might thus be arguable that the Chinese system, although attempts to walk a legal path,[9] has been restricted with administrative minds and eyes. The study on the practical constraints of Chinese arbitration hence reflects systematic problems in China. However, the problem seriously affects the quality of Chinese arbitration as a whole and has negatively impacted China's business reputation. Moreover, China will very much lose the competition in the international arbitration market to its regional competitors such as Hong Kong and Singapore which have been aligned with international arbitration standards. It is thus significantly argued that the unstable and dangerous "chair" of Chinese arbitration system should be amended right away. The power of arbitral tribunals should be essentially *increased* while that of the arbitration commission be significantly *decreased*. Meanwhile, the power of the people's court should be *maintained*, but its quality needs to be *improved* to exercise real checks and balances over arbitration. It is further argued that Chinese state control should be *decoupled* from the arbitration system for any future reform. **8.007**

2. PROSPECTIVE REFORMS FOR CHINESE ARBITRATION

The fact that there are practical constraints to the Chinese arbitration system does not mean that there is no room for improvement or change. The following discussions will focus on proposals for change with regard to the Arbitration Law, arbitration **8.008**

---

6   See discussions above under the headings "Enforcement of "non-signatory third party" and "Enforcement of "ambiguous arbitration commission" of Chapter 7.
7   See discussions above under the heading "Analysis of enforcement divergences and difficulties"of Chapter 7.
8   For example, United Kingdom and Hong Kong.
9   The PRC Constitution is amended in 1999 to incorporate "rule-of-law" as one of its basic principles.

commissions, China Arbitration Association (CAA) and people's courts. Among these proposals listed in Diagram 2 below, the author considers that the last three aspects of specific reforms will be helpful in addressing the practical constraints of Chinese arbitration.

Diagram 2: *Prospective reforms for Chinese arbitration system*

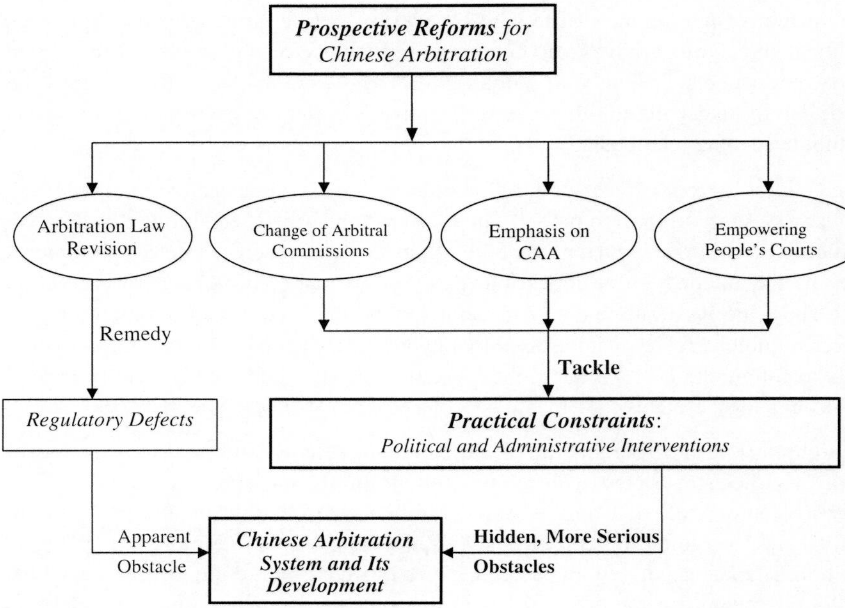

(a) Arbitration Law revision[10]

8.009　　As an *apparent obstacle* to the Chinese arbitration system and its development, the current Arbitration Law has been proved unable to cope with the practical needs. Revisions are therefore required to remedy the regulatory defects. It is notable that although the appeal to reform has been strong, no definite timetable has been set in the national legislative agenda thus far for revision.[11] It seems that now the conditions are ready for the Arbitration Law revision to take place in the near future. First, after more than a decade of practice, both positive and negative lessons have been drawn from the accumulation of experience of CIETAC and other experienced local arbitration commissions such as the Beijing Arbitration Commission (BAC). Secondly, the SPC interpretations on arbitration and its reforms of the judiciary over the past decade have prepared the courts to embrace a more pro-arbitration approach. Last but not the least, academic studies and research also provide the legislative reform with a solid theoretical ground.

---

[10]　See first limb in Diagram 2.
[11]　The Arbitration Law revision has not been included in the 2008, 2009, 2010 and 2011 NPC legislative agendas.

The Chinese legislature should take advantage of the best experience of international   **8.010**
arbitration norms, including the UNCITRAL Model Law, English Arbitration Act and
ICC Rules, in its legislative reform. Indeed, replacing the out-dated and rigid Arbitration
Law with an up-to-date and liberal *Arbitration Law* reflecting international standards
will benefit the Chinese market economy and be conducive to its integration with the
global economy. Reasons are straightforward. The adoption of international arbitration
norms and practices would significantly increase party and tribunal autonomy, thus
making arbitration in China more commercially-oriented and user-friendly. Evidently,
this serves the interests of the entire commercial sector, especially the commercial
interests of foreign-related parties who prefer using arbitration in resolving their trade
and investment disputes. It thus serves China's trade and investment interests and
hence, will be beneficial to China's integration into the global economy.

At the same time, in conducting the legislative revision, Chinese legislatures also   **8.011**
need to pay attention to its consistency with other types of arbitral regulations, whose
uncertain and even conflicting interactions with the Arbitration Law have been at
least partly blamed for distorting Chinese arbitral practices. In this regard, the revised
Arbitration Law should confirm the initiatives of the most recent SPC interpretations
on arbitration in 2006 so as to prevent any future inconsistencies. Another point
worth noting is that, the concept of "foreign-related arbitration commission"[12]
should be discarded, which has caused practical confusion concerning arbitral
jurisdiciton. Indeed, all arbitration commissions in China are now able to receive
both domestic and foreign-related disputes as a result of the State Council Notice in
1996 and subsequent revisions to the CIETAC Rules in 1998.[13] There are no longer
any jurisdictional divisions predicated on the characterisation of the arbitration
commissions. As such, only the concept of "foreign-related dispute" should be
retained (as in accordance with the judicial interpretations of both General Principles
of Civil Law and Civil Procedure Law).[14] Bifurcations should only be maintained
to the extent of different treatment of judicial review over arbitral awards resulting
from the two types of disputes; and grounds for reviewing domestic awards should
be narrowed only to procedural aspects.

Other problematic areas of Chinese arbitration may include, for example, interim   **8.012**
measures, in which the Arbitration Law falls significantly short in meeting practical
needs. Main defects are as follows. First, the arbitral tribunal has no authority to
entertain a party's motion for evidence[15] or property preservation.[16] The power is
either wholly in the hands of the people's court or shared by the court and arbitration

---

[12] Articles 66–73 of the Arbitration Law, under Chapter 7, "Special Provisions for Arbitration Involving Foreign
      Elements".
[13] See discussions above under the heading "Inconsistent ancillary rules" of Chapter 3.
[14] *Ibid.*
[15] Article 46 of the Arbitration Law provides for evidence preservation, "In the event that the evidence might be
      destroyed or if it would be difficult to obtain later on, a party may apply for the evidence to be preserved". A
      similar article regarding evidence preservation in foreign-related arbitration is found in art.68.
[16] Article 28 of the Arbitration Law provides for property preservation, "A party may apply for property preservation
      if it appears that an award may be impossible or difficult to enforce".

commission.[17] This recasts one of the principal weaknesses of the Chinese arbitral regulation which places over-emphasis on the arbitration commission. Secondly, the Arbitration Law is silent as to whether preservation may be ordered before arbitration takes place.[18] Although there is a high recognition among practitioners that it is very likely urgency could arise before the arbitral proceeding demanding interim measures, there has been a uniform practice among the judiciary and arbitration commissions denying pre-arbitration measures.[19] Thirdly, there is a further legal gap as to the grounds under which the interim measures can be ordered; and upon the order, whether parties will have a chance to present their case. Pursuant to arts.28 (property preservation) and 46 (evidence preservation) of the Arbitration Law, the "urgency of the measures sought" needs to be considered.[20] In practice, however, people's courts either construe the "urgency" very discretionarily[21] or they just want to make sure that the party applying the measures has supplied a sufficient security from which the opponent whom the measure is sought can be compensated once the measure is found wrong.[22] This is surely not a modern way of dealing with interim measures. In this regard, the UNCITRAL Working Group has lately suggested some very liberal amendments concerning interim measures in January 2006.[23] Among its various suggestions, the revised Model Law art.17(1) has confirmed the ordering of interim measures a default authority for arbitral tribunals, whereby the arbitrators are empowered to do so *unless* there is evidence that the parties did *not* intend to bestow that power.[24] In addition, art.17(1) also emphasises that an interim measure is any form of temporary measure, which parties can seek at *any* time prior to the issuance of the final award of the dispute.[25] Consistent with its previous suggestions, the Working Group further lays down in its para (2) of the revised art.17 grounds to order the interim measures by tribunals:

> "(a) harm not adequately reparable by an award of damages is likely to result if the measure is not ordered; (b) there is a reasonable possibility that the requesting party will succeed on the merits of the claim".[26]

---

[17]   The party seeking the interim measures is required to file the motion to the arbitration commission. And the arbitration commission then will redirect the motion to the competent people's court. See second half of art.46 of the Arbitration Law.

[18]   Indeed, in the text of the Civil Procedure Law, the interim measures can only be sought after the suit/action has been started (*qisu*). Is the "suit or action (*su*)" here restricted to litigation alone, i.e. is pre-arbitration interim measures prohibited in China as well? In this regard, the whole literature seems to take an expansive interpretation of what the "starting a suit" means to include both litigation and arbitration.

[19]   Lijun Cao, "Interim Measures of Protection in the Context of Arbitration in China", (2005) 8 *International Arbitration Law Review*, 104. And no case has been reported so far in which a party succeeds in applying for pre-arbitration interim measures.

[20]   See arts.28 and 46 of the Arbitration Law.

[21]   Cao, "Interim Measures of Protection in the Context of Arbitration in China" (2005), 105.

[22]   *Ibid*, 106.

[23]   The UNCITRAL settlement of uniform provisions on "interim measures of protection" in the Model Law art.17, passed by the Forty-forth session of the UNCITRAL Working Group (New York, 23–27 January 2006). See UNCITRAL document A/CN.9/WG.II/WP.141, available at http://daccessdds.un.org/doc/UNDOC/LTD/ V05/907/58/PDF/V0590758.pdf?OpenElement.

[24]   Article 17(1), sub-paragraph one, *ibid*.

[25]   Article 17(1), sub-paragraph two, *ibid*.

[26]   Article 17(2), *ibid*.

Moreover, under its revised para (4), immediately after the tribunal has made a **8.013** determination to order the interim measures, it shall give notice to the parties making the request and shall give an opportunity to any party against whom the measures are directed to present its case at the earliest practical time.[27] There are other new developments under the revised art.17 such as the burden of proof on the party seeking interim measures of protection,[28] its duty of disclosing any material change of circumstances on the basis of which the measure was requested or granted.[29] The UNCITRAL Arbitration Rules have also been revised accordingly under its art.26 in February 2008.[30]

Chinese legislative reform should borrow the experience of most advanced arbitration **8.014** norms and at least fulfill the following aspects in the new *Arbitration Law*: (1) that as a general principle, the arbitral tribunal rather than the arbitration commission or people's court should be empowered to order interim measures; (2) that pre-arbitration interim measures should be allowed; (3) that the measure can be granted only after both parties have the chance to be heard and certain prerequisites have been met such as "whether irreparable harm will follow if the measure is denied", and "reasonable likelihood of success on the merits"; (4) that people's courts should mainly be responsible for enforcing the tribunal-ordered measures. The discussion below will then focus on a series of *specific reforms* for tackling the "practical constraints" identified by the study.

(b) Restructuring of arbitration commissions[31]

This section argues for independent and professional arbitration commissions to be **8.015** developed in China drawing institutional experience from advanced arbitral institutions such as the ICC Court of Arbitration and Hong Kong International Arbitration Center (HKIAC). Two aspects should be achieved in reforming arbitration commissions.

One is that, structurally, arbitration commissions must be *decoupled* from the local **8.016** governments and thus achieve independence and self-sufficiency. This purports to eliminate the external intervention by political and administrative powers into arbitration commissions. For this purpose, arbitration commissions should be independent in both aspects of personnel and finance. The personnel composition within a commission, particularly that of its leadership should be selected from the legal professionals rather than representatives of administrative departments. On financial matters, arbitration commissions should rely on its arbitration fees for operation and development instead of being under the shelter of local governments.

This will push arbitration commissions in China to strive for quality development **8.017** under market competition, because whether or not an arbitration commission can

---

[27] Article 17(4), *ibid.*

[28] Article 17(6), *ibid.*

[29] Article 17(7), *ibid.*

[30] Article 26 of the Revision of the UNCITRAL Arbitration Rules, passed by 48th session of the UNCITRAL Working Group on Arbitration (New York, 4–8 February 2008). See UNCITRAL document A/CN.9/WG.II/WP.149, available at http://daccessdds.un.org/doc/UNDOC/LTD/V07/885/92/PDF/V0788592.pdf?OpenElement.

[31] See second limb in Diagram 2.

attract caseload ultimately depends on its quality and market competitiveness; and the local government should be prohibited from forcing local enterprises to use local arbitration commissions for playing upon localisation sentiment. In this regard, it is good to see that BAC has successfully restructured itself in terms of both integrity and quality; and BAC has further won itself rising fame in resolving commercial and technology disputes in the arbitration market.[32] The success of BAC tests the feasibility of structural reform of large numbers of locally based arbitration commissions in China. In the mean time, one has to realise that the restructuring might lead to survival problems for many local arbitration commissions. It is the current arbitration system that fails to rationally allocate the resources to some qualified arbitration commissions whereby qualified commissions have been outnumbered by other commissions throughout the country catering to local administrative needs rather than real market demand. The author thus advocates that those less developed commissions which have no or very little caseload to support its operation should be eliminated from the market.

8.018   The other aspect is to reform the power division within the arbitration commission and hence their *functions*, which aims at reducing any possible influences from practical constraints within the commission. Indeed, arbitral powers should be transferred from the commission back to the tribunal. Fundamentally, commissions should be denied powers in both merit adjudication and jurisdictional determination so that tribunals can play a key role in the arbitration process and their arbitral autonomy and power should be strengthened. Drawing experience from the ICC Court of Arbitration, a Chinese arbitration commission should mainly be responsible for managing daily institutional operations. The commission should also provide liberal arbitration rules for facilitating dispute resolution and helping to ensure compliance with the rules. In addition, the commission may exercise power to administer either arbitral procedures or make appointment of arbitrators when parties default in their choices. However, the purpose of their administrative power is to secure the procedural efficiency of the arbitration rather than to interfere or control the decision-making of arbitral tribunals. Moreover, the roles of staff of Chinese arbitration commissions should change. Commission staff should refrain from acting as arbitrators in the cases submitted to their commissions. In particular, the commission secretariat should not play any role in deciding procedural or substantive issues in individual cases. Finally, the remuneration of arbitrators should be duly raised, although it may take time to align the amount with international levels.

(c) Emphasis on China Arbitration Association in arbitrator regulation[33]

8.019   It has been illustrated in previous chapters that it is very likely party autonomy and interest would be endangered by tribunals formed under the closed-panel system. This is partly explained by the closing of the panels; and partly by the defective commission-controlled arbitrator qualifying scheme by each individual commission[34]

---

[32]   See discussions above under the heading "Reform suggestions and administrative challenges" of Chapter 5.
[33]   See third limb in Diagram 2.
[34]   See discussions above under the heading "Distinctive features of the commission panel" of Chapter 6.

which opens the door for large numbers of staff, official and local arbitrators under political, administrative and institutional influence.[35] Legislative suggestions have been made to adopt an open-styled panel system of arbitrator appointment in Chinese arbitration commissions. However, this disregards the question that if parties wish to choose legal and commercial experts outside the commission panel list, who can assure the qualifications of these people? This leads to the conclusion that if the open-panel has been adopted, but the power of accrediting outside arbitrators remains with the government, it would remain difficult to eliminate political and administrative influence. A change in the accreditation scheme of arbitrators will therefore be necessary.

It is advocated that accreditation should be managed by a self-regulatory body rather than controlled by arbitration commissions. The self-regulation of arbitrators would be a major improvement, because it can eliminate the institutional as well as political and administrative impacts on the screening process and thus help *delink* state involvement in arbitration. Previous studies have illustrated that the institutional panel system has been used in the days when Chinese arbitration was immature and there were only a few experts to handle commercial and trade disputes.[36] However, over the past fifteen years, arbitration intellectuals have developed dramatically. There is no shortage of experts today and conditions are now ripe for *self-regulation*. In this respect, the CAA should be the most appropriate authority for qualifying and overseeing arbitrators given its legal status to coordinate and supervise all Chinese arbitration commissions as a professional self-regulatory organisation.[37] Indeed, the establishment of the CAA should be settled as soon as possible, which has been a lingering issue[38] for more than a decade since the promulgation of the Arbitration Law.[39]

8.020

It is further advocated that the power of the CAA should develop to cover all areas of regulations of arbitrators, from qualifying/training to disciplining, so that powers can be transferred from the government back to the self-regulatory body. One point which is worth noting, however, is who should establish CAA? An ideal solution would be that CAA would be set up by all the non-governmental Chinese arbitration commissions, which is conditional upon these commissions first fulfilling their restructuring.[40] CAA should be independent from any Party and governmental bodies to prevent any potential danger of administrative influence and it must be self-financing by collecting fees from its members as practiced by, for example, the

8.021

---

[35] See discussions above under the heading "Hidden Obstacles to Tribunal Formation" of Chapter 6.

[36] See discussions above under the heading "Conclusion: State control vs party autonomy" of Chapter 6.

[37] See art.15, para 2 of the Arbitration Law.

[38] There have been concerns and worries that once arbitration commissions broke off from the supervision of the administrative bodies, they would be out of control. This to some extent might help explain why the establishment of CAA has been such a lingering issue. See, Wen Ge, "On the Lingering Establishment of China Arbitration Association: Worries by Arbitration Academics and Practitioners (Zhongcai Xiehui Huzhiyuchu: Yenei Renshi Youxinchongchong)", available at http://www.china-arbitration.com.

[39] It has been highly urged that the CAA should be established before the revision to the Arbitration Law. See Song Lianbin, "Seven Years' Critical Awaiting: Several Suggestions to the Draft Judicial Interpretations on Foreign-related Arbitration", in CIETAC South-China Sub-Commission (ed), *Judicial Review of the Foreign-Related Arbitration (Shewaizhongcai Sifa Shengcha)* (Beijing: China Law Press, 2006), 166.

[40] This suggestion is compatible to the legislative definition of CAA under art.15 of the Arbitration Law.

Chartered Institute of Arbitrators (CIArb) in London.[41] Since China has not had a tradition of arbitrator professionalism, further experience can be drawn from the CIArb with respect to organising standardised exams and training for Chinese and foreign citizens to become accredited and remain competent.[42] Moreover, preparing ethical and disciplinary codes for the conduct of arbitrators should also be within the ambit of the CAA. By doing so, CAA would provide its users, i.e. arbitral parties, with the confidence that its members have an assured level of training and experience in arbitration in China. The *detachment* of arbitrator accreditation from the commission will help implement the open-panel legislative proposal whereby parties can enjoy the freedom of appointing competent arbitrators both inside and outside the panels. Further, it will facilitate the introduction of *ad hoc* arbitration practice in China.

(d) Empowering people's courts[43]

8.022 As argued previously, Chinese government influence should pursue itself in a way of "legal control" as modern arbitration systems do—with ante-control by a modern *Arbitration Law*; and if the arbitral process fails to abide by the Law, then the people's court will step in providing effective judicial review as post-control (see Diagram 3 below).

Diagram 3: ***Modern system of state control on arbitration***

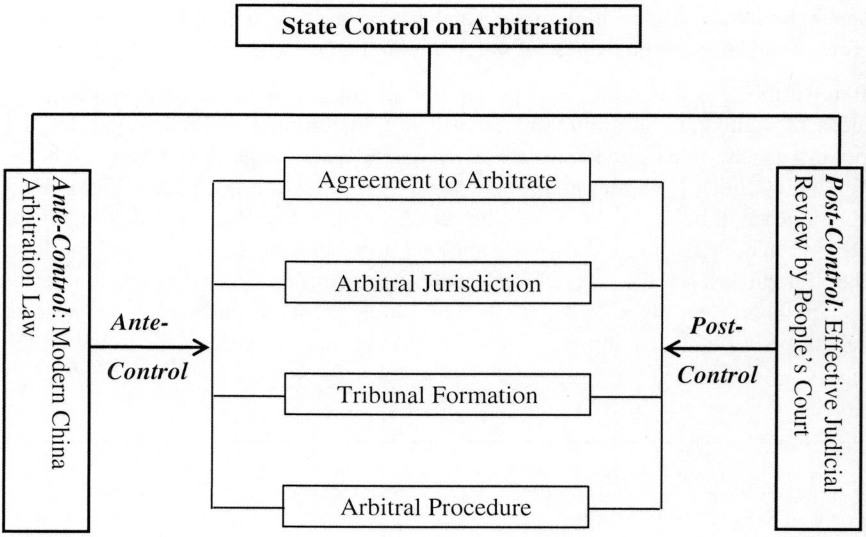

---

41 CIArb is a world recognized self-regulatory institutional leader in providing accreditation and training to arbitrators and mediators. The institute is accessible at http://www.arbitrators.org.

42 For example, see the "Catalogue of Course" offered to the different categories of CIArb members (Associate, Member and Fellow), accessible at, http://www.arbitrators.org/Courses/QualIntro.asp?pd=1.

43 See fourth limb in Diagram 2.

This will first rely on the clear power division between arbitration commissions and people's courts so as to live up to the international standard that "courts cannot intervene into the arbitral procedure unless otherwise clearly provided".[44] More importantly, significant improvement of judicial *integrity* as well as *quality* of the people's courts should be achieved in order to provide checks and balances to arbitration under a "legal system". It is encouragingly noted that the retarded Chinese court system has been seriously addressed in the past decade, especially the two rounds of SPC reforms of the people's courts in response to rising international pressures to establish an independent judiciary in China. Local protectionism and corruption may be mitigated by the SPC directives. The second SPC Five-Year-Reform-Outline (2004–2008) appears particularly bold in exploring a number of goals for upgrading the Chinese judicial system. It is fair to say that China is still struggling for its optimal judicial framework where the Party leadership is in a dilemma with respect to the role of the judiciary in Chinese society and governance. Although it has been strenuously argued that people's courts should be empowered to play a more active role from which enforcement of arbitration could benefit, fundamentally reforming Chinese courts will be a very difficult and complex task which needs an entire rule-of-law system to be established. The rule-of-law is increasingly pushed by the more civilised Chinese society for achieving effective prohibition of all kinds of external interferences in the adjudication and enforcement processes from the Party, government, or other sources.

8.023

Laws and policies from the Central Government are needed to officially support the SPC reforms with the expanding progress of the nation's rule-of-law agenda, under which the court should develop into an independent organ or branch of the state. This would suggest the judiciary gradually manage its own *financial* and *personnel* affairs. For example, the budget of each people's court would be determined and administered by the SPC to prevent local governments from using budgetary powers to influence adjudication and enforcement. This would further suggest that, the appointment and removal of judges would be centralised in the SPC, whereby impacts of the Party committee or local government on personnel affairs could be minimised. Specifically, to improve the quality of enforcement over arbitration (both arbitration agreements and arbitral awards), the overall quality of Chinese judges in terms of knowledge of and practical experience in arbitration should be enhanced. Judges at lower levels should understand properly SPC's liberal interpretations on arbitration, as well as international arbitration norms and the world-wide pro-arbitration judicial trend. Moreover, the education arrangement organised by the SPC should persist, and more international legal education programs should be promoted to the lower level people's courts.

8.024

(e) Hong Kong's experience

It is also advocated that Hong Kong' experience with respect to more advanced arbitral legislations and institutions, may draw immediate lessons to the development and

8.025

---

[44] For example, art.5 of the Model Law states that, "In matters governed by this Law, no court shall intervene except where so provided by this Law".

improvement of the arbitration system in China, particularly against the backdrop of the close economic relations between the two regions under the framework of "one country, two systems".[45]

8.026   First, the Arbitration Ordinance[46] works as a good model on harmonisation with international arbitration norms for Chinese arbitral regulations to draw experience from. Hong Kong has adopted the Model Law as part of its arbitral legal framework in 1996 to govern international arbitrations,[47] so does the HKIAC regarding its reception of the UNCITRAL Rules as early as 1993 in governing international arbitral procedures administered by the HKIAC.[48] These liberal arbitration regulations have placed Hong Kong in a significantly advantageous status in marketing its arbitration in line with international standards at a rather early stage. In addition, the Arbitration Ordinance makes it explicit that parties, irrespective of the nature of their disputes, can freely opt in and opt out of the domestic and international arbitration regimes to let the Model Law even be applicable to domestic disputes if the parties so wish.[49] The flexible opting system has maximised parties' autonomy in different types of arbitrations, as a praiseworthy adaptation contributed by Hong Kong to Model Law jurisprudence.[50] China should definitely catch up on the legislative point and lessons drawing from Hong Kong may push the revised *Arbitration Law* to first introduce the international standards to its foreign-related track which has historically been more developed than the domestic regime. Based on that, an opt-in/out-of mechanism may be allowed between dual tracks in the revised *Arbitration Law* as what the Arbitration Ordinance has enthusiastically pursued.

8.027   Secondly, institutional experience from the HKIAC can shed light on how to restructure Chinese arbitration commissions to be professional and market-oriented institutions. Specific proposals have already been made with respect to developing Chinese arbitral commissions to be delinked from the government and to achieve clear arbitral power divisions within the institution.[51] It is further noted that HKIAC's experience in compiling a larger institutional pool of potential arbitrators may draw lessons to the proposed open-panel system to be established in China. As mentioned in previous chapters, the open-panel system of the HKIAC is employed in a way of "three-step" formula.[52] In the first step, a group of experts is listed as its panel arbitrators. In the second step, a database of other arbitral talents is maintained who, albeit not as highly

---

[45]   China and Hong Kong signed a Closer Economic Partnership Arrangement (CEPA) in 2003, providing an unprecedented platform for the close economic ties between the two regions.

[46]   Arbitration Ordinance (Cap.341), revised in 1990, 1996, and 2009.

[47]   Hong Kong adopted the Model Law in 1996 to govern its international arbitration regime by its revision to the Arbitration Ordinance, listed as Part II. Domestic arbitrations taking place in Hong Kong still follow pretty much the stipulations of the English Arbitration Act 1996, listed as Arbitration Ordinance Part I. See Hong Kong Legal Information Institute official website, http://www.hklii.org/hk/legis/en/ord/341/.

[48]   The HKIAC adopts the UNCITRAL Arbitration Rules for international arbitral disputes submitted to it. See HKIAC official website, http://hkiac.org/HKIAC/HKIAC_English/main.html.

[49]   Sections 2L and 2M of the Arbitration Ordinance.

[50]   Katherine Lynch, *The Forces of Economic Globalization: Challenges to the Regime of International Commercial Arbitration* (The Hague: Kluwer Law International, 2003), 247.

[51]   See discussions above under the heading "Restructuring of Arbitration Commissions" with respect to the "Restructuring of Arbitration Commissions in China" drawing institutional experience of the ICC and HKIAC.

[52]   See discussions above in Section 1(a)(iii) of Chapter 6, entitled "Panel Appointment: Closed vs Open".

qualified as those experts being listed on the panel, may yet be available for parties' choice in suitable cases. In the last step, the parties will never be restricted to either the panel or the database such that they are free to appoint any persons they feel confident with. The formula has indeed made HKIAC a favorable institutional choice for arbitration, as the parties have not only a wider pool of arbitral talents to select from, but they may make full use of the institutional advantage of the batch of high expertise accumulated as well. Chinese arbitration commissions, particularly those leading commissions such as CIETAC and BAC, are as such strongly recommended to follow the three-step formula of HKIAC in implementing its open-panel scheme, for balancing both the party autonomy and institutional culture in a more market-oriented fashion.

Thirdly, the experience of the Hong Kong Institute of Arbitrators (HKIArb)[53] on nurturing arbitrator professionalism in Hong Kong could be borrowed by CAA for self-regulation of arbitrators in China. It has been suggested earlier that CAA may look at CIArb in London for organising standardised exams to get Chinese and foreign citizens accredited as arbitrators in China.[54] It is, however, more straightforward by looking at HKIArb for experience sharing. The common language culture and geographic convenience between the two regions are always the strongest arguments for reference. It is notable that HKIArb runs both English and Chinese courses for interested persons with different knowledge and experience levels of arbitration to get qualified. In addition, different packages of course materials and different sets of training workshops are provided, i.e. those at the elementary level to be accredited as "Associate" members and those at the senior level to be qualifed as "Fellow" members.[55] Moreover, a council is adopted within HKIArb to work as the board of governors for deciding on its major development issues and for reviewing the curriculum of the accrediting and training courses and workshops on a yearly basis.[56] The HKIArb Council, elected by members annually, are composed of prominent and experienced arbitrators in Hong Kong who erstwhile frequently serve as arbitrators in other jurisdictions.[57] This purports to ensure the highly professionalist feature of the self-regulatory institute and highly competitive quality of the arbitrators trained therein for fostering the arbitrator professionalism of Hong Kong. CAA can at least embark on the following two schemes as immediate lessons to be drawn from its Hong Kong counterpart. On one hand, a council or committee should be established within CAA to oversee its overall development and management of qualification programs. The personnel components of the CAA council or committee must be independent professionals such as renowned arbitration academics and practitioners. On the other hand, CAA could borrow from HKIArb specific experience with respect to curriculum

8.028

---

[53] The Hong Kong Institute of Arbitrators is set up by a group of professional people in Hong Kong who are experienced at arbitration, mediation and other kinds of dispute resolution. HKIArb is mainly involved in the training of arbitrators and mediators and the setting of standards of conduct for arbitrators and mediators in Hong Kong. See HKIArb's official introduction, at http://www.hkiarb.org.hk/index.htm.

[54] See discussions above under the heading "Emphasis on CAA in Arbitrator Regulation" with respect to the "self-regulation of arbitrators in China" drawing experience of the self-regulatory bodies such as the CIArb in London.

[55] See the HKIArb's official website on its membership program, available at http://www.hkiarb.org.hk/membership.htm.

[56] See the HKIArb's official website on its Council composition, at http://www.hkiarb.org.hk/council.htm.

[57] *Ibid.*

development, course design and workshop format on the qualification and training of its arbitrator members. Indeed, the availability of a Chinese-language set of HKIArb course materials facilitates the experience sharing. In this regard, trainers of HKIArb can even be invited to give lectures in the CAA programs and more exchanges are encouraged between the two organisations.

8.029   Lastly, the supportive role by the Hong Kong courts with respect to enforcement of both arbitration agreements and arbitral awards are role models for the Chinese judiciary. As we recall the landmark case of *Lucky-Goldstar International Ltd*,[58] courts in Hong Kong have developed a very liberal "intent-based" technique regarding the interpretation of defective arbitration agreements, and awards are generally enforced except for violation of public policy of Hong Kong such as "due process" concerns.[59] The more advanced judicial approach to arbitration in Hong Kong will be impactful upon the future improvement of the competence and quality of Chinese judges in handling arbitral disputes. People's courts in China shall follow suit when determining the existence and validity of arbitration agreements. They shall look into the intent of the parties and refrain from imposing judicial limitations through narrow textual interpretations. Chinese judges should bear in mind that the spirit of an agreement to arbitrate will prevail over any technical limitations. They shall further be refrained from using nationalist or local protectionist sentiment to deny enforcement of arbitral awards outside the jurisdiction. Although it is much more challenging to reform the judicial independence at the moment, it might be plausible to start with the improvement of the quality of Chinese judges first, who may then work more actively in preventing the political and administrative interferences in arbitral enforcement by resorting to legitimate grounds and standards of modern arbitration.

3. CONCLUDING REMARKS

8.030   While the author has argued that there are practical constraints to the Chinese arbitration system and its development, and as such, the most recent reforms led by CIETAC and SPC have been restricted in effect, one has to admit that these practical constraints are rooted in Chinese systematic problems. To thoroughly wipe out these deeply-rooted problems will be dependent on reforming the entire Chinese governance system or rule of law in general, but this would go beyond the scope of the study. This study is therefore not suggesting revolutions to the Chinese arbitration regime. However, it suggests *evolution* from an academic point of view, by providing a package of proposals on both legislative and practical aspects that can be adopted step by step by the Chinese government.

8.031   On one hand, the *legislative revisions* have been paying attention to the experience of most advanced international arbitration norms. The very reason for taking advantage of these best practices is that the author firmly believes that the Chinese arbitration

---

[58]   *Lucky-Goldstar International (HK) Ltd v Ng Moo Kee Engineering Ltd* [1993] 2 HKLR 73.

[59]   *Hebei Import and Export Corp v Polytek Engineering Co Ltd* [1999] 1 HKLRD 665.

legislation will finally develop to the international level as has already taken place in the regime of intellectual property laws.[60] This is because arbitration is important to the commercial sector and it serves the nation's trade and investment interests. Indeed, the author has explained that it is very likely that legislative changes will take place in the not too distant future.

On the other hand, the *specific proposals* suggested, such as restructuring of arbitration commissions, emphasis on CAA in arbitrator regulation and empowering people's courts in providing effective judicial review over arbitration, are not only urgent for redressing the practical constraints but also plausible for implementation in the near future. This is because a very positive scene has been observed in the development of modern Chinese local arbitration commissions such as BAC; moreover, there has been vigorous growth in arbitral talents and increasing recognition of the importance of judicial power in China over the past decade.

8.032

Last but not the least, the experience of Hong Kong's arbitration on both legislative and institutional development is impactful upon the future reform of the Chinese arbitration system. Apart from geographic and language convenience, the signing of the Arrangement on Reciprocal Recognition and Enforcement of Arbitral Awards between the Mainland and Hong Kong in 2000 has already shown the signal of convergence of arbitration practices between the two regions,[61] where China is more inclined towards adopting Hong Kong standards in conducting arbitrations.[62]

8.033

In conclusion, this is an academic work which provides academic insights into the reform of the arbitration system in China. It identifies the major pitfalls of the Chinese arbitration system by comparative study (with international arbitration norms and practices) and empirical research (of the actual operation of key arbitration role players). In order to tackle them, legislative and specific proposals are raised. The proposals are indeed forward-looking, as the author is confident and optimistic about the future of Chinese arbitration, that China will finally be aligned with international norms and standards and provide world-class arbitral service to its investors both at home and abroad.

8.034

---

[60] The most recently revised Copyright Law (2006), Patent Law (2007) and Trademark Law (2007) are very advanced legislations and they have been aligned with various international conventions on the protection of intellectual properties.

[61] Arrangement between the Mainland and Hong Kong Special Administrative Region on Reciprocal Recognition and Enforcement of Arbitral Awards (The Arrangement), was signed by the Department of Justice in Hong Kong and Supreme People's Court in China in 1999. The Arrangement was put into effect in both regions on 1 February 2000.

[62] For example, art.7(1) of the Arrangement lists the grounds for non-enforcement of awards from the other side, where China has adopted all the Hong Kong standards and grounds with respect to setting aside an international arbitral award. For detailed discussion, see Gu Weixia, "Recourse against Arbitral Awards: How Far Can a Court Go? Supportive and Supervisory Role of HK Courts as Lessons to Mainland China Arbitration", (2005) 4 *Chinese Journal of International Law*, 500.

Arbitration Law of the People's Republic of China

(Adopted by the 9th Meeting of the Standing Committee of the Eighth National People's Congress on 31 October 1994 and promulgated by the Decree No. 31 of the President of the People's Republic of China on 31 October 1994)

Chapter 1

General Provisions

Article 1

The law is formulated with a view to ensure fair and timely arbitration of economic disputes, reliable protection to legitimate rights and interests of parties concerned and a healthy development of the socialist market economy.

Article 2

Contractual disputes between citizens of equal status, legal persons and other economic organisations and disputes arising from property rights may be put to arbitration.

Article 3

The following disputes cannot be put to arbitration:

1. Disputes arising from marriage, adoption, guardianship, bringing up of children and inheritance.

2. Disputes that have been stipulated by law to be settled by administrative organs.

Article 4

In settling disputes through arbitration, an agreement to engage in arbitration should first of all be reached by parties concerned upon free will. Without such an agreement, the arbitration commission shall refuse to accept the application for arbitration by any one single party.

Article 5

Whereas the parties concerned have reached an agreement for arbitration, the people's court shall not accept the suit brought to the court by any one single party involved, except in case where the agreement for arbitration is invalid.

Article 6

The members of the arbitration commission shall be chosen by the parties concerned. Arbitration shall not be subject to the jurisdiction of administrative departments at any level and region.

Article 7

Arbitration shall be made based on true facts and relative laws to give out a fair and reasonable settlement for parties concerned.

Article 8

Arbitration shall be conducted independently according to law, free from interference of administrative organs, social groups or individuals.

Article 9

The arbitration award is final. After the award is given, the arbitration commission or the people's court shall not accept the re-application of the suit concerning the same dispute by any of the parties concerned.

Whereas the award cancelled or put in void under a rule by the people's court, the parties concerned for the dispute may reach another agreement for arbitration and apply for arbitration or bring a suit in the people's court.

Chapter 2

Arbitration Commission and Arbitration Association

Article 10

An arbitration commission may be set up in the domicile of the people's governments of municipalities directly under the Central Government (hereinafter referred to as municipalities), provinces and autonomous regions or in other places according to needs. It shall not be set up according to administrative levels.

An arbitration commission shall be set up by the relevant departments and chambers of commerce under the coordination of the people's governments of the cities prescribed in the preceding paragraph.

The establishment of an arbitration commission shall be registered with the judicial administrative departments of provinces, autonomous regions and municipalities.

Article 11

An arbitration commission shall meet the following requirements:

1. It shall have its own name, residence and statute.

2. It shall have necessary property.

3. It shall have its own members.

4. It shall have appointed arbitrators.

The statute of an arbitration commission shall be formulated according to this law.

Article 12

An arbitration commission shall be composed of a chairman, two to four vice-chairmen and 7 to 11 members.

The chairman, vice-chairmen and members of an arbitration commission shall be experts in law and economy and trade with practical work experience. Of the composition of an arbitration commission, experts in law, economy and trade shall be no less than two-thirds.

Article 13

Members of an arbitration commission shall be appointed from among the people who are fair and justice.

An arbitrator shall meet one of the following requirements:

1. At least eight years of work experience in arbitration.

2. At least eight years of experience as a lawyer.

3. At least eight years of experience as a judge.

4. Engaging in law research and teaching, with a senior academic title.

An arbitration commission shall prepare the list of arbitrators according to different specialities.

Article 14

An arbitration commission shall be independent of any administrative organ, without any subordinate relationship with administrative organs. Neither would there be any subordinate relations thereof.

Article 15

The China Arbitration Association is an institutional legal person with all the separate arbitration commissions as its members. The statute of the China Arbitration Association shall be formulated by the national congress of the association.

The China Arbitration Association is a self-disciplinary organisation for arbitration commissions to supervise over the latter and their members and arbitrators therein.

The China Arbitration Association shall formulate arbitration rules according to this law and the civil procedure law.

Chapter 3

Agreement for Arbitration

Article 16

An agreement for arbitration shall include the arbitration clauses stipulated in the contracts or other written agreements for arbitration reached before or after a dispute occurs.

An arbitration agreement shall contain the following:

1. The expression of application for arbitration.

2. Matters for arbitration.

3. The arbitration commission chosen.

Article 17

An agreement for arbitration shall be invalid in one of the following cases:

1. The matters agreed for arbitration exceed the scope of arbitration provided by law.

2. Agreements concluded by people being incapable or restricted in civil acts.

3. An agreement forced upon a party by the other party by means of coercion.

Article 18

Whereas an agreement for arbitration fails to specify or specify clearly matters concerning arbitration or the choice of arbitration commission, parties concerned may conclude a supplementary agreement. If a supplementary agreement cannot be reached, the agreement for arbitration is invalid.

Article 19

The effect of an agreement for arbitration shall stand independently and shall not be affected by the alteration, dissolution, termination or invalidity of a contract.

An arbitration tribunal has the right to establish the validity of a contract.

Article 20.

Whereas parties concerned have doubt on the validity of an agreement for arbitration, a request can be made to the arbitration commission for a decision or to the people's court for a ruling. If one party requests the arbitration commission for a decision while the other party requests the people's court for a ruling, the people's court shall pass a ruling.

A doubt to the effectiveness of an arbitration agreement, should be raised before the first hearing at the arbitration tribunal.

Chapter 4

Arbitration Procedure

Section 1: Application and Acceptance

Article 21

The parties concerned should meet the following requirements in applying for arbitration:

1. There is an agreement for arbitration.

2. There are specific requests for arbitration and facts and reasons.

3.   The matters to be put to arbitration shall fall into the limits of the authority of the arbitration commission.

Article 22.

In applying for arbitration, the parties concerned shall submit the agreement and the application for arbitration and their copies.

Article 23

The application for arbitration shall specify the following matters:

1.   Name, sex, age, profession, work unit and residence of parties concerned; the name, residence of legal persons or other organisations and the name and position of the legal representatives or principal leading members.

2.   The claimants's claim and the facts and evidence on which the claim is based.

3.   Evidence and sources of evidence and name and residence of witnesses.

Article 24

An arbitration commission shall accept the application within five days after the application is received if it deems the application conforming to requirements and notify the parties concerned. If it deems the application unconformable to requirements, it shall notify the parties concerned in writing and state the reasons.

Article 25

After an arbitration commission has accepted an arbitration application, it shall deliver the arbitration rules and the list of the panel of arbitrators to the claimant within the time limit prescribed in the arbitration rules and send the copies of the arbitration application and the arbitration rules and the list of the panel of arbitrators to the respondent.

After the respondent has received the copy of the application for arbitration, the aforesaid respondent shall file a counter-claim with the arbitration commission. After the arbitration commission has received the counter-claim of the respondent, it shall deliver the counter-claim to the claimant within the time limit set in the arbitration rules. If a respondent fails to submit a counter-claim, it does not affect the arbitration proceedings.

Article 26

When parties concerned have reached an agreement for arbitration but one party brings a suit in the people's court without notifying the court that there is an agreement for arbitration and, after the people's court has accepted the case, the other party submits the agreement for arbitration before the opening of the arbitration tribunal, the people's court shall reject the suit, except in the case that the agreement for arbitration is invalid. If the other party fails to raise objection to the acceptance of the case by the court before first hearing, it shall be regarded as having forfeited the agreement for arbitration and the people's court shall continue the hearing.

Article 27

A claimant may give up or alter its claims. The respondent may acknowledge or refute the claims and has the right to raise counter-claims.

Article 28

Whereas due to the acts of the other party or other reasons, the arbitration award cannot be or is hard to be executed, the parties concerned may apply for putting the property under custody.

Whereas a claimant has applied for a custody to the property, the arbitration commission shall, according to the relevant provisions of the Civil Procedure Law, submit the application of the claimant to the people's court.

Whereas there are errors in the application, the claimant shall compensate to the respondent for the losses arising from the custody to the property.

Article 29

The parties concerned or legal attorneys may entrust lawyers or other attorneys to handle matters relating to arbitration. In the case where lawyers or other attorneys are entrusted with the handling of arbitration matters, the attorneys shall produce a power of attorney to the arbitration commission.

Section 2: Composition of Arbitration Tribunal

Article 30

An arbitration tribunal may be composed of three arbitrators or one arbitrator. In the case of three arbitrators, there should be a chief arbitrator.

Article 31

Whereas the parties concerned agree that the arbitration tribunal is composed of three arbitrators, each of them shall chose one arbitrator or entrust the appointment to the chairman of the arbitration commission, with the third arbitrator jointly chosen by the parties concerned or appointed by the chairman of the arbitration commission jointly entrusted by the two parties. The third arbitrator shall be the chief arbitrator.

Whereas the parties concerned agree to have the arbitration tribunal composed of one arbitrator, the two parties shall jointly choose the arbitrator or entrust the choice of the arbitrator to the chairman of the arbitration commission.

Article 32

Whereas the parties concerned fail to decide on the composition of the arbitration tribunal or fail to choose arbitrators within the time limit prescribed in the arbitration rules, the chairman of the arbitration commission shall make the decision.

Article 33

After the formation of an arbitration tribunal, the arbitration commission shall notify in writing the composition of the arbitration tribunal matters.

Article 34

An arbitrator shall be withdrawn and the parties concerned have the right to request withdrawal, whereas:

1. The arbitrator is a party involved in the case or a blood relation or relative of the parties concerned or their attorneys.

2. The arbitrator has vital personal interests in the case.

3. The arbitrator has other relations with the parties or their attorneys involved in the case that might effect the fair ruling of the case.

4. The arbitrator meets the parties concerned or their attorneys in private or has accepted gifts or attended banquets hosted by the parties concerned or their attorneys.

Article 35

In requesting for withdrawal, the parties concerned shall state reasons before the first hearing of the tribunal. If the reasons are known only after the first hearing, they may be stated before the end of the last hearing.

Article 36

The withdrawal of an arbitrator shall be decided upon by the chairman of the arbitration commission. Whereas the chairman of the arbitration commission serves as an arbitrator, the withdrawal shall be decided upon collectively by the arbitration commission.

Article 37

Whereas an arbitrator is withdrawn or unable to perform his duty due to other reasons, another arbitrator shall be chosen or appointed according to the relevant provisions of this law.

Whereas re-selection or re-appointment of an arbitrator is made due to withdrawal, the parties concerned may apply for the re-start of the arbitration proceedings, but the final decision shall be made by the arbitration tribunal. The arbitration tribunal may also make its own decision as to whether or not the arbitration proceedings will restart.

Article 38

Whereas a case provided for in 4. of art.34 of this law is found with an arbitration and the case is very serious or a case provided for in 6. of art.58 of this law is found with an arbitrator, the arbitrator shall bear the legal responsibility according to law and the arbitration commission shall remove him from the panel of arbitrators.

Section 3: Hearing and Ruling

Article 39

An arbitration tribunal shall hold oral hearings to hear a case.

Whereas the parties concerned agree not to hold oral hearings, the arbitration tribunal may give the award based on the arbitration application, claims and counter-claims and other documents.

Article 40

The arbitration tribunal may not hear a case in open sessions. But when parties concerned agree to have the case heard in open sessions, the hearing may be held openly, except cases that involve State secrets.

Article 41

The arbitration commission shall notify the parties concerned the date of hearing within the time limit prescribed in the arbitration rules. With justifiable reasons, a party concerned may request the postponement of the hearing within the time limit set in the arbitration rules. Whether or not the hearing is postponed shall be decided upon by the arbitration tribunal.

Article 42

Whereas a claimant is absent from the hearing without justifiable reasons after receiving the written notice or withdraws from hearing half way without the prior permission by the arbitration tribunal, it may be regarded as a withdrawal of claims.

Whereas a respondent is absent from the hearing without justifiable reasons after receiving the written notice or withdraws from hearing half way without the prior permission by the arbitration tribunal, it may give the award by default.

Article 43

The parties concerned shall provide evidence to support their respective claims.

Whereas an arbitration tribunal deems it necessary to collect evidence, it may collect it on its own initiative.

Article 44

Whereas an arbitration tribunal deems it necessary to have the specialised issues appraised, it may submit them to the appraisal department chosen by the parties concerned by agreement or to the appraisal department designated by the arbitration tribunal.

At the request of the parties concerned or of the arbitration tribunal, the appraisal department shall send appraisers to the hearing. Parties concerned may, with the permission of the arbitration tribunal, raise questions to the appraisers.

Article 45

Evidence shall be produced during the course of hearing and the parties concerned may question or substantiate their evidence.

Article 46

Whereas evidences are vulnerable to be destroyed or missing and would be heard to be recovered, the parties concerned may apply to put the evidences on custody: When a party applies for custody of evidences, the arbitration commission shall submit the evidences of the party concerned to the people's court at the place where the evidences are obtained.

Article 47

The parties concerned have the right to debate during the process of hearing. At the end of the debate, the chief arbitrator or the sole arbitrator shall ask the parties concerned for the final statement.

Article 48

The arbitration tribunal shall record the hearings in writing. Whereas the parties concerned or other people involved in the arbitration find something in their statements left out in the recording or misrecorded, they have the right to apply for correction. Whereas corrections are not made, the application shall be recorded.

The written records of the hearings shall be signed or affixed with seals by the arbitrators, minute keepers, the parties concerned and other people participating in the arbitration.

Article 49

After the parties have applied for arbitration, they may reach reconciliation on their own initiative. Whereas a reconciliation agreement has been reached, a request may be made to the arbitration tribunal for an award based on the reconciliation agreement or the application for arbitration may be withdrawn.

Article 50

Whereas the parties concerned have gone back on their word after they have reached a reconciliation agreement, they may apply for arbitration according to the arbitration agreement.

Article 51

The arbitration tribunal may reconciliate a case before passing the award. Whereas the parties concerned accept the reconciliation effort of their own accord, the arbitration tribunal may conduct the reconciliation. Should the reconciliation fail, the arbitration tribunal shall pass the ruling in time.

Whereas an agreement is reached through reconciliation, the arbitration tribunal shall compile the reconciliation document or make an award based on the results of the agreement. The document of reconciliation and the arbitral award are equally binding legally.

Article 52

The document of reconciliation shall specify the arbitration claims and the result of the agreement between the parties concerned. The document of reconciliation shall be signed by the arbitrator and affixed with the seal of the arbitration commission before being delivered to the parties concerned.

The document of reconciliation becomes legally binding immediately upon received by parties concerned.

If any party concerned has gone back on his word after receiving the document of reconciliation, the arbitration tribunal shall make a timely ruling.

Article 53

An arbitral award shall be decided by the majority of the arbitrators and the views of the minority can be written down in the record. Whereas a majority vote cannot be reached, the award shall be decided based on the opinion of the chief arbitrator.

Article 54

The arbitral award shall specify the arbitration claims, facts in disputes, reasons for the award, result of the award, arbitration expenses and date of the award given. Whereas parties concerned object to the specification of the facts in dispute and reasons for the ruling, such specification and reasons may be omitted. The arbitral award shall be signed by arbitrators and affixed with the seals of the arbitration commission. An arbitrator holding differences of views may sign or may not sign the award.

Article 55

In arbitrating disputes, the arbitration tribunal may pass the ruling on part of the facts that have already been made clear.

Article 56

An arbitration tribunal should correct the errors involving context or computation and add things that have been omitted in the rulings in the arbitral award. The parties concerned may apply for correction with the arbitration tribunal within 30 days after the receipt of the award.

Article 57

The arbitral award takes legal effect upon its issuing.

Chapter 5

Application for Cancelling Arbitral Ruling

Article 58

If parties concerned have evidences to substantiate one of the following, they may apply for the cancellation of arbitral award with the intermediate people's court at the place where the arbitration commission resides.

1. There is no agreement for arbitration.

2. The matters ruled are out the scope of the agreement for arbitration or the limits of authority of an arbitration commission.

3. The composition of the arbitration tribunal or the arbitration proceedings violates the legal proceedings.

4. The evidences on which the ruling is based are forged.

5. Things that have an impact on the impartiality of ruling have been discovered concealed by the opposite party.

6. Arbitrators have accepted bribes, resorted to deception for personal gains or perverted the law in the ruling.

The people's court shall form a collegial bench to verify the case. Whereas one of the aforesaid cases should be found, arbitral award should be ordered to be cancelled by the court.

Whereas the people's court establishes that an arbitral award goes against the public interests, the award should be cancelled by the court.

Article 59

An application filed by the parties concerned for the cancellation of an arbitral award should be sent within six months starting from the date of receipt of the award.

Article 60

The people's court should rule to cancel the award or reject the application within two months after the application for cancellation of an award is received.

Article 61

After the people's court has accepted an application for the cancellation of an arbitral award and deems it necessary for the arbitration tribunal to make a new award, it shall notify the arbitration tribunal for a new ruling within a certain limit of time and order the termination of the cancellation procedure. In the case when the arbitration tribunal refuses a new ruling, the people's court shall rule that the cancellation procedure be restored.

Chapter 6

Enforcement

Article 62

The parties concerned shall execute the arbitral award. If one of the parties refuses to execute the award, the other party may apply for enforcement with the people's court according to the relevant provisions of the Civil Procedure Law. The people's court with which the application is filed should enforce it.

Article 63

If the respondent has produced evidences to substantiate one of the following cases provided for in the para 2 of art.217 of the Civil Procedure Law, the award shall not be enforced after the verification by the collegiate bench of the people's court.

Article 64

Whereas one party applies for an enforcement while the other applies for a cancellation of a award, the people's court shall order the termination of the performance of the award.

Whereas the people's court has ordered the cancellation of an award, it should also order the termination of performance of the award. Whereas an application for the cancellation of an award is rejected, the people's court shall order the restoration of the performance of the award.

Chapter 7

Special Provision on Arbitration Involving Foreign Interests

Article 65

The provisions in this chapter apply to arbitration of disputes arising from foreign economic cooperation and trade, transportation and maritime matters. Matters not covered by this chapter shall be handled according to other relevant provisions of this law.

Article 66

Foreign arbitration commissions may be formed by the China International Chamber of Commerce.

A foreign arbitration commission is composed of a chairman, a number of vice-chairmen and members.

The chairman, vice-chairmen and members of a foreign arbitration commission shall be appointed by the China International Chamber of Commerce.

Article 67

Members of a foreign arbitration commission may appoint arbitrators from among foreign nationals with specialised knowledge in law, economy and trade, science and technology.

Article 68

Whereas the parties involved in a foreign arbitration case apply for the custody of evidences, the foreign arbitration commission shall submit the application to the intermediate people's court at places where the evidences are produced.

Article 69

The foreign arbitration tribunal may write down its hearings on records or summary of records. The records shall be signed or affixed with the seals of the parties concerned and other people participating in the arbitration.

Article 70

Whereas the claimant has produced evidences to substantiate one of the cases as provided for in the para 1 of art.260 of the Civil Procedure Law, the People's court shall form a collegiate bench to verify the facts and order the cancellation of the award.

Article 71

Whereas the respondent has produced evidences to substantiate one of the cases as provided for in the para 1 of art.260 of the Civil Procedure Law, the people's court shall form a collegiate bench to verify the facts and order the non-performance of the award.

Article 72

Whereas a party involved in a foreign arbitration case applies for the enforcement of the award that has taken legal effect, the party shall apply directly with a foreign law court with the jurisdiction for recognition and enforcement if the party that should implement the award or its property is not in the territory of the People's Republic of China.

Article 73

The rules for foreign arbitration shall be formulated by the China International Chamber of Commerce according to this law and the relevant provisions of the Civil Procedure Law.

Chapter 8

Supplementary Provisions

Article 74

Whereas there is a limited effective period for the arbitration stipulated in the law, the limit shall apply. Whereas there is not a limited effective period for the arbitration stipulated by the law, the provisions about limits for proceedings shall apply.

Article 75

Before the China Arbitration Association has formulated arbitration rules, arbitration commissions may formulate interim rules for arbitration according to this law and the relevant provisions of the Civil Procedure Law.

Article 76

Parties concerned shall pay arbitration fees according to provisions.

The schedule of arbitration fees shall be submitted for approval by the pricing administrative department.

Article 77

The arbitration of labor disputes and disputes arising from the farm work contract inside the collective agricultural organisations shall be formulated separately.

Article 78

Whereas the relevant arbitration regulations formulated before the enforcement of this law come into conflict with the provisions of this law, the provisions of this law shall prevail.

Article 79

The arbitration organisation set up in cities where the people's governments of the municipalities, provinces and autonomous regions are located and other cities which have districts shall be reorganised according to the relevant provisions of this law. Those not reorganised shall be terminated in one year's time starting from the date of the implementation of this law.

Other arbitration organisations set up before the implementation of this law and are not in conformity to the provisions of this law shall be terminated starting from the date of the implementation of this law.

Article 80

The law shall enter into force as of 1 September 1995.

Civil Procedure Law of the People's Republic of China

(Adopted at the Fourth Session of the Seventh National People's Congress on 9 April 1991, and revised by virtue of the 'Decision of the Standing Committee of the National People's Congress on Revising the "Civil Procedure Law of the People's Republic of China"' issued at the Thirtieth Session of the Standing Committee of the Tenth National People's Congress on 28 October 2007)

PART I   General Provisions

Chapter 1

Aim, Scope of Application and Basic Principles

Article 1

The Civil Procedure Law of the People's Republic of China is formulated on the basis of the Constitution and in the light of the experience and actual conditions of our country in the trial of civil cases.

Article 2

The Civil Procedure Law of the People's Republic of China aims to protect the exercise of the litigation rights of the parties and ensure the ascertaining of facts by the people's courts, distinguish right from wrong, apply the law correctly, try civil cases promptly, affirm civil rights and obligations, impose sanctions for civil wrongs, protect the lawful rights and interests of the parties, educate citizens to voluntarily abide by the law, maintain the social and economic order, and guarantee the smooth progress of the socialist construction.

Article 3

In dealing with civil litigation arising from disputes on property and personal relations between citizens, legal persons or other organisations and between the three of them, the peoples' courts shall apply the provisions of this Law.

Article 4

Whoever engages in civil litigation within the territory of the People's Republic of China must abide by this Law.

Article 5

Aliens, stateless persons, foreign enterprises and organisations that bring suits or enter appearance in the people's courts shall have the same litigation rights and obligations as citizens, legal persons and other organisations of the People's Republic of China.

If the courts of a foreign country impose restrictions on the civil litigation rights of the citizens, legal persons and other organisations of the People's Republic of China, the people's courts of the People's Republic of China shall follow the principle of reciprocity regarding the civil litigation rights of the citizens, enterprises and organisations of that foreign country.

Article 6

The people's courts shall exercise judicial powers with respect to civil cases.

The people's courts shall try civil cases independently in accordance with the law, and shall be subject to no interference by any administrative organ, public organisation or individual.

Article 7

In trying civil cases, the people's courts must base themselves on facts and take the law as the criterion.

Article 8

The parties in civil litigation shall have equal litigation rights. The people's courts shall, in conducting the trials, safeguard their rights, facilitate their exercising the rights, and apply the law equally to them.

Article 9

In trying civil cases, the people's courts shall conduct conciliation for the parties on a voluntary and lawful basis; if conciliation fails, judgments shall be rendered without delay.

Article 10

In trying civil cases, the people's courts shall, according to the provisions of the law, follow the systems of panel hearing, withdrawal, public trial and the court of second instance being that of last instance.

Article 11

Citizens of all nationalities shall have the right to use their native spoken and written languages in civil proceedings.

Where minority nationalities live in aggregation in a community or where several nationalities live together in one area, the people's courts shall conduct hearings and issue legal documents in the spoken and written languages commonly used by the local nationalities.

The people's courts shall provide translations for any participant in the proceedings who is not familiar with the spoken or written languages commonly used by the local nationalities.

Article 12

Parties to civil actions are entitled in the trials by the people's courts to argue for themselves.

Article 13

The parties are free to deal with their own civil rights and litigation rights the way they prefer within the scope provided by the law.

Article 14

The people's procuratorates shall have the right to exercise legal supervision over civil proceedings.

Article 15

Where an act has infringed upon the civil rights and interests of the State, a collective organisation or an individual, any State organ, public organisation, enterprise or institution may support the injured unit or individual to bring an action in a people's court.

Article 16

The people's conciliation committees shall be mass organisations to conduct conciliation of civil disputes under the guidance of the grass-roots level people's governments and the basic level people's courts.

The people's conciliation committee shall conduct conciliation for the parties according to the Law and on a voluntary basis. The parties concerned shall carry out the settlement agreement reached through conciliation; those who decline conciliation or those for whom conciliation has failed or those who have backed out of the settlement agreement may institute legal proceedings in a people's court.

If a people's conciliation committee, in conducting conciliation of civil disputes, acts contrary to the law, rectification shall be made by the people's court.

Article 17

The people's congresses of the national autonomous regions may formulate, in accordance with the Constitution and the principles of this Law, and in conjunction with the specific circumstances of the local nationalities, adaptive and supplementary provisions. Such provisions made by an autonomous region shall be submitted to the Standing Committee of the National People's Congress for approval; those made by an autonomous prefecture or autonomous county shall be submitted to the standing committee of the people's congress of the relevant province or autonomous region for approval and to the Standing Committee of the National People's Congress for the record.

Chapter 2

Jurisdiction

Section 1: Jurisdiction by Forum Level

Article 18

The basic people's courts shall have jurisdiction as courts of first instance over civil cases, unless otherwise provided in this Law.

Article 19

The intermediate people's courts shall have jurisdiction as courts of first instance over the following civil cases:

1. major cases involving foreign element;

2. cases that have major impact on the area under their jurisdiction; and

3. cases as determined by the Supreme People's Court to be under the jurisdiction of the intermediate people's courts.

Article 20

The high people's courts shall have jurisdiction as courts of first instance over civil cases that have major impact on the areas under their jurisdiction.

Article 21

The Supreme People's Court shall have jurisdiction as the court of first instance over the following civil cases:

1. cases that have major impact on the whole country; and

2. cases that the Supreme People's Court deems it should try.

Section 2: Territorial Jurisdiction

Article 22

A civil lawsuit brought against a citizen shall be under the jurisdiction of the people's court of the place where the defendant has his domicile; if the place of the defendant's domicile is different from that of his habitual residence, the lawsuit shall be under the jurisdiction of the people's court of the place of his habitual residence.

A civil lawsuit brought against a legal person or any other organisation shall be under the jurisdiction of the people's court of the place where the defendant has his domicile.

Where the domiciles or habitual residences of several defendants in the same lawsuit are in the areas under the jurisdiction of two or more people's courts, all of those people's courts shall have jurisdiction over the lawsuit.

Article 23

The civil lawsuits described below shall be under the jurisdiction of the people's court of the place where the plaintiff has his domicile; if the place of the plaintiff's domicile is different from that of his habitual residence, the lawsuit shall be under the jurisdiction of the people's court of the place of the plaintiff's habitual residence:

1. those concerning personal status brought against persons not residing within the territory of the People's Republic of China;

2. those concerning the personal status of persons whose whereabouts are unknown or who have been declared as missing.

3. those brought against persons who are undergoing rehabilitation through labor; and

4. those brought against persons who are in imprisonment.

Article 24

A lawsuit brought on a contract dispute shall be under the jurisdiction of the people's court of the place where the defendant has his domicile or where the contract is performed.

Article 25

The parties to a contract may agree to choose in their written contract the people's court of the place where the defendant has his domicile, where the contract is performed, where the contract is signed, where the plaintiff has his domicile or where the object of the action is located to exercise jurisdiction over the case, provided that the provisions of this Law regarding jurisdiction by forum level and exclusive jurisdiction are not violated.

Article 26

A lawsuit brought on an insurance contract dispute shall be under the jurisdiction of the people's court of the place where the defendant has his domicile or where the insured object is located.

Article 27

A lawsuit brought on a bill dispute shall be under the jurisdiction of the people's court of the place where the bill is to be paid or where the defendant has his domicile.

Article 28

A lawsuit arising from a dispute over a railway, road, water, or air transport contract or over a combined transport contract shall be under the jurisdiction of the people's court of the place of dispatch or the place of destination or where the defendant has his domicile.

Article 29

A lawsuit brought on a tortious act shall be under the jurisdiction of the people's court of the place where the tort is committed or where the defendant has his domicile.

Article 30

A lawsuit brought on claims for damages caused by a railway, road, water transport or air accident shall be under the jurisdiction of the people's court of the place where the accident occurred or where the vehicle or ship first arrived after the accident or where the aircraft first landed after the accident, or where the defendant has his domicile.

Article 31

A lawsuit brought on claims for damages caused by a collision at sea or by any other maritime accident shall be under the jurisdiction of the people's court of the place where the collision occurred or where the ship in collision first docked after the accident or where the ship at fault was detained, or where the defendant has his domicile.

Article 32

A lawsuit instituted for expenses of maritime salvage shall be under the jurisdiction of the people's court of the place where the salvage took place or where the salvaged ship first docked after the disaster.

Article 33

A lawsuit brought for general average shall be under the jurisdiction of the people's court of the place where the ship first docked or where the adjustment of general average was conducted or where the voyage ended.

Article 34

The following cases shall be under the exclusive jurisdiction of the people's courts herein specified:

1. a lawsuit brought on a dispute over real estate shall be under the jurisdiction of the people's court of the place where the estate is located;

2. a lawsuit brought on a dispute over harbour operations shall be under the jurisdiction of the people's court of the place where the harbor is located; and

3. a lawsuit brought on a dispute over succession shall be under the jurisdiction of the people's court of the place where the decedent had his domicile upon his death, or where the principal part of his estate is located.

Article 35

When two or more people's courts have jurisdiction over a lawsuit, the plaintiff may bring his lawsuit in one of these people's courts; if the plaintiff brings the lawsuit in two or more people's courts that have jurisdiction over the lawsuit, the people's court in which the case was first entertained shall have jurisdiction.

Section 3: Transfer and Designation of Jurisdiction

Article 36

If a people's court finds that a case it has entertained is not under its jurisdiction, it shall refer the case to the people's court that has jurisdiction over the case. The people's court to which a case has been referred shall entertain the case, and if it considers that, according to the relevant regulations, the case referred to it is not under its jurisdiction, it shall report to a superior people's court for the designation of jurisdiction and shall not independently refer the case again to another people's court.

Article 37

If a people's court which has jurisdiction over a case is unable to exercise the jurisdiction for special reasons, a superior people's court shall designate another court to exercise jurisdiction.

In the event of a jurisdictional dispute between two or more people's courts, it shall be resolved by the disputing parties through consultation; if the dispute cannot be so resolved, it shall be reported to their common superior people's court for the designation of jurisdiction.

Article 38

If a party to an action objects to the jurisdiction of a people's court after the court has entertained the case, the party must raise the objection within the period prescribed for the submission of defence. The people's court shall examine the objection. If the objection is established, the people's court shall order the case to be transferred to the people's court that has jurisdiction over it; if not, the people's court shall reject it.

Article 39

The people's courts at higher levels shall have the power to try civil cases over which the people's courts at lower levels have jurisdiction as courts of first instance; they may also transfer civil cases over which they themselves have jurisdiction as courts of first instance to people's courts at lower levels for trial.

If a people's court at a lower level that has jurisdiction over a civil case as court of first instance deems it necessary to have the case to be tried by a people's court at a higher level, it may submit it to and request the people's court at a higher level to try the case.

Chapter 3

Trial Organisation

Article 40

The people's court of first instance shall try civil cases by a collegial panel composed of both judges and judicial assessors or of judges alone. The collegial panel must have an odd number of members.

Civil cases in which summary procedure is followed shall be tried by a single judge alone.

When performing their duties, the judicial assessors shall have equal rights and obligations as the judges.

Article 41

The people's court of second instance shall try civil cases by a collegial panel of judges. The collegial panel must have an odd number of members.

For the retrial of a remanded case, the people's court of first instance shall form a new collegial panel in accordance with the procedure of first instance.

If a case for retrial was originally tried at first instance, a new collegial panel shall be formed according to the procedure of first instance; if the case was originally tried at second instance or was brought by a people's court at a higher level to it for trial, a new collegial panel shall be formed according to the procedure of second instance.

Article 42

The president of the court or the chief judge of a division of the court shall designate a judge to serve as the presiding judge of the collegial panel; if the president or the chief judge participates in the trial, he himself shall serve as the presiding judge.

Article 43

When deliberating a case, a collegial panel shall observe the rule of majority. The deliberations shall be recorded in writing, and the transcript shall be signed by the members of the collegial panel. Dissenting opinions in the deliberations must be truthfully entered in the transcript.

Article 44

The judicial officers shall deal with all cases impartially and in accordance with the law.

The judicial officers shall not accept any treat or gift from the parties or their agents "ad litem."

Any judicial officer who commits embezzlement, accepts bribes, engages in malpractice for personal benefits or who perverts the law in passing judgment shall be investigated for legal responsibility; if the act constitutes a crime, the offender shall be investigated for criminal responsibility according to the law.

Chapter 4

Withdrawal

Article 45

A judicial officer shall of himself withdraw from the case, and the parties thereto shall be entitled to apply orally or in writing for his withdrawal in any of the following circumstances:

1.   he being a party to the case or a near relative of a party or an agent "ad litem" in the case;

2.   he being an interested party in the case; or

3.   he having some other kind of relationship with a party to the case, which might affect the impartiality of the trial.

The above provisions shall also apply to clerks, interpreters, expert witnesses and inspection personnel.

Article 46

In applying for the withdrawal, the party shall state the reason and submit the application at the beginning of the proceedings; the application may also be submitted before the closing of arguments in court if the reason for the withdrawal is known to him only after the proceedings begin.

Pending a decision by the people's court regarding the withdrawal applied for, the judicial officer concerned shall temporarily suspend his participation in the proceedings, with the exception, however, of cases that require the taking of emergency measures.

Article 47

The withdrawal of the presiding judge who is president of the court shall be decided by the judicial committee; the withdrawal of judicial officers shall be decided by the court president; and the withdrawal of other personnel by the presiding judge.

Article 48

The decision of a people's court on an application made by any party for withdrawal shall be made orally or in writing within three days after the application was made. If the applicant is not satisfied with the decision, he may apply for reconsideration which could be granted only once. During the period of reconsideration, the person whose withdrawal has been applied for shall not suspend his participation in the proceedings. The decision of a people's court on the reconsideration shall be made within three days after receiving the application and the applicant shall be notified of it accordingly.

Chapter 5

Participants in Proceedings

Section 1: Parties

Article 49

Any citizen, legal person and any other organisation may become a party to a civil action.

Legal persons shall be represented by their legal representatives in the litigation. Other organisations shall be represented by their principal heads in the proceedings.

Article 50

Parties to an action shall have the right to appoint agents, apply for withdrawals, collect and provide evidence, proffer arguments, request conciliation, file an appeal and apply for execution.

Parties to an action may have access to materials pertaining to the case and make copies thereof and other legal documents pertaining to the case. The scope of and rules for consulting and making copies of them shall be specified by the Supreme People's Court.

Parties to an action must exercise their litigation rights in accordance with the law, observe the procedures and carry out legally effective written judgments or rulings and conciliation statements.

Article 51

The two parties may reach a compromise of their own accord.

Article 52

The plaintiff may relinquish or modify his claims. The defendant may admit or rebut the claims and shall have the right to file counterclaims.

Article 53

When one party or both parties consist of two or more than two persons, their object of action being the same or of the same category and the people's court considers that, with the consent of the parties, the action can be tried combined, it is a joint action.

If a party of two or more persons to a joint action have common rights and obligations with respect to the object of action and the act of any one of them is recognised by the others of the party, such an act shall be valid for all the rest of the party; if a party of two or more persons have no common rights and obligations with respect to the object of action, the act of any one of them shall not be valid for the rest.

Article 54

If the persons comprising a party to a joint action are large in number, the party may elect representatives from among themselves to act for them in the litigation. The acts of such representatives in the litigation shall be valid for the party they represent. However, modification or waiver of claims or admission of the claims of the other party or pursuing a compromise with the other party by the representatives shall be subject to the consent of the party they represent.

Article 55

Where the object of action is of the same category and the persons comprising one of the parties is large but uncertain in number at the commencement of the action, the people's court may issue a public notice, stating the particulars and claims of the case and informing those entitled to participate in the action to register their rights with the people's court within a fixed period of time.

Those who have registered their rights with the people's court may elect representatives from among themselves to proceed with the litigation; if the election fails its purpose, such representatives may be determined by the people's court through consultation with those who have registered their rights with the court.

The acts of such representatives in the litigation shall be valid for the party they represent; however, modification or waiver of claims or admission of the claims of the other party or pursuing a compromise with the other party by the representatives shall be subject to the consent of the party they represent.

The judgments or rulings rendered by the people's court shall be valid for all those who have registered their rights with the court. Such judgments or rulings shall apply to those who have not registered their rights but have instituted legal proceedings during period of limitation of the action.

Article 56

If a third party considers that he has an independent claim to the object of action of both parties, he shall have the right to bring an action.

Where the outcome of the case will affect a third party's legal interest, such party, though having no independent claim to the object of action of both parties, may file a request to participate in the proceedings or the people's court shall notify the third party to participate. A third party that is to bear civil liability in accordance with the judgment of the people's court shall be entitled to the rights and obligations of a party in litigation.

Section 2: Agents ad Litem

Article 57

Any person with no legal capacity to engage in litigation shall have his guardian or guardians as statutory agents to act for him in a lawsuit. If the statutory agents try to shift responsibility as agents "ad litem" upon one another, the people's court shall appoint one of them to represent the person in litigation.

Article 58

A party to an action, or statutory agent may appoint one or two persons to act as his agents ad litem.

A lawyer, a near relative of the party, a person recommended by a relevant social organisation or a unit to which the party belongs or any other citizen approved by the people's court may be appointed as the party's agent ad litem.

Article 59

When a person appoints another to act on his behalf in litigation, he must submit to the people's court a power of attorney bearing his signature or seal.

The power of attorney must specify the matters entrusted and the powers conferred. An agent "ad litem" must obtain special powers from his principal to admit, waive or modify claims, or to compromise or to file a counterclaim or an appeal.

A power of attorney mailed or delivered through others by a citizen of the People's Republic of China residing abroad must be certified by the Chinese embassy or consulate accredited to that country. If there is no Chinese embassy or consulate in that country, the power of attorney must be certified by an embassy or a consulate of a third country accredited to that country that has diplomatic relations with the People's Republic of China, and then transmitted for authentication to the embassy or consulate of the People's Republic of China accredited to that third country, or it must be certified by a local patriotic overseas Chinese organisation.

Article 60

A party to an action shall inform the people's court in writing if he changes or revokes the powers of an agent " ad litem, and the court shall notify the other party of the change or revocation.

Article 61

A lawyer who serves as an agent "ad litem" and other agents "ad litem" shall have the right to investigate and collect evidence, and may have access to materials pertaining to the case. The scope of and rules for consulting materials pertaining to the case shall be specified by the Supreme People's Court.

Article 62

In a divorce case in which the parties to the action have been represented by their agents ad litem, the parties themselves shall still appear in court in person, unless they are incapable of expressing their own will. A party who is truly unable to appear in court due to a special reason shall submit his views in writing to the people's court.

Chapter 6

Evidence

Article 63

Evidence shall be classified as follows:

1. documentary evidence;

2. material evidence;

3. audio-visual material;

4. testimony of witnesses;

5. statements of the parties;

6. expert conclusions; and

7. records of inspection.

The above-mentioned evidence must be verified before it can be taken as a basis for ascertaining a fact.

Article 64

It is the duty of a party to an action to provide evidence in support of his allegations.

If, for objective reasons, a party and his agent "ad litem" are unable to collect the evidence by themselves or if the people's court considers the evidence necessary for the trial of the case, the people's court shall investigate and collect it.

The people's court shall, in accordance with the procedure prescribed by the law, examine and verify evidence comprehensively and objectively.

Article 65

The people's court shall have the right to make investigation and collect evidence from the relevant units or individuals; such units or individuals may not refuse to provide information and evidence.

The people's court shall verify the authenticity, examine and determine the validity of the certifying documents provided by the relevant units or individuals.

Article 66

Evidence shall be presented in court and cross-examined by the parties concerned. But evidence that involves State secrets, trade secrets and personal privacy shall be kept confidential. If it needs to be presented in court, such evidence shall not be presented in an open court session.

Article 67

The people's court shall take the acts, facts and documents legalised by notarisation according to legal procedures as the basis for ascertaining facts, unless there is evidence to the contrary sufficient to invalidate the notarisation.

Article 68

Any document submitted as evidence must be the original. Material evidence must also be original. If it is truly difficult to present the original document or thing, then reproductions, photographs, duplicates or extracts of the original may be submitted.

If a document in a foreign language is submitted as evidence, a Chinese translation must be appended.

Article 69

The people's court shall verify audio-visual materials and determine after their examination in the light of other evidence in the case whether they can be taken as a basis for ascertaining the facts.

Article 70

All units and individuals who have knowledge of a case shall be under the obligation of giving testimony in court. The persons-in-charge of the relevant units shall support the witnesses to give testimony. When it is truly difficult for a witness to appear in court, he may, with the consent of the people's court, submit a written testimony.

Any person who is incapable of expressing his will properly shall not give testimony.

Article 71

The people's court shall examine the statements of the parties concerned in the light of other evidence in the case to determine whether the statements can be taken as a basis for ascertaining the facts.

The refusal of a party to make statements shall not prevent the people's court from ascertaining the facts of a case on the basis of other evidence.

Article 72

When the people's court deems it necessary to make an expert evaluation of a problem of a technical nature, it shall refer the problem to a department authorised by the law for the evaluation. In the absence of such a department, the people's court shall appoint one to make the expert evaluation.

The authorised department and the experts designated by the department shall have the right to consult the case materials necessary for the evaluation and question the parties and witnesses when circumstances so require.

The authorised department and the experts it designated shall present a written conclusion of the evaluation duly sealed or signed by both. If the evaluation is made by an expert alone, the unit to which the expert belongs shall certify his status by affixing its seal to the expert's conclusion.

Article 73

When inspecting material evidence or a site, the inspector must produce his credentials issued by a people's court. He shall request the local grass-roots organisation or the unit to which the party to the action belongs to send persons to participate in the inspection. The party concerned or an adult member of his family shall be present; their refusal to appear on the scene, however, shall not hinder the inspection.

Upon notification by the people's court, the relevant units and individuals shall be under the obligation of preserving the site and assisting the inspection.

The inspector shall make a written record of the circumstances and results of the inspection, which shall be duly signed or sealed by the inspector, the party concerned and the participants requested to be present.

Article 74

Under circumstances where there is a likelihood that evidence may be destroyed or lost, or difficult to obtain later, the participants in the proceedings may apply to the people's court for preservation of the evidence. The people's court may also on its own initiative take measures to preserve such evidence.

Chapter 7

Time Periods and Service

Section 1: Time Periods

Article 75

Time periods shall include those prescribed by the law and those designated by a people's court.

Time periods shall be calculated by the hour, the day, the month and the year. The hour and day from which a time period begins shall not be counted as within the time period.

If the expiration date of a time period falls on a holiday, then the day immediately following the holiday shall be regarded as the expiration date.

A time period shall not include traveling time. A litigation document that is mailed before the deadline shall not be regarded as overdue.

Article 76

In case of failure on the part of a party to an action to meet a deadline due to force majeure or for other justified reasons, the party concerned may apply for an extension of the time limit within 10 days after the obstacle is removed. The extension applied for shall be subject to approval by a people's court.

Section 2: Service

Article 77

A receipt shall be required for every litigation document that is served and it shall bear the date of receipt noted by the signature or seal of the person on whom the document was served.

The date noted on the receipt by the person on whom the document was served shall be regarded as the date of service of the document.

Article 78

Litigation documents shall be sent or delivered directly to the person on whom they are to be served. If that person is a citizen, the documents shall, in case of his absence, be receipted by an adult member of his family living with him. If the person on whom they are to be served is a legal person or any other organisation, the documents shall be receipted by the legal representatives of the legal person or the principal heads of the other organisation or anyone of the legal person or the other organisation responsible for receiving such documents; if the person on whom they are to be served has an agent ad litem, the documents may be receipted by the agent ad litem; if the person on whom they are to be served has designated a person to receive litigation documents on his behalf and has informed the people's court of it, the documents may be receipted by the person designated.

The date put down in the receipt and signed by the adult family member living with the person or whom the litigation documents are to be served, or by the person responsible for receiving documents of a legal person or any other organisation, or by the agent ad litem, or the person designated to receive documents shall be deemed the date of service of the documents.

Article 79

If the person on whom the litigation documents are to be served or the adult family member living with him refuses to receive the documents, the person serving the documents shall ask representatives from the relevant grass-roots organisation or the unit to which the person on whom the documents are to be served belongs to appear on the scene, explain the situation to them, and record on the receipt the reasons of the refusal and the date of it. After the person serving the documents and the witnesses have affixed their signatures or seals to the receipt, the documents shall be left at the place where the person on whom they are to be served lives and the service shall be deemed completed.

Article 80

If direct service proves to be difficult, service of litigation documents may be entrusted to another people's court, or done by mail. If the documents are served by mail, the date stated on the receipt for postal delivery shall be deemed the date of service of the documents.

Article 81

If the person on whom the litigation documents are to be served is a military man, the documents shall be forwarded to him through the political organ of the unit at or above the regimental level in the force to which he belongs.

Article 82

If the person on whom the litigation documents are to be served is in imprisonment, the documents shall be forwarded to him through the prison authorities or the unit of reform through labor where the person is serving his term.

If the person on whom the litigation documents are to be served is undergoing rehabilitation through labor, the documents shall be forwarded to him through the unit of his rehabilitation through labor.

Article 83

The organisation or unit that receives the litigation documents to be forwarded must immediately deliver them to and have them receipted by the person on whom they are to be served. The date stated on the receipt shall be deemed the date of service of the documents.

Article 84

If the whereabouts of the person on whom the litigation documents are to be served is unknown, or if the documents cannot be served by the other methods specified in this Section, the documents shall be served by public announcement. Sixty days after the public announcement is made, the documents shall be deemed to have been served.

The reasons for service by public announcement and the process gone through shall be recorded in the case files.

Chapter 8

Conciliation

Article 85

In the trial of civil cases, the people's court shall distinguish between right and wrong on the basis of the facts being clear and conduct conciliation between the parties on a voluntary basis.

Article 86

When a people's court conducts conciliation, a single judge or a collegial panel may preside over it. Conciliation shall be conducted on the spot as much as possible.

When a people's court conducts conciliation, it may employ simplified methods to notify the parties concerned and the witnesses to appear in court.

Article 87

When a people's court conducts conciliation, it may invite the units or individuals concerned to come to its assistance. The units or individuals invited shall assist the people's court in conciliation.

Article 88

A settlement agreement reached between the two parties through conciliation must be of their own free will and without compulsion. The content of the settlement agreement shall not contravene the law.

Article 89

When a settlement agreement through conciliation is reached, the people's court shall draw up a conciliation statement. The conciliation statement shall clearly set forth the claims, the facts of the case, and the result of the conciliation.

The conciliation statement shall be signed by the judge and the court clerk, sealed by the people's court, and served on both parties.

Once it is receipted by the two parties concerned, the conciliation statement shall become legally effective.

Article 90

The people's court need not draw up a conciliation statement for the following cases when a settlement agreement is reached through conciliation:

1. divorce cases in which both parties have become reconciled after conciliation;

2. cases in which adoptive relationship has been maintained through conciliation;

3. cases in which the claims can be immediately satisfied; and

4. other cases that do not require a conciliation statement.

Any settlement agreement that needs no conciliation statement shall be entered into the written record and shall become legally effective after being signed or sealed by both parties concerned, by the judge and by the court clerk.

Article 91

If no agreement is reached through conciliation or if either party backs out of the settlement agreement before the conciliation statement is served, the people's court shall render a judgment without delay.

Chapter 9

Property Preservation and Advance Execution

Article 92

In the cases where the execution of a judgment may become impossible or difficult because of the acts of either party or for other reasons, the people's court may, at the application of the other party, order the adoption of measures for property preservation. In the absence of such application, the people's court may itself, when necessary, order the adoption of measures for property preservation.

In adopting property preservation measures, the people's court may enjoin the applicant to provide security; if the applicant fails to do so, his application shall be rejected.

After receiving an application, the people's court must, if the case is urgent, make a ruling within 48 hours; if the ruling for the adoption of property preservation measures is made, the execution thereof shall begin immediately.

Article 93

Any interested party whose lawful rights and interests would, due to urgent circumstances, suffer irretrievable damage without immediately applying for property preservation, may, before filing a lawsuit, apply to the people's court for the adoption of property preservation measures. The applicant must provide security; if he fails to do so, his application shall be rejected.

After receiving an application, the people's court must make an ruling within 48 hours; if the court orders the adoption of property preservation measures, the execution thereof shall begin immediately.

If the applicant fails to bring an action within 15 days after the people's court has adopted the preservation measures, the people's court shall cancel the property preservation.

Article 94

Property preservation shall be limited to the scope of the claims or to the property relevant to the case.

Property preservation shall be effected by sealing up, distraining, freezing or other methods as prescribed by the law.

After the people's court has frozen the property, it shall promptly notify the person whose property has been frozen.

The property that has already been sealed up or frozen shall not be sealed up or frozen for a second time.

Article 95

If the person against whom the application for property preservation is made provides security, the people's court shall cancel the property preservation.

Article 96

If an application for property preservation is wrongfully made, the applicant shall compensate the person against whom the application is made for any loss incurred from property preservation.

Article 97

The people's court may, upon application of the party concerned, order advance execution in respect of the following cases:

1. those involving claims for alimony, support for children or elders, pension for the disabled or the family of a decedent, or expenses for medical care;

2. those involving claims for remuneration for labor; and

3. those involving urgent circumstances that require advance execution.

Article 98

Cases in which advance execution is ordered by the people's court shall meet the following conditions:

1. the relationship of rights and obligations between the parties concerned is clear and definite, and denial of advance execution would seriously affect the livelihood or production operations of the applicant; and

2. the person against whom the application for advance execution is made is capable of fulfilling his obligations.

The people's court may enjoin the applicant to provide security; if the applicant fails to do so, his application shall be rejected. If the applicant loses the lawsuit, he shall compensate the person against whom the application is made for any loss of property incurred from the advance execution.

Article 99

If the party concerned is not satisfied with the ruling made on property preservation or execution, he may apply for reconsideration which could be granted only once. Execution of the ruling shall not be suspended during the time of reconsideration.

Chapter 10

Compulsory Measures Against Obstruction of Civil Proceedings

Article 100

If a defendant is required to appear in court, but, having been served twice with summons, still refuses to do so without justified reason, the people's court may constrain him to appear in court by a peremptory writ.

Article 101

Participants and other persons in the court proceedings shall abide by the court rules.

If a person violates the court rules, the people's court may reprimand him, or order him to leave the courtroom, or impose a fine on or detain him.

A person who seriously disrupts court order by making an uproar in the court or rushing at it, or insulting, slandering, threatening, or assaulting the judicial officers, shall be investigated for criminal responsibility by the people's court according to the law; if the offence is a minor one, the offender may be detained or a fine imposed on him.

Article 102

If a participant or any other person in the proceedings commits any one of the following acts, the people's court shall, according to the seriousness of the act, impose a fine on him or detain him; if the act constitutes a crime, the offender shall be investigated for criminal responsibility according to law:

1. forging or destroying important evidence, which would obstruct the trial of a case by the people's court;

2. using violence, threats or subornation to prevent a witness from giving testimony, or instigating, suborning, or coercing others to commit perjury;

3. concealing, transferring, selling or destroying property that has been sealed up or distrained, or property of which an inventory has been made and which has been put under his care according to court instruction, or transferring the property that has been frozen;

4. insulting, slandering, incriminating with false charges, assaulting or maliciously retaliating against judicial officers or personnel, participants in the proceedings, witnesses, interpreters, evaluation experts, inspectors, or personnel assisting in execution;

5. using violence, threats or other means to hinder judicial officers or personnel from performing their duties; or

6. refusing to carry out legally effective judgments or rulings of the people's court.

With respect to a unit that commits any one of the acts specified above, the people's court may impose a fine or detention on the main persons-in-charge or the directly liable person; if the act constitutes a crime, he shall be investigated for criminal liability according to law.

Article 103

Where a unit which is under an obligation to assist in investigation and execution commits any one of the following acts, the people's court may, apart from enjoining it to perform its obligation, also impose a fine:

1. refusing or obstructing the investigation and collection of evidence by the people's court;

2. refusing by banks, credit cooperatives or other units dealing with savings deposit, after receiving a notice for assistance in execution from the people's court, to assist in inquiring into, freezing or transferring the relevant deposit;

3. refusing by the unit concerned, after receiving a notice for assistance in execution from the people's court, to assist in withholding the income of the party subject to execution, in going through the formalities of transferring the relevant certificates of property rights or in transferring the relevant negotiable instruments, certificates, or other property; or

4. refusing to provide other obligatory assistance in the execution.

With respect to a unit that commits any one of the acts specified above, the people's court may impose a fine on its main persons-in-charge or the directly liable persons. If they still fail to perform the obligation of the assistance, the people's court may impose detention and may also put forward a judicial proposal for disciplinary action to the supervisory organ or any relevant organ.

Article 104

A fine on an individual shall not exceed RMB 10,000. A fine on a unit shall be not less than RMB 10,000 but not more than RMB 300,000.

The period of detention shall not be longer than 15 days.

The people's court shall deliver detained persons to a public security organ for custody. The people's court may decide to advance the time of release, if the detainee admits and mends his wrongdoings.

Article 105

Constrained appearance in court, imposition of a fine or detention shall be subject to the approval of the president of the people's court.

A peremptory writ shall be issued for constraining appearance in court.

A decision in writing shall be made for the imposition of a fine or detention. The offender, if dissatisfied with the decision, may apply to a people's court at a higher level for reconsideration which could be granted only once. The execution of the decision shall not be suspended during the time of reconsideration.

Article 106

Decision on the adoption of compulsory measures against obstruction of proceedings shall be made only by the people's court. Any unit or individual that extorts repayment of a debt by illegal detention of a person or illegal distrainment of property shall be investigated for criminal responsibility according to the law, or shall be punished with detention or a fine.

Chapter 11

Litigation Costs

Article 107

Any party filing a civil lawsuit shall pay court costs according to the rules. For property cases, the party shall pay other fees in addition to the court costs.

Any party that has genuine difficulty in paying litigation costs may, according to the relevant rules, apply to the people's court for deferment or reduction of the payment or for its exemption.

Particulars for payment of litigation costs shall be laid down separately.

PART II   Trial Procedure

Chapter 12

Ordinary Procedure of First Instance

Section 1: Bringing a Lawsuit and Entertaining a Case

Article 108

The following conditions must be met when a lawsuit is brought:

1. the plaintiff must be a citizen, legal person or any other organisation that has a direct interest in the case;

2. there must be a definite defendant;

3. there must be specific claim or claims, facts, and cause or causes for the suit; and

4. the suit must be within the scope of acceptance for civil actions by the people's courts and under the jurisdiction of the people's court where the suit is entertained.

Article 109

When a lawsuit is brought, a statement of complaint shall be submitted to the people's court, and copies of the statement shall be provided according to the number of defendants.

If the plaintiff has genuine difficulty in presenting the statement of complaint in writing, he may state his complaint orally; the people's court shall transcribe the complaint and inform the other party of it accordingly.

Article 110

A statement of complaint shall clearly set forth the following:

1. the name, sex, age, ethnic status, occupation, work unit and home address of the parties to the case; if the parties are legal persons or any other organisations, their names, addresses and the names and posts of the legal representatives or the principal heads;

2. the claim or claims of the suit, the facts and grounds on which the suit is based; and

3. the evidence and its source, as well as the names and home addresses of the witnesses.

Article 111

The people's court must entertain the lawsuits filed in conformity with the provisions of art.108 of this Law. With respect to lawsuits described below, the people's court shall deal with them in the light of their specific circumstances:

1. For a lawsuit within the scope of administrative actions in accordance with the provisions of the Administrative Procedure Law, the people's court shall advise the plaintiff to institute administrative proceedings;

2. If, according to the law, both parties have on a voluntary basis reached a written agreement to submit their contract dispute to an arbitral organ for arbitration, they may not institute legal proceedings in a people's court. The people's court shall advise the plaintiff to apply to the arbitral organ for arbitration;

3. In case of disputes which, according to the law, shall be dealt with by other organs, the people's court shall advise the plaintiff to apply to the relevant organ for settlement;

4. With respect to cases that are not under its jurisdiction, the people's court shall advise the plaintiff to bring a lawsuit in the competent people's court;

5. With respect to cases in which a judgment or ruling has already taken legal effect, but either party brings a suit again, the people's court shall advise that party to file an appeal instead, except when the ruling of the people's court is one that permits the withdrawal of a suit;

6. With respect to an action that may not be filed within a specified period according to the law, it shall not be entertained, if it is filed during that period;

7. In a divorce case in which a judgment has been made disallowing the divorce, or in which both parties have become reconciled after conciliation, or in a case concerning adoptive relationship in which a judgment has been made or conciliation has been successfully conducted to maintain the adoptive relationship, if the plaintiff files a suit again within six months in the absence of any new developments or new reasons, it shall not be entertained.

Article 112

When a people's court receives a statement of complaint or an oral complaint and finds after examination that it meets the requirements for acceptance, the court shall place the case on the docket within seven days and notify the parties concerned; if it does not meet the requirements for acceptance, the court shall make a ruling within seven days to reject it. The plaintiff, if not satisfied with the order, may file an appeal.

Section 2: Preparations for Trial

Article 113

The people's court shall send a copy of the statement of complaint to the defendant within five days after docketing the case, and the defendant shall file a defence within 15 days from receipt of the copy of the statement of complaint.

When the defendant files a defence, the people's court shall send a copy of it to the plaintiff within five days from its receipt. Failure by the defendant to file a defence shall not prevent the case from being tried by the people's court.

Article 114

The people's court shall, with respect to cases whose acceptance has been decided, inform the parties in the notification of acceptance and in the notification calling for response to the action of their relevant litigation rights and obligations of which the parties may likewise be informed orally.

Article 115

The parties shall be notified within three days after the members of the collegial panel are determined.

Article 116

The judicial officers must carefully examine and verify the case materials and carry out investigations and collection of necessary evidence.

Article 117

The personnel sent by a people's court to conduct investigations shall produce their credentials before the person to be investigated.

The written record of an investigation shall be checked by the person investigated and then signed or aled by both the investigator and the investigated.

Article 118

A people's court may, when necessary, entrust a people's court in another locality with the investigations.

The entrusting people's court shall clearly set out the matters for and requirements of the entrusted investigations. The entrusted people's court may on its own initiative conduct supplementary investigations.

The entrusted people's court shall complete the investigations within 30 days after receiving the commission in writing. If for some reason it cannot complete the investigations, the said people's court shall notify the entrusting people's court in writing within the above-mentioned time limit.

Article 119

If a party who must participate in a joint action fails to participate in the proceedings, the people's court shall notify him to participate.

Section 3: Trial in Court

Article 120

Civil cases shall be tried in public, except for those that involve State secrets or personal privacy or are to be tried otherwise as provided by the law.

A divorce case or a case involving trade secrets may not be heard in public if a party so requests.

Article 121

For civil cases, the people's court shall, whenever necessary, go on circuit to hold trials on the spot.

Article 122

For civil cases, the people's court shall notify the parties and other participants in the proceedings three days before the opening of a court session. If a case is to be tried in public, the names of the parties, the cause of action and the time and location of the court session shall be announced publicly.

Article 123

Before a court session is called to order, the court clerk shall ascertain whether or not the parties and other participants in the proceedings are present and announce the rules of order of the court.

At the beginning of a court session, the presiding judge shall check the parties present, announce the cause of action and the names of the judicial officers and court clerks, inform the parties of their relevant litigation rights and obligations and ask the parties whether or not they wish to apply for the withdrawal of any court personnel.

Article 124

Court investigation shall be conducted in the following order:

1. statements by the parties;
2. informing the witnesses of their rights and obligations, giving testimony by the witnesses and reading of the written statements of absentee witnesses;
3. presentation of documentary evidence, material evidence and audio-visual material;
4. reading of expert conclusions; and
5. reading of records of inspection.

Article 125

The parties may present new evidence during a court session.

With the permission of the court, the parties may put questions to witnesses, expert witnesses and inspectors.

Any request by the parties concerned for a new investigation, expert evaluation or inspection shall be subject to the approval of the people's court.

Article 126

Additional claims by the plaintiff, counterclaims by the defendant and third-party claims related to the case may be tried in combination.

Article 127

Court debate shall be conducted in the following order:

1. oral statements by the plaintiff and his agents "ad litem";

2. defence by the defendant and his agents "ad litem";

3. oral statement or defence by the third party and his agents "ad litem";

4. debate between the two sides.

At the end of the court debate, the presiding judge shall ask each side, first the plaintiff, then the defendant, and then the third party, for their final opinion respectively.

Article 128

At the end of the court debate, a judgment shall be made according to the law. Where conciliation is possible prior to the rendering of a judgment, conciliation efforts may be made; if conciliation proves to be unsuccessful, a judgment shall be made without delay.

Article 129

If a plaintiff, having been served with a summons, refuses to appear in court without justified reasons, or if he withdraws during a court session without the permission of the court, the case may be considered as withdrawn by him; if the defendant files a counterclaim in the mean time, the court may make a judgment by default.

Article 130

If a defendant, having been served with a summons, refuses to appear in court without justified reasons, or if he withdraws during a court session without the permission of the court, the court may make a judgment by default.

Article 131

If a plaintiff applies for withdrawal of the case before the judgment is pronounced, the people's court shall make a ruling on whether to approve it or not.

If the people's court has made a ruling to disapprove the withdrawal of the case but the plaintiff refuses to attend the court without justification after a summons has been served, the people's court may make a judgment by default.

Article 132

Under any of the following circumstances, the trial may be adjourned:

1. the parties concerned and other participants in the proceedings required to appear in court fail to do so for justified reasons;

2. any party concerned makes an extempore application for the withdrawal of a judicial officer; or

3. it is necessary to summon new witnesses to court, collect new evidence, make a new expert evaluation, new inspection, or to make a supplementary investigation; or

4. other circumstances that warrant the adjournment.

Article 133

The court clerk shall make a written record of the entire court proceedings, which shall be signed by him and the judicial officers.

The court record shall be read out in court, or else the parties and other participants in the proceedings may be notified to read the record while in court or within five days. If they consider that there are omissions or errors in the record of their own statements, the parties or other participants in the proceedings shall have the right to apply for rectifications. If such rectifications are not made, the application shall be placed on record in the case file.

The court record shall be signed or sealed by the parties and other participants in the proceedings. Refusal to do so shall be put on record in the case file.

Article 134

The people's court shall publicly pronounce its judgment in all cases, whether publicly tried or not.

If a judgment is pronounced in court, the written judgment shall be issued and delivered within ten days; if a judgment is pronounced later on a fixed date, the written judgment shall be issued and given immediately after the pronouncement.

Upon pronouncement of a judgment, the parties concerned must be informed of their right to file an appeal, the time limit for appeal and the court to which they may appeal.

Upon pronouncement of a divorce judgment, the parties concerned must be informed not to remarry before the judgment takes legal effect.

Article 135

A people's court trying a case in which the ordinary procedure is followed, shall conclude the case within six months after docketing the case. Where an extension of the period is necessary under special circumstances, a six-month extension may be allowed subject to the approval of the president of the court. Further extension, if needed, shall be reported to the people's court at a higher level for approval.

Section 4: Suspension and Termination of Litigation

Article 136

Legal Proceedings shall be suspended in any of the following circumstances:

1. one of the parties dies and it is necessary to wait for the heir or heiress to make clear whether to participate or not in the proceedings;

2.   one of the parties has lost the capacity to engage in litigation and his agent "ad litem" has not been designated yet;

3.   the legal person or any other organisation as one of the parties has dissolved, and the successor to its rights and obligations has not been determined yet;

4.   one of the parties is unable to participate in the proceedings for reasons of force majeure;

5.   the adjudication of the case pending is dependent on the results of the trial of another case that has not yet been concluded; or

6.   other circumstances that warrant the suspension of the litigation.

The proceedings shall resume after the causes of the suspension have been eliminated.

Article 137

Legal proceedings shall be terminated in any of the following circumstances:

1.   the plaintiff dies without a successor, or the successor waives the right to litigate;

2.   the decedent leaves no estate, nor any one to succeed to his obligations;

3.   one of the parties in a divorce case dies; or

4.   one of the parties dies who is a claimant to alimony, support for elders or children or to the termination of adoptive relationship.

Section 5: Judgment and Ruling

Article 138

A judgment shall clearly set forth the following:

1.   cause of action, the claims, facts and cause or causes of the dispute;

2.   the facts and causes as found in the judgment and the basis of application of the law;

3.   the outcome of adjudication and the costs to be borne; and

4.   the time limit for filing an appeal and the appellate court with which the appeal may be filed.

The judgment shall be signed by the judicial officers and the court clerk, with the seal of the people's court affixed to it.

Article 139

If some of the facts in a case being tried by the people's court are already evident, the court may pass judgment on that part of the case first.

Article 140

A ruling shall apply to the following matters:

1. refusal to entertain a case;

2. objection to the jurisdiction of a court;

3. rejection of a complaint;

4. property preservation and advance execution;

5. approval or disapproval of withdrawal of a suit;

6. suspension or termination of legal proceedings;

7. correction of errata in the judgment;

8. suspension or termination of execution;

9. refusal to enforce an arbitration award;

10. refusal to enforce a document of a notary office evidencing the rights of a creditor and entitling him to its compulsory execution;

11. other matters to be decided in the form of ruling.

An appeal may be lodged against a ruling in Item(1), (2) and (3) mentioned above.

A written ruling shall be signed by the judicial officers and the court clerk, with the seal of the people's court affixed to it. If the ruling is delivered orally, it shall be taken down in writing.

Article 141

All judgments and rulings of the Supreme People's Court, as well as judgments and rulings that may not be appealed against according to the law or that have not been appealed against within the prescribed time limit, shall be legally effective.

Chapter 13

Summary Procedure

Article 142

When trying simple civil cases in which the facts are evident, the rights and obligations clear and the disputes trivial in character, the basic people's courts and the tribunals dispatched by them shall apply the provisions of this Chapter.

Article 143

In simple civil cases, the plaintiff may lodge his complaint orally.

The two parties concerned may at the same time come before a basic people's court or a tribunal dispatched by it for a solution of their dispute. The basic people's court or the tribunal it dispatched may try the case immediately or set a date for the trial.

Article 144

In trying a simple civil case, the basic people's court or the tribunal dispatched by it may use simplified methods to summon at any time the parties and witnesses.

Article 145

Simple civil cases shall be tried by a single judge alone and the trial of such cases shall not be bound by the provisions of arts.122, 124, and 127 of this Law.

Article 146

The people's court trying a case in which summary procedure is followed shall conclude the case within three months after placing the case on the docket.

Chapter 14

Procedure of Second Instance

Article 147

If a party refuses to accept a judgment of first instance of a local people's court, he shall have the right to file an appeal with the people's court at the next higher level within 15 days after the date on which the written judgment was served.

If a party refuses to accept a ruling of first instance of a local people's court, he shall have the right to file an appeal with a people's court at the next higher level within 10 days after the date on which the ruling was served.

Article 148

For filing an appeal, a petition for the purpose shall be submitted. The content of the appeal petition shall include the names of the parties, the names of the legal persons and their legal representatives or names of other organisations and their principal heads; the name of the people's court where the case was originally tried; file number of the case and the cause of action; and the claims of the appeal and the reasons.

Article 149

The appeal petition shall be submitted through the people's court which originally tried the case, and copies of it shall be provided according to the number of persons in the other party or of the representatives thereof.

If a party appeals directly to a people's court of second instance, the said court shall within five days transmit the appeal petition to the people's court which originally tried the case.

Article 150

The people's court which originally tried the case shall, within five days after receiving the appeal petition, serve a copy of it on the other party, who shall submit his defence within 15 days from the receipt of such copy. The people's court shall, within five days after receiving the defence, serve a copy of it on the appellant. Failure by the other party to submit a defence shall not prevent the case from being tried by the people's court.

After receiving the appeal petition and the defence, the people's court which originally tried the case shall, within five days, deliver them together with the entire case file and evidence to the people's court of second instance.

Article 151

The people's court of second instance shall review the relevant facts and the application of the law being the subject matters of the appeal.

Article 152

With respect to a case on appeal, the people's court of second instance shall form a collegial panel to conduct the hearing. After verification of the facts of the case through consulting the files, making investigations and questioning the parties, if the collegial panel considers that it is not necessary to conduct a hearing, it may make a judgment or a ruling directly.

The people's court of second instance may hear a case on appeal at its own site or in the place where the case originated or where the people's court which originally tried the case is located.

Article 153

The appeal case heard by the people's court of second instance shall be disposed of in the light of the following circumstances:

1. if the facts were clearly ascertained and the law was correctly applied in the original judgment, the appeal shall be rejected in the form of a judgment and the original judgment shall be affirmed;

2. if the application of the law was incorrect in the original judgment, the said judgment shall be amended according to the law;

3. if in the original judgment the facts were incorrectly or not clearly ascertained and the evidence was insufficient, the people's court of second instance shall make a ruling to set aside the judgment and remand to case to the original people's court for retrial, or the people's court of second instance may amend the judgment after investigating and clarifying the facts; or

4. if there was violation of legal procedure in making the original judgment, which may have affected correct adjudication, the judgment shall be set aside by a ruling and the case remanded to the original people's court for retrial.

The parties concerned may appeal against the judgment or ruling rendered in a retrial of their case.

Article 154

The people's court of second instance shall invariably adopt the form of ruling in the appeal cases against the rulings made by the people's courts of first instance.

Article 155

In dealing with a case on appeal, a people's court of second instance may conduct conciliation. If an agreement is reached through conciliation, a conciliation statement shall be made and signed by the judicial officers and the court clerk, with the seal of the people's court affixed to it. After the conciliation statement has been served, the original judgment of the lower court shall be deemed as set aside.

Article 156

If an appellant applies for withdrawal of his appeal before a people's court of second instance pronounces its judgment, the court shall decide whether to approve the application or not.

Article 157

In the trial of a case on appeal, the people's court of second instance shall, apart from observing the provisions of this Chapter, follow the ordinary procedure for trials of first instance.

Article 158

The judgment and the ruling of the people's court of second instance shall be final.

Article 159

The people's court trying a case on appeal shall conclude the case within three months after docketing the case. Any extension of the period necessitated by special circumstances shall be subject to the approval of the president of the court.

The people's court trying a case on appeal against a ruling shall, within 30 days after docketing the case for second instance trial, make a ruling which is final.

Chapter 15

Special Procedure

Section 1: General Provisions

Article 160

When the people's courts try cases concerning the qualification of voters, the declaration of a person as missing or dead, the adjudgment of legal incapacity or restricted legal capacity of a citizen and the adjudgment of a property as ownerless, the provisions of this Chapter shall apply. For matters not covered in this Chapter, the relevant provisions of this Law and other laws shall apply.

Article 161

In cases tried in accordance with the procedure provided in this Chapter, the judgment of first instance shall be final. A collegial panel of judges shall be formed for the trial of any case involving the qualification of voters or of any major, difficult or complicated case; other cases shall be tried by a single judge alone.

Article 162

If a people's court, while trying a case in accordance with the procedure provided in this Chapter, finds that the case involves a civil dispute over rights and interests, it shall make a ruling to terminate the special procedure and inform the interested parties to otherwise institute an action.

Article 163

A people's court trying a case in which special procedure is followed shall conclude the case within 30 days after placing the case on the docket or within 30 days after expiration of the period stated in the public notice. Any extension of the time limit necessitated by special circumstances shall be subject to the approval of the president of the court, excepting, however, a case concerning the qualification of voters.

Section 2: Cases Concerning the Qualification of Voters

Article 164

If a citizen refuses to accept an election committee's decision on an appeal concerning his voting qualification, he may, five days before the election day, bring a suit in the basic people's court located in the electoral district.

Article 165

After entertaining a case concerning voting qualification, a people's court must conclude the trial before the election day.

The party who brings the suit, the representative of the election committee and other citizens concerned must participate in the proceedings.

The written judgment of the people's court shall be served on the election committee and the party who brings the suit before the election day; other citizens concerned shall be notified of the judgment.

Section 3: Cases Concerning the Proclamation of a Person as Missing or Dead

Article 166

With respect to a citizen whose whereabouts are unknown for two years in full, if the interested party applies for declaring the person as missing, the application shall be filed with the basic people's court in the locality where the missing person has his domicile.

The application shall clearly state the facts and time of the disappearance of the person missing as well as the motion; documentary evidence from a public security organ or other relevant organs concerning the disappearance of the citizen shall be appended to the application.

Article 167

With respect to a citizen whose whereabouts are unknown for four years in full or whose whereabouts are unknown for two years in full after an accident in which he was involved, or with respect to a citizen whose whereabouts are unknown after such an accident, and, upon proof furnished by the relevant authorities that it is impossible for him to survive, if the interested party applies for declaring such person as dead, the application shall be filed with the basic people's court in the locality where the missing person has his domicile.

The application shall clearly state the facts and time of the disappearance as well as the motion; documentary evidence from a public security organ or other relevant organs concerning the disappearance of the citizen shall be appended to the application.

Article 168

After entertaining a case concerning the declaration of a person as missing or dead, the people's court shall issue a public notice in search of the person missing. The period of the public notice for declaring a person as missing shall be three months, and that for declaring a person as dead shall be one year. Where a citizen's whereabouts are unknown after an accident in which he was involved and, upon proof furnished by the relevant authorities that it is impossible for him to survive, the period of the public notice for proclaiming such person as dead shall be three months.

On the expiration of the period of the public notice, the people's court shall, depending on whether the fact of the missing or death of the person has been confirmed, make a judgment declaring the person missing or dead or make a judgment rejecting the application.

Article 169

If a person who has been declared missing or dead by a people's court reappears, the people's court shall, upon the application of that person or of an interested party, make a new judgment and annul the previous one.

Section 4: Cases Concerning the Determination of Legal Incapacity or Restricted Legal Capacity of Citizens

Article 170

An application for adjudgment of legal incapacity or restricted legal capacity of a citizen shall be filed by the citizen's near relatives or any other interested party with the basic people's court in the locality where the citizen has his domicile.

The application shall clearly state the fact and grounds of the citizen's legal incapacity or restricted legal capacity.

Article 171

After accepting such an application, the people's court shall, when necessary, have an expert evaluation of the citizen of whom the determination of legal incapacity or restricted legal capacity is sought; if the applicant has already provided an evaluation conclusion, the people's court shall examine such conclusion.

Article 172

In the trial by the people's court of a case for the determination of legal incapacity or restricted legal capacity of a citizen, a near relative of the citizen shall be his agent, the applicant being excluded. If the near relatives of the citizen shift responsibility onto one another, the people's court shall appoint one of them as agent for the citizen. If the citizen's condition of health permits, the people's court shall also seek the opinion of the citizen on the matter.

If, through the trial, the people's court finds that the application is based on facts, a judgment of legal incapacity or restricted legal capacity of the citizen shall be made; if the court finds that the application is not based on facts, it shall make a judgment rejecting the application.

Article 173

If, upon the application of a person who has been determined as one of legal incapacity or restricted legal capacity or upon the application of his guardian, the people's court confirms that the causes of that person's legal incapacity or restricted legal capacity have been eliminated, a new judgment shall be made annuling the previous one.

Section 5: Cases Concerning the Determination of a Property as Ownerless

Article 174

An application for determining a property as ownerless shall be filed by a citizen, legal person or any other organisation with the basic people's court in the place where the property is located.

The application shall clearly state the type and quantity of the property and the grounds on which the application for determining the property as ownerless is filed.

Article 175

The people's court shall, after accepting such an application and upon examination and verification of it, issue a public notice calling on the owner to claim the property. If no one claims the property one year after the issue of the public notice, the people's court shall make a judgment determining the property as ownerless and turn it over to the State or the collective concerned.

Article 176

If, after a property has been determined by a judgment as ownerless, the owner of the property or his successor appears, such a person may file a claim for the property within the period of limitation specified in the General Principles of the Civil Law. The people's court shall, after examination and verification of the claim, make a new judgment, annuling the previous one.

Chapter 16

Procedure for Trial Supervision

Article 177

If the president of a people's court at any level finds definite error in a legally effective judgment or ruling of his court and deems it necessary to have the case retried, he shall refer it to the judicial committee for discussion and decision.

If the Supreme People's Court finds definite error in a legally effective judgment or ruling of a local people's court at any level, or if a people's court at a higher level finds some definite error in a legally effective judgment or ruling of a people's court at a lower level, it shall respectively have the power to bring the case up for trial by itself or direct the people's court at a lower level to conduct a retrial.

Article 178

If a party to an action considers that there is an error in a legally effective judgment or ruling, he may apply to the people's court at a next higher level for a retrial. However, execution of the judgment or ruling shall not be suspended.

Article 179

If an application made by a party meets any of the following conditions, the people's court shall retry the case:

1. there is new evidence to sufficiently set aside the original judgment or ruling;

2. lack of evidence to support the basic fact finding in the original judgment or ruling;

3. the main evidence supporting the fact finding in the original judgment or ruling is forged;

4. the main evidence supporting the fact finding in the original judgment or ruling has not been authenticated;

5. Regarding the evidence needed for trial of a case, the party concern is unable to collect it by itself for a certain objective reason and has made a written application to request the people's court to do so for examination. The people's court, however, fails to do so;

6. there was definite error in the application of the law in the original judgment or ruling;

7. the litigation took place in wrong court jurisdiction, which is contrary to laws;

8. the composition of the adjudicating penal does not comply with laws or a judicial officer ought to excuse himself from the case according to law has failed to do so;

9. where an incapacitated person has not sued by his next friend, or where a party which ought to be a litigation party has not joined the action for a reason not being his or his next friend's fault;

10. where the party concerned was deprived of his right to defence, contrary to laws;

11. where there was no summons issued, the party was absent thereby;

12. the relief granted by the original judgment or ruling has been omitted or has exceeded the relief sought by the party; or

13. the legal document relied upon by the original judgment or ruling has been annuled or revised.

The people's court shall order for a retrial where there is a breach of legal procedure that possibly affects the correctness of a judgment or ruling on the case, or where the judicial officer has practiced corruption or bribery, practiced favoritism and fraudulence, and perverted the law in trying the case.

Article 180

If a party concerned makes an application for retrial, such party shall submit a retrial application statement and other relevant materials. The people's court shall, within five days after receipt of the retrial application statement, serve a copy of the retrial application statement to the opposite party. The opposite party shall, within 15 days after receipt of copy of the retrial application statement, submit a written submission. However, the assessment by the people's court shall not be affected if no written submission is made. The people's court may request the applicant and the opposite party to supplement any relevant document and make inquiry of the relevant matters.

Article 181

The people's court shall complete the assessment within three months after receipt of the retrial application statement. If the application meets one of the circumstances stipulated in art.179 of this Law, a ruling for retrial shall be entered. If the application does not meet the provisions of art.179 of this Law, a ruling of dismissal shall be entered. If the period is required to be extended due to special circumstance, it shall be approved by the president of the court concerned.

The case ruled for retrial upon application by the party concerned shall be heard by the people's court superior than the intermediate people's court. The case ruled for retrial by the Supreme People's Court or the higher people's court shall be heard by such court or transferred to other people's court, or may also be heard by the people's court for first instance of such case.

Article 182

With respect to a legally effective conciliation statement, if evidence furnished by a party proves that the conciliation violates the principle of voluntariness or that the content of the conciliation agreement violates the law, the party may apply for a retrial. If the foregoing proves true after its examination, the people's court shall retry the case.

Article 183

The party concerned shall not make an application for retrial in respect of a judgment of dissolution of marriage which has already been in legal effect.

Article 184

An application for a retrial made by a party shall be submitted within two years after the judgment or ruling becomes legally effective. If the legal document relied upon by the original judgment or ruling is annuled or revised after two years, or if the judicial officer is found to have practiced corruption or bribery, practiced favoritism and fraudulence, and perverted the law in trying such case, the retrial application shall be made within three months after the said matters are known or ought to have known.

Article 185

When a decision is made to retry a case in accordance with the procedure for trial supervision, the execution of the original judgment shall be suspended by a ruling which shall be signed by the president of the court with the seal of the people's court affixed to it.

Article 186

With respect to a case pending retrial by a people's court in accordance with the procedure for trial supervision, if the legally effective judgment or ruling was made by a court of first instance, the case shall be tried in accordance with the procedure of first instance, and the parties concerned may appeal against the new judgment or ruling; if the legally effective judgment or ruling was made by a court of second instance, the case shall be tried in accordance with the procedure of second instance, and the new judgment or ruling shall be legally effective; if it is a case which was brought up for trial by a people's court at a higher level, it shall be tried in accordance with the procedure of second instance, and the new judgment or ruling shall be legally effective.

The people's court shall form a new collegial panel for the purpose of the retrial.

Article 187

In case that the Supreme People's Procuratorate discovers that a legally effective judgment or ruling made by the people's court at any level, or in case that the people's procuratorate at a higher level discovers that a legally effective judgment or ruling made by a people's court at a lower level involves any of the circumstances prescribed in art.179 of this Law, the Supreme People's Procuratorate or the people's procuratorate at a higher level shall respectively lodge a counterappeal.

If a local people's procuratorate at any level discovers that a legally effective judgment or ruling made by the people's court at the same level involves any of the circumstances prescribed in art.179 of this Law, it shall refer the matter to the people's procuratorate at a higher level for the counterappeal a t the people's court at such higher level.

Article 188

For a case of which the judgment or ruling is protested by the people's procuratorate, the people's court entertaining the protest shall make a ruling on retrial within 30 days from receiving the counterappeal submission. If there is a case within the meaning of item (1) to (5) of para 1 of art.179 of this Law, the retrial may be heard by the people's court at a next lower level.

Article 189

When a people's procuratorate decides to lodge a counterappeal against a judgment or ruling made by a people's court, the counterappeal submission shall be adopted.

Article 190

The people's court shall, in retrying a case in which counterappeal was lodged by a people's procuratorate, notify the procuratorate to send representative to attend the court session.

Chapter 17

Procedure for Hastening Debt Recovery

Article 191

When a creditor requests payment of a pecuniary debt or recovery of negotiable instruments from a debtor, he may, if the following requirements are met, apply to the basic people's court that has jurisdiction for an order of payment:

1. no other debt disputes exist between the creditor and the debtor; and

2. the order of payment can be served on the debtor.

The application shall clearly state the requested amount of money or of the negotiable instruments and the facts and evidence on the basis of which the application is made.

Article 192

After the creditor has submitted his application, the people's court shall within five days inform the creditor whether it accepts the application or not.

Article 193

After entertaining the application and upon examination of the facts and evidence provided by the creditor, if the relation of creditor's right and the debt is clear and legitimate, the people's court shall grant an order of payment to the debtor within 15 days after entertaining such application. If the application is found to be unsuccessful, a ruling of dismissal shall be entered.

The debtor shall, within 15 days after receipt of the order of payment, clear off his debts or submit to the people's court his written objection.

If the debtor has neither submitted the objection nor complied with the order of payment within the period specified in the preceding paragraph, the creditor may apply to the people's court for execution.

Article 194

After receiving the written objection submitted by the debtor, the people's court shall make a ruling to terminate the procedure of hastening debt recovery. The order of payment shall be null automatically. The creditor may lodge an action.

Chapter 18

Procedure for Publicising Public Notice for Assertion of Claims

Article 195

Any holder of a bill transferable by endorsement according to the law may, if the bill is stolen, lost, or destroyed, apply to the basic people's court of the place where the bill is to be paid for publication of public notice for assertion of claims. The provisions of this Chapter shall apply to other matters for which, according to the law, an application for publication of a public notice for assertion of claims may be made.

The applicant shall submit to the people's court an application which clearly states the main contents of the bill such as the face amount, the drawer, the holder, the endorser, and the facts and reasons in respect of the application.

Article 196

The people's court shall, upon deciding to accept the application, notify the payor concerned in the meantime to suspend the payment, and shall, within three days, issue a public notice for the interested parties to assert their rights. The period of the public notice shall be decided at the discretion of the people's court; however, it shall not be less than 60 days.

Article 197

The payor shall, upon receiving the notification by the people's court to suspend the payment, do so accordingly till the conclusion of the procedure for publicising public notice for assertion of claims.

Within the period of the public notice, assignment of rights on the bill shall be void.

Article 198

Interested party or parties as claimants shall report their claims to the people's court within the period of the public notice.

After receiving the report on the claims by interested party or parties, the people's court shall make a ruling to terminate the procedure for publicising public notice for assertion of claims, and notify the applicant and the payor.

The applicant or the claimants may bring an action in the people's court.

Article 199

If no claim is asserted, the people's court shall make a judgment on the basis of the application to declare the bill in question null and void. The judgment shall be published and the payor notified accordingly. As of the date of publication of the judgment, the applicant shall be entitled to payment by the payor.

Article 200

If an interested party for justified reasons was unable to submit his claim to the people's court before the judgment is made, he may, within one year after the day he knows or should know the publication of the judgment, bring an action in the people's court which has made the judgment.

PART III   Procedure of Execution

Chapter 19

General Stipulations

Article 201

The legally effective civil judgments or rulings, as well as the property in criminal judgments or rulings shall be executed by the people's court of first instance or the people's court at the same level of a place where the executed property is located.

Other legal documents which are to be executed by a people's court as prescribed by the law shall be executed by the people's court of the place where the person subjected to execution domiciles or where the property subject to execution is located.

Article 202

If the party concerned or the related party with interest therein is of the view that the execution violates the provisions of law, such party may submit a written objection to the people's court responsible for the execution. If the party concerned or the related party with interest therein submits a written objection, the people's court shall complete the assessment within 15 days from the receipt of written objection. If there is a valid ground, a ruling on the judgment or ruling be quashed or rectified shall be entered. If there is no valid ground, a ruling on dismissal shall be entered. If the party concerned or the related party with interest therein is aggrieved at the ruling, the party may apply for a review at the people's court at a next higher level within 10 days from the date of service of the ruling.

Article 203

If the people's court fails to execute the judgment or ruling for more than six months after receipt of the application statement for execution, the execution applicant may apply for the execution at the people's court a next higher level. Upon assessment, the people's court at a next higher level may order the original people's court for the execution to be done within a prescribed period or may also decide to execute itself or appoint another people's court for execution.

Article 204

If, in the course of the execution, an outsider to the case submits a written objection regarding the subject matter of the execution, the people's court shall complete the assessment within 15 days from the receipt of written objection. If there is valid ground, a ruling shall be made to cease the execution of such subject matter. If there is no valid ground, a ruling on dismissal shall be entered. If the party concerned or such outsider is aggrieved at the ruling and is of the view that there is error in the original judgment or verdict, the case shall be disposed of by the trial supervision procedure. For matter not related to the original judgment or ruling, the aggrieved party may lodge an action at the people's court within 15 days after service of the ruling.

Article 205

Execution work shall be carried out by the execution officer.

When carrying out a compulsory execution measure, the execution officer shall produce his credentials. After the execution is completed, the execution officer shall make a record of the particulars of the execution, and have it signed or sealed by the persons concerned on the scene.

The people's court may, if necessary, set up an execution institution.

Article 206

If a person or property subjected to execution is in another locality, the people's court in that locality may be entrusted with the carrying out of the execution. The entrusted people's court shall begin the execution within 15 days after receiving a letter of entrustment and shall not refuse to do so. After the execution has been completed, the entrusted people's court shall promptly inform the entrusting people's court, by letter, of the result of the execution. If the execution has not been completed within 30 days, the entrusted people's court shall also inform the entrusting people's court, by letter, of the particulars of the execution.

If the entrusted people's court does not carry out the execution within 15 days after receiving the letter of entrustment, the entrusting people's court may request the people's court at a higher level over the entrusted people's court to instruct the entrusted people's court to carry out the execution.

Article 207

If in the course of execution the two parties become reconciled and reach a settlement agreement on their own initiative, the execution officer shall make a record of the contents of the agreement, and both parties shall affix their signatures or seals to the record.

If either party fails to fulfill the settlement agreement, the people's court may, at the request of the other party, resume the execution of the legal document which was originally effective.

Article 208

In the course of execution, if the person subjected to execution provides a guaranty, the people's court may, with the consent of the person who has applied for execution, decide on the suspension of the execution and the time limit for such suspension. If the person subjected to execution still fails to perform his obligations after the time limit, the people's court shall have the power to execute the property he provided as security or the property of the guarantor.

Article 209

If the citizen subjected to execution dies, his debts shall be paid off from the deceased estate; if a legal person or any other organisation subjected to execution dissolves, the party that succeeds to its rights and obligations shall fulfill the obligations.

Article 210

After the completion of execution, if definite error is found in the executed judgment, ruling or other legal documents resulting in the annulment of such judgment, ruling or legal documents by the people's court, the said court shall, with respect to the property which has been executed, make a ruling that persons who have obtained the property shall return it. In the event of refusal to return such property, compulsory execution shall be carried out.

Article 211

The provisions of this Part shall be applicable to the execution of the conciliation statement as drawn up by the people's court.

Chapter 20

Application for Execution and Referral

Article 212

The parties concerned must comply with legally effective judgments or rulings in civil cases. If a party refuses to do so, the other party may apply to the people's court for execution, or the judge may refer the matter to the execution officer for enforcement.

The parties concerned must comply with the conciliation statement and other legal documents that are to be executed by the people's court. If a party refuses to do so, the other party may apply to the people's court for enforcement.

Article 213

If a party fails to comply with an award of an arbitral organ established according to the law, the other party may apply for execution to the people's court which has jurisdiction over the case. The people's court applied to shall enforce the award.

If the party against whom the application is made furnishes proof that the arbitral award involves any of the following circumstances, the people's court shall, after examination and verification by a collegial panel, make a ruling not to allow the enforcement:

1. the parties have had no arbitration clause in their contract, nor have subsequently reached a written agreement on arbitration;

2. the matters dealt with by the award fall outside the scope of the arbitration agreement or are matters which the arbitral organ has no power to arbitrate;

3. the composition of the arbitration tribunal or the procedure for arbitration contradicts the procedure prescribed by the law;

4. the main evidence for ascertaining the facts is insufficient;

5. there is definite error in the application of the law; or

6. the arbitrators have committed embezzlement, accepted bribes or done malpractice for personal benefits or perverted the law in the arbitration of the case.

If the people's court determines that the execution of the arbitral award is against the social and public interest, it shall make a ruling of non-execution.

The above-mentioned written ruling shall be served on both parties and the arbitral organ.

If the non-execution of an arbitral award is ruled by the people's court, the parties may, in accordance with a written agreement on arbitration reached between them, apply for arbitration again; they may also bring an action in the people's court.

Article 214

If a party fails to comply with a document evidencing the creditor's rights made enforceable according to the law by a notary office, the other party may apply to the people's court which has jurisdiction over the case for execution. The people's court applied to shall enforce such document.

If the people's court finds definite error in the document of creditor's rights, it shall make a ruling of non-execution and serve the written ruling on both parties concerned as well as the notary office.

Article 215

The limitation period for an application for execution shall be two years. The law on termination or discontinuance of limitation of actions shall be applicable in fixing the termination or discontinuance of the period of limitation.

The limitation period as prescribed by the preceding paragraph shall be calculated from the last day of the performance period specified by the legal document. If the legal document specifies the performance divided into stages, the limitation period shall be calculated from the last day of each specified stage of performance. If the legal document does not specify any performance period, it shall be calculated from the effective date of the legal document.

Article 216

The execution officer shall, after receiving the application for execution or the writ of referral directing execution, send an execution notice to the person subject to the execution, instructing him to comply within the specified time. If the person fails to comply accordingly, compulsory enforcement shall be carried out.

If a person subject to the execution fails to perform the obligations specified in the legal document, and will possibly hide or transfer his asset, the execution officer may immediately adopt the compulsory enforcement.

Chapter 21

Execution Measures

Article 217

If a person subject to the execution does not comply with the execution notice by failure to perform the obligations specified in the legal document, he shall declare his current assets and the status of his assets one year prior to the receipt of the execution notice. If a person subject to the execution refuses to declare or makes false declaration, the people's court may impose a fine or detention upon such person subject to the execution or his legal representative, the major person-in-charge or the directly liable person of the relevant unit based on the seriousness of the case.

Article 218

If the person subjected to execution fails to fulfill according to the execution notice the obligations specified in the legal document, the people's court shall be empowered to make inquiries with banks, credit cooperatives or other units that deal with savings deposit into the deposit accounts of the person subjected to execution, and shall be empowered to freeze or transfer his deposits; however, the inquiries, freezing or transfer of the deposits shall not exceed the scope of the obligations to be fulfilled by the person subjected to execution.

The people's court shall, in deciding to freeze or transfer a deposit, make a ruling and issue a notice for assistance in execution. Banks, credit cooperatives or other units that deal with savings deposit must comply with it.

Article 219

If the person subjected to execution fails to fulfill according to the execution notice the obligations specified in the legal document, the people's court shall be empowered to withhold or withdraw part of the income of the person subjected to execution, for the fulfillment of his obligations. However, it shall leave out the necessary living expenses for the person subjected to execution and his dependant family members.

The people's court shall, when withholding or withdrawing the income, make a ruling and issue a notice for assistance in execution. The unit in which the person subjected to execution works, banks, credit cooperatives or other units that deal with savings deposit must comply with the notice.

Article 220

If the person subjected to execution fails to fulfill according to the execution notice the obligations specified in the legal document, the people's court shall be empowered to seal up, distrain, freeze, sell by public auction, or sell off part of the property of the person subjected to execution for the fulfillment of his obligations. However, it shall leave out the necessaries of life for the person subjected to execution and his dependant family members.

The people's court shall make a ruling for the adoption of the measures specified in the preceding paragraph.

Article 221

When the people's court seals up or distrains a property, it shall, if the person subjected to execution is a citizen, notify him or an adult member of his family to appear on the scene; if the party subjected to execution is a legal person or any other organisation, it shall notify its legal representatives or its principal heads to be present. Their refusal to appear on the scene shall not hinder the execution. If the person subjected to execution is a citizen, his unit or the grass-roots organisation of the place where his property is located shall send a representative to attend the execution.

An inventory of the sealed-up or distrained property must be made by the execution officer and, after the inventory has been signed or sealed by the persons on the scene, a copy of it shall be given to the person subjected to execution. If the person subjected to execution is a citizen, another copy may be given to an adult member of his family.

Article 222

The execution officer may commit the sealed-up property to the person subjected to execution for safekeeping, and the person shall be held liable for any losses incurred due to his fault.

Article 223

After a property has been sealed up or distrained, the execution officer shall instruct the person subjected to execution to fulfill, within the prescribed period, the obligations specified in the legal document. If the person has not fulfilled his obligations upon expiration of the period, the people's court may, in accordance with the relevant legal provisions, entrust the relevant units with selling by public auction or selling off the sealed-up or distrained property. Articles which are prohibited from free trading by the State shall be delivered to and purchased by the relevant units at the price fixed by the State.

Article 224

If the person subjected to execution fails to fulfill his obligations specified in the legal document and conceals his property, the people's court shall be empowered to issue a search warrant and search him and his domicile or the place where the property was concealed.

In adopting the measure mentioned in the preceding paragraph, the president of the people's court shall sign and issue the search warrant.

Article 225

With respect to the property or negotiable instruments specified for delivery in the legal document, the execution officer shall summon both parties concerned and deliver them in their presence or the execution officer may forward them to the recipient, who shall sign and give a receipt.

Any unit concerned that has in possession the property or negotiable instruments shall turn them over to the recipient in accordance with the notice of the people's court for assistance in execution, and the recipient shall sign and give a receipt.

If any citizen concerned has in possession the property or negotiable instruments, the people's court shall notify him to hand them over. If he refuses to do so, compulsory execution shall be carried out.

Article 226

Compulsory eviction from a building or a plot of land shall require a public notice signed and issued by the president of a people's court, instructing the person subjected to execution to comply within a specified period of time. If the person subjected to execution fails to do so upon the expiration of the period, compulsory execution shall be carried out by the execution officer.

When compulsory execution is being carried out, if the person subjected to execution is a citizen, the person or an adult member of his family shall be notified to be present; if the party subjected to execution is a legal person or any other organisation, its legal representatives or principal heads shall be notified to be present; their refusal to be present shall not hinder the execution. If the person subjected to execution is a citizen, his work unit or the grass-roots organisation in the locality of the building or the plot of land shall send a representative for attendance. The execution officer shall make a record of the particulars of the compulsory execution, with the signatures or seals of the persons on the scene affixed to it.

The people's court shall assign personnel to transport the property removed in a compulsory eviction from a building to a designated location and turn it over to the person subjected to execution or, if the person is a citizen, to an adult member of his family; if any loss is incurred due to such person's refusal to accept the property, the loss shall be borne by the person subjected to execution.

Article 227

In the course of execution, if certain formalities for the transfer of certificates of property right need to be gone through, the people's court may issue a notice for assistance in execution to the relevant units, and they must comply with it.

Article 228

If the person subjected to execution fails to perform acts specified in a judgment or ruling or any other legal document according to the execution notice, the people's court may carry out compulsory execution or entrust the task to a relevant unit or other persons, and the person subjected to execution shall bear the expenses thus incurred.

Article 229

If the person subjected to execution fails to fulfill his obligations with respect to pecuniary payment within the period specified by a judgment or ruling or any other legal document, he shall pay double interest on the debt for the belated payment. If the person subjected to execution fails to fulfill his other obligations within the period specified in the judgment or ruling or any other legal document, he shall pay a charge for the dilatory fulfillment.

Article 230

After the adoption of the execution measures stipulated in arts.221, 222 and 223 of this Law, if the person subjected to execution is still unable to repay the debts, he shall continue to fulfill his obligations. If the creditor finds that the person subjected to execution has any other property, he may at any time apply to the people's court for execution.

Article 231

If a person subject to the execution fails to perform the obligations specified in the legal document, the people's court may adopt or inform the relevant unit to assist to adopt the departure restriction, put a record on the credit reference system, announce the non-performance of obligation through mass media and adopt other measures prescribed by laws.

Chapter 22

Suspension and Termination of Execution

Article 232

The people's court shall make a ruling to suspend execution under any of the following circumstances:

1.   the applicant indicates that the execution may be postponed;

2.   an outsider raises an obviously reasonable objection to the object of the execution;

3.   a citizen as one of the parties dies and it is necessary to wait for the successor to inherit the rights of the deceased or to succeed to his obligations;

4.   a legal person or any other organisation as one of the parties dissolves, and the party succeeding to its rights and obligations has not been determined; or

5.   other circumstances occur under which the people's court deems the suspension of execution necessary.

Execution shall be resumed when the circumstances warranting the suspension of execution have disappeared.

Article 233

The people's court shall make a ruling to terminate execution under any of following circumstances:

1.   the applicant has withdrawn his application;

2.   the legal document on which the execution is based has been revoked;

3.   the citizen subjected to execution dies and there is no estate that may be subjected to execution, nor anyone to succeed to his obligations;

4.   the person entitled to claim alimony or support for elders or children dies;

5.   the citizen subjected to execution is too badly off to repay his debts, has no source of income and has lost his ability to work as well; or

6.   other circumstances occur under which the people's court deems the termination of execution necessary.

Article 234

A ruling to suspend or terminate execution shall become effective immediately after being served on the parties concerned.

PART IV   Special Provisions for Civil Proceedings of Cases Involving Foreign Element

Chapter 23

General Principles

Article 235

The provisions of this Part shall be applicable to civil proceedings within the territory of the People's Republic of China in regard to cases involving foreign element. Where it is not covered by the provisions of this Part, other relevant provisions of this Law shall apply.

Article 236

If an international treaty concluded or acceded to by the People's Republic of China contains provisions that differ from provisions of this Law, the provisions of the international treaty shall apply, except those on which China has made reservations.

Article 237

Civil actions brought against a foreign national, a foreign organisation or an international organisation that enjoys diplomatic privileges and immunities shall be dealt with in accordance with the relevant law of the People's Republic of China and the provisions of the international treaties concluded or acceded to by the People's Republic of China.

Article 238

The people's court shall conduct trials of civil cases involving foreign element in the spoken and written language commonly used in the People's Republic of China. Translation may be provided at the request of the parties concerned, and the expenses shall be borne by them.

Article 239

When foreign nationals, stateless persons or foreign enterprises and organisations need lawyers as agents "ad litem" to bring an action or enter appearance on their behalf in the people's court, they must appoint lawyers of the People's Republic of China.

Article 240

Any power of attorney mailed or forwarded by other means from outside the territory of the People's Republic of China by a foreign national, stateless person or a foreign enterprise and organisation that has no domicile in the People's Republic of China for the appointment of a lawyer or any other person of the People's Republic of China as an agent "ad litem" must be notarised by a notarial office in the country of domicile and authenticated by the Chinese embassy or consulate accredited to that country or, for the purpose of verification, must go through the formalities stipulated in the relevant bilateral treaties between China and that country before it becomes effective.

Chapter 24

Jurisdiction

Article 241

In the case of an action concerning a contract dispute or other disputes over property rights and interests, brought against a defendant who has no domicile within the territory of the People's Republic of China, if the contract is signed or performed within the territory of the People's Republic of China, or if the object of the action is located within the territory of the People's Republic of China, or if the defendant has distrainable property within the territory of the People's Republic of China, or if the defendant has its representative office within the territory of the People's Republic of China, the people's court of the place where the contract is signed or performed, or where the object of the action is, or where the defendant's distrainable property is located, or where the torts are done, or where the defendant's representative office is located, shall have jurisdiction.

Article 242

Parties to a dispute over a contract concluded with foreign element or over property rights and interests involving foreign element may, through written agreement, choose the court of the place which has practical connections with the dispute to exercise jurisdiction. If a people's court of the People's Republic of China is chosen to exercise jurisdiction, the provisions of this Law on jurisdiction by forum level and on exclusive jurisdiction shall not be violated.

Article 243

If in a civil action in respect of a case involving foreign element, the defendant raises no objection to the jurisdiction of a people's court and responds to the action by making his defence, he shall be deemed to have accepted that this people's court has jurisdiction over the case.

Article 244

Actions brought on disputes arising from the performance of contracts for Chinese-foreign equity joint ventures, or Chinese-foreign contractual joint ventures, or Chinese-foreign cooperative exploration and development of the natural resources in the People's Republic of China shall fall under the jurisdiction of the people's courts of the People's Republic of China.

Chapter 25

Service and Time Period

Article 245

A people's court may serve litigation documents on a party who has no domicile within the territory of the People's Republic of China in the following ways:

1. in the way specified in the international treaties concluded or acceded to by both the People's Republic of China and the country where the person on whom service is to be made resides;

2. by making the service through diplomatic channels;

3. with respect to the person on whom the service is to be made and who is of the nationality of the People's Republic of China, service may be entrusted to the embassy or consulate of the People's Republic of China accredited to the country where the person resides;

4. by making the service on the agent "ad litem" who is authorised to receive the documents served;

5. by serving the documents on the representative office established in the People's Republic of China by the person on whom the service is to be made or on his branch office or business agents there who have the right to receive the documents;

6. by making service by mail if the law of the country where the person on whom the service is to be made resides so permits; in the event that the receipt of delivery is not returned six months after the date on which the documents were mailed, and that circumstances justify the assumption that service has been made, the service shall be deemed completed upon the expiration of the said time period; and

7. by making service by public notice, if none of the above-mentioned methods can be employed. The service shall be deemed completed six months after the date on which the public notice was issued.

Article 246

If a defendant has no domicile within the territory of the People's Republic of China, the people's court shall serve a copy of the statement of complaint on the defendant and notify him to submit his defence within 30 days after he receives the copy of the statement of complaint. Extension of the period requested by the defendant shall be at the discretion of the people's court.

Article 247

If a party who has no domicile within the territory of the People's Republic of China is not satisfied with a judgment or ruling made by a people's court of first instance, he shall have the right to file an appeal within 30 days from the date the written judgment or ruling is served. The appellee shall submit his defence within 30 days after receipt of a copy of the appeal petition. If a party who is unable to file an appeal or submit a defence within the period prescribed by the law requests an extension of the period, the people's court shall decide whether to grant it.

Article 248

The period for the trials of civil cases involving foreign element by the people's court shall not be restricted by the provisions of arts.135 and 159 of this Law.

Chapter 26

Property Preservation

Article 249

The parties to an action may, in accordance with the provisions of art.92 of this Law, apply to the people's court for property preservation.

Interested parties may, in accordance with the provisions of art.93 of this Law, apply to the people's court for property preservation before an action is brought.

Article 250

After a people's court makes a ruling on pre-litigation property preservation, the applicant shall bring an action within 30 days. If he fails to bring the action within the period, the people's court shall cancel the property preservation.

Article 251

After the people's court makes a ruling on property preservation, if the party against whom the application is made provides a guarranty, the people's court shall cancel the property preservation.

Article 252

If the application is wrongfully made, the applicant shall compensate the party against whom the application is made for losses incurred from the property preservation.

Article 253

If the property to be preserved by a people's court needs supervision, the court shall notify the unit concerned to be responsible for the supervision, and the party against whom the application is made shall bear the expenses.

Article 254

The order to cancel the preservation issued by a people's court shall be carried out by an execution officer.

Chapter 27

Arbitration

Article 255

In the case of a dispute arising from the foreign economic, trade, transport or maritime activities of China, if the parties have had an arbitration clause in the contract concerned or have subsequently reached a written arbitration agreement stipulating the submission of the dispute for arbitration to an arbitral organ in the People's Republic of China handling cases involving foreign element, or to any other arbitral body, they may not bring an action in a people's court.

If the parties have not had an arbitration clause in the contract concerned or have not subsequently reached a written arbitration agreement, they may bring an action in a people's court.

Article 256

If a party has applied for property preservation measures, the arbitral organ of the People's Republic of China handling cases involving foreign element shall refer the party's application for a decision to the intermediate people's court of the place where the party against whom the application is made has his domicile or where his property is located.

Article 257

In a case in which an award has been made by an arbitral organ of the People's Republic of China handling cases involving foreign element, the parties may not bring an action in a people's court. If one party fails to comply with the arbitral award, the other party may apply for its enforcement to the intermediate people's court of the place where the party against whom the application for enforcement is made has his domicile or where his property is located.

Article 258

A people's court shall, after examination and verification by a collegial panel of the court, make a ruling not to allow the enforcement of the award rendered by an arbitral organ of the People's Republic of China handling cases involving foreign element, if the party against whom the application for enforcement is made furnishes proof that:

1. the parties have not had an arbitration clause in the contract or have not subsequently reached a written arbitration agreement;

2. the party against whom the application for enforcement is made was not given notice for the appointment of an arbitrator or for the inception of the arbitration proceedings or was unable to present his case on the ground for which he is not responsible;

3. the composition of the arbitration tribunal or the procedure for arbitration was not in conformity with the rules of arbitration; or

4.   the matters dealt with by the award fall outside the scope of the arbitration agreement or which the arbitral organ was not empowered to arbitrate.

If the people's court determines that the enforcement of the award goes against the social and public interest of the country, the people's court shall make a ruling not to allow the enforcement of the arbitral award.

Article 259

If the enforcement of an arbitral award is disallowed by a ruling of a people's court, the parties may, in accordance with a written arbitration agreement reached between them, apply for arbitration again; they may also bring an action in a people's court.

Chapter 28

Judicial Assistance

Article 260

In accordance with the international treaties concluded or acceded to by the People's Republic of China or with the principle of reciprocity, the people's courts of China and foreign courts may make mutual requests for assistance in the service of legal documents, in investigation and collection of evidence or in other litigation actions.

The people's court shall not render the assistance requested by a foreign court, if it impairs the sovereignty, security or social and public interest of the People's Republic of China.

Article 261

The request for the providing of judicial assistance shall be effected through channels provided in the international treaties concluded or acceded to by the People's Republic of China; in the absence of such treaties, they shall be effected through diplomatic channels.

A foreign embassy or consulate accredited to the People's Republic of China may serve documents on its citizens and make investigations and collect evidence among them, provided that the laws of the People's Republic of China are not violated and no compulsory measures are taken.

Except for the conditions provided in the preceding paragraph, no foreign organisation or individual may, without the consent of the competent authorities of the People's Republic of China, serve documents or make investigations and collect evidence within the territory of the People's Republic of China.

Article 262

The letter of request for judicial assistance and its annexes sent by a foreign court to a people's court shall be appended with a Chinese translation or a text in any other language or languages specified in the relevant international treaties.

The letter of request and its annexes sent to a foreign court by a people's court for judicial assistance shall be appended with a translation in the language of that country or a text in any other language or languages specified in the relevant international treaties.

Article 263

The judicial assistance provided by the people's courts shall be rendered in accordance with the procedure prescribed by the laws of the People's Republic of China. If a special form of judicial assistance is requested by a foreign court, it may also be rendered, provided that the special form requested does not contradict the laws of the People's Republic of China.

Article 264

If a party applies for enforcement of a legally effective judgment or ruling made by a people's court, and the opposite party or his property is not within the territory of the People's Republic of China, the applicant may directly apply for recognition and enforcement to the foreign court which has jurisdiction. The people's court may also, in accordance with the relevant provisions of the international treaties concluded or acceded to by China, or with the principle of reciprocity, request recognition and enforcement by the foreign court.

If a party applies for enforcement of a legally effective arbitral award made by an arbitral organ in the People's Republic of China handling cases involving foreign element and the opposite party or his property is not within the territory of the People's Republic of China, he may directly apply for recognition and enforcement of the award to the foreign court which has jurisdiction.

Article 265

If a legally effective judgment or ruling made by a foreign court requires recognition and enforcement by a people's court of the People's Republic of China, the party concerned may directly apply for recognition and enforcement to the intermediate people's court of the People's Republic of China which has jurisdiction. The foreign court may also, in accordance with the provisions of the international treaties concluded or acceded to by that foreign country and the People's Republic of China or with the principle of reciprocity, request recognition and enforcement by a people's court.

Article 266

In the case of an application or request for recognition and enforcement of a legally effective judgment or ruling of a foreign court, the people's court shall, after examining it in accordance with the international treaties concluded or acceded to by the People's Republic of China or with the principle of reciprocity and arriving at the conclusion that it does not contradict the basic principles of the law of the People's Republic of China nor violates State sovereignty, security and social and public interest of the country, recognise the validity of the judgment or ruling, and, if required, issue a writ of execution to enforce it in accordance with the relevant provisions of this Law; if the application or request contradicts the basic principles of the law of the People's Republic of China or violates State sovereignty, security and social and public interest of the country, the people's court shall not recognise and enforce it.

Article 267

If an award made by a foreign arbitral organ requires the recognition and enforcement by a people's court of the People's Republic of China, the party concerned shall directly apply to the intermediate people's court of the place where the party subjected to enforcement domiciles or where his property is located. The people's court shall deal with the matter in accordance with the international treaties concluded or acceded to by the People's Republic of China or with the principle of reciprocity.

Article 268

This Law shall be effective as of the promulgation date. The "Civil Procedure Law of the People's Republic of China (for Trial Implementation)" shall be repealed simultaneously.

China International Economic and Trade Arbitration Commission Arbitration Rules

(Revised and adopted by the China Council for the Promotion of International Trade/ China Chamber of International Commerce on 11 January 2005. Effective as from 1 May 2005)

Chapter 1

General Provisions

Article 1 The Rules

These Rules are formulated in accordance with the Arbitration Law of the People's Republic of China and the provisions of other relevant laws, as well as the "Decision" of the former Administration Council of the Central People's Government and the "Notice" and the "Official Reply" of the State Council.

Article 2 Name and Structure

1. The China International Economic and Trade Arbitration Commission (originally named the Foreign Trade Arbitration Commission of the China Council for the Promotion of International Trade, later renamed the Foreign Economic and Trade Arbitration Commission of the China Council for the Promotion of International Trade, and currently called the China International Economic and Trade Arbitration Commission, hereinafter referred to as the CIETAC) independently and impartially resolves, by means of arbitration, disputes arising from economic and trade transactions of a contractual or non-contractual nature.

2. The CIETAC concurrently uses the "Court of Arbitration of the China Chamber of International Commerce" as its name.

3. Where an arbitration agreement or an arbitration clause contained in a contract provides for arbitration by the CIETAC or one of its Sub-Commissions or by the CIETAC using one of its prior names, the parties shall be deemed to have unanimously agreed that the arbitration shall be administered by the CIETAC or by one of its Sub-Commissions.

4. Where an arbitration agreement or an arbitration clause contained in a contract provides for arbitration by the China Council for the Promotion of International Trade/China Chamber of International Commerce or by the Arbitration Commission or the Court of Arbitration of the China Council for the Promotion of International Trade/China Chamber of International

Commerce, the parties shall be deemed to have unanimously agreed that the arbitration shall be administered by the CIETAC.

5. The Chairman of the CIETAC shall perform the functions and duties vested in him/her by these Rules while a Vice-Chairman may perform the Chairman's functions and duties with the Chairman's authorisation.

6. The CIETAC has a Secretariat, which handles its day-to-day work under the direction of its Secretary-General.

7. The CIETAC is based in Beijing, and has a South China Sub-Commission (formerly known as Shenzhen Sub-Commission) in Shenzhen Special Economic Zone and a Shanghai Sub-Commission in Shanghai. These Sub-Commissions are integral parts of the CIETAC. The Sub-Commissions have their respective secretariats, which handle their day-to-day work under the direction of the Secretaries-General of the respective Sub-Commissions.

8. The parties may agree to have their disputes arbitrated by the CIETAC in Beijing, the South China Sub-Commission in Shenzhen or the Shanghai Sub-Commission in Shanghai. In the absence of such an agreement, the Claimant shall have the option to submit the case for arbitration by the CIETAC in Beijing, the South China Sub-Commission in Shenzhen or the Shanghai Sub-Commission in Shanghai. When such option is exercised, the first choice by the party shall prevail. In case of any dispute, the final decision shall be made by the CIETAC.

9. The CIETAC may, in its discretion, establish arbitration centers for specific business sectors and issue arbitration rules therefore.

10. The CIETAC shall establish a Panel of Arbitrators, and may, in its discretion, establish Panels of Arbitrators for specific business sectors.

Article 3 Jurisdiction

The CIETAC accepts cases involving:

1. international or foreign-related disputes;

2. disputes related to the Hong Kong Special Administrative Region or the Macao Special Administrative Region or the Taiwan region; and

3. domestic disputes.

Article 4 Scope of Application

1. These Rules uniformly apply to the CIETAC and its Sub-Commissions. When arbitration proceedings are administered by a Sub-Commission, the functions and duties under these Rules allocated to the Chairman, the secretariat and the Secretary-General of the CIETAC shall be performed, respectively, by a Vice-Chairman authorised by the Chairman, a secretariat and a Secretary-General of the relevant Sub-Commission except for the power to make decisions on challenges to arbitrators.

2.   The parties shall be deemed to have agreed to arbitrate in accordance with these Rules whenever they have provided for arbitration by the CIETAC. Where the parties have agreed on the application of other arbitration rules, or any modification of these Rules, the parties' agreement shall prevail except where such agreement is inoperative or in conflict with a mandatory provision of the law of the place of arbitration.

3.   Where the parties agree to refer their disputes to arbitration under these Rules without providing the name of an arbitration institution, they shall be deemed to have agreed to refer the dispute to arbitration by the CIETAC.

4.   Where the parties agree to refer their dispute to arbitration under the CIETAC's arbitration rules for a specific business sector or profession and the dispute falls within the scope of such rules, the parties' agreement shall prevail; otherwise, these Rules shall apply.

Article 5 Arbitration Agreement

1.   The CIETAC shall, upon the written application of a party, accept a case in accordance with an arbitration agreement concluded between the parties, either before or after the occurrence of the dispute, in which it is provided that disputes are to be referred to arbitration by the CIETAC.

2.   An arbitration agreement means an arbitration clause in a contract concluded between the parties or any other form of written agreement providing for the settlement of disputes by arbitration.

3.   The arbitration agreement shall be in writing. An arbitration agreement is in writing if it is contained in a tangible form of a document such as a contract, letter, telegram, telex, facsimile, EDI, or Email. An arbitration agreement shall be deemed to exist where its existence is asserted by one party and not denied by the other during the exchange of the Request for Arbitration and the Statement of Defense.

4.   An arbitration clause contained in a contract shall be treated as a clause independent and separate from all other clauses of the contract, and an arbitration agreement attached to a contract shall also be treated as independent and separate from all other clauses of the contract. The validity of an arbitration clause or an arbitration agreement shall not be affected by any modification, rescission, termination, transfer, expiry, invalidity, ineffectiveness, revocation or non-existence of the contract.

Article 6 Objection to an Arbitration Agreement and/or Jurisdiction

1.   The CIETAC shall have the power to determine the existence and validity of an arbitration agreement and its jurisdiction over an arbitration case. The CIETAC may, if necessary, delegate such power to the arbitral tribunal.

2.   Where the CIETAC is satisfied by prima facie evidence that an arbitration agreement providing for arbitration by the CIETAC exists, it may make a

decision based on such evidence that it has jurisdiction over the arbitration case, and the arbitration shall proceed. Such a decision shall not prevent the CIETAC from making a new decision on jurisdiction based on facts and/or evidence found by the arbitral tribunal during the arbitration proceedings that are inconsistent with the prima facie evidence.

3. An objection to an arbitration agreement and/or jurisdiction over an arbitration case shall be raised in writing before the first oral hearing is held by the arbitral tribunal. Where a case is to be decided on the basis of documents only, such an objection shall be raised before the submission of the first substantive defense.

4. The arbitration shall proceed notwithstanding an objection to the arbitration agreement and/or jurisdiction over the arbitration case.

5. The aforesaid objections to and/or decisions on jurisdiction by the CIETAC shall include objections to and/or decisions on a party's standing to participate in the arbitration.

Article 7 Bona Fide Cooperation

The parties shall proceed with the arbitration in bona fide cooperation.

Article 8 Waiver of Right to Object

A party shall be deemed to have waived its right to object where it knows or should have known that any provision of, or requirement under, these Rules has not been complied with and yet participates in or proceeds with the arbitration proceedings without promptly and explicitly submitting its objection in writing to such non-compliance.

Chapter 2

Arbitral Proceedings

Section 1: Request for Arbitration, Defense and Counterclaim

Article 9 Commencement of Arbitration

The arbitral proceedings shall commence on the date on which the CIETAC or one of its Sub-Commissions receives a Request for Arbitration.

Article 10 Application for Arbitration

A party applying for arbitration under these Rules shall:

1. Submit a Request for Arbitration in writing signed by and/or affixed with the seal of the Claimant and/or its authorised representative(s), which shall, inter alia, include:

   (a) the names and addresses of the Claimant and the Respondent, including the zip code, telephone, telex, fax and telegraph numbers, Email addresses or any other means of electronic telecommunications;

(b)   a reference to the arbitration agreement that is invoked;

(c)   a statement of the facts of the case and the main issues in dispute;

(d)   the claim of the Claimant; and

(e)   the facts and grounds on which the claim is based.

2.   Attach to the Request for Arbitration the relevant evidence supporting the facts on which the Claimant's claim is based.

3.   Make payment of the arbitration fee in advance to the CIETAC according to its Arbitration Fee Schedule.

Article 11 Acceptance of a Case

1.   Upon receipt of the Request for Arbitration and its attachments, if the CIETAC after examination finds the formalities required for arbitration application to be incomplete, it may request the Claimant to complete them. Where the formalities are found to be complete, the CIETAC shall send a Notice of Arbitration to both parties together with one copy each of the CIETAC Arbitration Rules, the Panel of Arbitrators and the Arbitration Fee Schedule. The Request for Arbitration and its attachments submitted by the Claimant shall be sent to the Respondent under the same cover.

2.   The CIETAC or its Sub-Commission shall, after accepting a case, appoint a staff-member of its secretariat to assist the arbitral tribunal in the procedural administration of the case.

Article 12 Statement of Defense

1.   Within forty-five (45) days from the date of receipt of the Notice of Arbitration, the Respondent shall file a Statement of Defense in writing with the Secretariat of the CIETAC or its Sub-Commission. The arbitral tribunal may extend that time period if it believes that there are justified reasons. The Statement of Defense shall be signed by and/or affixed with the seal of the Respondent and/or its authorised representative(s), and shall, inter alia, include:

(a)   the names and addresses of the Respondent, including the zip code, telephone, telex, fax and telegraph numbers, Email addresses or any other means of electronic telecommunications;

(b)   the defense to the Request for Arbitration setting forth the facts and grounds on which the defense is based; and

(c)   the relevant evidence supporting the defense.

2.   The arbitral tribunal has the power to decide whether to accept a Statement of Defense submitted after expiration of the above time limit.

3.   Failure of the Respondent to file a Statement of Defense shall not operate to affect the arbitral proceedings.

Article 13 Counterclaim

1. Within forty-five (45) days from the date of receipt of the Notice of Arbitration, the Respondent shall file with the CIETAC its counterclaim in writing, if any. The arbitral tribunal may extend that time period if it believes that there are justified reasons.

2. When filing a counterclaim, the Respondent shall specify its counterclaim in its written Statement of Counterclaim and state the facts and grounds upon which its counterclaim is based with relevant evidence attached thereto.

3. When filing a counterclaim, the Respondent shall pay an arbitration fee in advance according to the Arbitration Fee Schedule of the CIETAC within a specified time period.

4. Where the formalities required for filing a counterclaim are found to be complete, the CIETAC shall send the Statement of Counterclaim and its attachments to the Claimant. The Claimant shall, within thirty (30) days from the date of receipt of the Statement of Counterclaim and the attachment, submit in writing its Statement of Defense to the Respondent's counterclaim.

5. The arbitral tribunal has the power to decide whether to accept a Statement of Defense submitted after expiration of the above time limit.

6. Failure of the Claimant to file a Statement of Defense to the Respondent's counterclaim shall not operate to affect the arbitral proceedings.

Article 14 Amendments to the Claim or Counterclaim

The Claimant may amend its claim and the Respondent may amend its counterclaim. However, the arbitral tribunal may not permit any such amendment if it considers that the amendment is too late and may delay the arbitral proceedings.

Article 15 Copies of Submissions

When submitting the Request for Arbitration, the Statement of Defense, the Statement of Counterclaim, evidence and other documents, the parties shall make the submissions in quintuplicate. Where there are more than two parties, additional copies shall be provided accordingly. Where the arbitral tribunal is composed of a sole arbitrator, the number of copies submitted may be reduced by two. Where the preservation of property or protection of evidence is applied for, the party shall forward one additional copy accordingly.

Article 16 Representation

1. A party may be represented by its authorised representative(s) in handling matters relating to the arbitration. In such a case, a Power of Attorney shall be forwarded to the CIETAC by the party or its authorised representative(s).

2. Either Chinese or foreign citizens may be authorised by a party to act as its representative(s).

Article 17 Preservation of Property

When any party applies for the preservation of property, the CIETAC shall forward the party's application for a ruling to the competent court at the place where the domicile of the party against whom the preservation of property is sought is located or where the property of the said party is located.

Article 18 Protection of Evidence

When a party applies for the protection of evidence, the CIETAC shall forward the party's application for a ruling to the competent court at the place where the evidence is located.

Section 2: The Arbitral Tribunal

Article 19 Duties of Arbitrator

An arbitrator shall not represent either party and shall remain independent of the parties and treat them equally.

Article 20 Number of Arbitrators

1. The arbitral tribunal shall be composed of one or three arbitrators.

2. Unless otherwise agreed by the parties or provided by these Rules, the arbitral tribunal shall be composed of three arbitrators.

Article 21 Panel of Arbitrators

1. The parties shall appoint arbitrators from the Panel of Arbitrators provided by the CIETAC.

2. Where the parties have agreed to appoint arbitrators from outside of the CIETAC's Panel of Arbitrators, the arbitrators so appointed by the parties or nominated according to the agreement of the parties may act as co-arbitrator, presiding arbitrator or sole arbitrator after the appointment has been confirmed by the Chairman of the CIETAC in accordance with the law.

Article 22 Three Arbitrators

1. Within fifteen (15) days from the date of receipt of the Notice of Arbitration, the Claimant and the Respondent shall each appoint one arbitrator or entrust the Chairman of the CIETAC to make such appointment. Where a party fails to appoint or to entrust the Chairman of the CIETAC to appoint an arbitrator within the specified time period, the arbitrator shall be appointed by the Chairman of the CIETAC.

2. Within fifteen (15) days from the date of the Respondent's receipt of the Notice of Arbitration, the presiding arbitrator shall be jointly appointed by the parties or appointed by the Chairman of the CIETAC upon the parties' joint authorisation.

3. The parties may each recommend one to three arbitrators as candidates for the presiding arbitrator and shall submit the list of recommended candidates to the CIETAC within the time period specified in para 2. Where there is only one common candidate in the lists, such candidate shall be the presiding arbitrator jointly appointed by the parties. Where there are more than one common candidate in the lists, the Chairman of the CIETAC shall choose a presiding arbitrator from among the common candidates based on the specific nature and circumstances of the case, who shall act as the presiding arbitrator jointly appointed by the parties. Where there is no common candidate in the lists, the presiding arbitrator shall be appointed by the Chairman of the CIETAC from outside of the lists of recommended candidates.

4. Where the parties have failed to jointly appoint the presiding arbitrator according to the above provisions, the presiding arbitrator shall be appointed by the Chairman of the CIETAC.

Article 23 Sole Arbitrator

Where the arbitral tribunal is composed of one arbitrator, the sole arbitrator shall be appointed pursuant to the procedure stipulated in Paras 2, 3 and 4 of Art.22.

Article 24 Multi-Party

1. Where there are two or more Claimants and/or Respondents in an arbitration case, the Claimant side and/or the Respondent side each shall, through consultation, jointly appoint or jointly entrust the Chairman of the CIETAC to appoint one arbitrator from the CIETAC's Panel of Arbitrators.

2. Where the Claimant side and/or the Respondent side fail to jointly appoint or jointly entrust the Chairman of the CIETAC to appoint one arbitrator within fifteen (15) days from the date of receipt of the Notice of Arbitration, the arbitrator shall be appointed by the Chairman of the CIETAC.

3. The presiding arbitrator or the sole arbitrator shall be appointed in accordance with the procedure stipulated in Paras 2, 3 and 4 of art.22. When appointing the presiding arbitrator or the sole arbitrator pursuant to Para 3 of art.22, the Claimant side and/or the Respondent side each shall, through consultation, submit a list of their jointly agreed candidates to the CIETAC.

Article 25 Disclosure

1. An arbitrator appointed by the parties or by the Chairman of the CIETAC shall sign a Declaration and disclose to the CIETAC in writing any facts or circumstances likely to give rise to justifiable doubts as to his/her impartiality or independence.

2. If circumstances that need to be disclosed arise during the arbitral proceedings, the arbitrator shall promptly disclose such circumstances in writing to the CIETAC.

3. The CIETAC shall communicate the Declaration and/or the disclosure of the arbitrator to the parties.

Article 26 Challenge of Arbitrators

1. Upon receipt of the Declaration and/or written disclosure of an arbitrator communicated by the CIETAC, a party who intends to challenge the arbitrator on the grounds of the facts or circumstances disclosed by the arbitrator shall forward the challenge in writing to the CIETAC within ten (10) days from the date of such receipt. If a party fails to file a challenge within the above time limit, it shall not challenge an arbitrator later on the basis of matters disclosed by the arbitrator.

2. A party who has justifiable doubts as to the impartiality or independence of an appointed arbitrator may make a request in writing to the CIETAC for that arbitrator's withdrawal. In the request, the facts and reasons on which the request is based shall be stated with supporting evidence.

3. A party may challenge an arbitrator in writing within fifteen (15) days from the date of its receipt of the Notice of Formation of the Arbitral Tribunal. Where a party becomes aware of the reasons for a challenge after the said receipt, the party may challenge the arbitrator in writing within fifteen (15) days after such reasons become known, but no later than the conclusion of the last oral hearing.

4. The CIETAC shall promptly communicate the challenge to the other party, the arbitrator being challenged and the other members of the arbitral tribunal.

5. Where an arbitrator is challenged by one party and the other party agrees to the challenge, or the arbitrator being challenged withdraws from his/her office, such arbitrator shall no longer be on the arbitral tribunal. Neither case implies that the challenge made by the party is sustainable.

6. In circumstances other than those specified in Para 5, the Chairman of the CIETAC shall make a final decision on the challenge with or without stating the reasons therefore.

7. An arbitrator who has been challenged shall continue to fulfill the functions of arbitrator until a decision on the challenge has been made by the Chairman of the CIETAC.

Article 27 Replacement of Arbitrator

1. In the event that an arbitrator is prevented de jure or de facto from fulfilling his/her functions, or he/she fails to fulfill his/her functions in accordance with the requirements of these Rules or within the time period specified in these Rules, the Chairman of the CIETAC shall have the power to decide whether the arbitrator shall be replaced. The arbitrator may also withdraw form his/her office.

2. In the event that an arbitrator is unable to fulfill his/her functions owing to his/her demise, removal from the CIETAC's Panel of Arbitrators, withdrawal, resignation or any other reasons, a substitute arbitrator shall be appointed within a time period specified by the CIETAC pursuant to the procedure applied to the appointment of the arbitrator being replaced.

3. After the replacement of the arbitrator, the arbitral tribunal shall decide whether the whole or a part of the previous proceedings of the case shall be repeated.

4. The Chairman of the CIETAC shall make a final decision on whether an arbitrator should be replaced or not with or without stating the reasons therefore.

Article 28 Majority to Continue Arbitration

In the event that, after the conclusion of the last oral hearing, an arbitrator on a three-member arbitral tribunal is unable to participate in the deliberation and/or render the award owing to his/her demise or removal from the CIETAC's Panel of Arbitrators, the other two arbitrators may request the Chairman of the CIETAC to replace the arbitrator pursuant to art.27. After consulting with the parties and upon the approval of the Chairman of the CIETAC, the other two arbitrators may continue the arbitration and make decisions, rulings or the award. The Secretariat of the CIETAC shall notify the parties of the above circumstances.

Section 3: Hearing

Article 29 Conduct of Hearing

1. The arbitral tribunal shall examine the case in any way that it deems appropriate unless otherwise agreed by the parties. Under any circumstance, the arbitral tribunal shall act impartially and fairly and shall afford reasonable opportunities to all parties for presentations and debates.

2. The arbitral tribunal shall hold oral hearings when examining the case. However, oral hearings may be omitted and the case shall be examined on the basis of documents only if the parties so request or agree and the arbitral tribunal also deems that oral hearings are unnecessary.

3. Unless otherwise agreed by the parties, the arbitral tribunal may adopt an inquisitorial or adversarial approach when examining the case, having regard to the circumstances of the case.

4. The arbitral tribunal may hold deliberation at any place or in any manner that it considers appropriate.

5. The arbitral tribunal may, if it considers it necessary, issue procedural directions and lists of questions, hold pre-hearing meetings and preliminary hearings, and produce terms of reference, etc., unless otherwise agreed by the parties.

Article 30 Notice of Oral Hearings

1. The date of the first oral hearing shall be fixed by the arbitral tribunal and notified to the parties by the Secretariat of the CIETAC at least twenty (20) days in advance of the oral hearing date. A party having justified reasons may request a postponement of the oral hearing. However, such request must be communicated to the arbitral tribunal at least ten (10) days in advance of the oral hearing date. The arbitral tribunal shall decide whether to postpone the oral hearing or not.

2. A notice of oral hearing subsequent to the first oral hearing and a notice of a postponed oral hearing shall not be subject to the twenty (20)-day time limit provided for in the foregoing paragraph.

Article 31 Place of Arbitration

1. Where the parties have agreed on the place of arbitration in writing, the parties' agreement shall prevail.

2. Where the parties have not agreed on the place of arbitration, the place of arbitration shall be the domicile of the CIETAC or its Sub-Commission.

3. The arbitral award shall be deemed as being made at the place of arbitration.

Article 32 Place of Oral Hearing

1. Where the parties have agreed on the place of oral hearings, the case shall be heard at that agreed place except for circumstances stipulated in Para 3 of art.69 of these Rules.

2. Unless the parties agree otherwise, a case accepted by the CIETAC shall be heard in Beijing, or if the arbitral tribunal considers it necessary, at other places with the approval of the Secretary-General of the CIETAC. A case accepted by a Sub-Commission of the CIETAC shall be heard at the place where the Sub-Commission is located, or if the arbitral tribunal considers it necessary, at other places with the approval of the Secretary-General of the Sub-Commission.

Article 33 Confidentiality

1. Hearings shall be held in camera. Where both parties request an open hearing, the arbitral tribunal shall make a decision.

2. For cases heard in camera, the parties, their representatives, witnesses, interpreters, arbitrators, experts consulted by the arbitral tribunal and appraisers appointed by the arbitral tribunal and the relevant staff-members of the Secretariat of the CIETAC shall not disclose to any outsiders any substantive or procedural matters of the case.

Article 34 Default

1. If the Claimant fails to appear at an oral hearing without showing sufficient cause for such failure, or withdraws from an on-going oral hearing without the permission of the arbitral tribunal, the Claimant may be deemed to have withdrawn its Request for Arbitration. In such a case, if the Respondent has filed a counterclaim, the arbitral tribunal shall proceed with the hearing of the counterclaim and make a default award.

2. If the Respondent fails to appear at an oral hearing without showing sufficient cause for such failure, or withdraws from an on-going oral hearing without the permission of the arbitral tribunal, the arbitral tribunal may proceed with the arbitration and make a default award. In such a case, if the Respondent has filed a counterclaim, the Respondent may be deemed to have withdrawn its counterclaim.

Article 35 Record of Oral Hearing

1. During the oral hearing, the arbitral tribunal may arrange a stenographic and/or audio-visual record. The arbitral tribunal may, when it considers it necessary, take minutes stating the main points of the oral hearing and request the parties and/or their representatives, witnesses and/or other persons involved to sign and/or affix their seals to the minutes.

2. The stenographic and/or audio-visual record of the oral hearing shall be available for the use and reference by the arbitral tribunal.

Article 36 Evidence

1. Each party shall have the burden of proving the facts relied on to support its claim, defense or counterclaim.

2. The arbitral tribunal may specify a time period for the parties to produce evidence and the parties shall produce evidence within the specified time period. The arbitral tribunal may refuse to admit any evidence produced beyond the period. If a party has difficulties to produce evidence within the specified time period, it may apply for an extension before the expiration of the period. The arbitral tribunal shall decide whether or not to extend the time period.

3. If a party having the burden of proof fails to produce evidence within the specified time period, or the produced evidence is not sufficient to support its claim or counterclaim, it shall bear the consequences thereof.

Article 37 Investigation by the Arbitral Tribunal

1. The arbitral tribunal may, on its own initiative, undertake investigations and collect evidence as it considers necessary.

2.   When investigating and collecting evidence by itself, the arbitral tribunal shall promptly notify the parties to be present at such investigation if it considers it necessary. In the event that one or both parties fail to be present, the investigation and collection shall proceed without being affected.

3.   The arbitral tribunal shall, through the Secretariat of the CIETAC, transmit the evidence collected by itself to the parties and afford them an opportunity to comment.

Article 38 Expert's Report and Appraiser's Report

1.   The arbitral tribunal may consult or appoint experts and appraisers for clarification on specific issues of a case. Such an expert or appraiser may either be a Chinese or foreign organisation or citizen.

2.   The arbitral tribunal has the power to request the parties to deliver or produce to the expert or appraiser any relevant materials, documents, or property and goods for checking, inspection and/or appraisal. The parties shall be obliged to comply.

3.   Copies of the expert's report and the appraiser's report shall be communicated to the parties, who shall be given an opportunity to comment on the report. At the request of either party and with the approval of the arbitral tribunal, the expert and appraiser may be heard at an oral hearing where, if considered necessary and appropriate by the arbitral tribunal, they may give explanations on their reports.

Article 39 Examination of Evidence

1.   All evidence submitted by a party shall be filed with the Secretariat of the CIETAC for transmission to the other party.

2.   Where a case is examined by way of an oral hearing, the evidence shall be exhibited at the hearing and examined by the parties.

3.   In the event that evidence is submitted after the hearing and the arbitral tribunal decides to admit the evidence without holding further hearings, the arbitral tribunal may require the parties to submit their opinions thereon in writing within a specified time period.

Article 40 Combination of Conciliation with Arbitration

1.   Where the parties have reached a settlement agreement by themselves through negotiation or conciliation without involving the CIETAC, either party may, based on an arbitration agreement concluded between them that provides for arbitration by the CIETAC and the settlement agreement, request the CIETAC to constitute an arbitral tribunal to render an arbitral award in accordance with the terms of the settlement agreement. Unless the parties agree otherwise,

the Chairman of the CIETAC shall appoint a sole arbitrator to form such arbitral tribunal, which shall examine the case in the procedure it considers appropriate and render an award in due course. The specific procedure and the time limit for rendering the award shall not be subject to other provisions of these Rules.

2.   Where both parties have the desire for conciliation or one party so desires and the other party agrees when approached by the arbitral tribunal, the arbitral tribunal may conciliate the case during the course of the arbitration proceedings.

3.   The arbitral tribunal may conciliate the case in the manner it considers appropriate.

4.   The arbitral tribunal shall terminate the conciliation and continue the arbitration proceedings if one of the parties requests a termination of the conciliation or if the arbitral tribunal believes that further efforts to conciliate will be futile.

5.   A settlement agreement reached between the parties during the course of conciliation by the arbitral tribunal but without the involvement of the arbitral tribunal shall be deemed as one reached through the conciliation by the arbitral tribunal.

6.   Where settlement is reached through conciliation by the arbitral tribunal, the parties shall sign a written settlement agreement. Unless otherwise agreed by the parties, the arbitral tribunal will close the case and render an arbitral award in accordance with the terms of the settlement agreement.

7.   Where conciliation fails, the arbitral tribunal shall proceed with the arbitration and render an arbitral award.

8.   Where conciliation fails, any opinion, view or statement and any proposal or proposition expressing acceptance or opposition by either party or by the arbitral tribunal in the process of conciliation shall not be invoked as grounds for any claim, defense or counterclaim in the subsequent arbitration proceedings, judicial proceedings or any other proceedings.

Article 41 Withdrawal and Dismissal

1.   A party may file a request with the CIETAC to withdraw its claim or counterclaim in its entirety. In the event that the Claimant withdraws its claim in its entirety, the arbitral tribunal shall proceed with its examination of the counterclaim and render an arbitral award thereon. In the event that the Respondent withdraws its counterclaim in its entirety, the arbitral tribunal shall proceed with the examination of the claim and render an arbitral award thereon.

2.   Where a case is to be dismissed before the formation of the arbitral tribunal, the decision shall be made by the Secretary-General of the CIETAC. Where

the case is to be dismissed after the formation of the arbitral tribunal, the decision shall be made by the arbitral tribunal.

3. Where a party files with the CIETAC a request for arbitration for a claim which has been withdrawn, the CIETAC shall decide whether or not to accept the request anew.

.

Chapter 3

Arbitral Award

Article 42 Time Limits

1. The arbitral tribunal shall render an arbitral award within six (6) months as from the date on which the arbitral tribunal is formed.

2. Upon the request of the arbitral tribunal, the Chairman of the CIETAC may extend said time period if he/she considers it truly necessary and the reasons for the extension truly justified.

Article 43 Making Award

1. The arbitral tribunal shall independently and impartially make its arbitral award on the basis of the facts, in accordance with the law and the terms of the contracts, with reference to international practices and in compliance with the principle of fairness and reasonableness.

2. The arbitral tribunal shall state in the award the claims, the facts of the dispute, the reasons on which the award is based, the result of the award, the allocation of the arbitration costs and the date on which and the place at which the award is made. The facts of the dispute and the reasons on which the award is based may not be stated in the award if the parties have agreed so, or if the award is made in accordance with the terms of a settlement agreement between the parties. The arbitral tribunal has the power to determine in the arbitral award the specific time period for the parties to execute the award and the liabilities to be borne by a party failing to execute the award within the specified time.

3. The CIETAC's stamp shall be affixed to the award.

4. Where a case is examined by an arbitral tribunal composed of three arbitrators, the award shall be rendered by all three arbitrators or a majority of the arbitrators. A written dissenting opinion shall be docketed into the file and may be attached to the award, but it shall not form a part of the award.

5. Where the arbitral tribunal cannot reach a majority opinion, the award shall be rendered in accordance with the presiding arbitrator's opinion. The written opinion of other arbitrators shall be docketed into the file and may be attached to the award, but it shall not form a part of the award.

6. Unless the award is made in accordance with the opinion of the presiding arbitrator or the sole arbitrator, the arbitral award shall be signed by a majority of arbitrators. An arbitrator who has a dissenting opinion may or may not sign his/her name on the award.

7. The date on which the award is made shall be the date on which the award comes into legal effect.

8. The arbitral award is final and binding upon both parties. Neither party may bring a suit before a law court or make a request to any other organisation for revising the award.

Article 44 Interlocutory Award and Partial Award

An interlocutory arbitral award or partial award may be made by the arbitral tribunal on any issue of the case at any time during the arbitration before the final award is made if considered necessary by the arbitral tribunal, or if the parties request and the arbitral tribunal accepts. Either party's failure to perform the interlocutory award will not affect the continuation of the arbitration proceedings, nor will it prevent the arbitral tribunal from making a final award.

Article 45 Scrutiny of Draft Award

The arbitral tribunal shall submit its draft award to the CIETAC for scrutiny before signing the award. The CIETAC may remind the arbitral tribunal of issues in the award on condition that the arbitral tribunal's independence in rendering the award is not affected.

Article 46 Fees

1. The arbitral tribunal has the power to determine in the arbitral award the arbitration fee and other expenses to be paid by the parties to the CIETAC.

2. The arbitral tribunal has the power to decide in the award, according to the specific circumstances of the case, that the losing party shall compensate the winning party for the expenses reasonably incurred by it in pursuing its case. In deciding whether the winning party's expenses incurred in pursuing its case are reasonable, the arbitral tribunal shall consider such factors as the outcome and complexity of the case, the workload of the winning party and/or its representative(s), and the amount in dispute, etc.

Article 47 Correction of Award

Within thirty (30) days from its receipt of the arbitral award, either party may request in writing for a correction of any clerical, typographical, or calculation errors or any errors of a similar nature contained in the award; if such an error does exist in the award, the arbitral tribunal shall make a correction in writing within thirty (30) days from the date of receipt of the written request for the correction. The arbitral tribunal may likewise correct any such errors in writing on its own initiative within a reasonable time after the award is issued. Such correction in writing shall form a part of the arbitral award.

Article 48 Additional Award

Within thirty (30) days from the date on which the arbitral award is received, either party may request the arbitral tribunal in writing for an additional award on any claim or counterclaim which was advanced in the arbitration proceedings but was omitted from the award. If such omission does exist, the arbitral tribunal shall make an additional award within thirty (30) days from the date of receipt of the written request. The arbitral tribunal may also make an additional award on its own initiative within a reasonable period of time after the arbitral award is issued. Such additional award shall form a part of the arbitral award previously rendered.

Article 49 Execution of Award

1. The parties must automatically execute the arbitral award within the time period specified in the award. If no time limit is specified in the award, the parties shall execute the arbitral award immediately.

2. Where one party fails to execute the award, the other party may apply to a competent Chinese court for enforcement of the award pursuant to Chinese laws, or apply to a competent court for enforcement of the award according to the 1958 United Nations Convention on Recognition and Enforcement of Foreign Arbitral Awards or other international treaties that China has concluded or acceded to.

Chapter 4

Summary Procedure

Article 50 Application

1. Unless otherwise agreed by the parties, this Summary Procedure shall apply to any case where the amount in dispute does not exceed RMB 500, 000 yuan, or to any case where the amount in dispute exceeds RMB 500, 000 yuan, yet one party applies for arbitration under this Summary Procedure and the other party agrees in writing.

2. Where no monetary claim is specified or the amount in dispute is not clear, the CIETAC shall determine whether or not to apply the Summary Procedure after a full consideration of such factors as the complexity of the case and the interests involved, etc.

Article 51 Notice of Arbitration

Where a Request for Arbitration is submitted to the CIETAC and is found to be acceptable for arbitration under the Summary Procedure, the Secretariat of the CIETAC or its Sub-Commission shall send a Notice of Arbitration to the parties.

Article 52 Formation of Arbitral Tribunal

An arbitral tribunal of a sole arbitrator shall be formed in accordance with art.23 of these Rules to hear a case under the Summary Procedure.

Article 53 Statement of Defense and Counterclaim

1.   Within twenty (20) days from the date of receipt of the Notice of Arbitration, the Respondent shall submit its Statement of Defense and relevant evidence to the Secretariat of the CIETAC; counterclaims, if any, shall also be filed with supporting evidence within the said time period. The arbitral tribunal may extend this time period if it considers it justified.

2.   Within twenty (20) days from the date of receipt of the counterclaim and its attachments, the Claimant shall file its Statement of Defense to the Respondent's counterclaim.

Article 54 Conduct of Hearing

The arbitral tribunal may examine the case in the manner it considers appropriate. The arbitral tribunal may in its full discretion decide to examine the case only on the basis of the written materials and evidence submitted by the parties or to hold oral hearings.

Article 55 Oral Hearing

1.   For a case examined by way of an oral hearing, the Secretariat of the CIETAC shall, after the arbitral tribunal has fixed a date for the oral hearing, notify the parties of the date at least fifteen (15) days in advance of the oral hearing date. A party having justified reasons may request the arbitral tribunal for a postponement of the oral hearing. However, such request must be communicated to the arbitral tribunal at least seven (7) days in advance of the oral hearing date. The arbitral tribunal shall decide whether to postpone the oral hearing or not.

2.   Where the arbitral tribunal decides to hear the case orally, only one oral hearing shall be held unless it is otherwise truly necessary.

3.   A notice of oral hearing subsequent to the first oral hearing and a notice of a postponed oral hearing shall not be subject to the fifteen (15)-day time limit provided for in the foregoing Para 1.

Article 56 Time Limits for Rendering Award

1.   The arbitral tribunal shall render an arbitral award within three (3) months from the date on which the arbitral tribunal is formed.

2.   Upon the request of the arbitral tribunal, the Chairman of the CIETAC may extend the time period if he/she considers it truly necessary and the reasons for the extension truly justified.

Article 57 Change of Procedure

The application of the Summary Procedure shall not be affected by any amendment to the claim or by the filing of a counterclaim. Where the amount in dispute of the amended claim or that of the counterclaim exceeds RMB 500,000 Yuan, the procedure of the case shall be changed from the Summary Procedure to the general procedure unless the parties have agreed to the continuous application of the Summary Procedure.

Article 58 Context Reference

As to matters not covered in this Chapter, the relevant provisions in the other Chapters of these Rules shall apply.

Chapter 5

Special Provisions for Domestic Arbitration

Article 59 Application

1. The provisions of this Chapter shall apply to domestic arbitration cases accepted by the CIEATC.

2. The provisions of the Summary Procedure of Chapter IV shall apply if a domestic arbitration case falls within the scope of art.50 of these Rules.

Article 60 Acceptance

1. Where a Request for Arbitration is found to meet the formality requirements specified in art.10 of these Rules, the CIETAC shall accept the Request and notify the parties accordingly within five (5) days from its receipt of the Request or immediately upon its receipt of the Request. Where a Request for Arbitration is found not in conformity with the formality requirements, the CIETAC shall notify the party in writing of its refusal of the Request with reasons stated.

2. Upon receipt of a Request for Arbitration, the CIETAC may request the party to make corrections within a specified time period if it finds the Request is not in conformity with the provisions of art.10 of these Rules.

Article 61 Formation of Arbitral Tribunal

The arbitral tribunal shall be formed in accordance with the provisions of arts.21, 22, 23 and 24 of these Rules.

Article 62 Statement of Defense and Counterclaim

1. Within twenty (20) days from the date of receipt of the Notice of Arbitration, the Respondent shall submit its Statement of Defense and relevant evidence to the CIETAC; counterclaims, if any, shall also be filed with supporting evidence within the said time period. The arbitral tribunal may extend this time period if it considers it justified.

2. Within twenty (20) days from the date of receipt of the counterclaim and its attachments, the Claimant shall file its Statement of Defense to the Respondent's counterclaim.

Article 63 Notice of Oral Hearing

1.   For a case examined by way of an oral hearing, the Secretariat of the CIETAC or its Sub-Commission shall notify the parties of the date of oral hearing at least fifteen (15) days in advance of the oral hearing date. The arbitral tribunal may hold the oral hearing ahead of the schedule with consent from both parties. A party having justified reasons may request the arbitral tribunal for a postponement of the oral hearing. However, such request must be communicated to the arbitral tribunal seven (7) days in advance of the oral hearing date. The arbitral tribunal shall decide whether to postpone the oral hearing or not.

2.   A notice of oral hearing subsequent to the first oral hearing and a notice of a postponed oral hearing shall not be subject to the fifteen (15)-day time limit provided in the foregoing Para 1.

Article 64 Record of Oral Hearing

1.   The arbitral tribunal shall make a brief written record of the oral hearing. Any party or participant in the arbitration may apply for a correction of the record if any omission or mistake is found in the record regarding its own statement. If the application is refused by the arbitral tribunal, it shall nevertheless be recorded into the file.

2.   The written record shall be signed or sealed by the arbitrator(s), the recorder, the parties, and other participants in the arbitration, if any.

Article 65 Time Limits for Rendering Award

1.   The arbitral tribunal shall render an award within four (4) months from the date on which the arbitral tribunal is formed.

2.   Upon the request of the arbitral tribunal, the Chairman of the CIETAC may extend this time period if he/she considers it truly necessary and the reasons truly justified.

Article 66 Context Reference

As to matters not covered in this Chapter, the relevant provisions in the other Chapters of these Rules shall apply.

Chapter 6

Supplementary Provisions

Article 67 Language

1.   Where the parties have agreed on the arbitration language, their agreement shall prevail. Absent such agreement, the Chinese language shall be the official language to be used in the arbitration proceedings.

2. At an oral hearing, if a party or its representative(s) or witness requires language interpretation, the Secretariat of the CIETAC or its Sub-Commission may provide an interpreter, or the party may bring its own interpreter.

3. The arbitral tribunal and/or the Secretariat of the CIETAC or its Sub-Commission may, if it considers necessary, request the parties to submit a corresponding version of the documents and evidence by the parties in Chinese or in other languages.

Article 68 Service of Documents

1. All documents, notices and written materials in relation to the arbitration may be sent to the parties and/or their representatives in person, or by registered mail or express mail, facsimile, telex, cable, or by any other means considered proper by the Secretariat of the CIETAC or its Sub-Commission.

2. Any written correspondence to a party and/or its representative(s) shall be deemed to have been properly served on the party if delivered to the addressee or delivered at his place of business, registration, domicile, habitual residence or mailing address, or where, after reasonable inquiries by the other party, none of the aforesaid addresses can be found, the written correspondence is sent by the Secretariat of the CIETAC or its Sub-Commission to the addressee's last known place of business, registered address, domicile, habitual residence or mailing address by registered mail or by any other means that provides a record of the attempt of delivery.

Article 69 Arbitration Fees and Actual Expenses

1. Apart from charging arbitration fees to the parties according to the Fee Schedule of the CIETAC, the CIETAC may collect from the parties other extra, reasonable and actual expenses including arbitrators' special remuneration and their travel and accommodation expenses incurred in dealing with the case, as well as the costs and expenses of experts, appraisers and interpreters appointed by the arbitral tribunal, etc.

2. Where a party has appointed an arbitrator who will incur extra expenses, such as travel and accommodation expenses, and fails to pay in advance as a deposit within a time period specified by the CIETAC, the party shall be deemed not to have appointed the arbitrator. In such event, the Chairman of the CIETAC may appoint an arbitrator for the party pursuant to art.22 or art.23 of these Rules.

3. Where the parties have agreed to hold an oral hearing at a place other than the CIETAC's domicile, extra expenses including travel and accommodation expenses incurred thereby shall be paid in advance as a deposit by the parties. In the event that the parties fail to do so, the oral hearing shall be held at the domicile of the CIETAC.

Article 70 Interpretation

1. The headings of the articles in these Rules shall not serve as interpretations of the contents of the provisions contained herein.

2. These Rules shall be interpreted by the CIETAC.

Article 71 Coming into Force

These Rules shall be effective as from 1 May 2005. For cases accepted by the CIETAC or by its Sub-Commissions before these Rules become effective, the Arbitration Rules effective at the time of acceptance shall apply, or these Rules shall apply where both parties agree.

Beijing Arbitration Commission Arbitration Rules

(Revised and adopted at the First Meeting of the Fifth Session of the Beijing Arbitration Commission on 20 September 2007. Effective as from 1 April 2008)

Chapter 1

General Provisions

Article 1 The Beijing Arbitration Commission

1. The Beijing Arbitration Commission the BAC. is an arbitration institution registered in Beijing, China for resolving contractual disputes and other disputes over rights and interests in property between natural persons, legal persons and other organisations.

2. The Chairman of the BAC the Chairman. or, with the authorisation of the Chairman, one of the Vice-Chairmen or Secretary-General of the BAC, shall perform the duties and obligations stipulated by the Arbitration Rules of the BAC the Rules..

3. The Secretariat of the BAC the Secretariat. shall handle the day-to-day affairs of the BAC. A member of its staff shall be appointed as the secretary of an Arbitral Tribunal to assist with case management, including administration of procedural matters.

Article 2 Application of the Rules

1. Where parties to a dispute provide for arbitration of the dispute by the BAC, these Rules shall apply, save to the extent that the parties have agreed to the application of a different procedure or a different set of arbitration rules, in which case their agreement must comply with the mandatory law of Arbitration seat and be enforceable.

2. Where the parties agree to apply the BAC rules, but do not choose a specific arbitration institution, they shall be deemed to agree to provide their disputes to the BAC.

Article 3 Waiver of Right to Object

A party who knows or should have known that any provision of these Rules or any term of the arbitration agreement has not been complied with, but nevertheless participates in the arbitration without promptly raising its objection to such non-compliance in writing shall be deemed to have waived its right to object.

Chapter 2

Arbitration Agreement

Article 4 Definition and Form of Arbitration Agreement

1. An arbitration agreement is an agreement by parties to submit to arbitration all or certain disputes which have arisen or which may arise in connection with the legal relationship between the parties. An arbitration agreement includes an arbitration clause in a contract or any other written agreement to arbitrate.

2. An arbitration agreement shall be in written form, including but not limited to contractual instruments, letters and electronic data messages including telegrams, telexes, facsimiles, EDIs and e-mails. and any other forms of communication where the contents are visible.

Article 5 Separability of Arbitration Agreement

An arbitration agreement shall be independent of and separate from the principal contract in which it is contained. The validity of an arbitration agreement shall not be affected by the modification, rescission, termination, invalidity, expiry, non-effectiveness, revocation, or non-establishment of the principal contract.

Article 6 Objections to Validity of Arbitration Agreement

1. A jurisdictional objection or an objection to the validity of an arbitration agreement shall be raised in writing before the first hearing. For a documents-only arbitration, the written objection shall be raised prior to the expiry of the time limit for the submission of the first defence.

2. If a party has not raised any objections pursuant to the provisions of the preceding paragraph, it shall be deemed to have accepted that the arbitration agreement is valid and that the BAC has jurisdiction over the arbitration.

3. If a party objects to the validity of an arbitration agreement, it may make an application to either the BAC or the competent People's Court for a decision on the issue. If one party makes an application to the BAC while the other party to the People's Court, then the objection shall be decided upon by the People's Court.

4. The BAC or, if authorised by the BAC, the Arbitral Tribunal, shall have the power to rule on jurisdictional objections and objections to the validity of an arbitration agreement. The Arbitral Tribunal can deliver its decision in the form of either an interim award or a final award.

Chapter 3

Application for Arbitration, Defence and Counterclaim

Article 7 Application for Arbitration

1. A party applying for arbitration shall submit the following documents collectively the Application for Arbitration.:

(a) the arbitration agreement;

(b) its Statement of Claim, containing the following information:

  (i) the names, addresses, zip codes, telephone numbers, facsimile numbers and any other convenient means of contact of the Claimant and the Respondent; (where a party concerned is a legal person or organisation, the name, position, address, zip code, telephone number, facsimile number and any other convenient means of contact of the legal representative or the person in charge);

  (ii) the claims and the facts and grounds on which the claims are based;

(c) evidence and the source of those evidence (together with a list thereof), and the names and addresses of its witnesses; and

(d) proof of the Claimant's identity.

2. A party applying for arbitration shall deposit an advance on costs, calculated in accordance with the provisions of the Arbitration Fee Schedule. An application for deferment of the deposit can be made to the BAC in the event of hardship. The BAC shall decide on such applications. If a party applying for arbitration has neither deposited the advance on costs nor applied for deferment, it shall be deemed to have withdrawn its Application for Arbitration.

Article 8 Case Acceptance

1. The BAC shall accept the Application for Arbitration within five days of its receipt if it finds that the requisite requirements for acceptance are met.

2. The applicant shall rectify its Application for Arbitration if it does not fulfill the requirements stipulated by art.7.

3. The arbitral proceedings shall be deemed to commence on the date of acceptance of the Application for Arbitration by the BAC.

Article 9 Notice of Arbitration

Within 10 days of the acceptance of the Application for Arbitration, the BAC shall send to the Claimant a Notice of Case Acceptance, a set of the Rules and the BAC's Panel of Arbitrators. The BAC shall send to the Respondent a Request for Submission of Defence, as well as a copy of the Application for Arbitration, its attachments, if any, a set of these Rules, and the BAC's Panel of Arbitrators.

Article 10 Defence

1. Within 15 days of the receipt of the Request for Submission of Defence, the Respondent shall submit to the BAC such documents listed below:

(a) Statement of Defence clarifying information listed below:

  (i) the names, addresses, zip codes, telephone numbers, facsimile numbers and any other convenient means of contact of the Respondent; (where a party concerned is a legal person or organisation, the name, position, address, zip code, telephone number, facsimile number and any other convenient means of contact of the legal representative or the person in charge);

(ii) the key points of its defence and the facts and grounds on which the defence is based;

(b) evidence and the source of the evidence (together with a list thereof), and the names and addresses of its witnesses; and

(c) proof of the Respondent's identity.

2. Within 10 days of the receipt of the Statement of Defence, the BAC shall send a copy of the Statement of Defence to the Claimant.

3. The progress of the arbitral proceedings shall not be affected by any party's failure to submit its Statement of Defence.

Article 11 Counterclaim

1. Within 15 days of the receipt of the Request for Submission of Defence, the Respondent shall submit to the BAC its Counterclaim. If the Counterclaim is not submitted within the stipulated period of time, the Arbitral Tribunal, or if the Arbitral Tribunal has not been constituted, the BAC, shall decide whether to accept the Counterclaim.

2. The provisions of art.7 shall apply to the submission of the Counterclaim.

3. Within 10 days of the acceptance of the Counterclaim, the BAC shall send to the Claimant a Request for Submission of Defence to Counterclaim, as well as the Counterclaim and its attachments, if any.

4. The provisions of art.10 shall apply to the Claimant's submission of its Statement of Defence to Counterclaim.

5. Any other items concerning the counterclaim not being stipulated by these Rules shall refer to those of application for arbitration.

Article 12 Amendment to Claim or Counterclaim

An application to amend the Claim or Counterclaim shall be made in writing. The application shall be decided by the Arbitral Tribunal, or if the Arbitral Tribunal has not been constituted, by the BAC.

Article 13 Number of Copies of Documents to be Submitted

The Statement of Claim, the Statement of Defence, the Counterclaim, evidence and other written documents should be submitted in quintuplicate. If there are more than two parties, additional copies should be provided accordingly. If the Arbitral Tribunal is composed of a sole arbitrator, the number of copies can be reduced by two.

Article 14 Preservation of Property

1. A party may apply for an order for the preservation of property if the enforcement of any award that it may obtain subsequently is likely to be impossible or difficult, as a result of the conduct of the other party or other factors.

2. If a party applies for an order for the preservation of property, the BAC shall submit the application to the competent People's Court of the place where the Respondent is domiciled or where the Respondent's property is situated.

Article 15 Preservation of Evidence

1. A party may apply for an order for the preservation of evidence if the evidence may be destroyed or lost, or may subsequently be inaccessible.

2. If a party applies for an order for the preservation of evidence, the BAC shall submit the application to the competent People's Court of the place where the evidence is located.

Article 16 Representation

Where a party is represented by its authorised representatives, a power of attorney setting out the matters specifically entrusted and the scope of the authorised representatives' authority should be submitted to the BAC.

Chapter 4

Composition of Arbitral Tribunal

Article 17 Panel of Arbitrators

Arbitrators shall be chosen by the parties from the Panel of Arbitrators maintained by the BAC.

Article 18 Appointment of Arbitrator

1. Within 15 days of the receipt of the Notice of Arbitration, the parties shall nominate or entrust the Chairman to appoint their arbitrators from the BAC's Panel of Arbitrators. If the parties fail to nominate the arbitrator in accordance with the aforementioned provisions, the arbitrator shall be appointed by the Chairman.

2. Within 15 days of the receipt of the Notice of Arbitration, the parties shall jointly nominate or jointly entrust the Chairman to appoint the presiding arbitrator. The parties may each nominate 1–3 arbitrators as the candidates for the presiding arbitrator within the time limit in accordance with the aforementioned provisions. According to the application or agreement of parties, the BAC may also provide a list of 5–7 candidates for the presiding arbitrator from which the parties shall select 1–3 as candidates within the time limit fixed by para 1 above. Where there is only one common candidate on either both parties' list of nomination or both parties' list of selection the Candidate., such candidate shall be the presiding arbitrator jointly nominated by both parties. If there are two or more such candidates, the Chairman shall, taking into consideration the specific circumstances of the case, confirm one of them as the presiding arbitrator, who shall be regarded as being jointly nominated by the parties. If there are no such candidates, the Chairman shall appoint the presiding arbitrator from outside of the lists of nomination and lists of selection.

3. If the parties fail to jointly nominate the presiding arbitrator in accordance with the aforementioned provisions, the presiding arbitrator shall be appointed by the Chairman.

4. For a party comprising two or more persons or organisations, they should, through consultations, jointly nominate or jointly entrust the Chairman to appoint the arbitrator. If, within 15 days of the receipt by the last party of the notice of arbitration, they have not agreed on the joint nomination of the arbitrator or the joint authorisation of the Chairman, the arbitrator shall be appointed by the Chairman.

5. The party shall bear the burden of the arbitrator's increased travel expense incurred necessarily by hearing the cases, if the party nominates the arbitrator living outside Beijing. If a party has not deposited the advance on expenses within the period stipulated by the BAC, it shall be deemed not to select the arbitrator. The Chairman could appoint the arbitrator for the party in accordance with these Rules.

6. The party shall re-nominate another arbitrator within five days of its receipt of the notice of re-nomination, if the arbitrator refuses to accept the party's nomination or can not attend to hear the case, due to the illness or other factors that may affect performing an arbitrator's duty.

Article 19 Notice of Constitution of Arbitral Tribunal

Within five days of the constitution of the Arbitral Tribunal, the BAC shall notify the parties accordingly. The secretary of the Arbitral Tribunal shall transmit the case file to the Arbitral Tribunal promptly thereafter.

Article 20 Disclosure by Arbitrator

1. Upon accepting the appointment, the arbitrator shall sign a declaration of independence and impartiality, a copy of which shall be transmitted to each party.

2. If an arbitrator is aware of circumstances relating to the parties or their authorised representatives, which might lead any one of the parties to doubt his independence or impartiality, the arbitrator shall disclose those circumstances in writing.

3. Within five days of the receipt of such disclosure, the parties shall state in writing if they intend to challenge the arbitrator.

4. The provisions of paras 1, 2, 4, 5, and 6 of art.21 shall apply to the challenge of an arbitrator on the basis of circumstances disclosed by the arbitrator.

5. A party who fails to challenge an arbitrator within the period of time specified in para 3 shall not be permitted to challenge the arbitrator based on the circumstances already disclosed by the arbitrator.

Article 21 Challenge of Arbitrator

1. In the circumstances set out below, the arbitrator shall have an obligation to withdraw from his appointment and the parties shall have a right to challenge the arbitrator:

(a) the arbitrator is a party to the arbitration, or a close relative of any party or any party's authorised representatives;

(b) the arbitrator has personal interests in the dispute;

(c) the arbitrator has any other relationships with any party or its authorised representatives which may affect the arbitrator's impartiality; or

(d) the arbitrator met with any party or its authorised representatives in private, or accepted from any party or its authorised representatives offers of entertainment or gift.

2. A challenge shall be made in writing and accompanied by grounds of the challenge and supporting evidence.

3. A challenge shall be raised before the first hearing. A challenge based on circumstances known after the first hearing can be raised prior to the close of the final hearing, except for the situation referred to in para 3, art.20.

4. The secretary of the Arbitral Tribunal shall promptly transmit the notice of challenge to the other party and each member of the Arbitral Tribunal.

5. When a party challenges an arbitrator and the other party agrees to the challenge, or the challenged arbitrator withdraws voluntarily upon being informed of the challenge, such arbitrator shall no longer participate in the arbitration. In neither case does it imply acceptance of the validity of the grounds for the challenge.

6. The Chairman shall decide on the challenge, except in the situation referred to in para 5. The decision of the Chairman shall be final.

7. A party who, after being aware of the composition of the Arbitral Tribunal, appoints authorised representatives who may give rise to grounds for challenge of any arbitrator as set forth in this Chapter shall be deemed to have waived its right to challenge the arbitrator on those grounds. However, the other party's right to challenge the arbitrator shall not be affected. The additional costs resulting from any delay to the arbitral proceedings shall be borne by the party responsible for causing the grounds of challenge.

Article 22 Replacement of Arbitrator

1. An arbitrator shall be replaced if the arbitrator becomes unable to conduct the arbitration as a result of death or illness, withdraws from the arbitration due to personal reasons, is ordered to withdraw from the arbitration by the Chairman or is requested by both parties to withdraw from the arbitration.

2. An arbitrator may also be replaced on the BAC's initiative if it decides that the arbitrator is prevented de jure or de facto from fulfilling functions as an arbitrator, or is not fulfilling necessary functions in accordance with the Rules.

3. Before making any decision pursuant to the provisions of para 2, the BAC shall give both parties and all members of the Arbitral Tribunal an opportunity to comment in writing.

4. If the arbitrator to be replaced was nominated by a party, that party shall re-nominate another arbitrator within five days of its receipt of the notice of replacement. If the arbitrator to be replacéd was appointed by the Chairman, the Chairman shall appoint another arbitrator and, within five days of such appointment, notify the parties of the appointment. After the nomination or appointment of a new arbitrator, the parties may request that prior arbitral proceedings be repeated, in which case the Arbitral Tribunal shall determine if such repetition is necessary. The Arbitral Tribunal may also on its own accord decide if prior arbitral proceedings shall be repeated. The time limit stipulated in arts.43, 52 and 59 shall be re-calculated from the date of the reconstitution of the Arbitral Tribunal, if the arbitral tribunal dcides to repeat the arbitral proceedings.

Chapter 5

Arbitral Proceedings

Article 23 Mode of Hearing

1. The Arbitral Tribunal shall hold a hearing to examine the case.

2. If the parties agree on documents-only arbitration, or if the Arbitral Tribunal considers a hearing to be unnecessary and has the consent of the parties, the Arbitral Tribunal may decide the case on the basis of documents submitted by the parties.

3. Regardless of the mode of hearing adopted, the Arbitral Tribunal shall treat the parties fairly and impartially and give each party a reasonable opportunity to present and argue its case.

Article 24 Confidentiality

1. An arbitration hearing shall be conducted in private, unless both parties agree otherwise. Arbitrations involving state secrets shall be conducted in private in any event.

2. Where an arbitration is conducted in private, the parties, their authorised representatives, witnesses, arbitrators, experts consulted by the Arbitral Tribunal, appraisers appointed by the Arbitral Tribunal and staff of the BAC shall not disclose to third parties any matter concerning the arbitration, whether substantive or procedural.

Article 25 Place of the Arbitration

1. The place of arbitration shall be the premises of the BAC, unless agreed upon by the parties;

2. The arbitral award shall be deemed as rendering at the place of the arbitration.

Article 26 Place of Hearing

1. Hearings shall be held at the BAC's premises, or at other locations if the parties so agree.

2.   The resulting additional costs shall be borne by the parties, if the parties agree upon hearing at other locations. The parties shall deposit an advance in the additional costs upon the proportion stipulated in their agreement or decided by the Arbitral Tribunal within the period stipulated by the BAC, or otherwise the hearing shall be held at the BAC's premises.

Article 27 Consolidation of Arbitrations

1.   The Arbitral Tribunal may, on the application of any party and with the approval of all other parties concerned, order the consolidation of two or more related arbitrations or arbitrations involving a similar subject matter.

2.   The provisions of the preceding paragraph shall not apply if the compositions of the Arbitral Tribunals are different.

Article 28 Notice of Hearing

1.   The Arbitral Tribunal shall notify the parties of the date of the first hearing at least 10 days before the hearing. The date may be brought forward with the agreement of the parties and the approval of the Arbitral Tribunal. A party may request a postponement of the date of the first hearing, at least five days before the hearing, if there are grounds justifying a postponement. The Arbitral Tribunal shall decide on the request.

2.   Notification of the date of any hearing subsequent to the first one is not subject to the 10-day requirement.

Article 29 Default of Appearance

1.   If the Claimant, having been duly notified in writing of the hearing, fails to appear at the hearing without any justifiable reason or withdraws from an ongoing hearing without the permission of the Arbitral Tribunal, the Claimant shall be deemed to have withdrawn its Application for Arbitration. Whereas it shall not affect the hearing on the Respondent's Counterclaim.

2.   If the Respondent, having been duly notified in writing of the hearing, fails to appear at the hearing without any justifiable reason or withdraws from an ongoing hearing without the permission of the Arbitral Tribunal, the Arbitral Tribunal may proceed with the hearing. Upon such failure, the Respondent shall be deemed to have withdrawn its Counterclaim if there is any.

Article 30 Production of Evidence

1.   Each party shall bear the burden of proving the facts relied upon to support its case.

2.   The Arbitral Tribunal shall have the power to require the parties to produce their evidence within a specified period of time and the parties shall comply accordingly. The Arbitral Tribunal shall have the power to reject any evidence not produced within the specified period of time, unless the parties agree otherwise.

3. If a party having the burden of proof fails to produce evidence within the specified period of time, or if the evidence produced is insufficient to discharge its burden of proof, it shall bear the consequences of such failure.

4. Each party shall properly categorise and compile the evidence it produces, state briefly the source and contents of the evidence and what the evidence is sought to prove, affix its signature and seal on the evidence list, and indicate the date on which the evidence is produced.

5. A reproduction, photograph, duplicate copy, and abridged version of a document or thing shall be deemed to be identical to the original document or thing unless the other party challenges its authenticity.

6. Unless otherwise agreed by the parties, evidence and documentation in a foreign language should be accompanied by a Chinese translation. The Arbitral Tribunal may, if necessary, require the parties to provide a translation of the evidence and documentation into Chinese or other languages.

Article 31 Collection of Evidence by Arbitral Tribunal

1. The Arbitral Tribunal may, if any party so requests or it considers necessary, undertake investigations or collect evidence. If the Arbitral Tribunal considers it necessary to require the parties' presence when it is undertaking investigations or collecting evidence, it shall promptly notify the parties. The Arbitral Tribunal may proceed with the investigations or the collection of evidence even if one or both parties fail to appear after being notified.

2. The parties may challenge the authenticity, admissibility and relevance of the evidence collected by the Arbitral Tribunal.

Article 32 Appraisal

1. If any party requests an appraisal and the Arbitral Tribunal consents, or if the Arbitral Tribunal of its own motion considers it necessary, the Arbitral Tribunal may require the parties to jointly nominate an appraisal organisation or appraisal expert within a period of time specified by the Arbitral Tribunal. If the parties fail to do so, the appraisal organisation or appraisal expert shall be appointed by the Arbitral Tribunal.

2. The parties shall deposit an advance in appraisal costs according to the agreement by the parties or the proportion confirmed by the Tribunal. The Tribunal has the power to decide not to carry out the appraisal, if the parties do not deposit an advance in costs.

3. The Arbitral Tribunal shall have the power to require the parties to produce to the appraiser any document, material, property or any other article required for the appraisal and the parties shall comply accordingly.

The Arbitral Tribunal shall decide on any disagreement between any party and the appraiser as to whether the document, material, property or article required for the appraisal is relevant to the case.

4. A copy of the appraiser's report shall be sent by the Arbitral Tribunal to each party. The parties may submit their comments on the report.

5. If the Arbitral Tribunal considers it necessary or if the parties so request, the Arbitral Tribunal shall notify the appraiser to attend the hearing. The parties may, with the permission of the Arbitral Tribunal, question the appraiser on issues of the report.

6. The time limit stipulated in arts.43, 52, and 59 shall exclude any period of time taken to conduct an appraisal.

Article 33 Hearing-related Measures

If the Arbitral Tribunal considers it necessary, it may, prior to the hearing, authorise the presiding arbitrator to summon the parties to exchange their evidence and jointly draw up a list of the disputed issues and define the scope of the hearing. Prior to the hearing or at any stage during the hearing, the Arbitral Tribunal also may, if necessary, require the parties to produce evidence and to respond to questions.

Article 34 Examination and Authentication

1. In the event of a hearing, evidence exchanged between the parties prior to the hearing shall be presented for examination during the hearing. Evidence may be used as proof of the facts relied upon without being produced at the hearing if the Arbitral Tribunal affirms during the hearing that the evidence has been exchanged, admitted as authentic, and put on record.

2. Where evidence is produced by any party during or after the hearing and the Arbitral Tribunal decides to admit the evidence without holding further hearings, the Arbitral Tribunal may require the parties to submit in writing any challenge to the authenticity, admissibility and relevance of the evidence within a specified period of time.

3. The evidence shall be verified by the Arbitral Tribunal. The Arbitral Tribunal shall decide whether to adopt the appraiser's report.

4. If a party has neither admitted nor denied facts alleged by the other party, and refuses to express any opinion on those facts despite explanation and inquiry by the Arbitral Tribunal, it shall be deemed to have admitted those facts.

5. If a party has admitted to adverse facts or evidence, whether in the Application for Arbitration, Statement of Defence, its statements or other written opinions, those facts or evidence shall be confirmed by the Arbitral Tribunal, unless the party subsequently withdraws the admissions and produces evidence to rebut those facts or evidence.

6. If a party can prove that the other party possesses evidence that it refuses to disclose without any justifiable reason, and that such evidence would have had an adverse impact on the case of the party possessing the evidence, adverse inferences may be drawn from such refusal to disclose.

Article 35 Debate

The parties have a right to debate during the hearing.

Article 36 Closing Statement

At the close of the hearing, the Arbitral Tribunal shall solicit final comments from the parties, which may be presented orally during the hearing or in writing within a period of time specified by the Arbitral Tribunal.

Article 37 Record of Hearing

1. The Arbitral Tribunal shall keep minutes of the hearing, except in relation to conciliation proceedings.

2. The Arbitral Tribunal may make an audio or video record of the hearing.

3. The parties and other participants in the arbitration shall have a right to request a rectification of any error and omission in the minutes of their testimony. The request shall be recorded if the Arbitral Tribunal does not allow the rectification.

4. The Arbitral Tribunal, the reporter, the parties, and other participants in the arbitration shall sign or affix their seals on the minutes.

Article 38 Withdrawing the Application for Arbitration

1. The Claimant may also withdraw the Application for Arbitration after it has been submitted. If the parties reach a settlement after submission of the Application for Arbitration, they may request the Arbitral Tribunal to make an award incorporating the terms of the settlement agreement.

2. If the Claimant withdraws the Application for Arbitration, the Arbitral Tribunal shall decide on the dismissal of the case. If the Arbitral Tribunal has not been constituted at the time of withdrawal, the BAC, shall decide on the dismissal.

3. If the Claimant withdraws the Application for Arbitration before the constitution of the Arbitral Tribunal, the BAC shall refund the case acceptance fees paid in advance but may, depending on the circumstances of the case, retain a portion of the case handling fees paid in advance. If the Claimant withdraws the Application for Arbitration after the constitution of the Arbitral Tribunal, the BAC shall, depending on the circumstances of the case, charge a portion or all of the case acceptance fees and the case handling fees paid in advance.

Article 39 Conciliation by the Tribunal

1. The Arbitral Tribunal may, at the request of both parties or upon obtaining the consent of both parties, conciliate the case in a manner it considers appropriate.

2. If the conciliation leads to a settlement, the parties may withdraw their claims and counterclaims if any, or request the Arbitral Tribunal to issue a Statement of Conciliation or make an award in accordance with the terms of the settlement.

3. The statement of conciliation shall state the claims and the settlement agreement reached by the parties. It shall be signed by the Arbitral Tribunal and affixed with the seal of the BAC before being sent to both parties and shall be binding once both parties have acknowledged receipt of it.

4. If the conciliation fails to lead to a settlement, neither party shall invoke any of the statements, opinions, views or proposals expressed by the other party or the Arbitral Tribunal during the conciliation as grounds for any claim, defence or counterclaim in the arbitral proceedings, other judicial proceedings or any other proceedings.

Article 40 Private Conciliation by the Parties

During the arbitral proceedings, the parties may enter into private conciliation or apply to the BAC for mediation in accordance with the Mediation Rules of the BAC.

Article 41 Suspension of Arbitral Proceedings

1. The arbitral proceeding may be suspended upon the joint request of the parties or if special circumstances occur during the proceeding that makes suspension of proceeding necessary;

2. The suspension shall be decided by the Arbitral Tribunal, or if the Arbitral Tribunal has not been constituted, by the BAC.

Chapter 6

Arbitral Award

Article 42 Decision on Procedural Matters

1. Any decision of an Arbitral Tribunal composed of three arbitrators shall be made by a majority of the arbitrators. If the Arbitral Tribunal fails to reach a majority decision, the decision of the presiding arbitrator shall prevail.

2. With the consent of the parties or the authorisation of the other arbitrators of the Arbitral Tribunal, the presiding arbitrator may also decide on procedural matters.

Article 43 Time Limit for the Award

The Arbitral Tribunal shall render its award within four months of its constitution. If there are special circumstances justifying an extension, the Secretary-General may, at the request of the presiding arbitrator, approve a suitable extension of the time limit.

Article 44 Arbitral Award

1. The award of an Arbitral Tribunal composed of three arbitrators shall be made by a majority decision. The dissenting opinion of the minority may be put on record. If the Arbitral Tribunal fails to reach a majority decision, the award shall be made in accordance with the decision of the presiding arbitrator.

2. The award shall state the claims, the facts of the dispute, the reasons upon which the award is based, the result of the award, the allocation of the costs of the arbitration, the date of the award and the place where the award is made. The award need not state the factual background to the dispute or the reasons upon which the award is based if the parties so agree, or if the award is made in accordance with the terms of a settlement between the parties.

3. The award shall be signed by each member of the Arbitral Tribunal. The dissenting arbitrator may choose not to sign the award. An arbitrator who chooses not to sign the award shall issue a dissenting opinion, which shall be sent to the parties together with the award but does not form part of the award. If the arbitrator who chooses not to sign the award does not issue a statement of personal opinion, the arbitrator shall be deemed to have refused to sign the award without any justifiable reason.

4. After the award has been signed by the arbitrator or arbitrators, the BAC's seal shall be affixed to it.

5. The award shall be legally effective as of the date it is made.

6. The Arbitral Tribunal may, prior to the final award, make an interim or partial award on any disputed issue in the arbitration if necessary, or if the parties so request and it consents. Any party's failure to perform an interim or partial award shall neither affect the progress of the arbitral proceedings nor prevent the Arbitral Tribunal from making its final award.

Article 45 Allocation of Costs

1. The Arbitral Tribunal shall have the power to fix in its award the costs of the arbitration and the expenses incurred to be borne by the parties.

2. The costs of the arbitration shall in principle be borne by the losing party. If the parties are only partially successful in their respective cases, the Arbitral Tribunal shall decide on the proportion of each party's share of the costs based on each party's responsibilities. If the parties reach a settlement, whether or not as a result of the Arbitral Tribunal's conciliation, they may determine the proportion of their respective share of the costs through consultation.

3. The Arbitral Tribunal shall also have the power to order in its award, at the request of the winning party, that the losing party bears the cost and expenses reasonably incurred by the winning party in the arbitration.

Article 46 Rectification to Award and Supplementary Award

1. The Arbitral Tribunal shall correct in its award any error in computation, any clerical or typographical error, and any omission from its decision of claims on which it has made a judgment in its reasoning. In the event any claim is omitted entirely from the award, the Arbitral Tribunal shall make a supplementary award.

2.   Any party may, on discovering the existence of any of the circumstances stipulated in the preceding paragraph, request in writing within 30 days of the date of receipt of the award that the Arbitral Tribunal rectify the award or make a supplementary award.

3.   Any rectification by or supplementary award of the Arbitral Tribunal shall be an integral part of the original arbitral award.

Chapter 7

Summary Procedure

Article 47 Application of Summary Procedure

1.   Unless otherwise agreed by the parties, the summary procedure set out in this chapter the Summary Procedure. shall apply if the amount in dispute does not exceed RMB ¥1,000,000.

2.   The parties may agree to apply the Summary Procedure even if the amount in dispute exceeds RMB ¥1,000,000, in which case the costs of the arbitration shall be reduced accordingly.

3.   If the parties choose to apply the Ordinary Procedure non-summary procedure. even if the amount in dispute does not exceed RMB ¥1,000,000, they shall bear any ensuing additional costs of the arbitration.

Article 48 Composition of Arbitral Tribunal

1.   Cases applying the Summary Procedure shall be heard by a sole arbitrator.

2.   Within 10 days of the receipt of the notice of arbitration, the parties shall jointly nominate or jointly entrust the Chairman to appoint a sole arbitrator from the BAC's Panel of Arbitrators. The sole arbitrator may be selected in the manner prescribed by para 2 of art.18. If the parties fail to jointly nominate or jointly entrust the Chairman to appoint the sole arbitrator within the specified period of time, the Chairman shall make the appointment immediately.

Article 49 Time Limit for Defence and Counterclaim

Within 10 days of the receipt of the Request for Submission of Defence (30 days for international commercial cases), the Respondent shall submit to the BAC its Statement of Defence and any relevant supporting document. A Counterclaim, if any, shall also be submitted within the same period of time, together with any relevant supporting document.

Article 50 Notice of Hearing

1.   In the event of a hearing, the Arbitral Tribunal shall notify the parties of the date of the hearing at least three days before the hearing 10 days for international commercial cases..

2. If the Arbitral Tribunal is deciding the case by way of a hearing, it shall hold one hearing only. The Arbitral Tribunal may decide to hold subsequent hearings if necessary. Notification of the date of any hearing subsequent to the first one is not subject to the three-day requirement 10-day for international commercial cases..

Article 51 Termination of Summary Procedure

1. The application of the Summary Procedure is not affected by mere reason that, as a result of any amendments to the Application for Arbitration or the submission of a Counterclaim, the amount in dispute exceeds RMB ￥1,000,000. However, if the sole arbitrator finds that the application of the Summary Procedure may be affected, he may make a request to the Chairman for the Arbitral Tribunal to be constituted by three arbitrators, unless otherwise agreed upon by the parties.

2. In the event of a change from the Summary Procedure to the Ordinary Procedure, the parties shall, within five days of the receipt of notice of change of procedure, nominate or entrust the Chairman to appoint their arbitrators in accordance with the provisions of these Rules. Unless otherwise agreed by the parties, the original sole arbitrator shall become the presiding arbitrator.

3. The re-constituted Arbitral Tribunal shall decide whether or not to repeat the arbitral proceedings conducted prior to the re-constitution. The Summary Procedure shall not apply to arbitral proceedings conducted after the re-constitution.

Article 52 Time Limit for the Award

The Arbitral Tribunal shall render its award within 75 days of the date of its constitution. For an international commercial case, the award shall be rendered within 90 days of the date of its constitution. If there are special circumstances justifying an extension, the Secretary-General may, at the request of the sole arbitrator, approve a suitable extension of the time limit.

Article 53 Application of Other Provisions of these Rules

For matters not covered in this Chapter, the other relevant provisions of these Rules shall apply.

Chapter 8

Special Provisions for International Commercial Arbitration

Article 54 Application of this Chapter

1. Unless otherwise agreed by the parties, the provisions of this Chapter shall apply to international commercial cases. For matters not covered in this Chapter, the other relevant provisions of these Rules shall apply.

2. Cases relating to Hong Kong SAR, Macao SAR and the Taiwan region may be handled by reference to the provisions of this Chapter.

3.   Any dispute between the parties as to the existence of international elements shall be referred to the Arbitral Tribunal for a decision.

Article 55 Composition of Arbitral Tribunal

1.   Arbitrators could be chosen by the parties from or outside the Panel of Arbitrators maintained by the BAC.

2.   If the parties want to select arbitrators outside the Panel of Arbitrators maintained by the BAC, they shall submit the resume and means of contact of the candidate to the BAC. The candidate selected outside the Panel may act as an arbitrator with the confirmation of the BAC, and with a term to expire at the closing of the case, unless the BAC decides on listing the arbitrator on the Panel of Arbitrators.

3.   Within 20 days of the receipt of the notice of arbitration, the parties shall, pursuant to the provisions of art.18, nominate or entrust the Chairman to appoint their arbitrators and jointly nominate or jointly entrust the Chairman to appoint a third arbitrator who shall be the presiding arbitrator. If the parties fail to nominate their arbitrators or jointly nominate the presiding arbitrator in accordance with the provisions of the preceding paragraph, the arbitrators or the presiding arbitrator shall be appointed by the Chairman.

4.   As a party agrees to increase the compensation for international arbitrators, the party shall deposit an advance on the resulting additional costs within the period stipulated by the BAC. If a party has not deposited the advance on costs, it shall be deemed not to select the arbitrator. The Chairman could appoint the arbitrator for the party in accordance with these Rules.

Article 56 Defence and Counterclaim

1.   Within 45 days of the receipt of the Request for Submission of Defence, the Respondent shall submit to the BAC its Statement of Defence and any relevant supporting document.

2.   The Respondent shall also submit its Counterclaim in writing, if any, within 45 days of the receipt of the Request for Submission of Defence.

Article 57 Notice of Hearing

1.   The Arbitral Tribunal shall notify the parties of the date of the hearing at least 30 days before the hearing. The date may be brought forward with the agreement of the parties and the approval of the Arbitral Tribunal. A party may request a postponement of the date of the hearing, at least 12 days before the hearing, if there are grounds justifying a postponement. The Arbitral Tribunal shall decide on the request.

2.   Notification of the date of any hearing subsequent to the first one is not subject to the 30-day requirement.

Article 58 Conciliation by the Tribunal

1. The Arbitral Tribunal may, with the consent of both parties, conduct conciliation of the case.

2. If, upon the termination of unsuccessful conciliation proceedings, both parties request a replacement of an arbitrator on the ground that the results of the award may be affected by the conciliation proceedings, the Chairman may approve the request. The resulting additional costs shall be borne by the parties.

Article 59 Time Limit for the Award

The Arbitral Tribunal shall render its award within six months of the date of its constitution. If there are special circumstances justifying an extension, the Secretary-General may, at the request of the presiding arbitrator, approve a suitable extension of the time limit.

Article 60 Applicable Law

1. The Arbitral Tribunal shall apply the law agreed upon by the parties to the merits of the dispute. Unless otherwise agreed by the parties, the agreed applicable law refers to the substantive rules of law but not the rules of conflict of laws.

2. In the absence of an agreed choice of law, the Arbitral Tribunal shall apply the law, with which the dispute has the most significant relationship.

3. In all cases, the Arbitral Tribunal shall decide the case in accordance with the terms of the valid agreement and take into account the relevant international trade usages.

Article 61 Application of Summary Procedure

Where a case falls within the scope of art.47, the relevant provisions on Summary Procedure in Chapter VII shall be applicable.

Chapter 9

Supplementary Provisions

Article 62 Calculating Time Limits

1. A period of time specified in or fixed in accordance with these Rules shall start to run on the day following the date on which such period commences. The day on which such period commences does not form part of the period of time.

2. If the day following the date on which the period of time commences is an official holiday or a non-business day at the place of the addressee, the period of time shall begin to run on the first following business day. Official holidays or non-business days occurring within such period are included in calculating the period of time. If the last day of the relevant period of time falls on an official holiday or a non-business day, the period of time shall expire on the first following business day.

3. Time for delivery shall not be included in the period of time. Any arbitral document, notice or material that has been mailed or dispatched prior to expiry of the period of time shall not be regarded as overdue.

4. If a party breaches a time limit because of force majeure events or other justifiable reasons, it may apply for an extension of time within 10 days of the removal of the obstacle. The BAC or the Arbitral Tribunal shall decide on the request.

Article 63 Service

1. All relevant arbitral documents, notices and other materials may be served on the parties or their authorised representatives in person or by mail, courier, telex, facsimile or any other means that the BAC or the Arbitral Tribunal considers appropriate.

2. An arbitral document, notice and material shall be deemed to have been served if it has been delivered to the addressee in person or by mail to the addressee's place of business, place of habitual residence or other mailing address provided by the addressee or the counterparty.

3. If despite reasonable inquiries, the addressee's place of business, place of habitual residence or other mailing address cannot be found, service shall be deemed to have been effected if the document, notice or material is delivered to the addressee's last known place of business, place of habitual residence or other mailing address by mail, courier or by any other means of delivery with proof of attempt to deliver.

Article 64 Language

1. Chinese is the official language of the BAC. If the parties have agreed otherwise, their agreement shall prevail.

2. If translation services are required by the parties or their authorised representatives or witnesses during hearings, translators may be provided by the BAC or by the parties themselves. The parties shall bear the cost of translation.

Article 65 Interpretation of the Rules

The power to interpret these Rules is vested in the BAC. Other documents issued by the BAC do not constitute part of these rules, unless the BAC has otherwise statement.

Article 66 Official Versions of the Rules

Each of the Chinese, English and other language versions of the Rules published by the BAC is official. In the event of any conflict between the different versions, the Chinese version shall prevail.

Article 67 Implementation of the Rules

These Rules are effective as of 1 April 2008. For cases accepted by the BAC before these Rules came into effect, the Arbitration Rules effective at the time of such acceptance shall apply. In such a case, these Rules may apply if the parties so agree and the BAC consents.

Interpretation of the Supreme People's Court on Several Issues Concerning Application of the Arbitration Law of the People's Republic of China

The "Interpretation of the Supreme People's Court on Several Issues Concerning Application of the Arbitration Law of the People's Republic of China" was adopted at the 1375th Session of the Judicial Committee of the Supreme People's Court on 23 August 2006. This Interpretation is hereby promulgated and shall come into effect as of 8 September 2006.

According to the provisions of the "Arbitration Law of the People's Republic of China" and the "Civil Procedure Law of the People's Republic of China", several issues concerning the application of law by the people's courts in hearing arbitration cases are hereby interpreted as follows:

Article 1

The arbitral agreement "in other written forms" as prescribed by art.16 of the Arbitration Law shall include the agreements on request for arbitration that are concluded in the forms of contract, letter and data teletext (inclusive of telegraph, telex, facsimile, electronic data interchange and electronic mail).

Article 2

Where the parties concerned intend to agree on general contractual disputed matters to be subject to arbitration, the disputes arising from formation, validity, alteration, transfer, performance, liabilities for breach, interpretation and rescission of contracts may also be regarded as matters subject to arbitration.

Article 3

Where the name of the arbitration institution agreed in the arbitration agreement is inaccurate, but such particular arbitration institution can be ascertained, such arbitration institution shall be regarded as the chosen arbitration institution.

Article 4

Where the arbitration clause has only agreed on the arbitration rules applied in disputes, it shall be deemed that the arbitration institution has not been ascertained unless the parties concerned are able to ascertain the arbitration institution by reaching a supplementary agreement or through the agreed arbitration rules.

Article 5

Where the arbitration agreement has stipulated two or more arbitration institutions, the parties concerned may apply for arbitration by choosing either one of the arbitration institutions. However, if the parties concerned fail to reach a unanimous agreement concerning the choice of arbitration institution, the arbitration agreement shall be null and void.

Article 6

Where the arbitration agreement has agreed that the arbitration shall be conducted by an arbitration institution in a certain area and there is only one arbitration institution in such area, the arbitral institution therein shall be deemed to be the agreed arbitration institution. Where there are two or more arbitration institutions in such area, the parties concerned may apply for the arbitration at either arbitration institution. Where the parties concerned fail to reach to an agreement concerning the choice of arbitration institution, the arbitral clause shall be null and void.

Article 7

If the parties concerned agree to make an application to the arbitral institution or institute a lawsuit to the people's court in case of dispute, the arbitral clause shall be null and void except that one side has applied for arbitration but the other side has not raise any objection within the time limit as prescribed in para 2 of art.20 of the Arbitration Law.

Article 8

Where the parties concerned merge or split after concluding an arbitral agreement, the arbitral agreement shall be binding on the inheritor of the rights and obligations thereof.

Where the parties concerned died after concluding an arbitral agreement, the arbitral agreement shall be binding on the inheritor to the rights and obligations in the arbitration matters thereof.

The circumstances as prescribed in the two preceding paragraphs shall be followed unless otherwise separately agreed by the parties concerned concluding the arbitration agreement.

Article 9

Where the creditor's right and debt have been completely or partially transferred, the arbitral agreement shall be binding on the transferee, unless otherwise separately agreed by the parties concerned, or clearly objected by the transferee in transferring the creditor's right and debt or having no knowledge of the separate arbitral agreement.

Article 10

Where the contract fails to come into effect or being set aside after the conclusion, the provisions of para 1 in art.19 of the Arbitration Laws shall apply to the determination of the effectiveness of the arbitral agreement.

Where the parties concerned have reached an arbitral agreement in respect of any dispute arising from concluding the contract, the contract which has not yet been concluded shall not affect the arbitral agreement.

Article 11

Where the valid arbitration clauses in other contracts or documents applicable to dispute resolution have been agreed on the contract, the parties concerned shall request for the arbitration under the arbitration clauses in case of dispute over the contract occurred.

If there is any arbitration provision in the relevant international treaties applicable to the foreign-related contracts, the parties concerned shall request for the arbitration under the arbitration clauses in the international treaties in case of dispute over the contract occurred.

Article 12

Regarding the case in which the party concerned makes an application to the people's court to confirm the validity of an arbitral agreement, it shall be within the jurisdiction of the intermediate people's court at the place where the arbitration institution designated under the arbitral agreement is located. Where the arbitral institution stipulated by an arbitral agreement is unclear, the case shall be within the jurisdiction of the intermediate people's court of the place where the arbitration agreement is signed, or of the place of domicile of the applicant or the party against whom the application is filed.

Cases in which an application for confirmation of validity of foreign-related arbitration agreement shall be within the jurisdiction of the intermediate people's court at the place where the arbitration institution designated under an arbitration agreement is located, or of the place where the arbitration agreement is signed, or of the place of domicile of the applicant or the party against whom the application is filed.

Cases concerning the validity of the arbitration agreement for maritime disputes shall be within the jurisdiction of the maritime court of the place of the arbitration institution stipulated by an arbitration agreement, or of the place where the arbitration agreement is signed, or of the place of domicile of the applicant or the party against whom the application is filed. If there has no maritime court in the above prescribed places, the case shall be within the jurisdiction of the maritime court nearby.

Article 13

Where a party concerned has not raised objection to the validity of the arbitration agreement before the first hearing of the arbitration tribunal, but applied to the people's court for confirmation of nullity of the arbitration agreement thereafter, the people's court shall not entertain such application according to the provisions of para 2 of art.20 of the Arbitration Law.

A people's court shall not entertain the application of a party concerned for confirmation of validity of an arbitration agreement or setting aside an arbitral award after the arbitration institution has made a decision to the validity of the arbitration agreement.

Article 14

The "first hearing" as prescribed in art.26 of the Arbitration Law shall mean the first hearing for judgment organised by the people's court after the closing of the defence, and shall not include all the activities in the pre-trial procedure.

Article 15

For ruling a case for confirmation of validity of an arbitration agreement, the people's court shall form a collegiate bench to conduct the examination, and shall inquire the parties concerned.

Article 16

The applicable law agreed by the parties concerned shall apply to the examination on the validity of foreign-related arbitration agreement. Where the parties concerned have failed to agree on the applicable law but have agreed on the arbitration place, the law of the arbitration place shall apply. Where the parties concerned have neither agreed on the applicable law nor the arbitration place, or the arbitration place is unclear, the law of the place where the court is located shall apply.

Article 17

The people's court shall not entertain the application of a party concerned for setting aside of the arbitral award on the ground that the matter does not fall within the provisions in art.58 of the Arbitration Law or art.260 of the Civil Procedure Law.

Article 18

"No arbitration agreement" as prescribed in Item 1 under para 1 of art.58 of the Arbitration Law shall mean the parties concerned has not concluded an arbitration agreement. Where an arbitration agreement was deemed as invalid or being set aside, it shall be regarded as the situation of no arbitration agreement.

Article 19

Where a party concerned applies for setting aside the arbitral award on the ground of the arbitral award matter exceeding the scope of arbitration agreement, the people's court shall set aside the exceeding part of the arbitral award upon examination. If the exceeding part is inalienable to other arbitral matters, the people's court shall set aside the arbitral award.

Article 20

"Not in conformity with the statutory procedure" as prescribed in art.58 of the Arbitration Law shall mean the circumstances that violating the arbitration procedure prescribed by the Arbitration Law and the arbitration rules chose by the parties concerned may affect the right judgment of the case.

Article 21

Where the case in which a party concerned applies for setting aside domestic arbitral award falls within one of the following circumstances, the people's court may notify the arbitration tribunal to conduct a fresh arbitration within a time limit according to the provisions in art.61 of the Arbitration Law:

1.   the evidences on which the award is based are forged; or

2.   the other party has withheld the evidence which is sufficient to affect the impartiality of the arbitration.

The people's court shall describe the specific reasons for re-arbitration in the notice.

Article 22

Where the arbitration tribunal starts to re-arbitrate within the time limit designated by the people's court, the people's court shall make a ruling to end the setting-aside procedure. Where the re-arbitration failed to be started, the people's court shall rule to resume the setting-aside procedure.

Article 23

If a party concerned does not satisfied with the re-arbitral award, he may apply to the people's court for setting aside within six months after receiving the re-arbitration award according to the provisions of art. 58 of the Arbitration Law.

Article 24

The people's court shall form a collegial bench to rule the case applied by a party concerned for setting aside the arbitral award, and inquire the parties concerned.

Article 25

If the people's court has entertained the application of a party concerned for setting aside the arbitral award before the other party concerned applied to enforce the identical arbitral award, the people's court which has entertained the enforcement application shall make a ruling to terminate the enforcement after entertaining the case.

Article 26

Where the application made by the party concerned to the people's court for setting aside the arbitral award was dismissed, and subsequently submitted a defence against the enforcement on the identical ground in the enforcement procedure, the people's court shall not rule in its favour.

Article 27

Where a party concerned fails to raise objection in respect of the validity of the arbitration agreement in the arbitration procedure, and insist to set aside the arbitral award or submit a defence against the enforcement by using the ground of the arbitration agreement to be invalid after the arbitral award has been made, the people's court shall not rule in its favour.

Where a party concerned raises objection in respect of the validity of the arbitration agreement in the arbitration procedure, and insist to set aside the arbitral award or submit a defence against the enforcement on the identical ground after the arbitral award has been made, the people's court shall support it upon verification to be in compliance with the provisions of art.58 of the Arbitration Law or art.217 and art.260 of the Civil Procedure Law.

Article 28

Where a party concerned applied for non-performance of the reconciliation document for arbitration or the arbitral award made according to the reconciliation agreement between the parties concerned, the people's court shall not rule in its favour.

Article 29

The case of which the party concerned makes an application for enforcing the arbitral award shall be within the jurisdiction of the intermediate people's court of the place of domicile of the party that should implement the award or the place where the property to be implemented is located.

Article 30

The people's court may request the arbitration institution to make description or ask for reviewing the file of the arbitration case to the relevant arbitration institution according to the actual need for ruling of the case in respect of setting-aside or enforcement of the arbitral award.

Any judgment made by the people's court in the course of handling the case involving arbitration may be delivered to the relevant arbitration institution.

Article 31

This Interpretation shall come in effect as of the promulgation date.

Where the previous judicial interpretations promulgated by the Court are inconsistent to this Interpretation, this Interpretation shall prevail.

Arrangement Between the Mainland and Hong Kong Special Administrative Region on Reciprocal Recognition and Enforcement of Arbitral Awards

[Promulgation Date] 2000-01-24   [Effective Date] 2000-02-01

In accordance with art.95 of the Basic Law of Hong Kong Special Administrative Region of the People's Republic of China, through the mutual consultation of the Supreme People's Court and the Government of the Hong Kong Special Administrative Region (hereinafter referred to as the "HKSAR"), the courts of the HKSAR agree to enforce the awards made by the Mainland arbitral institutions in accordance with the Arbitration Law of the People's Republic of China, and the people's courts in the Mainland agree to enforce the awards made by the HKSAR in accordance with the Arbitration Ordinance of the HKSAR. We hereby make the Arrangement on Reciprocal Enforcement of Arbitral Awards between the Mainland and HKSAR as follows.

Article 1

If one party to an arbitral award made in the mainland or HKSAR fails to perform the arbitral award, the other party may apply to the concerned court with the jurisdiction over his residence or the place where his property is located for enforcement.

Article 2

The said courts in the previous paragraph refer to, for the part of the mainland, the intermediate people's courts with the jurisdiction over the residence of the party subject to application or the place where the property of the party subject to application is located; and for the part of HKSAR, the High Court of HKSAR.

Where the residence of the party subject to application or the places where the property of the party subject to application are scattered in or spread over jurisdictional areas of different people's courts in the mainland, the applicant may choose one of the courts to apply for enforcement and shall not submit application to two or more people's courts respectively.

Where the residence of the party subject to application or the places where the property of the party subject to application are scattered in the mainland and in HKSAR simultaneously, the applicant shall not submit application to the courts of both places simultaneously. If the enforced property by the court of one region is not enough to pay off the debt, then he may apply to the court of the other region for enforcement. The total amount obtained from the consecutive enforcement of the arbitral award shall not exceed the total amount awarded.

Article 3

The applicants apply for the enforcement of the arbitral awards decided in mainland or in HKSAR shall submit the following documents:

1. Application for enforcement;

2. Arbitral award; and

3. Agreement on arbitration.

Article 4

Applications for enforcement shall contain the following contents:

1. Under the condition that the applicant is a natural person: the name and address of the applicant; under the condition that the applicant is a legal person or any other organisation: the name, address of the legal person or any other organisation and the name, address of the legal representative;

2. Under the condition that the party subject to application is a natural person: the name and address; under the condition that the party subject to application is a legal person or any other organisation: the name, address of the legal person or any other organisation and the name, address of the legal representative;

3. If the applicant is a legal person or any other organisation, it shall submit the duplicate copy for enterprise business registration certificate. If the applicant is a legal person or any other organisation of foreign nationality, the corresponding notarisation and accreditation materials shall be furnished; and

4. The reasons for the application of enforcement and contents of application, the place of the property and financial status of the party subject to application.

The application for enforcement shall be in Chinese text, if the award or the agreement on arbitration has no Chinese text, the party subject to application shall furnish officially certified translated Chinese version as well.

Article 5

The time limit for applying for enforcement of the arbitral awards made in the mainland or in HKSAR shall refer to the provisions of the relevant laws on the time limit of the place where the enforcement is carried out.

Article 6

Concerned courts shall, upon receiving the applications from the applicants, handle and enforce according to the legal procedure of the place where the enforcement is sought.

Article 7

When the parties subject to application furnish sufficient evidence upon receiving the notice and prove the arbitral awards applied for enforcement in the mainland or in HKSAR involve any of following circumstances, the concerned courts may, upon verification, make orders rejecting the application for enforcement:

1. The parties to the agreement on arbitration, in accordance with the law applicable to them, are in a certain incapable circumstance; or the agreements on arbitration,

accordance with the agreed governing law, the agreement on arbitration are invalid, or there is no indication of the governing law, according to the law of the place of award, this invalidates the agreements on arbitration;

2. The parties subject to application haven't received the proper notice from the dispatched arbitrator or fail to make statement due to other reasons;

3. The dispute decided by the award is not the subject put for arbitration or not covered within the terms and conditions of the agreement on arbitration; or the award carries decisions beyond the scope put for arbitration; while the decisions for the matters within the scope put for arbitration can be separable from the decisions on matters beyond the scope for arbitration, the decisions for the matters within the scope put for arbitration shall be enforced;

4. The formation of the arbitral tribunal or the procedure of the arbitral tribunal is inconsistent with the agreement on arbitration or the law of the place of arbitration when such an agreement is not existing; and

5. The award is still not binding on the parties yet or has been vacated by the courts of the place of arbitration or terminated in accordance with the law of the place of arbitration.

If concerned courts consider the disputed matters can not be settled through arbitration in accordance with the law of the place of enforcement, then the award may not be granted for enforcement.

If the courts of the mainland consider executing the arbitral award in the mainland violates the social public interests of the mainland, or the courts of HKSAR consider executing the arbitral awards violates the public policy of HKSAR, they may choose not to enforce the arbitral awards.

Article 8

Applicants, when applying to concerned courts for enforcement of arbitral awards made in the mainland or in HKSAR, shall pay the enforcement fee in accordance with the measures on collection of litigation costs of the place of enforcement.

Article 9

Applications for enforcement of arbitral awards made in the mainland or in HKSAR submitted after 1 July 1997 shall be handled in accordance with the Arrangement.

Article 10

For the applications between 1 July and the date of effectiveness of the Arrangement, both parties agree as follows:

Any applicant failing to apply for enforcement for special reasons in the mainland or in HKSAR during 1 July 1997 and the date of effectiveness of the Arrangement may, if the applicant is a legal person, or any other organisation, submit the applications within six months upon effectiveness of the Arrangement; if the applicant is a natural person, then he may submit his application within one year upon the effectiveness of the Arrangement.

With regard to cases on the arbitral awards that the courts of the mainland or HKSAR refuse to accept or refuse to enforce between 1 July 1997 and the date of effectiveness, the parties shall be permitted to apply for enforcement again.

Article 11

In case of any problem and amendment in the enforcement of the Arrangement, the Supreme People's Court and the Government of Hong Kong Special Region shall resolve through friendly consultation.

BIBLIOGRAPHY

ENGLISH REFERENCES

A. Books and Texts

1. International arbitration norms

Adam Samuel, *Jurisdictional Problems in International Commercial Arbitration: A Study of Belgian, Dutch, English, French, Swedish, Swiss, US and Western German Law* (The Hague: Kluwer Law International, 1989).

Alan Redfern and Martin Hunter, *Law and Practice of International Commercial Arbitration* (4th ed.) (London: Sweet & Maxwell, 2004).

Albert Jan van den Berg, *The New York Arbitration Convention of 1958* (Deventer: Kluwer Law and Taxation, 1981).

Albert Jan van den Berg (ed), I*nternational Dispute Resolution: Towards an International Arbitration Culture*: *ICCA Congress Series No.8* (The Hague: Kluwer Law International, 1996).

Albert Jan van den Berg (ed), *Improving the Efficiency of Arbitration Agreements and Awards: 40 Years of Application of the New York Convention: ICCA Congress Series No. 9* (The Hague: Kluwer Law International, 1998).

Albert Jan van den Berg (ed), *New Horizons in International Commercial Arbitration and Beyond: ICCA Congress Series No.12* (The Hague: Kluwer Law International, 2005).

Brad Roberts (ed), *New Forces in the World Economy* (Cambridge, Mass.: MIT Press, 1996).

Center for Transnational Law, ICC (ed), *Understanding Transnational Commercial Arbitration* (Munster, Germany: Quadis Publishing, 2000).

Chia-Jui Cheng (ed), *Clive M. Schmitthoff's Selected Essays on International Trade Law* (The Hague: Kluwer Law International, 1988).

Christian Buhring-Uhle, *Arbitration and Mediation in International Business: Designing Procedures for Effective Conflict Management* (The Hague, London: Kluwer Law International, 1996).

Craig, Park and Paulsson, *International Chamber of Commerce Arbitration* (3rd ed.) (New York: Oceana Publications, 2000).

David Sutton and Judith Gill, *Russell on Arbitration* (22nd ed.) (London: Sweet & Maxwell, 2003).

D. Barry and R.C. Keith, *Regionalism, Multilateralism and the Politics of Global Trade* (Vancouver: University of British Columbia Press, 1999).

Emmanuel Gaillard and John Savage (ed), *Fouchard Gaillard Goldman on International Commercial Arbitration* (The Hague: Kluwer Law International, 1999).

Enid A. Marshall, *Gill: The Law of Arbitration* (4th ed.) (London: Sweet & Maxwell, 2001).

Famon J. Alvins and Victorino J. Tejera-Prerez, *The International Comparative Legal Guide to: International Arbitration* (Boston, NY: Global Legal Group, 2004).

F. Jameson and M. Miyoshi, *The Cultures of Globalization* (Durham, NC: Duke University Press, 1998).

F. J. Lechner and J. Boli, *The Globalization Reader* (Malden, Mass.: Blackwell, 2000).

Geoffrey M. B. Hartwell (ed) *The Commercial Way to Justice: The 1996 International Conference of the Chartered Institute of Arbitrators* (The Hague: Kluwer Law International, 1997).

Gerold Hermann (ed), *International Arbitration Culture* (The Hague: Kluwer Law International, 1998).

Henri C. Alvarez, Neil Kaplan QC and David W. Rivkin, *Model Law Decisions: Cases Applying the UNICTRAL Model Law on International Commercial Arbitration* (1985–2001) (The Hague: Kluwer Law International, 2001).

Howard M. Holtzman and Joseph E. Neuhaus, *A Guide to the UNCITRAL Model Law on International Commercial Arbitration: Legislative History and Commentary* (The Hague: Kluwer Law and Taxation Publishers, 1989).

ICC (ed), *ICC International Court of Arbitration Bulletin: International Commercial Arbitration in Asia (Special Supplement)* (The Hague: Kluwer Law International, 1998).

International Chamber of Commerce (ed), *60 Years of ICC Arbitration—A Look at the Future ICC* (The Hague: Kluwer Law International, 1985).

Jeochim G. Frick, *Arbitration and Complex International Contracts* (The Hague: Kluwer Law International, 2001).

John Tackaberry QC *et al*, *International Commercial Arbitration for Today & Tomorrow: a View of Arbitration in the Nineties & Beyond* (London: Euro Conferences Ltd, 1991).

Julian D. M. Lew, *Applicable Law in International Commercial Arbitration: a study in commercial arbitration awards* (New York: Oceana Publications, 1978).

Julian D. M. Lew (ed), *Contemporary Problems in International Arbitration* (London: Sweet & Maxwell, 1978).

Julian D. M. Lew, *Comparative International Commercial Arbitration* (The Hague: Kluwer Law International, 2003).

J. C. Schultz and A. J. van den Berg, *The Art of Arbitration* (Deventer: Kluwer Law and Taxation Publishers, 1982).

J. Tomlinson, *Globalization and Culture* (Chicago: University of Chicago Press, 1999).

Karl Mackie *et al*, *The ADR Practice Guide: Commercial Dispute Resolution* (2nd ed.) (London: Butterworths, 2000).

Katherine Lynch, *The Forces of Economic Globalization: Challenges to the Regime of International Commercial Arbitration*, (The Hague: Kluwer Law International, 2003).

Liljana Biukovic, *Court Intervention in Arbitral Proceedings in Countries Adopting the UNCITRAL Model Law on International Commercial Arbitration: An Impact of Legal Culture on Reception (Case Studies of Canada, Hong Kong and Russia)* (National Library of Canada, 2000).

Marc Blessing, *Introduction to Arbitration—Swiss and International Perspectives* (Helbing & Lichtenhahn, 1999).

Martin Domke, *Domke on commercial arbitration: The law and practice of commercial arbitration* (3rd ed.) ([St. Paul, Minn.]: Thomson/West, 2003).

Martin Hunter, Arthur Marriott and V. V. Veeder (ed), *The Internationalization of International Arbitration: The LCIA Centenary Conference* (London: Graham & Trotman/Martinus Nijhoff, 1994).

Michael Reisman, *Systems of Control in International Adjudication and Arbitration* (NY: Oceana Publishing, 1992).

M. Bogdan, *Comparative Law* (The Hague: Kluwer Law & Taxations Publishers, 1994).

M.J. Mustill and S.C. Boyd, *The Law and Practice of Commercial Arbitration in England* (2nd ed.) (London: Butterworths, 1989).

M. Huleatt-James, *International Commercial Arbitration: A Handbook* (New York: LLP, 1996).

Peter Binder, *International Commercial Arbitration in UNCITRAL Model Law Jurisdictions* (London: Sweet & Maxwell, 2000).

Peter Sarcevic (ed), *Essays on International Commercial Arbitration* (London: Martinus Nijhoff, 1989).

Pieter Sanders (ed), *UNCITRAL's Project for a Model Law on International Commercial Arbitration: ICCA Congress Series No.2* (Deventer: Kluwer Law & Taxation Publishers, 1984).

Pieter Sanders, *Quo Vadis Arbitration? Sixty Years of Arbitration Practice: A Comparative Study* (The Hague: Kluwer Law International, 1999).

Pieter Sanders and Albert Jan van den Berg (ed), *International Handbook on Commercial Arbitration: National Reports/ Basic Legal Texts* (The Hague: Kluwer Law International, 2002).

Pieter Sanders, *The Work of UNCITRAL on Arbitration and Conciliation* (2nd ed.) (The Hague: Kluwer Law International, 2004).

Ramon J. Alvins and Victorino J. Tejera-Prerez, *The International Comparative Legal Guide to: International Arbitration* (London: Global Legal Group, 2004).

Rene David, *L'arbitrage dans le commerce international* (Paris: Economica, 1981).

Rene David, *Arbitration in International Trade* (Deventer: Kluwer Law International, 1985).

Thomas E. Carboneau (ed), *Resolving Transnational Disputes through International Arbitration* (Charlottesville: University of Virginia Press, 1984).

Thomas E. Carbonneau (ed), *Lex Mercatoria and Arbitration* (Boston: Kluwer Law International, 1990).

Thomas E. Carbonneau, *Cases and Materials on the Law and Practice of Arbitration* (3rd ed.) (New York: Juris Pub., 2002).

Tibor Varady, John J. Barcelo III and Arthur T. Von Mehren, *International Commercial Arbitration: A Transnational Perspective* (St. Paul, Minn.: Thomson/ West, 1999).

UN (ed), *UNCITRAL Model Arbitration Law* (New York: United Nations, 1994).

UNCITRAL (ed), *Uniform Commercial Law in the Twenty-First Century: Proceedings of the Congress of the United Nations Commission on International Trade Law* (New York: United Nations, 1995).

WTO Secretariat (ed), *Guide to the GATS: An Overview of Issues for Further Liberalization of Trade in Services* (The Hague: Kluwer Law International, 2001).

Yves Derains and Eric A. Schwartz, *A Guide to the New ICC Rules of Arbitration* (The Hague: Kluwer Law International, 1998).

2. Arbitration in China

Ben Beaumont *et al*, *Commentary on the Chinese Arbitration Act 1994* (London: Simmonds & Hill Pub.: 1995).

Cheng Dejun, Michael J. Moser and Wang Shengchang, *International Arbitration in the People's Republic of China: Commentary, Cases and Materials* (2nd ed.) (Hong Kong: Butterworths Asia 2000).

China Chamber of International Commerce, Arbitration Research Institute (ed), *Essays on International Commercial Arbitration (English-Chinese)* (Beijing: China Foreign Economic and Trade Publishing, 1998).

Chris Hunter *et al*, *Dispute Resolution in the PRC: A Practical Guide to Litigation and Arbitration in China* (Hong Kong: Asia Law & Practice Ltd. Press, 1995).

Daniel R. Fung and Wang Shengchang (ed), *Arbitration in China: A Practical Guide* (Hong Kong: Sweet & Maxwell Asia, 2004).

Freshfields (ed), *Doing Business in China* (The Hague: Kluwer Law International, 2000).

Guo Xiaowen, *Case Studies of China International Economic and Trade Arbitration* (Hong Kong: Sweet & Maxwell, 1996).

G. A. Cornia & C. Popov (ed), *Transition and Institutions: the Experience of Gradual and Late Reformers* (Oxford: Oxford University Press, 2001).

Jianfu Chen, Yuwen Li and Jan Michiel Otto (ed), *Implementation of Law in the People's Republic of China* (The Hague: Kluwer Law International, 2002).

Jingzhou Tao, *Arbitration Law and Practice in China* (2nd ed.) (The Hague: Kluwer Law International, 2004).

John Shijian Mo, *Arbitration Law in China* (Hong Kong: Sweet & Maxwell Asia, 2001).

Nanping Liu, *Judicial Interpretation in China: Opinions of the Supreme People's Court* (Hong Kong: Sweet & Maxwell Asia, 1997).

Neil Kaplan, Jill Spruce and Michael J. Moser, *Hong Kong and China Arbitration: Cases and Materials* (2nd ed.) (Hong Kong: Butterworths, 2000).

Stanley B. Lubman, *Bird in a Cage: Legal Reform in China after Mao* (California: Stanford University Press 1999).

The Legislative Affairs Commission of the Standing Committee of the National People's Congress of the PRC (ed), *Arbitration Laws of China* (Hong Kong: Sweet & Maxwell Asia, 1997).

Pitman B. Potter, *The Contract Law of China: Legitimation and Contract Autonomy in the PRC* (Seattle and London: University of Washington Press, 1992).

Pitman B. Potter (ed), *Domestic Law Reforms in Post-Mao China* (Armonk, NY & London: M. E. Sharp, 1994).

Pitman B. Potter, *Chinese Foreign Business Law: Past Accomplishments, Future Challenges* (San Francisco: 1990 Institute, 1995).

Pitman B. Potter, *The Chinese Legal System: Globalization and Local Legal Culture—Series of Routledge Studies On China in Transition* (London & New York: Routledge, 2001).

Randall Peerenboom, *China's Long March towards Rule of Law* (Cambridge University Press, 2002).

Wang Guiguo and Wei Zhenyin (eds), *Legal Developments in China: Market Economy and Law* (Hong Kong: Sweet & Maxwell Asia, 1996).

Wang Shengchang, *Resolving Disputes in the PRC: A Practical Guide to Arbitration and Conciliation in China* (Hong Kong: FT Law & Tax Asia, 1997).

Wang Shengchang, *Resolving Disputes through Arbitration in Mainland China* (Beijing: China Law Press, 2003).

World Bank, *China 2020: Development Challenges in the New Century* (Washington D.C.: World Bank, 1997).

Y.M. Lin (ed), *Philip Yang on Shipping Practice in China* (Dalian: Dalian Maritime University Press, 1995).

B. Journal Articles and Conference Papers

1. International arbitration norms

Adam Samuel, "Arbitration in Western Europe—A Generation of Reform", (1991) 2 *Arbitration International.*

Alan Uzelac, "Jurisdiction of the Arbitral Tribunal: Current Jurisprudence and Problem Areas under the UNCITRAL Model Law", [2005] *International Arbitration Law Review.*

Bond, "How to Draft an Arbitration Clause", (1989) 6(2) *Journal of International Arbitration.*

Christoph Liebscher, "Interpretation of the Written Form Requirement Art. 7(2) UNCITRAL Model Law", [2005] *International Arbitration Law Review.*

C. M. Schmitthoff, "Defective Arbitration Clauses", (1975) 4 *Journal of Business Law.*

David J. Howell, "An Overview of Arbitration Practice in Asia", [2001] *International Arbitration Law Review.*

David Leebron, "Seoul Conference on International Trade Law: Integration, Harmonization and Globalization", (1996) 10(2) *Columbia Journal of Asian Law.*

Doug Jones, "The Growth And Development of International Commercial Arbitration in the Asia Pacific Region", [2003] *International Arbitration Law Review.*

D. Wallace, Q.C., "Control by the Courts: a Plea for More, Not Less", (1990) 3 *Arbitration International.*

Fabien Gelinas, "Arbitration and the Challenge of Globalization", (2000) 17(4) *Journal of International Arbitration.*

Gerald Hermann, "Does the World Need Additional Uniform Legislation on Arbitration?" (1999) 15(3) *Arbitration International.*

GU Weixia, "Confidentiality Revisited: Blessing or Curse in International Commercial Arbitration", (2004) 15(3–4) *American Review of International Arbitration.*

GU Weixia and Joshua Lindenbaum, "The NYPE 93 Arbitration Clause: Where Ends the Open- end?", (2006) 37(2) *Journal of Maritime Law and Commerce.*

G. Walker & M. Fox, "Globalization: An Analytical Framework", (1996) 3 *Indiana Journal of Global Legal Studies.*

Herrmann, "Does the World Need Additional Uniform Legislation on Arbitration? The 1998 Freshfields Lectureship", (1999) 15 *Arbitration International.*

Hong-Lin Yu, "Total Separation of International Commercial Arbitration and National Court Regime", (1998) 15(2) *Journal of International Arbitration.*

Hong-Lin Yu and Eric Sauzier, "From Arbitrator's Immunity to the Fifth Theory of International Commercial Arbitration" [2003] *International Arbitration Law Review.*

Hong-Lin Yu, "Explore the Void—An Evaluation of Arbitration Theories: Part II", [2005] *International Arbitration Law Review.*

James T. Peter, "Med-Arb in International Arbitration", (1997) 83(8) *American Review of International Arbitration.*

J. Bagwell, "Enforcement of Arbitration Agreements: The Severability Doctrine in the International Arena", (1992) 22 *Georgia Journal of International Comparative Law.*

J. Werner, "An Agenda for the Millennium," (1999) 16(3) *Journal of International Arbitration.*

K-H Bockstiegel, "The Role of Party Autonomy in International Arbitration", (1997) 52(3) *Dispute Resolution Journal.*

K. Lionnet, "Should the Law Applicable to International Arbitration Be Denationalized or Unified? The Answer of the Model Law", (1991) 8(3) *Arbitration International.*

Lando, "The *Lex Mercatoria* in International Commercial Arbitration", (1985) 34 *International Comparative Law Quarterly.*

Martin Boodman, "The Myth of Harmonization of Laws", (2000) 39 *American Journal of Comparative Law.*

Martin Hunter, "International Commercial Dispute Resolution: The Challenge of the 21st Century", (2000) 16 *Arbitration International.*

M. J. Mustill, "A New Arbitration for the UK? The Response of the Departmental Advisory Committee to the Model Law", (1990) 6(3) *Arbitration International.*

M. Kerr, "Arbitration and the Courts: The UNCITRAL Model Law", (1985) 34 *International Comparative Law Quarterly*, 16.

W. L. Craig, "Uses and Abuses of Appeal from Awards", (1988) 4(3) *Arbitration International.*

M. McNerney and C.E. Esplugues, "International Commercial Arbitration: The UNCITRAL Model Law", (1989) 9 *Boston College International and Comparative Law Review.*

M. Sornarajah, "The UNICTRAL Model Law: A Third World Viewpoint", (1989) 7(6) *Journal of International Arbitration.*

Pieter Sanders, "International Arbitration—Liber Amicorum for Martin Domke", (1986) 2 *Arbitration International.*

Pieter Sanders, "Unity and Diversity in the Adoption of the Model Law", (1995) 1 *Arbitration International.*

Professor Dr Alan Uzelac "Jurisdiction of the Arbitral Tribunal: Current Jurisprudence and Problem Areas under the UNCITRAL Model Law", [2005] *International Arbitration Law Review.*

Professor William Tetley, "Good Faith in Contract: Particularly in the Contracts of Arbitration", (2004) 35 *Journal of Maritime Law and Commerce.*

"Resolutions of the Working Group II: Arbitration and the Courts", in Proceedings of the Sixth International Arbitration Congress, Mexico City, 13–16 March 1978.

Stone, "A Paradox in the Theory of Commercial Arbitration" (1966) 21 *Arbitration Journal.*

S. Jarvin, "The Sources and Limits of the Arbitrator's Powers", (1994) 4 *Arbitration International.*

Tatsuya Nakamura, "Salient Features Of The New Japanese Arbitration Law Based Upon The UNCITRAL Model Law On International Commercial Arbitration", (2003) 18(9) *Mealey's International Arbitration Report.*

Thieffry and Thieffry, "Negotiating Settlement of Disputes Provisions in International Business Contracts", (1990) 45 *Journal of Business Law.*

Thomas E. Carboneau, "Arbitral Law-Making", in *Diversity or Cacophony? New Sources of Norms in International Law Symposium,* (2000) 25 *Michigan Journal of International Law.*Thomas E. Carbonneau, "The Exercise of Contract Freedom in the Making of Arbitration Agreement", (2003) 36(4) *Vanderbilt Journal of Transnational Law.*

T. Waelde and J. Gunderson, "Legislative Reform in Transition Economies: Western Transplants—short-Cut to Social Market Economy Status", (1994) 43 *International Comparative Law Quarterly.*

Weixia GU, "Security for Costs in International Commercial Arbitration", (2005) 22(3) *Journal of International Arbitration.*

W. Laurence Craig, "Some Trends and Developments in the Laws and Practice of International Commercial Arbitration", (1995) 30 *Texas International Law Journal.*

2. Arbitration in China

Arias, Jose and Tomas Gomez, "Relationship Marketing Approach to Guanxi", (1998) 32 *European Journal of Marketing.*

Arthur Anyuan Yuan, "Enforcing and Collecting Money Judgments in China from a U.S. Creditor's Perspective", (2004) 36 *George Washington International Law Review.*

Cao Lijun, "Letters—CIETAC's Integrity", (2005) 168(7) *Far Eastern Economic Review.*

Chao Xi, "In Search for an Effective Monitoring Board Model: Board Reforms and the Political Economy of Corporate Law in China", (2006) 22(1) *Cornell Journal of International Law.*

Charles Kenworthey Harner, "Arbitration Fails to Reduce Foreign Investors' Risk in China", (1998) 8 *Pacific Rim Law and Policy Journal.*

Chen Luming, "International Commercial Arbitration in China", (1996) 13(2) *Journal of International Arbitration.*

Christopher Wing To, "Developments of the Hong Kong International Arbitration Center", (2000) 12 *International Business Lawyer.*

Chua Eu Jin, "Arbitration in the People's Republic of China", (2005) 1 *Asian International Arbitration Journal*.

Darren Fitzgerald, "CIETAC's New Arbitration Rules: Do the Reform Go Far Enough?" [2005] *Asian Dispute Review*.

Donald C. Clarke, "Regulation and Its Discontents: Understanding Economic Law in China", (1992) 28(2) *Stanford Journal of International Law*.

Ellen Reinstein, "Finding a Happy Ending for Foreign Investors: The Enforcement of Arbitration Awards in the People's Republic of China", (2005) 16 *Indiana Journal of International Law*.

G. Liu and A. Lourie, "International Commercial Arbitration in China: History, New Developments and Current Practice", (1995) 28 *John Marshall law Review*.

Ge Lui and Alexandar Lourie, "International Commercial Arbitration in China: History, New Developments, and Current Practice", (1995) 28 *Journal of Marshall Law Review*.

Gu Weixia and Robert Morgan, "Improving Commercial Dispute Resolution in China", [2005] *Asian Dispute Review*.

Gu Weixia, "Recourse against Arbitral Awards: How Far Can a Court Go? Supportive and Supervisory Role of HK Courts as Lessons to Mainland China Arbitration", (2005) 4(2) *Chinese Journal of International Law*.

Guiguo Wang, "The Unification of the Dispute Resolution System in China", (1996) 13(2) *Journal of International Arbitration*.

Heng Wang, "Chinese Views on Modern Marco Polos: New Foreign Trade Amendments after WTO Accession", (2006) 39 *Cornell International Law Journal*.

Howard Yinghao Yang, "CIETAC Arbitration Clauses: Tips and Pitfalls", (2007) 2 *China Law & Practice*.

Hui Chin and George Graen, "Guanxi and Professional Leadership in Contemporary Sino-American Joint Ventures in Mainland China", (1997) 8 *Leadership Quarterly*.

Jerome A. Cohen, "International Commercial Arbitration in China: Some Thoughts from Experience", paper presentation at the *International Economic Law and China in Its Economic Transition Joint Conference*, Xiamen, 4–5 November 2004.

Jerome A. Cohen, "Time to Fix China's Arbitration", (2005) 168(2) *Far Eastern Economic Review*.

Jerome A. Cohen, "China's Legal Reform at the Crossroads", (2006) 174(2) *Far Eastern Economic Review*.

John Mo, "Dilemma of 'Foreign Related' Arbitration in PRC", [1999] *Arbitration and Dispute Resolution Law Journal*.

John Mo, "Reform of Chinese Arbitration System after the WTO", (2003) 41(4) *China Law*.

Johnson Tan, "The Panel System in Chinese Arbitration", Speech at the *Dispute Resolution Forum* co-held by the Jones Day, Revies & Pogue, Freshfields Bruckhaus Derigner and Lovell's, Shanghai, 15–16 February 2006.

Jun Ge, "Mediation, Arbitration and Litigation: Dispute Resolving in the People's Republic of China", (1996) 15 *UCLA Pacific Basin Law Journal.*

Kang Ming, "*Ad Hoc* Arbitration in China", [2003] *International Arbitration Law Review.*

Katherine Lynch, "The New Arbitration Law", (1996) 16 *Hong Kong Law Journal.*

Kong Yuan, "Revision of China's 1994 Arbitration Act—Some Suggestions from A Judicialization Perspective", (2005) 22(4) *Journal of International Arbitration.*

Laifan Lin, "Judicial Independence in Japan: A Re-investigation for China", (1999) 13 *Columbia Journal of Asian Law.*

Li Hu, "Setting aside an Arbitral Award in the People's Republic of China", (2001) 12 *American Review of International Arbitration.*

Li Hu, "Feature International—An Introduction to Commercial Arbitration in China", (2003) 58 *Dispute Resolution Journal.*

Liu Xiaohong and Gu Weixia, "The Validity of Arbitration Agreements—Critical Comparison between Hong Kong SAR and Mainland China", (2005) 2(2) *Asia Law Review.*

Mei Ying Gechlik, "Judicial Reform in China: Lessons from Shanghai", (2005) 19 *Columbia Journal of Asian Law.*

Michael J. Moser, "China's New International Arbitration Rules," (1994) 11(3) *Journal of International Arbitration.*

Michael J. Moser, "China's New Arbitration Law", (1995) 1 *World Arbitration & Mediation Report.*

Michael J. Moser, "The New 2005 CIETAC Arbitration Rules", speech at the symposium *Developments in the Settlement of International Commercial and Investment Disputes—Chinese and German Perspectives*, co-organized by the Hong Kong International Arbitration Center and German Institution of Arbitration, Hong Kong, 8 December 2006.

Philip J. McConnaughay, "Rethinking the Role of Law and Contracts in East-West Commercial Relationships", (2001) 41 *Vanderbilt Journal of International Law.*

Philip Yang Liangyi, "The Current Development of the Chinese Arbitration" in the Symposium *Comparative Arbitration in the East and West,* HKIAC, 26 March 2004.

Pitman B. Potter, "Globalization and Economic Regulation in China: Selective Adaptation of Globalized Norms and Practices", (2003) 2 *Washington University Global Studies Law Review.*

Pitman B. Potter, "Legal Reform in China: Institutions, Culture, and Selective Adaptation", (2004) 29(2) *Law & Social Inquiry.*

Randall Peerenboom, "Globalization, Path Dependency and the Limits of Law: Administrative Law Reform and Rules of Law in the People's Republic of China", (2001) 19 *Berkeley Journal of International Law*.

Robb M. LaKritz, "Taming a 5,000 Year-old Dragon: Toward a Theory of Legal Development in Post-Mao China", (1997) 11 *Emory International Law Review*.

Robert PE and Michael Polkinghorne, "Two Steps Forward, One Step … Sideways: Recent Developments in Arbitration in China", (2008) 25(3) *Journal of International Arbitration*.

Sarah Catherine Peck, "Playing By a New Set of Rules—Will China's New Arbitration Laws and Recent Membership in the ICC Improve Trade With China?", (1995) 12(4) *Journal of International Arbitration*.

Song Lianbin, Zhao Jian and Li Hong, "Approaches to the Revision of the 1994 Arbitration Act of the People's Republic of China", (2003) 20(2) *Journal of International Arbitration*.

S. Huang, "Several Problems in Need of Resolution in China by Legislation on Foreign Affairs Arbitration", (1993) 10(3) *Journal of International Arbitration*.

Tao Jingzhou and Zhao Jing, "CIETAC: Revising Its Arbitration Rules", (2005) 10(1) *Arbitration Newsletter of the International Bar Association*.

Taroh Inoue, "Introduction to International Commercial Arbitration in China", (2006) 36(1) *Hong Kong Law Journal*.

Urs Martin Lauchli, "Cross-Cultural Negotiations, With A Special Focus on ADR with the Chinese", (2000) 26 *John Marshall Law Review*.

Wang Guiguo, "The Unification of Dispute Resolution System in China: Cultural, Economic and Legal Contributions", (1996) 13 *Arbitration International*.

Wang Liming and Xu Chuanxi, "Fundamental Principles of China's Contract Law", (1999) 13(1) *Columbia Journal of Asian Law*.

Wang Shengchang, "Resolving Disputes Through Conciliation and Arbitration in Mainland China", speech delivered at the seminar jointly organized by the CIETAC, HKIAC, Macau Investment and Trade Promotion Bureau and Macau World Trade Center, Macau, 24 October 2001.

Wang Shengchang, "The Globalization of Economy and China's International Arbitration", paper delivered at the *Seminar on Globalization and Arbitration* jointly sponsored by the International Chamber of Commerce (ICC) and the ICC China, Beijing, 15 October 2002.

Wang Shengchang, "The Arbitration Law after China's Accession to the WTO", (2002) 37 *China Law*.

Wang Shengchang, "Roundtable Arbitration and Conciliation Concerning China: CIETAC's Perspective", paper for the 17th ICCA Conference, Beijing, 6–18 May 2004.

Wang Shengchang, "The Relation between Arbitration and Conciliation", (2004) 49 *China Law*.

Wang Shengchang and Cao Lijun, "Towards a Higher Degree of Party Autonomy and Transparency: The CIETAC Introduces Its 2005 New Rules", [2005] *International Arbitration Law Review*.

Wang Shengchang, "China Arbitration Law v UNCITRAL Model Law", [2006] *International Arbitration Law Review*.

Wang Wenying, "Distinctive Features of Arbitration in China: A Historic Perspective", (2006) 23(1) *Journal of International Arbitration*.

Xiabin Xu and George D. Wilson, "One Country, Two—International Commercial Arbitration—Systems", (2000) 48(17) *Journal of International Arbitration*.

Xin Ren, "Tradition of the Law and Law of the Tradition: Law, State, and Social Control in China", (1997) 20(1) *Columbia Journal of Asian Law*.

Yu Jianlong, Talk on *Managing Business Disputes in China Conference*, New York, 26 March 2007.

Zhang Yulin, "Towards the UNCITRAL Model Law: A Chinese Perspective", (1994) 11(1) *Journal of International Arbitration*.

Zhong Jianhua and Yu Guanghua, "Establishing the Truth on Facts: Has the Chinese Civil Process Achieved This Goal", (2003) 13 *Journal of Transnational Law & Policy*.

C. Newspapers and Magazines

Bei Hu, "Key Arbitration Center Loses Western Appeal", *South China Morning Post*, 13 May 2002, 4.

D. Hughes, "IMF Predicts No Way Back on the Road to Globalization", *South China Morning Post*, 20 May 1997, 16.

He Guanghui, "Reform of the Chinese Economic Structure", *FBIS Daily Report of China*, 23 March 1990, 21.

Jane Moir, "Foreign Business are Being Urged by Their Lawyers Not to Go to China's Official Arbitration Commission", *South China Morning Post*, 3 October 2001, 4.

Jerome A. Cohen, "The Delicate Art of Arbitration", *Financial Times (Asian Edition)*, 30 November 2005, 16.

"Speech by Qiao Shi at Closing of NPC", *FBIS Daily Report: China*, 1 April 1993, 22.

Wang Wenying, "China: CIETAC to Expand Arbitration Scope", *China Daily*, 29 April 1998, 8.

Xinhua English Service (22 March 1993), "The Amendments to Constitution Discussed", reprinted in *FBIS Daily Report of China*, 23 March 1993, 13.

Xinhua Domestic Service (1 September 1983), "Arbitration Committees to Handle Contract Disputes", reprinted in *FBIS Daily Report of China*, 2 September 1983, pp.K3–K4.

D. Legal Documents

Communication from the People's Republic of China—Assessment of Trade in Services, PRC Ministry of Commerce Document, TN/S/W/9 (19 Dec. 2002).

Commission Report on the UNCITRAL Model Law on International Commercial Arbitration:

UN Document, A/CN.9/207.

UN Document A/40/17.

UN Document A/CN.9/264.

UN Document A/CN.9/SR.309.

UN Document A/40/935.

UN Document A/CN.9/207.

UN Document A/CN.9/216.

UNCITRAL Document A/CN.9/WG.II/WP.141, Forty-forth session of the UNCITRAL Working Group on Arbitration (New York, 23–27 January 2006).

UNCITRAL Document A/CN.9/WG.II/WP.149, Forty-eighth session of the UNCITRAL Working Group on Arbitration (New York, 4–8 February 2008).

Report of the UNCITRAL on its 35th Session, 17–28 June 2002, Part III "Revised Draft UNCITRAL Model Law on International Commercial Arbitration".

E. Online Resources

Asia Pacific Law Club Newsletter (University of British Columbia), vol.9, issue 1, http://faculty.law.ubc.ca/aplc/9-1.pdf.

Case Law on UNCITRAL Texts (CLOUT) is available online *via* the UNCITRAL website, www.uncitral.org.

European Arbitrators Association, www.european-arbitrators.org/.

HKIAC, http://www.hkiac.org/.

ICC Arbitration, http://www.iccwbo.org/court/english/arbitration/rules.asp.

Jones Day (Jones, Day, Reavies & Porgue) Law Library on arbitration, http://www.jonesday.com/search/search.aspx?qu=arbitration.

Kluwer Law International Web, www.kluwerarbitration.com.

Lex Mercatoria, www.lexmercatoria.org.

Mealey's Publication on International Legal News, http://www.mealeys.com/legalnews/international.html.

New York Convention member states,

http://www.uncitral.org/uncitral/en/uncitral_texts/arbitration/NYConvention_status.html.

SIAC, http://www.siac.org.sg.

The Asia Pacific Dispute Resolution (APDR) project led by Professor Pitman Potter in the Faculty of Law, University of British Columbia,

http://www.apdr.iar.ubc.ca/description%202.htm.

The Chartered Institute of Arbitrators (CIArb), http://www.arbitrators.org/.

The Explanatory Note by the UNCITRAL Secretariat,

http://www.unicitral.org/english/texts/arbconc/ml-arb.htm.

The Hong Kong Institute of Arbitrators, http://www.hkiarb.org.hk/.

UNCITRAL Model Law adopting jurisdictions,

http://www.uncitral.org/uncitral/en/uncitral_texts/arbitration/1985Model_arbitration_status.html.

CHINESE REFERENCES

A. Books and Texts

Chen Zhidong, *International Commercial Arbitration Law (Guoji Shangshi Zhongcai Fa)* (Beijing: China Law Press, 1998).

CIETAC (ed), *Symposium Essays on Economic and Trade Arbitration across the Taiwan Straits (Haixia Liang'an Jingmao Zhongcai Yantaohui Wenji)* (Beijing: China Law Press, 2001).

CIETAC (ed), *Arbitration and Law Yearbook 2001 (Zhongcai yu Falv 2001 Niankan)* (Beijing: China Law Press, 2002).

CIETAC (ed), *Selected Jurisdictional Decisions of the CIETAC (Zhongguo Guoji Jingji Maoyi Zhongcaiweiyuanhui Guanxiaquan Jueding Xuanbian)* (Beijing: China Commercial Publishing House, 2004).

CIETAC South-China Sub-Commission (ed), *Judicial Review of the Foreign-related Arbitration (Shewai Zhongcai Sifa Shencha)* (Beijing: China Law Press, 2006).

CIETAC and CMAC (ed), *China International Commercial Arbitration Yearbook (Zhongguo Guoji Shangshi Zhongcai Nianjian) (1994–1995)* (Beijing: China Law Press, 1995).

CIETAC and CMAC (ed), *China International Commercial Arbitration Yearbook (Zhongguo Guoji Shangshi Zhongcai Nianjian) (1996–1997)* (Beijing: China Law Press, 1997).

CIETAC and CMAC (ed), *China International Commercial Arbitration Yearbook (Zhongguo Guoji Shangshi Zhongcai Nianjian) (2000–2001)* (Beijing: China Law Press, 2001).

CIETAC and CMAC (ed), *China International Commercial Arbitration Yearbook (Zhongguo Guoji Shangshi Zhongcai Nianjian) (2002–2003)* (Beijing: China Law Press, 2003).

Department of Coordination of the Legislative Affairs Office of the State Council (ed), *An overview of the Chinese Arbitration Institution (Zhongguo Zhongcai Jigou Gailan)* (Beijing: China Pricing Press, 2001).

Ding Linghua, *History of Chinese Legal System (Zhongguo Falv Zhidu Shi)* (Beijing: China Law Press, 1999).

Gou Chengwei and Zhang Peitian, *Practical Handbook of Arbitration (Zhongcai Shiyong Quanshu)* (Beijing: China University of Politics & Law Press, 1993).

Han Jian, *Theory and Practice on Modern International Commercial Arbitration (Xiandai Guoji Shangshi Zhongcai de Lilun yu Shijian)* (Beijing: China Law Press, 2000).

Institute for Practical Legal Research of the SPC (ed), *Selected Cases of the People's Court (Vol.6) (Renmin Fayuan Anli Xuanbian Diliujuan)* (Beijing: People's Court Publishing House, 1993).

Jiang Xianming and Li Ganggui, *Study of Chinese Arbitration Law (Zhongguo Zhongcai Faxue)* (Nanjing: Southeast University Press, 1996).

Kang Ming, *A Study on Commercial Arbitration Service* (Shangshi Zhongcai Fuwu Yanjiu) (Beijing: China Law Press, 2005).

Legislative Affairs Commission of the NPCSC, *Interpretative Comments on the Arbitration Law of the PRC (Zhonghuarenmingongheguo Zhongcaifa Shiping)* (Beijing: China Law Press, 1997).

Li Shuangyuan, *New Comments on Law and Practice of the International Economy and Trade (Guoji Jingji Maoyi Falv yu Shiwu Xinlun)* (Changsha: Hunan University Press, 1995).

Liu Xiaohong, *Jurisprudence and Empirical Research of International Commercial Arbitration Agreement (Guoji Shangshi Zhongcai Xieyi de Fali yu Shizheng Yanjiu)* (Beijing: Commercial Publishing House, 2005).

Qiao Xin, *Comparative Commercial Arbitration (Bijiao Shangshi Zhongcai)* (Beijing: China Law Press, 2004).

Research Office of the Legislative Affairs Office of the State Council (ed), *Handbook on Reorganizing Arbitration Institutions (Chongxin Zujian Zhongcai Jigou Shouce)* (Beijing: China Legal System Publishing, 1995).

Shen Hong, *Transitional Economics of China (Zhongguo Zhuanxing Jingjixue)* (Shanghai: Shanghai Sanlian Press & Shanghai People's Press, 1995).

Song Lianbin, *Studies on Jurisdictional Problems in International Commercial Arbitration (Guoji Shangshi Zhongcai Guanxiaquan Yanjiu)* (Beijing: China Law Press, 2000).

Song Yaowu (ed), *International Commercial Dispute Resolution Review (Vol.1) (Guoji Shangshi Zhengyi Jiejue Luocong Diyijuan)* (Harrbin: Harrbin Industrial University Publishing, 2004).

SPC (ed), *The Bulletin of the Supreme People's Court, Bulletin No.3* (Zuigao Renmin Fayuan Juanzong San) (Beijing: People's Court Publishing, 1998).

SPC, *Gazette of the SPC 2003 (Zhonghuarenmingongheguo Zuigaorenminfayuan Gongbao 2003)* (Beijing: People's Court Publishing, 2003).

Tan Bin, *Research on the Chinese Arbitration System (Zhongguo Zhongcai Zhidu Yanjiu)* (Beijing: Law Press, 1995).

Tang Dehua and Sun Xiujun, *Arbitration Law and New Judicial Interpretations (Zhongcaifa ji Peitao Guiding Xinshi Xinjie)* (Beijing: People's Court Publishing, 2003).

Wan Erxiang (ed), *China Trial Guide—Guide on Foreign-related Commercial and Maritime Trial (Zhongguo Shewai Shangshi Haishi Shenpan Zhidao)* (Beijing: People's Court Publishing, 2005).

Wang Baoshu (ed), *Collected Essays on Commercial Law, Vol.3 (Shangshi Falv Lunwenxuan Disan Juan)* (Beijing: China Law Press, 2001).

Wang Shengchang (ed), *The Theory and Practice of Combining Arbitration with Mediation (Zhongcai yu Tiaojie Xiangjiehe de Lilun yu Shiwu)* (Beijing: China Law Press, 2001).

Xie Shisong, *Commercial Arbitration Law (Shangshi Zhongcai Faxue)* (Beijing: Higher Education Press, 2003).

Zhang Binsheng, *New Theories on Arbitration Law (Zhongcaifa Xinlun)* (Xiamen: Xiamen University Press, 2002).

Zhao Jian, *Research on Judicial Supervision over International Commercial Arbitration (Guoji Shangshi Zhongcai de Sifa Jiandu)* (Beijing: China Law Press, 2000).

Zhao Xiuwen, *Studies on the International Commercial Arbitration and Its Applicable Law (Guoji Shangshi Zhongcai jiqi Shiyong Falv Yanjiu)* (Beijing: Beijing University Press, 2002).

Zhu Jianlin, *Comments and Analyses on International Commercial Arbitration Cases (Guoji Shangshi Zhongcai Anli Pingxi)* (Beijing: Citic Publishing, 2002).

Zhu Suli, *Constitutionality and Its Local Resources (Fazhi jiqi Bentu Ziyuan)* (Beijing: China University of Politics & Law Publishing, 1996).

B. Journal Articles and Conference Papers

Chen Dejun, "The New Milestone in the Arbitration History of Our Country (Woguo Zhongcaishi shang de Lichengbei)," (1994) 4 *Arbitration and Law (Zhongcai yu Falv)*.

Cheng Furong and Su Shunmin, "Several Counter-measures for Reforming the System of Institutions during the Period of Transition (Zhuangui Shiqi Shiye Danwei Tizhi Gaige de Jidian Duice)", (2002) 3 *Hangzhou College of Commerce Review (Hangzhou Shangxueyuan Xuebao)*.

Feng Kefei, "The Theory of Competence-Competence and Its Practical Application in Our Country (Guanxiaquan/Guanxiaquan Lilun jiqi zai Woguo de Shijian)", (2002) 71 *Arbitration and Law (Zhongcai yu Falv)*.

Gao Fei, "Support and Supervision towards Arbitration by Chinese Courts (Zhongguo Fayuan dui Zhongcai de Zhichi yu Jiandu)", (2001) 66 *Arbitration in China (Zhongguo Zhongcai)*.

Gao Fei, "Interview with Lu Yunhua, Chief of the Department of Coordination on Government Legal Affairs Office, Legislative Affairs Office of the State Council (Fang Guowuyuanfazhiban Zhengfuwawuxietiaosi Sizhang Luyunhua)", 2 (2007) *Arbitration and Judicature in China (Zhongguo Zhongcai yu Sifa)*.

Gu Weixia, "Thinking about the Application of Subrogation in China's Commercial Arbitration (Guanyu Daiwei Qingqiuquan zai Zhongguo Shangshi Zhongcai zhong Yingyong de Sikao)", (2004) 88 *Arbitration and Law (Zhongcai yu Falv)*.

Hu Kangsheng, Vice-director of the Legislative Affairs Commission of the NPCSC, speech at the Seminar *Resolving Differences in China (Zhengyi Jiejue zai Zhongguo)*, reprinted in 70 (2001) *Arbitration and Law (Zhongcai yu Falv)*.

Li Hai, "Thinking about the Several Questions Regarding the Validity of the Arbitration Clause in the Bill of Lading (Guanyu Tidan Zhongcai Tiaokuan Xiaoli Ruogan Wenti de Sikao)", (2005) 94 *Arbitration and Law (Zhongcai yu Falv)*.

Li Hu, "Retrospect and Prospect of the 50 Years' History of CIETAC (Huigu yu Zhanwang Maozhong Wushinian)", (2004) 335 *China's Foreign Trade (Zhongguo Waimao)*.

Liang Huixin, "To Advance from the Three-Pillar Law System to a Unified Contract Law (Cong Sanzudingli Zouxiang Tongyi de Hetongfa)", (1995) 3 *Chinese Jurisprudence (Zhongguo Faxue)*.

Lin Yifei, "Understanding the New Judicial Interpretation on the Arbitration Law (Zhongcaifa Xin Sifajieshi Jiedu)", (2007) 60 *Arbitration in Beijing (Beijing Zhongcai)*.

Liu Maoliang, "*Ad Hoc* Arbitration Should Be Slow for Implementation in China (Linshizhongcai yingdang Huanxing)", (2005) 54 *Arbitration in Beijing (Beijing Zhongcai)*.

Lu Yunhua, *Speech in the Symposium on the Development of Nationwide Arbitration Works (Quanguo Zhongcai Gongcheng Fazhan Yantaohui de Yanjiang)*, CIETAC, 2003, unpublished.

Qiao Xin, "Supporting Arbitration and Developing Arbitration (Zhichi Zhongcai, Fazhan Zhongcai)", (2007) 60 *Arbitration in Beijing (Beijing Zhongcai)*.

Qu Guangming and Cai Xiao, "Two Cornerstones of the Application of Law in Foreign Contracts and Private International Law (Shewai Hetong Falv Shiyong yu Guoji Sifa de Liang Da Jishi)", (1995) 2 *Studies in Law and Commerce (Fa Shang Yanjiu)*.

Shen M., "New Developments in Our Country's Arbitration System (Lun Woguo Zhongcai Zhidu de Xin Fazhan)", (1995) 4 *Wuhan University Law Review (Faxue Pinglun)*.

Shen Sibao and Xue Yuan, "On the Positioning and Reform of the Chinese Commercial Arbitration System (Lun Woguo Shangshi Zhongcai Zhidu de Dingwei jiqi Gaige)", (2006) 4 *Legal Science Monthly (Faxue Yuekan)*.

Song Lianbin, "On the Principle of *Competence-Competence* in International Commercial Arbitration (Lun Guoji Shangshi Zhongcai zhong de Guanxiaquan Yuanze)", (2000) 2 *Jurisprudence Review (Faxue Pinglun)*.

Song Lianbin, "From Ideology to Rules: Several Issues Worthy of Attention for the Revision of Arbitration Law (Linian Zouxiang Guize: Zhongcaifa Gaige ying Zhuyi de Jige Wenti)", (2005) 52 *Arbitration in Beijing (Beijing Zhongcai)*.

Song Lianbin, "Comments on the Judicialization Trend of the Arbitration (Zhongcai Susonghua Qushi zhi Pingxi)", (2005) 55 *Arbitration in Beijing (Beijing Zhongcai)*.

Song Lianbin, "Comments on the SPC Interpretation on Several Issues in Applying the PRC Arbitration Law (Ping Zuigaorenminfayuan guanyu Shiyong Zhonghua Renmin Gongheguo Zhongcaifa Ruogan Wenti de Jieshi)", (2007) 60 *Arbitration in Beijing (Beijing Zhongcai)*.

Sun Yuxi, "Support and Supervision to Arbitration of the Beijing Higher People's Court (Beijingshi Gaojirenminfayuan dui Zhongcai de Zhichi yu Jiandu)", at the Forum *Protection of International Investment and Financing (Baohu Guoji Tourongzi)*, Beijing, 16 July 2005.

Sun Peng, "Contemporary Development of Contract Law (Qiyuefa de Xiandai Fazhan)", (1998) 4 *Contemporary Legal Studies (Xiandai Faxue)*.

Wang Baoshu, "The Socialist Market Economy and Research in Economic Law" (Shehuizhuyi Shichangjingji yu Minshangfa Yanjiu", (1993) 3 *Chinese Legal Science (Zhongguo Faxue)*.

Wang Chengjie and Qu Zhujun, "Several Comments on the Opinion by the Shanghai Higher People's Court on the Some Issues Regarding the Implementation of the Arbitration Law of the People's Republic of China" (Dui Shanghaishi Gaojirenminfayuan Guanyu Zhixing <Zhonghuarenmingongheguo Zhongcaifa> Ruogan Wenti de Chuli Yijian de Jidian Pingshu), (2001) 66 *Arbitration and Law (Zhongcai yu Falv)*.

Wang Hongsong, "Existing Problems of the Arbitration Law and Reform Suggestions (Zhongcaifa Cunzai de Wenti ji Xiugai Jianyi)", (2005) 52 *Arbitration in Beijing (Beijing Zhongcai)*.

Wang Hongsong, "Speech on the 2005 Spring Tea Reception for the BAC Arbitrators (Zai 2005 Nian Zhongcaiyuan Chunjie Chahuahui Shang de Jianghua)", (2005) 54 *Arbitration in Beijing (Beijing Zhongcai)*.

Wang Hongsong, "Keep abreast the Spirit of Arbitration Law, Establish the Modern Arbitration Institution (Linghui Zhongcaifa Jingshen, Jianshe Xiandaihua de Zhongcai Jigou)", (2005) 57 *Beijing Arbitration (Beijing Zhongcai)*.

Wang Wenying, "Studies on the Arbitral Independence in China (Zhongguo Zhongcai Dulixing Wenti Yanjiu)", (2004) 89 *Arbitration and Law (Zhongcai yu Falv)*.

Wang Wenying, "Comparative Research on Arbitration Rules and Revision of the CIETAC Rules (Zhongcai Guize Bijiao Yanjiu ji Maozhong Guize de Xiugai)", (2005) 94 *Arbitration and Law (Zhongcai yu Falv)*.

Wu Tong, "Where is Our Arbitration of Domestic Economic Contracts Going (Woguo Guonei Jingji Hetong Zhongcai xiang Hechu Zou)", (1991) 2 *Chinese Jurisprudence (Zhongguo Faxue)*.

Wang Shengchang, "The Chinese Characteristic System of Arbitral Jurisdiction Determination (Zhongguo Tese de Zhongcai Guanxiaquan Jueding Zhidu)", (2003) 75 *Arbitration and Law (Zhongcai yu Falv)*.

Wang Zhengbang, "The Modern Market Economy as a Rule of Law Economy (Shichang Jingji Nai Fazhi Jingji)", (1994) 25 *Studies in Law (Faxue Yanjiu)*.

Xiao Yang, President of the SPC of the PRC, "Report of the SPC Work (Zuigaorenminfayuan Gongzuo Baogao)", 4th *Session of the* 9th *National People's Congress*, Beijing, 10 March 2001.

Xu Zhiqing and Dai Shu, "China Should Establish the Tribunal's *Competence-Competence* (Woguo ying Queli Zhongcaiting Zicaiguanxiaquan Yuanze)", (2005) 95 *Arbitration and Law (Zhongcai yu Falv)*.

Yang Lin, "On the Legal Status of Arbitration Institution—Revisiting the Arbitration Law of Our Country (Lun Zhongcai Jigou de Falv Diwei—Jianji Woguo Zhongcaifa de Xiugai)", (2005) 98 *Arbitration and Law (Zhongcai yu Falv)*.

Ye Yu, "The Ascertaining of the Party to the Arbitration Agreement in Foreign-related Agency (Shewai Daili xia Zhongcaixieyi Dangshiren de Queding)", (2005) 94 *Arbitration and Law (Zhongcai yu Falv)*.

Zhang Wenxian, "Reflections on Macro-economic Control and its Law and Policy (Guanyu Hongguanjingji Tiaokong jiqi Falv yu Zhengce de Sikao)", (1994) 1 *Peking University Law Review (Zhongwai Faxue)*.

Zhang Wenxian, "Market Economy and the Spirit of Modern Law (Shichangjingji yu Xiandai Fazhi Jingshen)", (1994) 6 *Chinese Legal Science (Zhongguo Faxue)*.

Zhao Chengbi, "Rethinking of the Nature and Feature of Arbitration in Our Country (Dui Woguo Zhongcai de Xingzhi ji Tedian de Zaitantao)", (2005) 95 *Arbitration and Law (Zhongcai yu Falv)*.

Zhao Jian, "Reviews and Prospects: Chinese International Commercial Arbitration at the Turn of the Century (Huigu he Zhanwang: Shiji Zhijiao de Zhongguo Guoji Shangshi Zhongcai)", (2001) 51 *Arbitration and Law (Zhongcai yu Falv)*.

C. Newspapers and Magazines

Beijing Municipal Government, "The Biggest Support of Government to Arbitration Commissions is Non-interference (Dui Zhongcaiweiyuanhui Zuida de Zhichi jiushi Buganyu)", *Shanghai Justice Daily (Shanghai Fazhi Bao)*, 12 December 2004.

Michael J. Moser, "New Rules, New Breakthroughs (Xin Guize, Xin Tupuo)", *Legal Daily (Fazhi Ribao)*, 20 April 2005.

President Hu Jingtao, "China Will Remain in the Initial Stage of the Socialist Market Economy (Zhongguo Jiang Ren Chuzai Shehuizhuyi Shichangjingji Chujijieduan), *People's Daily (Renmin Ribao)*, 21 November 2006.

Qiu Shi, "Arbitration: Why is Self-contradictory—A Perspective of an Arbitration Case on a Dispute Arising from a Purchase Contract (Zhongcai Zixiang Maodun Wei Na Ban—Yiqi Gouxiao Hetong Jiufen An Toushi)", *Legal Daily (Fazhi Ribao)*, 30 May 1998.

Wen Jiabao, "Several Issues on the Historic Tasks and Foreign Policies that China Face in the Initial Period of Socialism (Guanyu Shehuizhuyi Chujijieduan de Lishi Renwu he Woguo Duiwai Zhengce de Jige Wenti), *Xinhua News Net*, Beijing, 26 February 2007.

Xia Zhong and Chen Gang, "On the Contribution of the Government-supported Industries to the Local Economy (Lun Zhengfu Zhongdian Fuchi Chanye dui Dangdi Jingji de Gongxian)", *China Economy Times (Zhongguo Jingji Shibao)*, 12 May 2005.

Zhang Jianhua, "The Separability of Arbitration Agreement (Zhongcaixieyi de Dulixing)", *Newsletter of Beijing Arbitration (Beijing Zhongcai Tongxun)*, 28 April 2000.

Zhao Jian, "Positioning and Behaving of the Arbitration System of Our Country in New Era (Xinshiqi Woguo Zhongcai Zhidu de Dingwei yu Zuowei)", *Brief Newsletter of the CIETAC Arbitration Research Institute (Zhongcai Yanjiusuo Jianbao)*, 13 November 2004.

D. Online Resources

Beijing Arbitration Commission, http://www.bjac.com.cn.

China Arbitration Net, http://www.china-arbitration.com/.

China Civil Law Net: www.civillaw.com.cn/.

China Foreign-related Commercial and Maritime Trial Net: http://www.ccmt.org.cn/.

China Judge Net, http://www.china.judge.com/.

China International Economic and Trade Arbitration Commission, http://www.cietac.org/.

Guangzhou Arbitration Commission, http://www.gzac.org.

Wuhan Arbitration Commission, http://www.whac.org.

Hangzhou Arbitration Commission, http://www.hzac.gov.cn/.

Legislative Affairs Office of the State Council, http://www.chinalaw.gov.cn.

People's Court Net, www.chinacourt.org.

Shanghai Arbitration Commission, http://www.accsh.org.

Shenzhen Arbitration Commission, http://www.szac.org/.

Xinhua News Net, http://news.xinhuanet.com.

INDEX